Currency Risk
and the Corporation

Edited by
Boris Antl

Published by Euromoney Publications

Published by
Euromoney Publications Limited,
Nestor House, Playhouse Yard,
London, EC4

ISBN 0 903121 14 X

Text set in 10/11 pt Linotron 202 Times,
printed and bound in Great Britain at
The Pitman Press, Bath

Acknowledgements

Working with the authors of this study has been an extremely gratifying experience, and I deeply appreciate the sharing of their knowledge by contributing chapters to this study.

I am particularly grateful to Albert C. Henry of Price Waterhouse & Co., Richard Ensor of *Euromoney*, and Dr. Alan Teck of Chemical Bank. Al Henry encouraged me to develop this book and commented on large portions of the manuscript at various stages of its development. He made valuable suggestions which I have used to the best of my ability. Richard Ensor provided considerable assistance in compiling the individual chapters of the manuscript. Alan Teck gave me constructive advice on the overall organization of the book. His contribution will be appreciated particularly by practitioners and students of the discipline, as it provides an underlying logic of the subject matter from both practical and pedagogical perspectives.

I would also like to thank for assistance in researching the tax areas Jay B. Schwartz of Price Waterhouse & Co., and Barry L. Salkin of Kelley Drye & Warren. Also, many thanks to the following individuals for reviewing and commenting on individual chapters of the book: Douglas E. Bender, Price Waterhouse & Co.; Robert J. E. Henrey, Coopers & Lybrand; Ralph J. Massey, Chemical Bank; Alice Kerr, Chemical Bank; Philip Y. Lee, Citibank; Henry Meininger, American Business Systems; David W. Bodenberg, Merrill Lynch Pierce & Smith; Robert LeStrange Rose, Salomon Brothers; Gail Lieberman, RCA Corporation; D. Gregory Lambert, Chemical Bank; and Marvin C. Feinstein, Citibank.

Finally, special thanks to *Harvard Business Review, Business International Money Report* and *Euromoney* who gave me the permission to use some material from their publications.

I am also indebted to Sondra Schwartz for typing numerous versions of the manuscript.

B.A.
New York, May 5, 1980

Contents

Introduction

Interest in defining and managing exposure to gains and losses caused by fluctuating exchange rates has increased dramatically in recent years. This concern is expected to become even more widespread as large and often unpredictable currency movements continue to be an important part of the international business environment in the years ahead. At the same time, often after experiencing serious losses, financial officers in virtually every country are becoming more aware of the diversity and complexity of their currency related problems. In addition to the need for improved exchange rate forecasts and for timely information and financial forecasts from within the company, there is a continuing search for analytical techniques to deal with specific situations and for a general framework that will provide a logical and comprehensive approach to the entire problem. It is with these needs in mind that Boris Antl, a recognized expert in foreign exchange matters, has designed and edited this book.

The book has four main objectives: first, to make the reader aware of the wide range of economic, financial, accounting, tax, regulatory and strategic issues that can affect the foreign exchange decisions of a multinational company. Second, to discuss specific information about the many factors that must be considered in today's environment. Third, to provide analytical tools and a conceptual framework so the reader can consider his particular problems within a broader context. Fourth, to present some issues that deserve further research.

To discuss these diverse problems, Mr. Antl has turned to practitioners from a wide range of business, accounting and banking organizations and to international economists from the academic community. Each author specializes in currency and exposure management problems and was selected because of an established reputation in this field. In addition, Mr. Antl has drawn on his experience and research to write many of the sections for which the available information is limited, particularly topics concerning the definition and measurement of foreign exchange exposure and forward contracts.

The book is organized to reflect a logical approach to the foreign exchange problems faced by multinational companies. Following Mr. Burtle's general discussion of exposure management, Chapter II analyzes different methods for defining and measuring a company's exposure to gains and losses that might occur as currency values change. As the presentation indicates, there are many valid ways to define exposure, depending on whether the emphasis is on cash or accounting considerations. The chapter examines each major type of asset and liability and indicates some of the more important relationships between the balance sheet and the income statement. The underlying concepts are applicable regardless of the accounting standards used in individual countries.

Chapters III and IV recognize that all strategies for dealing with changing currency values can be classified in one of three broad categories. First, after estimating its expected gains, losses and risks, a company can elect to do nothing. In other words, it can be self insured by deciding to remain exposed to possible losses. In this situation, the company can either try to recover its currency losses by raising prices or treat the losses as an expense of doing international business. Second, a company can eliminate or adjust its exposure by changing its assets and liabilities denominated in foreign currencies. In most situations, there are literally dozens of ways to do this, and each way has a cost or gain that can be compared with the costs or gains of the other alternatives. Third, a company can hedge its exposures by dealing in the forward foreign exchange markets. It will do this for actively traded currencies when the related costs are smaller or the gains larger than the expected costs or gains of remaining exposed or using other protective strategies.

Chapter III discusses many of the ways that a company can adjust its assets and liabilities denominated in foreign currencies. This can be done to eliminate an exposure at the subsidiary or parent company level, or to establish a net asset position in a currency expected to strengthen or a net liability denominated in a currency expected to weaken. The presentation evaluates some of the better known techniques such as leading and lagging (the rapid collection of receivables and delay of payments) as well as some of the more complex methods for borrowing in domestic and international money markets and investing in foreign assets. Many numerical examples illustrate the methods for measuring the advantages, costs and risks associated with each type of protective action.

Chapter IV provides a detailed explanation of the different ways that the forward exchange markets can be used, depending on the type of exposure to be protected. In many countries, the cash, accounting and tax treatments of a foreign exchange contract can be different depending on whether the transaction hedges a specific receivable or payable, a net balance sheet exposure, an intracompany account, or some other type of actual or anticipated exposure.

Chapter V deals with three subjects that are an integral part of every international company's foreign exchange decisions: currency forecasting, international tax and foreign regulations. Every financial manager should receive forecasts from within his organization and from outside sources to determine where he thinks exchange rates will be at various times in the future. These forecasts—for each currency in which the company has an exposure—are necessary to compare the expected gains, losses and risks of remaining exposed with the costs or gains of alternative protective actions. Dr. Levich discusses ways to evaluate and use these currency forecasts.

After having the currency forecasts, alternative protection strategies should be analyzed with consideration for the company's local and global tax situation. Tax effects can vary greatly depending on the type of action being considered and the countries in which they can be implemented. Moreover, there can be different tax effects on the company's cash flow, on the one hand, and its financial reports, on the other hand. Also, the financial officer must consider the constantly changing regulations that define, and in many countries severely limit, the options for moving funds and implementing financial strategies.

Chapter VI recognizes that exposure management requires decisions that must be based on a dual analysis which considers both a company's most likely expectations and the risks associated with each expectation. Objectives must be defined, policies established and strategies selected that not only minimize expenses but also permit contingency plans to be implemented quickly when conditions change. To an important extent, the basic concepts of exposure management are similar to those that have been used for years in other business programmes that involve planning for the future, such as marketing, acquisition analysis and budgeting. These activities typically require primary plans based on the organization's most likely expectations and contingency plans to be used if necessary. The chapter considers long term results of alternative protection strategies, some of the dynamic relationships between the balance sheet and income statement, and selected cash and accounting effects. Not all of these issues are fully resolved, and Dr. Adler's and Dr. Dumas' section on optimal hedging strategies is one subject about which there continues to be considerable discussion.

Chapter VII takes a more detailed look at some of the conflicts inherent in exposure management. These include divergent interests at the local and parent company levels, different cash, accounting and reporting effects, conflicts in the selection of protection strategies, and differences in objectives (for example, whether to incur expenses to minimize variations in the earnings stream or to forego such expenses in order to maximize short-term earnings per share). In most instances, these conflicts have to be resolved by judgements that represent the good of the entire company.

Finally, Chapter VIII discusses issues related to disclosure and management of information for proper control and evaluation of international profit performance.

Recent trends

Although this book provides a general framework for analyzing exposure management practices, it is obvious that every international company faces its own unique combination of problems caused by factors such as the currencies and countries in which it operates, its accounting, tax and regulatory considerations, the extent to which its financial decisions are centralized or dispersed, its management objectives, its products, market shares, profit margins, etc. Each company has different requirements which are constantly changing over time. Therefore, it may be useful to mention some longer term trends so the exposure management practices of individual organizations can be seen in a broader context.

For many years companies engaged in business with foreign nations were called international because the flow of their merchandise and capital tended to be mostly bilateral, with the country in which the parent company is located usually being at one end of each transaction. In recent years, a growing number of companies have become multinational as their trade and capital flows have moved increasingly among a number of nations, with many transactions not even involving the parent company. It has been increasingly common for goods to be manufactured in one country, assembled in another, and sold around the world; there is a more global approach to raising, managing and investing capital; and many companies have established regional headquarters with considerable autonomy, as well as foreign tax havens and reinvoicing centres in different parts of the world. This shift from international to multinational has profound implications for foreign exposure management.

Another trend in recent years is the centralization of data flows and the greater co-ordination of exposure management decisions. This accelerated abruptly in the United States in 1976 when the Financial Accounting Standards Board issued Statement No. 8 which changed the accounting methods for dealing with foreign exchange gains and losses in the consolidated financial statements. It has also become increasingly apparent in virtually all countries that completely decentralized exposure management can lead to suboptimal decisions or to conflicts between the individual subsidiaries and the consolidated interest of the parent company. Even if accounting standards are changed the movement toward greater co-ordination of exposure management decisions is likely to continue.

A different longer term trend involves the constantly broadening definition of exposure. Until the late 1960s, the exposure management concerns of most financial officers were concentrated almost entirely on specific transactions denominated in foreign currencies and on translation effects: the unrealized gains and losses that had to be reported in each accounting period when the foreign financial statements were consolidated into the accounts of the parent company. More recently, many companies have gone beyond the traditional considerations and have started including in their definition of exposure *all* assets and liabilities subject to currency gains and losses as well as *anticipated* foreign currency commitments expected to have an impact on the company's long term cash flow. There is a persistent movement away from concentrating entirely on the results reported in each accounting period to a more fundamental consideration of the longer-term changes in cash flow.

During the early years of the floating rate period, many financial officers maintained a policy of either always hedging or never hedging their foreign currency exposures. Those who always hedged did not want "to get involved in currency speculation". Those who never hedged argued that "currency gains and losses tend to offset each other in the long run". However, it became apparent over time that "always hedging" often involves costs that exceed the losses related to remaining exposed. It also became clear that currency values often move around a trend line that is sharply up or sharply down, with companies on the wrong side of the movement experiencing substantial losses. Today, virtually all financial managers are willing to make judgements about whether or not to obtain protection against adverse exchange rate movements after comparing the risks of remaining exposed with the cost of alternative strategies.

Another recent trend has been a growing awareness of the over-widening range of protection alternatives available to most multinational companies. Companies use to view their only options as remaining exposed to possible currency losses or taking protective positions in the foreign exchange markets. Most financial officers are now aware that there are literally dozens of protection possibilities ranging from better known activities such as leading and lagging payables and receivables, borrowing in weaker currencies and investing in assets denominated in stronger currencies to more complex activities such as multicountry netting and pooling systems, back-to-back loans, currency swaps and offshore reinvoicing centres. Today most financial managers are willing to make judgements about whether or not to obtain protection against adverse exchange rate movements after comparing the risk of remaining exposed with the cost of various forms of protection.

Methods have also changed with respect to making and using currency forecasts. Until the early 70s, it was common to make single point estimates for particular points of time. All currency forecasters, however, have been wrong so often in recent years that it is now fairly common to project not only a most likely exchange rate for various times in the future but also quantitative estimates of the risk that the exchange rate might vary considerably from the most likely forecast if more optimistic or more pessimistic conditions develop. Some forecasters quantify their most pessimistic and most optimistic forecasts as the minimum and maximum exchange rates that could materialize on selected future dates; others forecast a range of possible outcomes, with probabilities attached to each possibility; still others use a weighted average rather than a single most likely exchange rate. But regardless of the method, practitioners have become increasingly aware that numerical indications of the expected risks are equally as important as the most likely forecast when comparing the advantages or costs of remaining exposed with alternative protection strategies.

An additional development involves the increased use of exchange rate forecasts based on analysis and judgement rather than on rigidly applied econometric techniques or mechanical rules, such as using either the current spot rate or the forward rate as the best indicator of future spot rates. Those who use econometric models often gain insights into interrelationships among independent variables, but before using the actual forecast they generally adjust it based on judgemental considerations. The availability of timely data, the state of the econometric art, and the number of qualitative relationships that must be considered—how much pessimism or optimism has the current spot rate already discounted?—makes it hazardous to rely entirely on the unadjusted output of an econometric model.

People who use the current spot rate as the best indication of future spot rates generally subscribe to the random walk concept which assumes that the current spot rate has already discounted all known future events. Others assume that the forward exchange rate discounts all known future events and is, therefore, the best indicator of future spot rates. However, most practitioners have learned that they can usually estimate future spot rates more accurately than using either the current spot rate or forward rates. Projections based on knowledge, analysis and judgement continue to be more widely used than econometric techniques or fixed rules involving the random walk concept or forward exchange rates.

Another major trend concerns taxes. Until the mid 70s, it was fairly common to leave tax considerations out of exposure management decisions. Taxes were either regarded as too complicated, the problem of another department, or it was assumed that all exposure management strategies had similar tax effects and, therefore, that a pre-tax analysis was sufficient. Financial managers have learned, however, that different effective tax rates in different countries, tax loss carry forwards, differences between income and capital gains tax, offshore tax havens, etc., can be very important when selecting the least-cost strategy and the location for implementation. With many organizations paying taxes at effective rates of 40–50% and even higher, the number of companies that are integrating tax analysis into their exposure management strategies on a global as well as country-by-country basis is steadily growing.

With respect to rules and regulations, two trends have become apparent: first, virtually all written summaries of regulations concerning international movements of currency and trade are either out of date or too succinct to be useful. Companies are increasingly turning to their local personnel or to outside consultants for making direct contact with the authorities in the countries involved. Second, recognition has been growing that regulations are frequently the key factor for determining whether or not some of the more advanced exposure management techniques such as netting, pooling, parallel loans and establishing reinvoicing centres can be used in particular countries. There has been a growing awareness of the importance of knowing the limitations and flexibilities of the regulations in each country.

There has also been a rapidly expanding use of computers for exposure management by multinational companies, for gathering and organizing the organization's data, reviewing financial and currency forecasts, and simulating protection strategies. Computer models permit a company to use any definition or combination of definitions when measuring exposure, to enter any degree of detail for any number of locations, to examine any number of currency and financial projections for any number of time periods, to evaluate different tax assumptions and to simulate different protection strategies in a matter of minutes. Computers also facilitate the preparation of reports that allow the financial officer to measure the results of past actions and to monitor present positions as often as necessary. With the cost of computers declining, with an increasing number of people entering the labour force with good computer knowledge, and with a worldwide availability of in-house and time-sharing capabilities, the move toward greater use of computers is expected to continue.

Conclusion

In recent years, the liquid funds available to private market participants have increased dramatically in actual amounts and in relation to the resources held by central banks. Consequently, central banks can no longer maintain exchange rates at artificial levels for more than very brief periods when there is a disparity between the current rates and the levels that private market participants consider more appropriate. The longer artificial levels are maintained the greater will be the subsequent adjustments. Large and often unexpected movements in exchange rates will continue to be an important part of the international business environment and the primary cause of an increased concern for exposure management in the future.

These observations should not give the impression, however, that floating exchange rates have made it impossible to engage in profitable international business. Quite the contrary, international trade, investment and profits have increased persistently in real terms since the collapse of the Bretton Woods System, except during two years when there was a marked slowdown in worldwide economic activity. For many companies, international activities are more profitable than domestic activity even after adjusting for currency losses and the cost of protection. This book contributes to the knowledge that can be used to become progressively more efficient in maintaining acceptable levels of currency risk and managing currency exposures in a period of floating exchange rates.

Alan Teck, New York, April 2, 1980

CHAPTER I

Framework of foreign exchange exposure management

1. Introduction

Most companies agree that foreign exchange management is a form of risk management. Few company executives will permit their foreign exchange managers to take currency positions that have nothing to do with company operations. That would be speculation, narrowly defined, and most companies agree that losses from such speculation are scandalous and gains are low quality earnings. But there the agreement ends. There is a lack of a common viewpoint on (1) identifying the foreign exchange risks – the so-called exposure problem, (2) the extent that foreign exchange risks should be hedged, (3) the choice of a hedging strategy and (4) the organization of a hedging operation, e.g. centralized vs. decentralized. As is stressed throughout this book, a company's answers to these questions – its decisions on the objectives and operational methods of its foreign exchange management function – will depend on its corporate philosophy and the structure of the business. But it is clear that a company should decide on its objectives and methods at an early stage. It is not advantageous to wait until there is a foreign exchange crisis and then attempt to decide what is the company policy.

2. Foreign exchange risk and the exposure problem

One of the most controversial questions in foreign exchange management is the exact definition of what is at risk from exchange rate changes. When this risk is put into a quantified form, it is known as *exposure*. For example, if a foreign exchange manager says that he is positively exposed in $5 million in French francs, it is understood that he would gain $500,000 from a 10% appreciation of the French franc and would lose $500,000 from a 10% depreciation. Thus, the *consequences* of exposure are generally clear, but the *measurement* of exposure remains an area of debate and uncertainty.

Many of the disagreements in defining exposure arise because different companies operate with different objectives and are subject to different constraints. What is an appropriate definition of exposure for one company's operations may be totally inapplicable for another company.

Chapter VI–C, Part 4 focuses on the extremes in defining exposure. The broadest possible alternative is to define exposure as the extent that the market value of the firm's outstanding securities at a specified future date would be raised or lowered by future exchange rate changes. In some cases this impact would appear in the price/earnings ratio for the company i.e. a gain or loss of one dollar's worth of per share earnings from foreign exchange would have the same effect on the price of the stock as a dollar's worth of any other earnings. In other cases, however, gains in per share earnings from currency changes would be considered low quality earnings and have minimum effects on the stock price.

But the above definition of exposure is not appropriate for a company that does not have widely traded securities or for a company that, as a matter of policy, is disinterested in the value of its marketed securities. A narrower but, nevertheless, very broad definition of exposure is known as *economic exposure*. This can be defined as the impact of exchange rate changes on discounted cash flow of the company at a specified future date.[1] Choosing a suitable rate of discount is one difficulty in applying this definition of exposure.

In another variant of economic exposure, as proposed in Chapter VI–C, Part 4, it is defined as the effect of exchange rate changes on the book value of the company at a specific date in the future. Under this definition exposure easily breaks down into three parts:

---

[1] See "Measuring and Controlling Multinationals' Exchange Risk" by Rita Rodriguez in *Financial Analysts Journal*, November/December 1979.

1. Transaction exposure
2. Translation exposure
3. Operational exposure

Transaction exposure arises when a company has agreed to make a payment or to receive a payment at a future date and the payment is denominated in a foreign currency. A future payment or receipt that is foreign to a subsidiary (for example, pounds to a French subsidiary) is also a transaction exposure. Examples of transaction exposure arise from merchandise shipments, dividend remittances, foreign debt amortization, and settlements of foreign exchange contracts. Transaction exposure in general is discussed in Chapter II–B. Chapter II–E considers the problems of intercompany transaction exposure with special reference to third country and tax effects.

Translation exposure is concerned with changes in the valuation of overseas assets and liabilities as a result of exchange rate changes. For example, if a U.S. company plans to sell its output for sterling, this is transaction exposure. If there is a devaluation of sterling, the company will receive less, converted into dollars, from this sale. On the other hand, if its subsidiary has a sterling bank account, this is translation exposure. In the event of sterling devaluation the account would be worth less in terms of dollars.

While the basic concept of translation exposure is simple, there has been widespread controversy as to what assets and liabilities are exposed to translation gains and losses. In this book the treatment of major elements of translation exposure is considered in Chapter II–D on inventory exposure, II–F on fixed asset exposure and II–G on long term debt exposure. Accounting standards for reporting translation exposure are reviewed in Chapter II–A. Chapter II–C is concerned with the preparation of income statements showing the impact of exchange rate changes on both translation and transaction exposure.

Operational exposure, as discussed in Chapter VI–C is the third element in overall economic exposure and arises from the indirect effects of exchange rate changes on revenues and expenses of operating abroad. For example, if a U.S. company is operating an exporting business in the United Kingdom it may gain on translation exposure if there is a rise in the pound sterling. But the higher exchange rate for the pound may create economic losses because of a lower export volume as a result of the stronger sterling. Likewise, if a revaluation of sterling were to lower the prices in local currency of the company's imports of raw materials, the company might be able to cut sterling prices and expand sales. All of such complex risks and opportunities from exchange rate changes that arise neither from commitments (transaction exposure) nor from valuation adjustments (translation exposure) are considered part of operational exposure.

As already noted, the choice of a definition of exposure should not be the same for all companies. An export–import company with few assets and liabilities abroad may well confine its foreign exchange management to transaction exposure. A U.S. company operating almost entirely in a foreign country, with its business little affected by exports and imports, may get along very well by considering only translation exposure. In other cases, however, when a large company operates abroad with a vast network of inter-connected subsidiaries, it may be giving itself gross misinformation if it does not take full economic exposure into account in its foreign exchange management. Put another way, exposure data are information, and information is costly. Thus for some companies a broadly defined exposure definition will entail more costs than potential benefits. For other companies, however, a narrowly defined exposure definition may, by penny pinching on information costs, deny the company the benefits of adequate exposure management.

3. What exposures should be covered

Once exposure is defined, a company must confront the issue of whether or not exposure should always be covered. Here cover refers to a strategy whereby foreign exchange risk embodied in an exposed position is eliminated or reduced. It might seem self-evident that all exposures should be covered. But such action is not necessarily desirable because, as explained in Chapters III and IV, cover costs hard cash, for example, in the form of premiums or discounts on foreign exchange contracts or in paying interest differentials on borrowing costs. In many cases the costs of cover are too expensive when compared with the risks of likely foreign exchange losses on a particular exposed position.

Moreover, there is an opinion, widely held by academics, that apparent losses from foreign exposures are offset by gains elsewhere. Thus, in this view, much coverage of exposure is actually a redundant exercise. For example, if there is a devaluation, the apparent losses are likely to be offset by higher prices and gains on profit margins. If there are losses on long term debt, there are likely to be offsetting gains because interest rates may be lower in countries where borrowing is susceptible to this kind of foreign exchange loss. These alleged offsets depend, however, on market perfections that are by no means general. For example, price controls in many countries may stand in the way of price increases offsetting devaluation losses. Also, as discussed in Chapter VI–C–2, a company may go bankrupt before it gets the benefits of favourable offsets to exchange rate changes.

Perhaps worst of all are inconsistent company strategies that swing between policy extremes. For example, instructions may emanate from topside to cover all exposures. Such as strategy is strongly risk averse but cannot be faulted on logical grounds. Risk aversion, however, may give way when it is discovered that the company is paying heavily because foreign exchange contracts have to be settled in cold cash while offsetting gains on exposed positions may not be immediately realized. Then a sharp strategy reversal, forbidding foreign exchange contracts, returns the company to a state of uncovered exposure. Companies with frequent strategy reversals of this kind are probably the most prone to foreign exchange losses simply because (1) very little practical foreign exchange management experience is gained by operating under blanket rules, (2) opportunities for effective cover or non-cover are necessarily passed by and (3) in extreme 'cover everything' situations, some offsetting exposures within the company may be covered unnecessarily.

4. When should exposures be covered

Suppose that a company decides to leave selected exposed positions uncovered; in implementing this decision it should consider three basic forecasts:

1. The future value of foreign currencies. This is the difficult problem of forecasting exchange rates as discussed in Chapter V–B.
2. The future cost of foreign exchange cover. For example, a foreign exchange manager will want to cover an exposed position. But he expects the cost of cover to decline. He therefore postpones covering the exposed position.
3. The company's own exposed position. Sometimes an exposed position will be covered but then goes away because, for example, accounts receivable are paid off and converted into another currency. So it may turn out that the foreign exchange manager has unnecessarily put the company to the expense of a forward contract.

The first and second required forecasts depend on economic and statistical analysis. The third kind of forecasting depends on the company reporting accurately not only its existing financial data but also expected major changes in its currency positions.

With these three sets of forecasts a money manager has a good beginning for covering exposures against currency risk. If exposed assets are greater than exposed liabilities, the company is vulnerable to devaluation. On the other hand, if exposed liabilities are greater than exposed assets—a short position—then the company is vulnerable to revaluation. Long positions threatened by devaluation can be protected by selling forward in the foreign exchange market. On the other hand, short positions can be protected by buying forward. In both cases, however, the extent of coverage should depend on the company's risk aversion i.e. be considered against probable losses if exposed positions are not covered.

While the forward market is widely used as a hedge against currency losses, as discussed in Chapter III, borrowing or placing money abroad may be preferable to foreign exchange contracts. In some cases interest rate differentials may turn out to be cheaper than foreign exchange contracts. In other cases intercompany accounts can be operated as hedges. Finally, exposures *per se* may be avoided by restructuring balance sheets. Such methods may, however, involve serious trade-offs. For example, a company may attempt to reduce its translation exposure to devaluation by lowering its accounts receivable. But such a policy may result in loss of customers, therefore not justifying its foreign exchange savings.

Finally, it should be stressed that every exposure management policy should be formulated with careful reference to the tax (Chapters V–C, D, E and F) and exchange control policies (Chapter V–G) of the relevant countries.

5. Organization of foreign exchange management

The foreign exchange management function, if it is to be effective, must be consistent with the company's existing organizational structure and style. If a company is highly decentralized, foreign exchange management may operate mainly by offsetting undesired exposures that originate in affiliates. Here the clear requirement is that affiliates report exposure on an accurate and timely basis. Such a system may work better than attempts to control exposure generation, but clearly there needs to be some constraints on the extent that the managers can borrow, extend credit or incur other major financial positions. Such rules, aside from foreign exchange management considerations, are required for prudent management generally.

One danger in too much top management instruction to affiliate management is that it may be counter-productive for marketing or production. For instance, as already noted, top management may decide to restructure a balance sheet by cutting accounts receivable, but this may be a sure way to lose customers. If inventories are considered exposed (contrary to FASB-8 as of March 1980), top management may want to reduce inventories. Above a certain level, however, inventories in, for instance, spare parts may be essential to maintaining production. These logical inconsistencies can become conflicts if a centralized foreign exchange management function is imposed on an organization accustomed to decentralization.

In a decentralized organization, a key requirement for control is an adequate flow of accurate information. There is, however, a trade-off in information between frequency and accuracy. Out of date information is useless. On the other hand, companies who boast about the frequency of exposure reporting may find to their sorrow that data submitted are at a hopelessly low level of accuracy. Sometimes a quick reporting system may be instituted with the understanding that some estimating will be required. But estimating easily becomes guessing so that frequent data may be of worthlessly low quality.

While co-ordination of top management and affiliate management is widely emphasized, in many cases the worst co-ordination problems are among top managers within walking distance of one another. A corporate finance group may arrange a large international loan without considering its possible exposure to loss if the borrowed currency appreciates, as for example in Swiss franc borrowings in the early 1970s. Shareholder relations may brag far too much about how well a company is managing its foreign exchange when it ought to be realized that some years will show better results than others. It is a game in which modesty ought to be encouraged.

Another top management problem is in choosing an optimal number of persons responsible for making decisions. Optimality in this area is probably not a large number because of the limited personnel with really adequate training in this relatively new field. If a small group (e.g. two or three people) manage foreign exchange, it is obvious that they should inform management of the results of their work. The danger here is in management euphoria from profits and depression from losses, when both ought to be recognized as inevitable. Neglect of adequate attention to a function can be easily replaced by demands for above-optimal day-by-day, hour-by-hour information with the result that the foreign exchange managers have no time left to think about what they are supposed to be doing.

A large group managing foreign exchange can easily become a debating society. As has been stressed in such conflicts rationality is only one of three likely model situations. In alternative models the forecast can become a matter of applying bureaucratic rules or it can lead to analytically meaningless compromise.[2] Also, there is a time constraint to the decision making process. Costly resources can easily be wasted two or three times per day in meetings and simply talking about reasons for the latest exchange rate movements when such fluctuations may be mainly random. A longer term perspective somewhere between the tape watcher and the historian is required.

6. Conclusion

An international company should decide on its definition of exposure. It should then adopt and stick with a policy toward exposure risk that will accurately reflect its risk aversion. If it decides to leave some positions uncovered the company should be willing to pay more for data analysis and collection. In particular it should be prepared to forecast exchange rates, costs of cover of exposed positions and—last but not least—the company's own future exposed positions. Against this background and with an organizational structure consistent with the rest of the company, a foreign exchange management function can contribute significantly to company earnings.

---

[2] Graham Allison, *The Essence of Decision* (Little, Brown paperback, 1971).

CHAPTER II

Definitions and measurement of exposure

A. Accounting standards and exposure

The first and most crucial element of any exposure management programme is identification of the exposure. While accountants do not have a commonly accepted definition, a firm's attitude towards risk and the steps it takes to manage its exposure will depend upon how it defines exposure. Management, working with accountants, must decide what is exposed and must select appropriate exchange rates for translating each item on the balance sheet and income statement. This section discusses exposures from an accounting perspective: balance sheet exposure and the relevant translation methods, and income statement exposure and the selection of appropriate exchange rates for translation of the individual items. The section concludes by highlighting a number of the controversial issues the corporate treasurer faces when defining currency exposures. The following sections then analyze in greater detail individual components of exposure from both accounting and treasury perspectives.

1. Translation methods: balance sheet

There are four main accounting conventions used to translate balance sheets denominated in foreign currencies: (1) closing, or current, rate method; (2) monetary/non-monetary method; (3) current/noncurrent method, and (4) temporal method. Each of these methods looks to an item's specific attribute in order to categorize it as either exposed, employing the current exchange rate, or non-exposed, employing the historical rates of exchange.

The closing rate method translates all the assets and liabilities in the financial statements at the current rate. The rationale underlying this method is that the subsidiary's activities are being conducted in a foreign environment and its cash flows are denominated in a foreign currency. It is not a conglomeration of individual parts at risk, but the sum of the parts. The entire operation, the firm's net investment, is considered exposed.[1]

The current/non-current method classifies items based on their maturity, or holding period, within the subsidiary's books. All current items are translated at the current exchange rate, while non-current items are translated at historical rates. Accordingly, all current assets and liabilities are considered to be exposed to exchange risk while all non-current items are not. Potentially unrealistic exchange gains and losses are thus avoided as long term debt and fixed assets are not retranslated at each balance sheet date.

Under the monetary/non-monetary translation convention, the distinction between exposed and non-exposed is made on the basis of the financial nature of the item. All monetary items, where monetary is defined as fixed in the number of foreign currency units, are translated at the current exchange rate. All non-monetary items, essentially inventory and fixed assets, are translated at the historical rates of exchange. The rationale of this method is that as monetary items are fixed in terms of foreign currency units, any change in the exchange rate will result in a change in the base currency value. Non-monetary items are forms of wealth whose money value can change; in other words, price inflation or deflation is assumed to compensate for any changes in currency values.

The temporal method is similar to the monetary/non-monetary.[2] It is based on the concept that

---

[1] In a literal sense, equity is not *translated* at the current rate, although obviously it is in a net investment sense or the balance sheet would not balance.

[2] The key differences between the monetary/non-monetary and temporal methods relate to definitions rather than applications. Prior to the development of the temporal principle, companies using the monetary/non-monetary method realized that translation rates depended on the timing of money amounts rather than on the timing of an item's acquisition or incurrence. For instance, inventory is always non-monetary and therefore should be translated at historical exchange rates, but when the inventory was written down to year-end market value it was recognized that the applicable historical exchange rate was the current rate; the rate attached to the money amount, not to the physical goods. ". . .Market value by definition is a current concept and translation should be at the closing free exchange rate" (from a discussion of inventories translated using a monetary/non-monetary approach)—"Handbook of Modern Accounting," Sidney Davidson, Editor-in-Chief; McGraw Hill Book Company, 1970; *Foreign Exchange Transactions and Translations,* George C. Watt, p. 33.

the subsidiary is an extension of the activities of the parent. The translation process reflects transactions of the group as though it were a single enterprise, using the base currency as a unit of measure. Under this method all accounts which are measured on a historical basis are translated at the exchange rate in effect when these accounts were initially recorded. In a similar fashion, those accounts measured on a current (or market) basis are valued at the exchange rate in effect at the date of the balance sheet.

The choice of a translation method affects the accounting exposure by determining whether specific items will be translated at current or historical exchange rates. Accordingly, exposure definition is likely to affect the amount and direction of the hedge. It is possible for a company to be short from an FASB-8 or monetary/non-monetary viewpoint due to long term debt, more balanced if the current/non-current approach is used, and long under the current rate method, as illustrated in Exhibit 1.

Exhibit 1—Translation of balance sheet

Subsidiary's balance sheet		Accounting exposure computation		
		Monetary/non-monetary or temporal method	Current/Non-current method	Closing rate method
Current monetary assets	500	500	500	500
Inventory	500		500	500
Fixed assets	500			500
Land	500			500
	2,000			
Current monetary liabilities	(500)	(500)	(500)	(500)
Long term debt	(500)	(500)		(500)
Owners' equity	(1,000)			
	(2,000)			
Balance sheet exposure		(500)	500	1,000

Motivated by the first definition, to cover the exposure the company would buy forward LC* (Local currency) 500; in the second case it would sell LC 500; and in the third case it would sell LC 1,000. Each of the four methods is based on fundamentally different underlying philosophies. And, although there has been discussion for many years as to the right method, no solution has gained worldwide acceptance nor appears likely to in the foreseeable future. To illustrate, Appendix A summarizes current accounting practice in this regard in major countries.

2. Translation of income statement

A similar controversy over which rates to use is applicable to the income statement. Revenues and expenses can be translated at the current rate, historical rates or at average rates; average rates are more a question of practicality than anything else. If the closing rate is used to translate the subsidiary's income statement, the original accounting relationships are preserved when expressed in terms of parent currency (PC): only the measurement scale has been changed. Assuming an exchange rate of LC1 = PC1 at the beginning of the accounting period, this is illustrated in Exhibit 2, Column 1.

Exhibit 2—Translation of income statement

				Impact analysis in PC terms			
		(1) Closing rate		(2) Closing/hist. rates		(3) Average/hist. rates	
Subsidiary's income statement	LC	Exchange rate (ER)	PC	ER	PC	ER	PC
(1) Sales	1,000	0·9	900	0·9	900	0·95	950
(2) Expenses	(500)	0·9	(450)	0·9	(450)	0·95	(475)
(3) Depreciation	(300)	0·9	(270)	1·0	(300)	1·00	(300)
(4) Income before-tax	200		180		150		175
(5) Tax (60%)	(120)	0·9	(108)	0·9	(108)	0·95	(114)
(6) Income after-tax	LC 80	PC	72	PC	42	PC	61
(7) Gross profit margin	20%		20%		16·7%		18·4%
(8) Net profit margin	8%		8%		4·7%		6·4%

*Throughout the book the following abbreviations are used: local currency, LC; parent company, PC; third currency, TC; exchange rate, ER; after-tax, AT; before-tax, BT and foreign exchange, FX.

The gross profit margin of 20% and net profit margin of 8% are maintained despite the change in the exchange rate from PC (parent currency) 1·0 to PC 0·9. It must be stressed, however, that the reduction of PC 20 in income before-tax (line 4) is hidden from the reader of conventionally prepared financial statements.

If some income statement items are translated at the current rate while others are at historical rates, distortions occur in the original double entry accounting relationships. They occur, for instance, if sales revenues are translated at the current rate, while depreciation on a fixed asset used to generate those sales is translated at the rate in effect when the asset was acquired. This deformity is illustrated in Exhibit 2, Column 2, where the depreciation expense is fixed in PC terms. Since all other expenses are translated into PC at a lower exchange rate, the use of the historical exchange rate for depreciation results in a reduction of PC 50 in income before tax (line 4). The gross and net profit margins declined to 16·7% (from 20%) and 4·7% (from 8%), respectively.

Finally, if some items in the income statement are translated at the average exchange rate of the period, the financial impact recorded in the financial statements will differ further. Referring to Column 3 of Exhibit 2, the gross profit margin in this case is 18·4% while the net profit margin is 6·4%. The negative variance in income before tax is PC 25 (line 4).

3. Accounting exposure and the corporate treasurer

The preceding discussion makes it apparent that *exchange exposure cuts across the classifications used by accountants*. However, all translation methods ultimately result in the same gain or loss because the differences between accounting methods relate only to the timing of recognition of the gains and losses. Long term debt provides an example of this. Any change in the exchange rate will definitely lead to a change in the value of the liability; but if a major portion of this debt is not to be repaid for many years, of what relevance is the accountants' recognition of these changes in each period? The current/non-current method considers the long term debt as not exposed. But will there be a portion payable relatively soon? The closing and monetary/non-monetary methods tag the long term debt as exposed. But what about the portion not payable for many years?

A more precise definition of exchange exposure is needed. Accounting procedures may lead to arbitrary hedging decisions. Within this context, financial executives should take into account the following additional issues when defining currency exposures. First, he should recognize that accounting conventions are based on accrual accounting. At the extreme, accounting exposure will only point to the current impact of recorded transactions, and even then it may have an illusory nature because of the accrual concept. A more realistic definition of exposure must therefore be based on a cash flow basis which would account for all future flows. From a conceptual point of view this issue poses a question: which of the exchange differences will be realized in the proximate period of time? Which of these exchange differences is going to have a real impact on the firm? If one adopts a continuous concern approach many of these exchange differences will not be borne out. The erratic and sometimes reversing nature of the exchange markets may turn this week's loss into next week's gain. A loss recognized due to an appreciating long term debt is not likely to have a substantial impact on the firm for years to come; yet, under a monetary/non-monetary translation convention the total impact would be reported now.

This problem can also be levelled at current accounts, which are most often regarded as exposed to currency changes. Take for example a subsidiary with a receivable in a weak local currency:

> "Without a doubt . . . everyone would agree that if the receivable were in a foreign currency on the parent's books, a loss would have occurred. Why? Because that loss will have to be realized when the receivable is collected. But things are different when the receivable is collected by the subsidiary. Rather the loss will only be realized when the subsidiary is sold or liquidated by its parent, and that is generally only a remote possibility. So the loss is for the most part only a paper loss."[3]

Second, the corporate treasurer must be aware that whereas accounting results are historically oriented, exposure is computed on a *pro-forma* basis. There must be an anticipatory element in order to properly quantify the risks inherent in operations conducted in a foreign currency. In this sense, transaction exposure for the firm should not only be identifying the existing book exposure, but also the exposure arising from future transactions. The importance of this concept was illustrated by Prindl:

> "A number of U.S. companies which do not forecast (their cash positions) and started a period with a net short position in pounds have allowed that supposed position to remain in anticipation of sterling weakening. In several of the companies, the net short position moved to neutral or long in pounds

³ Ankrom, Robert: *"Treasurer's Viewpoint of Foreign Exchange Risk"*—written text of speech delivered in Paris, October 1977, p. 2.

without the parent being aware soon enough of the changed risk. In the worst of these cases, the swing also corresponded with a depreciation of the pound against the dollar. The overall strategy to remain short in sterling was overtaken by the real, unperceived swing in their positions, with the result that actual and sometimes material losses were suffered, without awareness until after the fact. Any tactics used to implement a strategy based on obsolete data could make that problem worse."[4]

Finally, it should be recognized that the use of the current rate within historical cost accounting is tenuous within today's inflationary environment. It may be argued that the use of a current exchange rate with historical cost accounting can only provide distorted valuations. Specifically, the argument states that until the complete implementation of current cost accounting is accomplished, it makes little sense to recognize changes in asset values overseas, while not doing so on a domestic basis. This was well stated in the discussion to FASB-8:

> "Translation is a poor valuation process for assets carried in financial statements at cost because it reflects only the exchange price between the dollar and a single foreign currency, and does not adequately reflect prices in other markets in which a foreign operation could buy and sell those assets. Thus, multiplying the historical foreign currency cost of an asset by the current rate cannot, except by coincidence, measure the value of an asset."[5]

Within this framework, the following sections discuss and analyze exposures generated by various items of the financial statements. Specifically, Section B starts with current monetary assets and liabilities; Section C deals with income statement items and Section D with inventory exposure. Intercompany flows are analyzed in Section E and fixed assets and long term debt in Section F and G, respectively. Chapter II concludes with a section on economic exposure within the framework of inflation accounting.

---

[4] Prindl, A., *Foreign Exchange Risk,* p. 30.
[5] Financial Accounting Standards Board, *Statement of Financial Accounting Standards No. 8,* October 1978, Paragraph 148, p. 66.

Appendix A—Accounting translation methods used in selected countries

	Closing or current							Current/ non-current							Monetary/ non-monetary							Temporal						
	Required	Insisted upon	Predominant practice	Minority practice	Rarely or not found	Not accepted	Not permitted	Required	Insisted upon	Predominant practice	Minority practice	Rarely or not found	Not accepted	Not permitted	Required	Insisted upon	Predominant practice	Minority practice	Rarely or not found	Not accepted	Not permitted	Required	Insisted upon	Predominant practice	Minority practice	Rarely or not found	Not accepted	Not permitted
Argentina					■							■							■					■				
Australia			■								■								■							■		
Austria							■							■							■							
Bahamas				■							■						■								■			
Belgium					■							■							■							■		
Bermuda					■		■					■							■					■				
Bolivia																												
Botswana			■								■							■							■			
Brazil					■							■							■							■		
Canada							■							■							■							
Chile				■								■						■						■				
Colombia			■									■							■							■		
Costa Rica					■					■							■								■			
Denmark			■								■							■							■			
Dominican Rep.						■							■							■			■					
Ecuador					■							■							■						■			
El Salvador					■					■									■					■				
Fiji			■								■							■								■		
France			■							■							■								■			
Germany				■							■						■								■			
Greece			■								■							■							■			
Guatemala				■							■								■							■		
Honduras					■						■							■							■			
Hong Kong			■								■								■							■		
India			■							■								■								■		
Iran					■							■							■							■		
Ireland, Rep. of			■								■							■							■			
Italy				■							■							■							■		

22

Ivory Coast

Jamaica

Japan

Jersey, Channel Is.

Kenya

Korea

Malawi

Malaysia

Morocco

Mexico

Netherlands

New Zealand

Nicaragua

Nigeria

Norway

Pakistan

Panama

Paraguay

Peru

Philippines

Portugual

Senegal

Singapore

South Africa

Spain

Sweden

Switzerland

Taiwan

Trinidad and Tobago

United Kingdom

United States

Uruguay

Venezuela

Zaire

Zambia

Zambabwe Rhodesia

Source: "International Survey of Accounting Principles and Reporting Practices", edited by R. D. Fitzgerald, A. D. Stickler and T. R. Watts, Price Waterhouse International, 1979.

B. Current monetary assets and liabilities

Current monetary exposure arises when a corporation holds current monetary assets and/or liabilities denominated in a foreign currency on its own books and/or when it operates abroad and generates current monetary assets and/or liabilities on the subsidiary's books. These exposures, from an exposure management viewpoint, are frequently defined as transaction, translation or consolidated after-tax.

Transaction exposure relates to actual transactions in foreign currencies, while translation exposure deals with the valuation of overseas operations. Transaction exposure frequently occurs at both the parent and the subsidiary level. For the parent it occurs whenever a transaction is denominated in a currency other than the parent currency; at the subsidiary level it arises when a transaction is denominated in a currency other than the local currency. These gains or losses, whether at the parent or subsidiary level, are taxable or tax deductible by the local tax authorities. The key point is that transaction exposure has tax impacts and affects directly the cash flows of the trading entity.

Translation exposure is a major issue only from the consolidated viewpoint. Translation gains and losses are recognized for accounting purposes by the consolidated entity upon translating the foreign subsidiary's financial statement (as reported in local currency (LC) terms) to the parent currency. Translation gains or losses do not normally represent immediate cash gains or losses. Also, translation exposure frequently can be assumed to have no tax effect upon consolidation; the parent currency (PC) translation gain or loss has no tax effect for the subsidiary and the parent often does not provide for tax effects of foreign earnings considered to be reinvested—each company's tax situation must be evaluated to avoid making unwarranted assumptions, but for illustration purposes it is assumed below that translation gain or loss has no tax effect.

Consolidated after-tax exposure, as the term indicates, combines the translation component *and* the tax effect of the transaction component of the exposure from a consolidated after-tax viewpoint. Accordingly, this definition of exposure, though not an accounting concept, accounts properly for the gain, loss and the tax effects of movements of the individual currencies *vis-à-vis* the parent currency. The concept of after-tax exposure is used extensively by corporations with a centralized exposure management function.

This section discusses current monetary exposure from the parent's, the subsidiary's and the consolidated viewpoints. The exchange rate assumptions are identical throughout the section and are summarized below:

$$31/12/X0 \ldots \ldots \text{TC } 1 = \text{LC } 1 = \text{PC } 1$$
$$28/02/X1 \ldots \ldots \text{LC } 1 = \text{PC } 0.93$$
$$31/03/X1 \ldots \ldots \text{LC } 1 = \text{PC } 0.9$$
$$\text{TC } 1 = \text{PC } 0.8$$
$$\text{TC } 1 = \text{LC } 0.8889$$

In other words, *unless* indicated otherwise, on the *last day* of the accounting period, LC devalues by 10% against PC and TC (third currency) by 20% against PC.

1. Parent's exposures in foreign currencies

A. Transaction exposure

In this example, presented in Exhibit 1, let us assume that the only exposure on the parent's books is an account receivable of TC 1,000. This account receivable is worth PC 1,000 on 31/12/XO. As the TC devalues by 20% vs. the PC on 31/3/X1, the receivable is then worth PC 800 and a before-tax transaction loss of PC 200 is recorded by the parent company (line 4). This loss is assumed to be taxable at the rate of 40% and results in a net after-tax loss of PC 120 (line 6) and an after-tax negative cash impact of PC 120 (line 7).

Exhibit 1—Parent's exposure: transaction

	31/12/X0	31/3/X1
(1) Exposure (TC)	1,000	1,000
(2) ER (PC/TC)	1·0	0·8
(3) PC equivalent	1,000	800
(4) FX gain/(loss) B.T.		(200)
(5) Tax (40%)		80
(6) FX gain/(loss) A.T.		(120)
(7) Cash impact A.T.		(120)

B. Dividend exposure

Anticipated or declared dividends from foreign subsidiaries are exposed to foreign exchange fluctuations as any other exposed monetary assets on the parent's books. This is because the value of the dividend in terms of the parent currency changes in line with the exchange rate change between the LC and PC. It is worth noting, however, that dividend exposure differs from other *transaction* exposures on the parent's books in that it is an intercompany transaction between the subsidiary and the parent with complex tax implications. These are discussed in greater detail in Chapter IV, Section E, and Chapter V, Section D.

Referring to Exhibit 2, we assume that on 31/12/X0 the parent anticipates a dividend of LC 1,000 to be declared on February 28 and remitted on March 3, 19X1. That dividend is originally valued by the parent at PC 1,000. By the time the dividend is declared, however, the LC has depreciated to PC 0·93 and the dividend is worth PC 930. When the dividend is remitted on March 31, the LC has declined further to PC 0·90 and the dividend is worth only PC 900. The cumulative before-tax cash impact thus amounts to PC 100 (line 4).

Exhibit 2—Parent's exposure: dividend

	31/12/X0	28/02/X1	31/03/X1	Cumulative
(1) Exposure (LC)	1,000	1,000	1,000	
(2) ER (PC/LC)	1·0	0·93	0·90	
(3) PC equivalent	1,000	930	900	
(4) Cash impact B.T.		(70)	(30)	(100)

2. Subsidiary's exposures

Whereas exposures on the parent's books impact only the parent, exposures on the subsidiary's books may affect either the subsidiary, the consolidated results or both. Accordingly, in order to understand fully the impact of a subsidiary's exposures it is useful to differentiate between at least three categories of exposure, namely those denominated in: (i) local currency, (ii) parent currency, and (iii) third currencies. A brief analysis of each category follows.

A. Local currency exposure

In this example, we assume that the only exposure on the subsidiary's books on December 31, 19X0, is an account receivable of LC 1,000. From the consolidated viewpoint, this receivable is originally worth PC 1,000, as illustrated in Exhibit 3. On March 31, the PC value of the receivable decreases to PC 900 and a translation loss of PC 100 is recognized in consolidation (line 4). This loss is a valuation loss and has no immediate cash impact. The subsidiary is not affected, as the receivable is denominated in local currency.

Exhibit 3—Subsidiary's exposure: local currency

	31/12/X0	31/3/X1
(1) Exposure (LC)	1,000	1,000
(2) ER (PC/LC)	1·0	0·9
(3) PC equivalent	1,000	900
(4) FX gain/(loss)		(100)

B. Parent currency exposure

In this example we assume that the subsidiary has an account receivable of PC 1,000 on its books on December 31, 19X0. That exposure has an impact on both the subsidiary's and consolidated financial statements, as illustrated in Exhibit 4.

Impact on subsidiary: If there is a change in the exchange rate between the local currency and the parent currency, then the subsidiary will report foreign exchange gains or losses. These gains and losses, in turn, may be taxable by the local tax authorities. Referring to Exhibit 4, whereas on December 31, the subsidiary expected to receive LC 1,000 (for PC 1,000) it will receive LC 1,111·11 on March 31, resulting in a transaction gain of LC 111·11 (line 4). This gain, assumed to be taxable at the rate of 40% in our example, results in an after-tax gain of LC 66·67 (line 6).

Exhibit 4—Subsidiary's exposure: parent currency

A. Subsidiary	31/12/X0	31/3/X1
(1) Exposure (PC)	1,000	1,000
(2) ER (LC/PC)	1·0	1·111
(3) LC equivalent	1,000	1,111·11
(4) FX gain/(loss) B.T.		111·11
(5) Tax (40%)		(44·44)
(6) FX gain/(loss) A.T.		66·67
(7) Cash impact A.T.		66·67
B. Consolidation		
(8) Exposure (PC)	1,000	1,000
(9) ER (PC/PC)	1·0	1·0
(10) PC equivalent	1,000	1,000
(11) FX gain/(loss) B.T.		0
(12) ER (PC/LC)	1·0	0·9
(13) PC equivalent of tax; (5) × (12)		(40)
(14) FX gain/(loss) A.T.; (11) + (13)		(40)

Impact on consolidation: As the receivable on the subsidiary's books is denominated in parent currency, there is no translation effect from the consolidated before-tax viewpoint. If, however, the tax impact on the subsidiary is taken into account, it becomes obvious that 40% of the receivable is exposed to the PC/LC exchange rate. This is because only 40% of the subsidiary's gain constitutes a tax event. The remaining 60% of the subsidiary's gain is no gain to the consolidated entity, as it only maintains its value in PC terms. In other words, it is only the subsidiary's tax that is exposed.

The LC tax exposure and the related gain/loss to the consolidated entity are computed as follows:

Exposure	ER (PC/LC)	PC equivalent	1- tax rate	PC after-tax	Change in ER	PC gain/ (loss)
(1) LC 1,000	1·00	1,000	1	1,000		
(2) (LC 1,000)	1·00	(1,000)	0·6	(600)		
(3) LC tax exposure				400	−10%	(PC 40)

The after-tax exposure of PC 400 equivalent results in an after-tax loss of PC 40 to the consolidated entity if the local currency devalues by 10% against the parent currency. Inversely, should the local currency revalue, the after-tax impact would be positive, as illustrated in Chart 1.

Chart 1–Consolidated after-tax impact of PC exposure on subsidiary's books

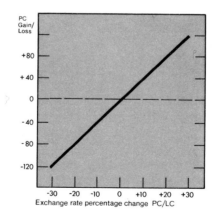

C. Third currency exposure

In this example we assume that the only exposure on the subsidiary's books on December 31, 19X0 is an account receivable of TC 1,000. That exposure will impact both the subsidiary's and consolidated financial statements, as presented in Exhibit 5.

Impact on subsidiary: From the subsidiary's viewpoint the TC has depreciated by 11·11% against the LC and the receivable is now worth LC 888·89, resulting in a transaction loss of LC 111·11 (line 4). This loss is assumed to be taxable by the local authorities at the rate of 40% and results in an after-tax loss of LC 66·67 (line 6).

Exhibit 5—Subsidiary's exposure: third currency

A. Subsidiary	31/12/X0	31/03/X1
(1) Exposure (TC)	1,000	1,000
(2) ER (LC/TC)	1·0	0·8889
(3) LC equivalent	1,000	888·89
(4) FX gain/(loss) B.T.		(111·11)
(5) Tax (40%)		44·44
(6) FX gain/(loss) and cash impact—A.T.		(66·67)
B. Consolidation		
(7) Exposure (TC)	1,000	1,000
(8) ER (PC/TC)	1·0	0·8
(9) PC equivalent	1,000	800
(10) FX gain/(loss) B.T.		(200)
(11) ER (PC/LC)	1·0	0·9
(12) PC equivalent of tax; (5) × (11)		40
(13) FX gain/(loss) A.T.; (10 + (12)		(160)

Impact on consolidation: From the consolidated viewpoint, as the TC has depreciated by 20% *vs.* the PC, the receivable is now worth PC 800 producing a translation loss of PC 200, which is assumed not to be taxable by the parent (line 10). The subsidiary's tax credit is translated and consolidated and, added to the translation loss of PC 200, yields an after-tax loss of PC 160 (line 13).

The after-tax loss of PC 160 can be interpreted as follows: If the receivable of TC 1,000 was collected by the subsidiary on March 31, and immediately remitted to the parent, it would be worth to the parent PC 840 (*vs.* PC 1,000 on 31/12). This valuation is the sum of the PC value of the receivable—PC 800 and the PC equivalent of the tax credit received by the subsidiary—PC 40.

The after-tax exposures and the related gains/losses in this situation are computed as follows:

Exposure	ER (PC/LC)	PC equivalent	1- tax rate	PC after-tax	Change in ER (PC/LC)	PC gain/(loss)
(1) LC 1,000	1·00	1,000	1	1,000		
(2) (LC 1,000)	1·00	(1,000)	0·6	(600)		
(3) LC tax exposure				400	−10%	(40)

Exposure	ER (PC/LC)	PC equivalent	1- tax rate	PC after-tax	Change in ER (PC/TC)	
(4) TC 1,000	1·00	1,000	0·6	600		
(5) TC after tax exposure				600	−20%	(120)
(6) Total after-tax gain/(loss)						(160)

The above computations indicate that from a consolidated after-tax viewpoint, 40% of the receivable is exposed to the PC/LC exchange rate while the remaining 60% is exposed to the PC/TC rate. This is because 40% of the subsidiary's loss constitutes a tax event in LC terms, while the remaining 60% of the receivable maintains its value in TC terms. The impact of these exposures under various exchange rate assumptions is presented graphically in Chart 2.

Chart 2—Consolidated after-tax impact of TC exposure on subsidiary's books

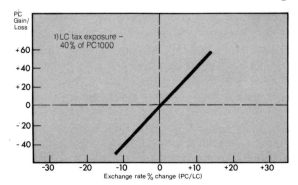
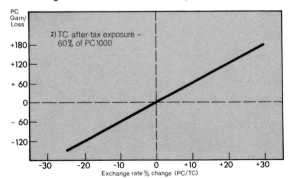

C. Income statement

Income statement exposure quantifies the negative or positive impact of currency fluctuations on the operating income and/or the translation adjustment of a reporting entity. As the value of a foreign currency changes relative to the currency of the reporting entity, the revenues and expenses from operations within a country, when expressed in the reporting currency, show an increase or decrease. But this increase or decrease is generally not reported as a foreign exchange gain or loss. Instead, it is usually quantified as an *operating variance,* affecting the operating income, as discussed in detail in Chapter VIII, Section B. Concomitantly, however, the revenues and expenses generate assets and liabilities on the books of the reporting entity. The *net* assets generated, in turn, impact the *translation adjustment* of the reporting entity if, at the end of the exposure period, they are translated at an exchange rate different from the transaction rate at which they had been originally recorded. This translation adjustment is conceptually identical to the one discussed in Section B of this chapter. This section discusses and analyzes income statement exposure as it arises at the parent and subsidiary levels.

1. Parent income statement

If the parent company's revenues and expenses are denominated in a foreign currency, the parent currency equivalent of revenues and expenses will be altered if the exchange rate between the foreign currency (FC) and parent currency changes during the exposure period. This section discusses the parent's income statement and balance sheet exposure, and the relationship between the two using different assumptions as to the timing in exchange rate changes. Accordingly, Scenario 1 in Exhibit 1 assumes that the foreign currency devalues by 10% at the end of the exposure period and Scenario 2 a devaluation of 10% at the beginning of the period. Scenario 3 assumes a gradual depreciation of the FC over the period, with a 10% depreciation by the end of the period. We assume that the exchange rate at the beginning of the exposure period is FC 1 = PC 1.

Stable foreign currency: control statement: If the exchange rate between the foreign currency and the parent currency does not change over the exposure period, the results in terms of the parent currency will represent exactly the PC equivalent of the FC earnings. In our case, where the exchange rate remains at par throughout the period, the FC and PC results are identical. This situation is presented as the control statement in Exhibit 1 where sales of FC 10,000 by the parent company have no impact on either the variance or the translation adjustment (columns 5 and 6).

Exhibit 1—Income statement exposure of the parent company

| | (1) FC revenues | PC equivalent stated at | | | PC impact analysis | | |
Item		(2) Opening rate	(3) Transaction rate	(4) Closing rate	(5) Operating variance	(6) Translation adjustment	(7) Total impact
Control statement	10,000	10,000	10,000	10,000	0	0	0
Scenario 1	10,000	10,000	10,000	9,000	0	(1,000)	(1,000)
Scenario 2	10,000	10,000	9,000	9,000	(1,000)	0	(1,000)
Scenario 3	10,000	10,000	9,500	9,000	(500)	(500)	(1,000)

Foreign currency devalues at the end of the period: If the foreign currency devalues on the last day of the accounting period, the parent will report a translation loss of PC 1,000. This is because the net assets generated by the net income at the exchange rate of PC 1·0 are translated at the end of the period at the exchange rate of PC 0·9. The translation loss of PC 1,000 is shown under Scenario 1 in the Exhibit (column 6).

Foreign currency devalues at the beginning of the period: If the FC devalues at the beginning of the period, revenues will be recorded at the exchange rate of PC 0·9. Since the exchange rate remains at PC 0·9 throughout the whole quarter, the income generated during the period will remain on the books on March 31, 19X1 at the same exchange rate of PC 0·9. *No translation* gain/loss will be reported and the decline in income would show as a negative variance of PC 1,000, as illustrated under Scenario 2 (column 5).

Foreign currency depreciates gradually over the period: If the foreign currency depreciates gradually over the exposure period, revenues and expenses generally are translated at the lower average exchange rate of the period. Furthermore, if the local currency continues to decline after the revenues and costs have been booked at the average rate, the assets generated, i.e. FC 10,000 will decline in value when expressed in PC terms and result in a translation loss. In Scenario 3 the total decline of PC 1,000 in income (column 7) is due to a negative variance of PC 500 (column 5) and a translation loss of PC 500 (column 6).

Reconciliation of impact recognition: The above analysis indicates that the timing of the exchange rate changes influences the manner in which impact of foreign exchange fluctuations is reported. Column 7 of Exhibit 1 indicates that the *net impact of the exchange rate changes is identical under* the three scenarios where the foreign currency depreciates by 10% against the parent currency *by the end* of the accounting period. They key difference between the three situations is therefore only a matter of accounting cosmetics.

2. Subsidiary income statement

When a subsidiary generates revenues and/or incurs expenses, these transactions give rise to currency exposures at either the subsidiary or the consolidated level or both, depending on the currency denomination of these transactions. Accordingly, in the following pages, we analyze a subsidiary's income statement exposure where revenues and expenses are denominated in the local currency of the subsidiary, the parent currency and a third currency. We assume that the exchange rates at the beginning of the exposure period are LC 1 = PC 1 = TC 1.

A. Local currency denomination

If the subsidiary's transactions are only denominated in local currency, there is no impact on subsidiary's variance or translation adjustment as these transactions are denominated in the subsidiary's own currency. From the consolidated viewpoint, however, the financial statements will reflect an increase or decrease in earnings when stated in the parent currency if the exchange rate between the local and parent currency changes during the exposure period. This impact on the consolidated entity is analyzed in the same manner as in the case of the income statement of the parent company.

In the example that follows we assume that the subsidiary's revenues are LC 10,000 and the local currency depreciates gradually over the exposure period, with a 10% decline by the end of the period.

Exhibit 2—Subsidiary income statement: LC denomination—consolidated impact

	PC data stated at			PC impact analysis		
LC revenues	Opening rate	Transaction rate	Closing rate	Operating variance	Translation adjustment	Net impact
10,000	10,000	9,500	9,000	(500)	(500)	(1,000)

Exhibit 2 indicates that the LC decline against the PC results in a negative currency variance of PC 500 and a translation loss of PC 500, i.e. net nagative impact of PC 1,000.

B. Parent currency denomination

Subsidiaries frequently have operating transactions denominated in currencies other than the local currency. The impact of transactions denominated either in the parent or a third currency on the subsidiary's and consolidated financial statements is discussed and analyzed below.

If the transactions are denominated in the parent currency and the exchange rate between the LC and PC changes during the exposure period, then the local currency value of the transaction will change. The increase or decrease in the LC value of the transaction, in turn, alters the subsidiary's tax position which is also reflected in the consolidated accounts.

To illustrate this impact, we assume that the subsidiary generates revenues during the exposure period on the basis of a PC sales price. In our example, this creates an inflow of PC 10,000 either in the form of a receipt of PC denominated cash or the creation of an account receivable denominated in PC. Given an appreciation of the parent currency from LC 1·0 to LC 1·11 on the first day of the exposure period, the impact on the subsidiary and the consolidated entity is presented below.

Impact on subsidiary: The subsidiary's pre-tax income increases by LC 1,111·11 as shown in the net impact column of Exhibit 3–A. The translation adjustment is unaffected as the rate change took place at the beginning of the period.

Exhibit 3—Subsidiary's income statement exposure: PC demonination

A. Impact on subsidiary

Revenues	LC equivalent stated at			LC impact analysis		
	Opening rate	Transaction rate	Closing rate	Operating variance	Translation adjustment	Net impact
PC 10,000	10,000	11,111·11	11,111·11	1,111·11	0	1,111·11

B. Consolidated impact

Revenues	PC equivalent stated at			PC impact analysis		
	Opening rate	Transaction rate	Closing rate	Operating variance	Translation adjustment	Net impact
PC 10,000	10,000	10,000	10,000	0	0	0

Consolidated impact: When expressed in the parent currency, revenues remain at PC 10,000 and no impact is recognized at the consolidated level on a pre-tax basis. This is illustrated in Exhibit 3–B. If taxes are taken into account, however, the increase in the subsidiary's taxable income by LC 1,111·11 increases local tax by LC 444·44, which translated into PC at the closing rate of PC 0·9 amounts to PC 400. The decline of PC 400 in consolidated after-tax income is computed as follows:

Exposure	ER (PC/LC)	PC equivalent	1-tax rate	PC after-tax	Change in ER	PC gain/(loss)
LC 10,000	1·0	10,000	1·0	10,000		
(LC 10,000)	1·0	(10,000)	0·6	(6,000)		
LC tax exposure and impact				4,000	−10%	(400)

These computations indicate that if local currency selling prices are maintained in PC terms, the subsidiary will report higher local currency revenues than that established prior to the devaluation of the local currency. The higher local currency profit results in an increase in local taxes, which must be translated into PC at current rates upon consolidation. Therefore, even in cases where local currency selling prices can be adjusted to offset a currency devaluation, after-tax profits in PC terms will be lower by the amount of increase in taxes payable than that anticipated prior to the local currency devaluation.

C. Third currency denomination

In the following example we assume that a subsidiary exports to a third country and generates revenues of TC 10,000 denominated in the third currency. The exchange rates are at par on December 31, 19X0. On January 1, 19X1 the LC devalues by 10% and the TC by 20% against the PC as shown below:

```
31/12/X0 . . . . . . TC 1 = LC 1 = PC 1
01/01/X1 . . . . . . TC 1 = PC 0·8; LC 1 = PC 0·9; TC 1 = LC 0·8889
31/03/X1 . . . . . . TC 1 = PC 0·8; LC 1 = PC 0·9; TC 1 = LC 0·8889
```

Impact on subsidiary: Chart 1 indicates that the subsidiary's pre-tax revenues declined by LC 1,111·11, thereby decreasing the subsidiary's tax liability by LC 444·44. The net negative after-tax impact on the subsidiary is thus LC 666·67, as shown in the left-hand column of the Chart.

Chart 1: Subsidiary's income statement exposure

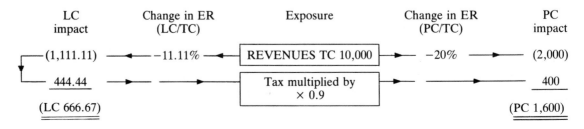

30

The subsidiary's exposure due to third currency transactions and its impact on the subsidiary are computed as follows:

Exposure	ER (LC/TC)	LC equivalent	1-tax rate	LC after-tax	Change in ER	LC gain/(loss)
TC 10,000	1·0	10,000	0·6	6,000		
Subsidiary's after-tax exposure				6,000	−11·11%	(666·67)

Consolidated impact: In parent currency terms, revenues decline by PC 2,000 upon consolidation as a result of the 20% devaluation of the third currency against the parent currency. This is illustrated in Exhibit 4–B.

Exhibit 4—Subsidiary's income statement exposure: TC denomination

A. Impact on subsidiary

	LC equivalent stated at			LC impact analysis		
Revenues	Opening rate	Transaction rate	Closing rate	Operating variance	Translation adjustment	Net impact
TC 10,000	10,000	8,888·89	8,888·89	(1,111·11)	0	(1,111·11)

B. Impact on consolidation

	PC equivalent stated at			PC impact analysis		
Revenues	Opening rate	Transaction rate	Closing rate	Operating variance	Translation adjustment	Net impact
TC 10,000	10,000	8,000	8,000	(2,000)	0	(2,000)

The decrease in the subsidiary's pre-tax revenues of LC 1,111·11, however, decreases the tax liability of the subsidiary by LC 444·44. Translated into PC at the closing rate of PC 0·9, the decrease of PC 400 in consolidated taxes is presented as follows:

- Total decrease in subsidiary's revenues   (LC 1,111·11)
- Tax (40%) on revenues (decrease)   LC 444·44
- PC equivalent of tax at ending rate of PC 0·9   PC 400

The decline in consolidated income of PC 1,600 is due to a decline of PC 2,000 in revenues and a tax credit of PC 400 due to subsidiary's decrease in operating income as illustrated in the right-hand column of Chart 1. The decline of PC 1,600 is computed as follows:

Exposure	ER (PC/LC)	PC equivalent	1-tax rate	PC after-tax	Change in ER	PC gain/(loss)
LC 10,000	1·0	10,000	1·0	10,000		
(LC 10,000)	1·0	(10,000)	0·6	(6,000)		
LC tax exposure and impact				4,000	−10%	(400)
TC 10,000	1·0	10,000	0·6	6,000		
TC after-tax exposure and impact				6,000	−20%	(1,200)
Net after-tax impact						(PC 1,600)

D. Inventory exposure

Inventory exposure arises when a corporation holds and sells inventory abroad. As exchange rates change over time, the value and the costs associated with these inventories change when translated into the parent currency. Accordingly, translation adjustments and/or increases or decreases in the operating profit are reported upon consolidation. The magnitude of the reported impact, in turn, depends on a number of accounting rules and conventions, namely, (1) the translation method, i.e.

at current or historical exchange rate; (2) the accounting method used to arrive at cost, e.g. FIFO or LIFO; and, (3) the lower of cost or market rule.

In this section we discuss inventory exposure of subsidiaries within the framework of these rules and conventions. In Part 1 of the section we review the two translation methods, i.e. current and historical; in Part 2 the accounting method used to arrive at cost, i.e. FIFO and LIFO; in Part 3 we analyze and define inventory exposure under the various translation and costing methods. Finally in Part 4 we review the lower of cost or market rule as it relates to inventory exposure.

In order to avoid unnecessary repetition, the exchange rate assumptions are identical in all of the examples used in this section unless indicated otherwise. For convenience, they are summarized below:

December 31, 19X0	. . . . . . LC 1 = PC1
March 31, 19X1	. . . . . . LC 1 = PC 0·9
Transaction rate for the period	. . . . . . LC 1 = PC 0·95

1. Translation methods: current and historical

As discussed in Section A of this chapter, accounting methods differ with regard to translation of inventory. From the accounting viewpoint, the difference is essentially between those which translate inventory at current exchange rate and others which use historical rates. Although the overall impact of inventory exposure is the same under both methods, they differ in the deferral of accounting gains or losses under the historical method and their immediate recognition under the current rate method.

Inventory carried at current rate: Let us assume that a subsidiary holds inventory worth LC 500 when the exchange rate is LC 1·00 = PC 1·00. Under the current rate method the inventory is exposed because if the local currency depreciates the inventory will be less valuable in terms of the parent currency. In our case the translation loss of PC 50 is computed by multiplying the inventory exposure of PC 500 equivalent by the 10% depreciation of the local currency against the parent currency.

Inventory carried at historical rate: If inventory is carried at historical rates, it is assumed not to be exposed to currency fluctuations. Accordingly, no translation gains or losses result if the exchange rate between the LC and PC changes while the inventory is held. Assuming that the inventory from the previous example is carried at the historical rate of PC 1·0, no translation gain or loss will be reported on consolidation at the end of the accounting period.

Reconciliation of the two methods: The above computations indicate that the translation method used for valuation of inventory influences the manner in which the foreign exchange impact is recognized in the financial statements. Under the current rate, on one hand, gains or losses in the carrying value of inventory are recognized as exchange rates change. Under the historical translation of inventory, on the other hand, the recognition of the impact is deferred until the inventory is sold.

Returning to the previous examples and assuming that the inventory of LC 500 is sold for LC 1,000 in the second quarter of 19X1 at the exchange rate of LC 1 = PC 0·9, the *net* impact of the two methods is summarized and reconciled in Exhibit 1.

Exhibit 1—Reconciliation of timing differences between current and historical translation methods

			Current rate		Historical rate	
Item	LC data	PC equivalent stated at opening rate	PC equiv. stated at end rate	FX impact	PC equiv. stated at end rate	FX impact
Opening inventory	500	500	450	(50)	500	0
Revenues	1,000	1,000	900	(100)	900	(100)
Cost of goods sold	(500)	(500)	(450)	50	(500)	0
Net impact of foreign exchange fluctuations		PC 0		(PC 100)		(PC 100)

The above computations indicate that the only difference between the two translation methods is in timing. Under the current rate method the translation loss of PC 50 during the first quarter is offset by a lower cost of goods sold during the second quarter. Under the historical rate method, the inventory has no foreign exchange impact in parent currency terms in either of the two quarters. The *net* foreign exchange impact of negative PC 100 under each of the two methods is thus an operating variance traceable to the subsidiary's revenues of LC 1,000 during the second quarter of 19X1.

2. Accounting methods to arrive at cost: FIFO and LIFO

Revenues are generally translated at an average exchange rate of the period in which the inventory is sold, regardless of whether FIFO or LIFO valuation is used. Costs, however (i.e. cost of goods sold), are translated at historical rates, i.e. at the rates of the period in which the inventory was acquired. Accordingly, gains and losses due to inventory arise because of changes in exchange rates between the purchase and selling dates of the inventory. In other words, it is a cost/revenue relationship in parent currency terms that determines the gain or loss for the consolidated entity. Yet, as this cost/revenue relationship differs under the two costing methods, the foreign exchange impact of inventories differs under the two methods as well.

FIFO (first-in, first-out): Under FIFO goods are assumed to be used in the order in which they are purchased. Here, the first goods purchased are the first used or sold and the inventory remaining therefore represents the most recent purchases. An example of this method is presented in Chart 1. In the example we make the following assumptions: beginning inventory of LC 500 purchased on December 31, 19X0 at the rate of PC 1·00; and sales of LC 1,000 and purchases of LC 500 at the transaction rate of PC 0·95.

Chart 1—FIFO flows

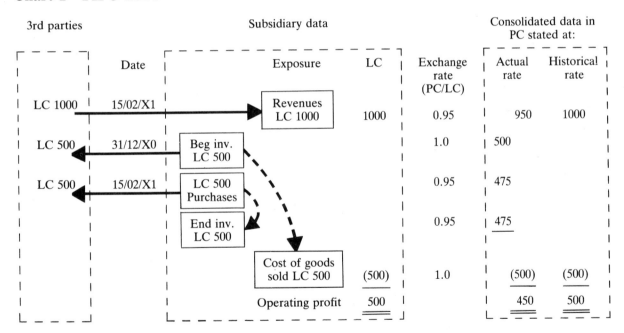

In Chart 1, if the exchange rate remained at par throughout the period, the operating profit would be LC 500 or PC 500 (right-hand column). With the local currency depreciating gradually over the period, however, the operating profit declines from PC 500 to PC 450 as a result of decrease in revenues from PC 1,000 to PC 950. The original inventory of PC 500 equivalent is transferred to cost of goods sold of PC 500 equivalent without having impact on the operating profit.

LIFO (last-in; first-out): LIFO allocates costs on the assumption that the last goods purchased are used first. Though the concept seems simple, in practice LIFO accounting is complex, since it is based on classes or pools of identifiable inventory.[6] Even for accounting purposes, the translation of

---

[6] LIFO is quite rare outside of the United States, where it is used primarily as a tax saver, allowing companies to expense the most recently acquired—and presumably the most expensive—inventory.

inventory is often done by using reasonable estimates. The exposure manager therefore has to make some overall assumptions, as discussed below.

Using the data of the preceding example, the flows of goods and funds under LIFO are presented in Chart 2.

Chart 2—LIFO flows

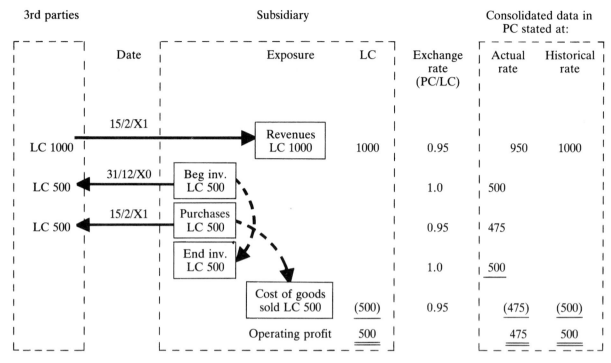

In this example, both sales and costs of goods sold are translated at the same average exchange rate of PC 0·95. The beginning inventory is transferred into the ending inventory and remains on the balance sheet at the historical exchange rate of LC 1 = PC 1. The decrease in the operating profit from PC 500 (with no exchange rate change) to PC 475 (with a 10% depreciation of the LC) is due to a decline of PC 50 in sales and a decline of PC 25 in cost of goods sold.

Reconciliation of FIFO and LIFO: FIFO and LIFO yield different results with the same set of data. Under FIFO we recorded operating profit of PC 450, under LIFO it amounted to PC 475. This is because under LIFO a loss of PC 25 is being deferred until the time the original layer of inventory is sold. Thus, if the exchange rate remained at LC 1 = PC 0·95 in the second quarter of 19X1 and all inventories were then liquidated, the operating profit under FIFO and LIFO would be PC 475 and PC 450 respectively, as illustrated in Exhibit 2.

Exhibit 2—FIFO and LIFO: 2nd quarter

Item	FIFO			LIFO		
	LC	ER	PC	LC	ER	PC
Revenues	1,000	0·95	950	1,000	0·95	950
CGS	500	0·95	475	500	1·00	500
Oper. profit	500		475	500		450

If the results are combined for the two periods, under each of the two methods, the *net* impact is identical as illustrated in Exhibit 3.

Exhibit 3—Reconciliation of FIFO and LIFO

Operating profit

Period	FIFO	LIFO
1st quarter	PC 450	PC 475
2nd quarter	PC 475	PC 450
Cumulative	PC 925	PC 925

Exhibit 3 shows that if the results of the two periods are combined, the operating profit is PC 925 under both FIFO and LIFO. The key difference between the two methods is again in timing. Under LIFO there is less *income statement* distortion; yet, *balance sheet* distortions here are more pronounced. Under LIFO the difference between *accounting* cost and *current replacement* cost varies, and the difference is part of the economic net worth. In that sense, the inventory is very much exposed.

3. Inventory exposure

The impact of inventory differs under the various inventory translation and costing methods. The differences under both methods are attributable primarily to the timing in the recognition of the impact. And although the concepts and principles discussed above are straightforward, they are difficult to apply in practice. Accordingly, in the following pages we consider inventory exposure in a number of situations; namely: (1) historical rate with LIFO; (2) historical rate with FIFO; and, (3) current rate with FIFO. Additionally, we discuss cases where prices of goods are fixed in terms of currencies other than the local currency.

A. Current rate—FIFO

If inventories are translated at current rates of exchange, and if cost of sales is stated in PC by using the same average rate as for other expenses, the exposure and its impact are defined and analyzed as follows: (1) opening inventory is exposed as any other current asset on the opening balance sheet, giving rise to translation gains or losses; and, (2) cost of goods sold decreases an asset valued at a current rate of exchange, impacting either the operating income, the translation adjustment or both. In brief, the exposure is equal to the opening inventory less cost of goods sold.

Assuming opening inventory of LC 500, cost of goods sold of LC 500 and closing inventory of LC 500, the inventory exposure is analyzed in Exhibit 4.

Exhibit 4—Current rate: stable inventory: FIFO

Item	LC	ER	Actual	PC data Variance	Translation	Totals	PC exposure
(1) Opening inventory	500	0·9	450*	N.A.	(50)	(50)	500
(2) Cost of production	500	0·95	475†				
(3) Closing inventory	500	0·9	450*				
(4) Cost of goods sold	(500)	0·95	(475)†	25	25	50	(500)
(5) Operating profit				25	(25)	0	0
(6) Exposure							0

* At closing rate of PC 0·9
† At transaction rate of PC 0·95

These computations indicate the net impact of inventory on financial statements is nil as the loss of PC 50 on the opening inventory is offset by a positive impact of the cost of goods sold of the same amount:

Opening inventory (line 1)	. . . .	(PC 50)
Cost of goods sold (line 4)	. . . .	PC 50
Operating profit (line 5)		PC 0

Inventory exposure in this example is zero, i.e. opening inventory of PC 500 less cost of goods sold of PC 500; accordingly, the impact of exposure is zero (line 6).[7]

B. Historical rate—FIFO

When inventory is translated at historical rate the analysis of the financial statement impact is complicated by two additional factors. First, as inventory brought forward from the previous period is stated at its historical PC value, under FIFO it will have an impact on the income statement of the current period to the extent the opening inventory is sold. Second, as purchases and/or production of inventory results in freezing a historical PC value of an asset, they are responsible directly for the magnitude of the translation gain/loss of the current period.

To illustrate, turning to Exhibit 5, let us assume that LC 500 were spent on purchasing and producing inventory during the first quarter. The opening and closing inventories are LC 500 and the LC figure for cost of goods sold is LC 500. Inventory brought forward from the preceding

---

[7] An additional example where inventory exposure is not zero is provided in the appendix.

period, however, is stated in the opening balance sheet at a historical rate of PC 1·08. Accordingly, the financial statements in this situation are affected in *two* ways:

Exhibit 5—Historical rate: stable inventory: FIFO

Item	LC	Historical valuation ER	PC	Actual	PC valuation Variance	Translation	Deferral	Total	PC exposure
(1) Opening inventory	500	1·08	540	500*			40	40	500
(2) Cost of production	500	0·95	475	450†	N.A.	25		25	
(3) Closing inventory	500	0·95	475	450†			(25)	(25)	
(4) Cost of goods sold	(500)	1·08	(540)	(500)*	(40)	N.A.		(40)	(500)
(5) Operating profit					(40)	25	15	0	
(6) Exposure									0

* At opening rate
† At closing rate

First, the PC equivalent of cost of goods sold for the period is penalized by PC 40 because LC 500 are transferred from a historic rate asset valued at 540. The penalty is measured by comparing what the PC value of the LC 500 would have been using the beginning and historical rates of exchange. And since all sales for the period are recorded at the PC 0·95 average rate, the result of the carry over of inventory with a historic exchange value is a misleading decrease in the operating gross profit when the earnings are stated in terms of parent currency. The translation adjustment is unaffected.

Second, the LC 500 spent during the period on purchasing and producing inventory will, to the extent that the inventory so purchased and produced is unsold at the end of the period, have a frozen PC value of PC 475, i.e. LC 500 at the average rate of PC 0·95. The result is that when the LC is declining against the PC, a translation loss of PC 25 is foregone. That loss would have been the difference between the inventory recorded at the historic PC 0·95 and PC 0·90 period-end rates. In this case only the translation adjustment is affected.

The net impact of the two elements is that the earnings of the period have been affected by timing differences. At the beginning of the period, overvalued inventory brought forward resulted in a penalty to current earnings of PC 40; the foregone translation loss is PC 25. The net income impact is therefore negative PC 15.

An additional consequence is that the overvaluation of the closing inventory by PC 25, achieved at the expense of the translation adjustment for the current period, will not have a negative impact on the translation adjustment of the subsequent period. It will instead affect the cost of sales of the subsequent period by overstating it and, therefore, decreasing gross profit.

Thus, the operating profit decreases by PC 15 because of two factors: (1) transfer of inventory valued at the historical cost of PC 540 into cost of goods sold, in effect increasing cost of goods sold by PC 40; and, (2) a translation gain of PC 25 resulting from freezing LC 500 at the rate of PC 0·95 instead of leaving it exposed to the end of the period when the rate is PC 0·90. The negative impact of PC 15 on the financial statements is summarized as follows:

Cost of goods sold (line 4)	(PC 40)
Cost of production (line 2)	PC 25
Operating profit (line 5)	(PC 15)

In this situation exposure itself is the sum of the opening inventory and the cost of goods sold, i.e. zero in our example, also resulting in zero gain/loss in PC terms. The exposure data in this situation is reconciled with the financial statements results as follows:

Gain/(loss) on inventory exposure of zero (line 6)	PC 0
Overvaluation of opening inventory (line 1)	(PC 40)
Overvaluation of closing inventory (line 3)	PC 25
	(PC 15)

C. Historical rate: LIFO

This situation is conceptually similar to the one discussed above, differing only with regard to cost allocation. More specifically, the positive impact of PC 50 on the operating profit results from (1) lower cost of goods sold than would have been the case had the opening inventory been sold; and, (2) the freezing of a monetary asset of LC 500 in inventory at the rate of PC 0·95 instead of leaving it exposed while the rate declines to PC 0·90.

36

Exhibit 6—Historical rate: stable inventory: LIFO

Item	LC	Historical valuation ER	PC	Actual	PC valuation Variance	Translation	Deferrals	Total	PC exposure
(1) Opening inventory	500	1·08	540	500*			40	40	500
(2) Cost of production	500	0·95	475	450†	N.A.	25		25	
(3) Closing inventory	500	1·08	540	450†			(90)	(90)	
(4) Cost of goods sold	(500)	0·95	(475)	(500)*	25	N.A.	—	25	(500)
(5) Operating profit					25	25	(50)	0	
(6) Exposure									0

* At opening rate
† At closing rate

The positive impact of PC 50 on the financial statements is summarized as follows:

Cost of goods sold (line 4)	PC 25
Cost of production (line 2)	PC 25
Operating profit (line 5)	PC 50

Exposure in this situation is again zero, resulting also in a zero gain/loss in PC terms. The exposure data is reconciled with the financial statements results as follows:

Gain/(loss) on inventory exposure of zero (line 6)	PC 0
Overvaluation of opening inventory (line 1)	(PC 40)
Overvaluation of closing inventory (line 3)	PC 90
	PC 50

Comparing the above LIFO results with those obtained under FIFO in the previous example, we notice larger balance sheet distortions under LIFO than under FIFO. Under LIFO the overvaluation on the closing inventory is PC 90 whereas under FIFO it amounts to only PC 25. These deferred amounts are computed in Exhibits 5 and 6. Conversely, the income statement impact is less pronounced under LIFO than under FIFO; under LIFO cost of sales is translated at the rate of PC 0·95, the same rate as used for translation of revenues. Under FIFO, on the other hand, inventory flows through the income statement at the rate of PC 1·08, considerably higher than the rate used for translating revenues of the current period.

D. PC priced inventory

Thus far we have assumed that both revenues and costs are stable in terms of the local currency. Yet, overseas subsidiaries often buy, sell and/or hold inventory with value fixed in a currency other than the local currency. In such circumstances, costs change in terms of the local currency and impact the profit margins in terms of the local currency. The increased or decreased profit margins, in turn, affect the tax position of both the subsidiary and the consolidated entity.

In the analysis that follows we assume that the subsidiary buys inventory with value fixed in terms of the parent currency. This, for example, would be the case where a subsidiary imports inventory from the parent company's country. Assuming current rate translation and FIFO costing methods, this situation is presented in Exhibit 7.

Exhibit 7—PC priced inventory, current rate: stable inventory: FIFO

Item	PC	Historical valuation ER	LC	Actual	LC valuation Variance	Translation	Total	LC exposure
(1) Opening inventory	500	2·0	1,000‡	1,250†	N.A.	250	250	1,000
(2) Cost of production	750	2·25	1,500‡	1,678·5*				
(3) Closing inventory	500	2·5	1,000‡	1,250†				
(4) Cost of goods sold	(500)	2·25	(1,000)‡	(1,125)*	(125)	(125)	(250)	(1,000)
	(250)	2·25	(500)‡	(562·5)*	(62·5)	(62·5)	(125)	(500)
(5) Operating profit					(187·5)	62·5	(125)	
(6) Exposure								(500)

* At transaction rate of PC 1 = LC 2·25
† At closing rate of PC 1 = LC 2·5
‡ At opening rate of PC 1 = LC 2·00

On December 31, 19X0, the subsidiary has on its books inventory worth PC 500, purchased earlier at the rate of LC 2·0. During the first quarter of 19X1 the subsidiary purchases inventory for PC 750 and sells PC 750 of the inventory at the transaction rate of PC 1 = LC 2·25. The exchange rate moves as follows:

December 31, X0	PC 1 = LC 2·0 or LC 1 = PC 0·5
March 31, X1	PC 1 = LC 2·5 or LC 1 = PC 0·4
Transaction rate	PC 1 = LC 2·25 or LC 1 = PC 0·444

Impact on subsidiary: Referring to Exhibit 7, the impact on the subsidiary's financial statements is summarized as follows:

Opening inventory (line 1)	LC 250
Cost of goods sold (line 4)	(LC 375)
Operating profit (line 5)	(LC 125)

Using the exposure of negative PC 500 (line 6), we compute the decline of LC 125 in the subsidiary's operating profit as follows:

Impact on operating profit = inventory exposure × change in LC/PC exchange rate = 500 × (−25%) = (LC 125)

Impact on consolidation: Since the inventory is assumed to maintain its intrinsic value in terms of the parent currency, the consolidated balance sheet and income statement will not be affected on a pre-tax basis. If, however, taxes are taken into account, the tax impact of the decline of the subsidiary's taxable income by LC 125 is reflected in the consolidated books as follows:

Decrease in subsidiary's income	(LC 125)
Tax (40%)	LC 50
PC equivalent of tax rate at closing rate of PC 0·4	PC 20

The consolidated after-tax impact of PC 20 is computed as follows:

LC exposure	LC	ER (PC/LC)	PC equivalent	Tax rate	PC after-tax	Change in ER	PC gain/(loss)
Opening inventory	1,000	0·5	500	0·4	200		
Cost of goods sold	(1,500)	0·5	(750)	0·4	(300)		
Tax exposure					(100)	−20%	PC 20

These computations indicate that if inventory costs remain stable in PC terms, the subsidiary will report lower operating profit than that established prior to the parent currency appreciation. The lower operating profit of the subsidiary results in a decrease in local taxes, which must be translated into PC at current rates upon consolidation. Therefore, in cases where costs are variable in local currency terms, a depreciation of the LC has a positive consolidated after-tax impact while an appreciation has the opposite effect.

4. Lower of cost or market rule

A major departure from adherence to the historical cost principle is made in the area of inventory valuation. If the inventory declines in value below its original cost for whatever reason (e.g. price level changes), the inventory is written down to reflect this loss. The general rule is that the historical cost principle is abandoned when the future utility of the asset is no longer as great as its original cost.

In such circumstances inventories are valued on the basis of lower of cost or market instead of on an original cost basis. The term market in the phrase "the lower of cost or market" means the cost to replace the item. Market, however, is limited to an amount that should not exceed the net realizable value (i.e. estimated selling price in the ordinary course of business less reasonably predictable cost of completion and disposal) and "should not be less than net realizable value reduced by an allowance for an approximately normal profit margin".

FASB–8 and FASB Interpretation No. 17

In the United States Paragraph 14 of FASB Statement No. 8 and FASB Interpretation No. 17

require that the rule of cost or market, whichever is lower, be applied in dollars. When applying the literal rule of cost or market, whichever is lower, in translated financial statements, translated market is the current foreign currency replacement cost translated at the current rate, except that:

a. Translated market shall not exceed foreign currency net realizable value translated at the current rate; and,
b. Translated market shall not be less than foreign currency net realizable value reduced by an allowance for an approximately normal profit margin translated at the current rate.

Literal application of the rule of cost or market, whichever is lower, requires an inventory write-down in dollar financial statements for locally acquired inventory if the value of the foreign currency had declined in relation to the dollar between the date the foreign operation acquired the inventory and the date of the foreign operation's balance sheet unless foreign currency replacement costs or selling prices have increased sufficiently so that translated market measured in dollars exceeds translated historical cost. In these circumstances, inventory write-downs are not translation exchange losses and *are not included in the aggregate exchange gain or loss* required to be disclosed pursuant to Paragraph 32 of Statement No. 8. The application of the rule is illustrated below, using examples presented in FASB–8's Interpretation No. 17.[8]

Example 1—Write-down required

Assume the following:

- When the rate is FC 1 = $2·40, a foreign subsidiary of a U.S. company purchases a unit of inventory at a cost of FC 500 (measured in dollars, $1,200);
- At the foreign subsidiary's balance sheet date, the current rate is FC 1 = $2·00 and the current replacement cost of the unit of inventory is FC 560 (measured in dollars, $1,120);
- Net realizable value (NRV) is FC 630 (measured in dollars, $1,260);
- Net realizable value reduced by an allowance for approximately normal profit margin is FC 550 (measured in dollars, $1,100).

Because current replacement cost measured in dollars ($1,120) is less than translated historical cost ($1,200) and falls between the NRV of $1,260 and NRV minus profit of $1,100, an inventory write-down of $80 is required in the dollar financial statements.

Example 2—No write-down required

Assume the same information as given in the preceding example except that the current replacement cost at the foreign subsidiary's balance sheet date is FC 620. Because market measured in dollars (FC 620 × $2·00 = $1,240) exceeds translated historical cost (FC 500 × $2·40 = $1,200), an inventory write-down is not required in the dollar financial statements.

---

[8] FASB Interpretation No. 17, "Applying the Lower of Cost or Market Rule in Translated Financial Statements: An Interpretation of FASB Statement No. 8", Financial Accounting Standards Board, Stamford, Connecticut, 1977.

Appendix A—Additional example of inventory exposure

Item	Opening inventory	Less: CGS	Add: purchases	Closing inventory	PC impact
Currency of denomination	LC 1,000	LC (600)	LC 500	LC 900	
Opening rate (PC/LC)	1·0	1·0			
Transaction rate (PC/LC)		0·95	0·95		
Closing rate (PC/LC)	0·9	0·9	0·9	0·9	
Current FIFO in PC terms					
Inventory at opening rate	1,000	(600)			
Inventory at transaction rate		(570)			
Inventory at closing rate	900	(540)			
Operating variance		30			30
Translation G/(L)	(100)	30			(70)
	(100)	60			(40)
Historical FIFO in PC terms					
Historical rate (PC/LC)	1·08	1·08	0·95	1·00778	
Inventory at historical rate	1,080	(648)	475	907	
Inventory at opening rate	1,000	(600)			
Inventory at closing rate			450	810	
Operating variance		(48)			(48)
Translation G/(L)			25		25
Impact of inventory		(48)	25		(23)
Timing differences	80			(97)	(17)
Net impact	80	(48)	25	(97)	(40)
Historical LIFO in PC terms					
Historical rate (PC/LC)	1·08	0·97167	0·95	1·08	
Inventory at historical rate	1,080	(583)	475	972	
Inventory at opening rate	1,000	(600)			
Inventory at closing rate			450	810	
Operating variance		17			17
Translation G/(L)			25		25
Impact of inventory		17	25		42
Timing differences	80			(162)	(82)
Net impact	80	17	25	(162)	(40)

Inventory exposure	LC	ER (PC/LC)	PC equivalent	Change in ER	PC impact
Opening inventory	1,000				
Cost of goods sold	(600)				
Net exposure	400	1·0	400	−10%	(PC 40)

E. Intercompany accounts

In analyzing intercompany exposures, a distinction between translation and transaction concepts is important. This is because translation of intercompany accounts does not normally give rise to accounting gains or losses on the consolidated books whereas their transaction effect does. Intercompany translation exposure is zero regardless of the currency denomination of the intercompany accounts. This is because, from a consolidated viewpoint, the two parties involved (e.g. the parent and the subsidiary) are long and short in the same currency, by the same amount, and for the same maturity. Thus, upon consolidation, exposures resulting from intercompany assets and liabilities normally cancel each other.

The individual legal entities involved, however, keep their books in their own currencies while intercompany accounts may be denominated in currencies other than the respective reporting currencies. Transaction gains and losses may therefore be reported at the subsidiary level (if there is a change in the exchange rate between the local currency and the currency of denomination of the intercompany account) or the parent level (if there is a change in exchange rate between the parent currency and the currency of denomination of the intercompany account). These transaction gains and losses may, in turn, be taxable or tax deductible by the local authorities. The tax effect is reflected in the consolidated accounts.

In essence, therefore, in intercompany exposures there is no translation effect from the consolidated viewpoint and only the tax impacts—translated at the appropriate exchange rate—would be recorded upon consolidation.

The concept of intercompany exposure is illustrated and discussed below within the context of parent/subsidiary and subsidiary/subsidiary transactions. The exchange rate assumptions are identical throughout the section unless indicated otherwise.

    31/12/X0   TC 1 = LC 1 = PC 1
    31/03/X1   LC 1 = PC 0·9
                TC 1 = PC 0·8 = LC 0·8889

In other words, on the last day of the accounting period, LC devalues by 10% against PC and TC by 20% against PC.

1. Parent-subsidiary intercompany exposure

Intercompany exposures between the parent company and a subsidiary are analyzed below with respect to parent, local, and third currency denominations.

A. Denomination in parent currency

In the following example let us assume that the subsidiary has an intercompany account payable of PC 1,000 to the parent on December 31, 19X0. On March 3, 19X1 no translation gain or loss will be recorded as the PC equivalent of the intercompany account is eliminated upon consolidation. This is illustrated below with the use of simple T-accounts:

● On December 31, 19X0, the PC equivalent of the intercompany account is eliminated (by the use of a circle in our examples) as follows:

	Parent	Subsidiary			
			LC	ER	PC
Interco A/R (accounts receivable)	PC 1000	Interco A/P (accounts payable)	1000	1.0	1000

● On March 31, 19X1, the PC equivalent of the intercompany remains at PC 1000 and is again eliminated:

	Parent	Subsidiary			
			LC	ER	PC
Interco A/R	PC 1000	Interco A/P	1111.11	0.9	1000

In the above example, the intercompany exposure of PC 1,000 results in zero pre-tax translation gain or loss for the consolidated entity. This is because on the translation side the payable on the subsidiary's books is fully offset by the receivable on the parent's books. On the transaction side, however, whereas on 31/12/X0 the subsidiary needed LC 1,000 to repay the debt, on 31/03/X1 it will need LC 1,111·11 to repay the liability. The subsidiary thus has a transaction loss of LC 111·11. The loss is assumed to be taxable at the rate of 40% by the subsidiary, resulting in a tax credit of LC 44·44 and an after-tax loss of LC 66·67. The subsidiary's tax credit is reflected in the consolidated accounts after translation at the new exchange rate as illustrated below:

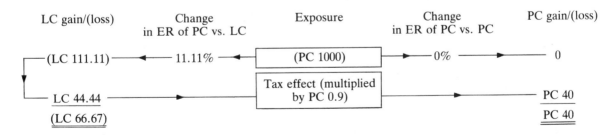

The consolidated after-tax gain of PC 40 identified above is computed as follows:

Exposure	ER (PC/LC)	PC equivalent	1-tax rate	PC after-tax	Change in ER	PC gain/(loss)
(1) (LC 1,000)	1·00	(1,000)	1	(1,000)		
(2) LC 1,000	1·00	1,000	0·6	600		
(3) LC tax exposure				(400)	−10%	PC 40

In this case, from a consolidated point of view only the subsidiary's tax effect is exposed, i.e. 40% of the PC equivalent of exposure. The remaining 60% of the exposure is not exposed from the consolidated viewpoint, as it maintains its parent currency value.

This situation is summarized below and presented in Exhibit 1 as follows:

Exhibit 1—Parent/subsidiary intercompany exposure denominated in parent currency

A. Subsidiary	31/12/X0	31/03/X1
(1) Exposure (PC)	(1,000)	(1,000)
(2) ER (LC/PC)	1·0	1·1111
(3) LC equivalent; (1) × (2)	(1,000)	(1,111·11)
(4) FX gain/(loss) B.T.		(111·11)
(5) Tax (40%)		44·44
(6) FX gain/(loss) A.T.		(66·67)
B. Parent		
(7) Exposure (PC)	1,000	1,000
(8) FX gain/(loss) B.T.		0
(9) FX gain/(loss) A.T.		0
C. Consolidation		
(10) Exposure B.T.; (1) + (7)	0	0
(11) FX gain/(loss) B.T.		0
(12) ER (PC/LC)		0·9
(13) PC equivalent of tax; (5) × (12)		40
(14) FX gain/(loss) A.T.; (11) + (13)		40

Subsidiary's exposure: The subsidiary's transaction exposure of PC 1,000 (line 1) results in foreign exchange losses of LC 111·11 (line 4) and LC 66·67 (line 6) before- and after-tax respectively.

Parent's exposure: The parent has no exposure, as the intercompany account is denominated in the parent currency. Accordingly, no foreign exchange gains or losses are recorded by the parent company (lines 8 and 9).

Consolidated exposure: From the consolidated after-tax perspective, the subsidiary's incremental tax impact of LC 44·44 (line 5) is translated into the parent currency (at the closing exchange rate of LC 1 = PC 0·9 in our example), yielding an after-tax gain of PC 40 (line 14).

B. Denomination in local currency

The concept of intercompany exposure denominated in local currency is illustrated in Exhibit 2. In this example let us assume that the subsidiary has on its December 31, 19X0 balance sheet an intercompany payable of LC 1,000 to the parent company.

The parent's exposure data is summarized in Section A of the exhibit, and indicates a foreign exchange loss of PC 100 before-tax (line 4), an incremental tax credit of PC 40 (line 5) and an after-tax loss of PC 60 (line 6). The subsidiary's exposure data is presented in Section B of the exhibit. Here, as the subsidiary's exposure is denominated in the local currency, it has no foreign exchange impact on its financial statements (line 8).

Exhibit 2—Parent/subsidiary intercompany exposure denominated in local currency

A. Parent	31/12/X0	31/03/X1
(1) Exposure (LC)	1,000	1,000
(2) ER (PC/LC)	1·0	0·9
(3) PC equivalent; (1) × (2)	1,000	900
(4) FX gain/(loss) B.T.		(100)
(5) Tax (40%)		40
(6) FX gain/(loss) A.T.		(60)
B. Subsidiary		
(7) Exposure (LC)	(1,000)	(1,000)
(8) FX gain/(loss) B.T.		0
(9) FX gain/(loss) A.T.		0
C. Consolidation		
(10) Exposure; (1) + (7)	0	0
(11) FX gain/(loss) B.T.		0
(12) Tax impact; line 5		40
(13) FX gain/(loss) A.T.; (11) + (12)		40

The consolidated exposure data is shown in Section C and reflects the incremental tax credit of PC 40 (line 12), traceable to the parent company's foreign exchange loss of PC 100. Accordingly, the consolidated after-tax impact is PC 40, as indicated on line 13 of the exhibit.

C. Denomination in third currency

When intercompany accounts are denominated in a third currency, no translation exposure exists, as explained above. Nonetheless, transaction exposure may give rise to foreign exchange gains and/or losses at either parent, or the subsidiary level, or both. These gains/losses, in turn, have tax effects which are reflected in the consolidated books.

The parent will report a transaction gain or loss if the exchange rate between the parent and third currency changes; the subsidiary will report a gain or loss if the exchange rate between the local and third currency changes. In the real world, however, it is likely that the third currency will change in value by various amounts against each, the local and the parent currency. Foreign exchange gains and/or losses will thus be recorded by both legal entities, depending on the cross-rate movements between the relevant currencies. These gains and/or losses of the subsidiary and the parent company are normally taxable or tax deductible within the respective tax jurisdictions. The tax effects, in turn, are reflected, after their translation at appropriate exchange rates, in the consolidated accounts.

2. Inter-subsidiary exposure

We have discussed intercompany exposures arising between the parent company and a subsidiary. Intercompany exposures also arise between the individual subsidiaries. Here, the concepts outlined above apply as well. More specifically, from a translation point of view, there is no exposure at the consolidated level, as the payable and receivable are denominated in the same currency, in the same amount and for the same maturity. This applies regardless of the currency denomination of the inter-subsidiary account, be it the parent currency, the currency of one of the subsidiaries, or a third currency. On the transaction side, however, each subsidiary will report a foreign exchange gain or loss if the two following conditions are met: (1) the intercompany account is denominated in a currency other than the local currency, and (2) the exchange rate between the local currency and the currency of denomination of the account changes during the exposure period. The resulting foreign exchange gains/losses of the various subsidiaries, in turn, may be taxable or tax deductible within the respective tax jurisdictions. The parent currency equivalent of these tax events is reflected in the consolidated books, as discussed above.

Since the concepts involved in intersubsidiary exposure are identical regardless of the currency denomination of the account, within this subsection we analyze only one situation, an intersubsidiary exposure denominated in one of the subsidiaries' currencies. More specifically, in the following example we assume a sterling receivable of £10,000 on the books of a German subsidiary owed by the British subsidiary. Exchange gains/losses are assumed to be taxable/tax deductible at a rate of 40% in Germany. Both subsidiaries are fully owned by a U.S. parent and the exchange rate is assumed to move as follows:

December 31, 19X0   £1 = DM 3·0 = $1·5
March 31, 19X1   £1 = DM 2·9 = $1·595, i.e.
                    DM 1 = $0·55

This situation is presented in Exhibit 3.

Exhibit 3—Subsidiary/subsidiary intercompany exposure

A. German subsidiary	31/12/X0	31/03/X1
(1) Exposure (£)	10,000	10,000
(2) ER (DM/£)	3·0	2·9
(3) DM equivalent	30,000	29,000
(4) FX gain/(loss) B.T.		(1,000)
(5) Tax (40%)		400
(6) FX gain/(loss) A.T.		(600)
B. U.K. subsidiary		
(7) Exposure (£)	(10,000)	(10,000)
(8) FX gain/(loss)		0
C. Consolidation		
(9) ER ($/DM)	0·5	0·55
(10) Exposure; (1) + (7)	0	0
(11) FX gain/(loss) B.T.		0
(12) $ equivalent of tax; (5) × (9)		220
(13) FX gain/(loss) A.T.; (11) + (12)		220

The German subsidiary reports a foreign exchange loss of DM 1,000 before-tax (line 4) which gives rise to a tax credit of DM 400 (line 5). Accordingly, the subsidiary's after-tax loss is DM 600, as shown on line 6. The British subsidiary's data is shown in Section B of the exhibit. Here, as the intercompany payable of £10,000 is denominated in sterling, the U.K. subsidiary has no transaction exposure and reports no foreign exchange gains or losses. The U.S. consolidated results, summarized in Section C, reflect the dollar equivalent of the German subsidiary's tax credit of DM 400, i.e. $220 (line 12). The consolidated after-tax impact is therefore $220, as computed on line 13 of the exhibit.

F. Fixed assets

As discussed in Section A of this chapter, translation methods differ with regard to the treatment of fixed assets. Essentially, the difference is between those which translate the asset at current rates and others which use historical rates. Although the net impact of fixed asset exposure is the same under both methods, the key difference between them is in the immediate recognition of accounting gains or losses when the asset is carried at current rates and their deferral if it is carried at historical rates.

When compared to other assets, fixed assets have at least two distinguishing features. First, instead of being for sale in the normal course of business, they are retained for use in earning revenues. Second, during the time they are earning revenues, they may be—depending on the nature of the asset—consumed and are therefore depreciable. The depreciation expense is usually charged against income and allocated over the life of the asset.

This section discusses fixed asset exposure—i.e. acquisition, depreciation and disposal of fixed assets—within the context of the two translation methods. Throughout the section we use an identical example where a subsidiary, reporting in local currency, purchases a fixed asset worth LC 1,000 on December 31, 19X0 with a expected life of four years. The subsidiary's tax rate is 40% and the exchange rate moves as follows:

31/12/X0	LC 1·0 = PC 1·0
31/12/X1	LC 1·0 = PC 0·9
Average rate for 19X1	LC 1·0 = PC 0·95
31/12/X2	LC 1·0 = PC 0·8
31/12/X3	LC 1·0 = PC 0·7
31/12/X4	LC 1·0 = PC 0·6

1. Acquisition of fixed assets

If the fixed asset is carried at current rates of exchange the underlying assumption is that if the local currency depreciates, the asset will be less valuable in terms of the parent currency. Accordingly, smaller revenues in parent currency equivalents will be generated by the goods it produces for sale. More specifically, under the current rate method, by purchasing a fixed asset, exposed monetary assets are converted into exposed fixed assets and translation gains or losses are accrued each time the books of the subsidiary are translated and consolidated. In our example the asset valued at LC 1,000 or PC 1,000 on December 31, 19X0, gives rise to a translation loss of PC 100 on December 31, 19X1. This is illustrated in Exhibit 1–A in the translation adjustment column and the last three columns where the exposure of PC 1,000 equivalent is multiplied by the 10% devaluation of the local currency against the parent currency, yielding the translation loss of PC 100.

Exhibit 1—Fixed asset exposure: current rate method

| Item | Historical value | | | Actual | PC impact analysis | | | PC exposure | Change in ER | PC impact |
	LC	ER	PC		Operating variance	Translation adjustment	Net impact			
A. Fixed asset exposure										
Fixed asset	1,000	1·0	1,000	900*	—	(100)	(100)	1,000	−10%	(100)
B. Depreciation expense exposure										
Depreciation expense	(250)	1·0	(250)	(225)*	12·5	12·5	25	(250)	−10%	25
						Net impact	(PC 75)			(PC 75)

* At closing rate of PC 0·9

44

In other words, on December 31, 19X1, the value of the fixed asset is written down from PC 1,000 to PC 900 resulting in a translation loss of PC 100.

Under historical rate method investment in fixed assets results in freezing the parent currency value of a local currency denominated asset. In other words, it is assumed that the asset maintains its intrinsic value in terms of the parent currency and foreign exchange gains or losses are foregone as current monetary assets are transferred into a historically valued fixed asset. Accordingly, in our example, by investing LC 1,000 in a fixed asset on December 31, 19X0, the company has eliminated its monetary exposure of LC 1,000, thereby foregoing a potential translation loss of PC 100 as follows:

	LC amount	PC gain/(loss)
● Current asset on December 31, 19X0	1,000	(100)
● Acquisition of F.A. at rate of PC 1·0 instead of holding cash till LC declines to PC 0·9	(1,000)	100
● End of period exposure and impact	LC 0	PC 0

2. Depreciation of fixed assets

The fixed asset exposure is complicated further for depreciable assets because the value of the asset decreases over its life, in line with the periodic depreciation charge. Three issues are important for analyzing the impact of depreciation expenses on exposure: (1) the translation method; (2) the interrelationship between depreciation expense and cash flows; and (3) the relationship between accelerated depreciation, cash flows, and deferred taxes.

Translation methods: The depreciation expense under the current rate method is translated at the average exchange rate of each accounting period. Accordingly, from an accounting point of view, depreciation charges under the current rate method alter expenses when expressed in the parent currency in the consolidated income statement. Returning to our example and assuming depreciation expense of LC 250 during 19X1, we identify a positive variance of PC 12·5 and a translation gain of PC 12·5 (Exhibit 1–B). If the positive impact of PC 25 traceable to depreciation is added to the translation loss of PC 100 identified above, the net impact of the fixed asset is a negative PC 75 during 19X1.

Under the historical rate method, on the other hand, depreciation charges are not exposed from an accounting point of view. To illustrate, let us assume an operating profit of LC 450 and a depreciation charge of LC 250 during the exposure period. Here, the decline of PC 45 in income results only from the translation of the operating profit, as illustrated below:

			PC stated at		
	LC	ER	Actual rate	Historical rate	PC impact
(1) Operating profit	450	0·9	405	450	(45)
(2) Less: depreciation	(250)	1·0	(250)	(250)	
(3) Net profit	200		155	200	(45)
(4) Add: depreciation	250	1·0	250	250	
(5) Cash flow	450	0·9	405	450	(45)

The above table indicates that the depreciation expense of the subsidiary has no foreign exchange impact on the consolidated entity. The decline in income of PC 45 results solely from the translation of operating profit of LC 450 (line 1).

Depreciation expense and cash flows: It is frequently assumed that depreciation provides funds for the replacement of fixed assets. This assumption, however, is incorrect, since depreciation expense—being a non-cash item—merely reduces retained earnings. The funds for the replacement of the assets come from revenues, without which no profits and cash inflows result.

To illustrate why depreciation does not generate funds for the replacement of the fixed assets, let us assume that a fixed asset, valued at LC 1,000 on December 31, 19X0, has an expected life of four years. The estimated salvage value of the asset is zero and the subsidiary's beginning balance sheet is:

Fixed assets	LC 1,000	Equity	LC 1,000

Taking the extreme example where the subsidiary has no revenues over the four year period, the respective income statements are:

	19X1	19X2	19X3	19X4
(1) Revenues	0	0	0	0
(2) Less: depreciation	(250)	(250)	(250)	(250)
(3) Income	(250)	(250)	(250)	(250)
(4) Add: depreciation	250	250	250	250
(5) Cash flow	0	0	0	0

The resulting balance sheet on December 31, 19X4 is as follows:

Fixed assets	0	Equity	0

The above points out that depreciation in no way provides funds for the replacement of the asset. Rather, firms purchase fixed assets if these permit an increase in volume and an acceptable return on the investment. The sales value of the additional output, net of the related income tax, generates liquid funds for the subsidiary. To illustrate, let us assume again a fixed asset valued at LC 1,000 on December 31, 19X0, with an expected life of four years and an estimated salvage value of zero. The subsidiary in this example generates revenues of LC 250 in each of the four years, while depreciation charges are determined on a straight-line basis. The taxable income and cash flows are computed as follows:

Year	(1) Sales amount	(2) Depreciation expense	(3)=(1)–(2) Taxable income	(4) Tax payable	(5)=(1) Net cash flow
19X1	250	(250)	0	0	250
19X2	250	(250)	0	0	250
19X3	250	(250)	0	0	250
19X4	250	(250)	0	0	250

The cash flow generated in the above example is LC 250 per year, as indicated in Column 5. The cash flows generated create exposures, and the foreign exchange impact of these exposures depends on where and how the funds generated are used. In the table below we examine two alternative uses: (1) retention of funds by the subsidiary; and, (2) remittance of the funds to the parent company:

Year	LC cash flow (1)	Opening rate (2)	Stated in PC at Closing rate of the year (3)	Closing rate of 19X4 (4)	PC impact Funds remitted (5) = (2) − (3)	PC impact Funds retained (6) = (2) − (4)
19X1	250	250	225	150	(25)	(100)
19X2	250	250	200	150	(50)	(100)
19X3	250	250	175	150	(75)	(100)
19X4	250	250	150	150	(100)	(100)
					(250)	(400)

If funds are remitted as earned, the loss is PC 250, as indicated in Column 5. If however, the funds are retained by the subsidiary till the end of 19X4 the loss is PC 400, as shown in Column 6.

Accelerated depreciation and deferred taxes: Whereas accounting income is measured in accordance with generally accepted accounting principles, taxable income is computed in accordance with prescribed tax regulations and rules. And as tax rules are different from accounting principles, differences between taxable income and accounting income exist. These differences give rise to tax differences, some of which must be reported in the financial statements.

Timing differences arise with regard to depreciation of fixed assets. To induce companies to expand their plants, tax laws frequently permit them to deduct "accelerated depreciation" in their income tax returns, thereby lowering the tax burden and increasing cash flows in the early years of the asset. This is illustrated below with the additional assumptions of annual revenues of LC 450 and a depreciation expense computed by the "sum-of-the-years–digits" method.

Exhibit 2—Financial and tax accounting for depreciation expense

A. Tax accounting

Year	(1) Sales amount	(2) Depreciation expense	(3)=(1)−(2) Taxable income	(4)=(3)×0·4 Tax payable	(5)=(1)−(4) Cash flow
19X1	450	(400)*	50	(20)	430
19X2	450	(300)*	150	(60)	390
19X3	450	(200)*	250	(100)	350
19X4	450	(100)*	350	(140)	310
				(320)	1,480

B. Financial accounting

Year	(1) Sales amount	(2) Depreciation expense	(3)=(1)−(2) Financial income	(4)=(3)×0·4 Tax payable	(5)=(1)−(4) Cash flow
19X1	450	(250)	200	(80)	370
19X2	450	(250)	200	(80)	370
19X3	450	(250)	200	(80)	370
19X4	450	(250)	200	(80)	370
				(320)	1,480

* Depreciation expense: In year 19X1 = 4/10 × 1,000 = LC 400; In year 19X2 = 3/10 × 1,000 = LC 300; In year 19X3 = 2/10 × 1,000 = LC 200, etc.

Referring to Exhibit 2, tax accounting results in lower taxes and higher cash flows in year 19X1 and 19X2 when compared to financial accounting. This is reversed in years 19X3 and 19X4, with the cumulative results being identical under both approaches.

The above computations indicate that taxable income will differ from accounting results if accelerated depreciation is used for tax computations. Accordingly, to avoid misleading income statements, companies enjoying this temporary tax advantage must show in their income statements an amount for income tax expenses that is related to its reported income before taxes. The difference between this amount and the tax actually due for the year is credited or debited to "deferred income taxes", as illustrated below:

Year	Financial accounting tax	Tax payable	Deferred tax
19X1	(80)	(20)	(60)
19X2	(80)	(60)	(20)
19X3	(80)	(100)	20
19X4	(80)	(140)	60
	(320)	(320)	0

The existing accounting rules in the United States require that the offsetting liability, i.e. deferred income tax, be recorded at historic exchange rates. Consequently, timing problems of the nature discussed in connection with inventory carried at historical rates arise.

3. Disposal of fixed assets

The foreign exchange impact of fixed assets differs under the two translation methods. This difference is due to the timing in the recognition of that impact under the respective methods. These timing differences, however, will be reversed upon the sale of the asset, as illustrated below.

Given opening fixed assets of LC 1,000 and a depreciation charge of LC 250 during the first year, let us assume that the subsidiary sells the asset at the end of the first year. The net impact of the sale under each of the translation methods is presented in Exhibit 3.

Exhibit 3—Reconciliation of two translation methods

PC impact analysis

Item	Fixed asset sold at current rate value		Fixed asset sold at historical rate value	
	Current method (1)	Historical method (2)	Current method (3)	Historical method (4)
Impact as *per financial* statements (Exhibit 1)	(75)	0	(75)	0
Book value at end of period	(675)	(750)	(675)	(750)
Market value at end of period	675	675	750	750
Gain/(loss) on sale	0 0	(75) (75)	75 75	0 0
Net impact	(75)	(75)	0	0

- If the asset is sold for its current book value of PC 675, then under both methods, the net impact is negative PC 75, as computed in columns 1 and 2 of the table.
- If the asset is sold for its historical book value of PC 750, then under both the current and historical rate the net impact is zero, as indicated in columns 3 and 4 of the table.

To summarize, the *net* foreign exchange impact of fixed asset exposure is identical under the two methods regardless of the resale value of the asset. The only difference is in the timing of recognition of that impact, with the current rate method reporting it as exchange rates change and historical method deferring it until its sale. Within this context care should be exercised in applying either the historical or current rates to fixed assets. The book value of the asset may grossly over or understate its market or replacement value and upon sale of the asset unexpected gains/losses may have to be reported. To illustrate, if the asset (from example above) is sold for an assumed market value of PC 575, the net impact under both methods is a loss of PC 175, as indicated in Exhibit 4.

Exhibit 4—Asset sold at market value

PC impact analysis
Fixed asset sold at market value

Item	Current method		Historical method	
Impact as *per financial* statements	(75)		0	
Book value at end of period	(675)		(750)	
Market value at end of period	575		575	
Gain/(loss) on sale	(100)	(100)	(175)	(175)
Net impact		(175)		(175)

G. Long term debt

Long term debt consists of present obligations that are not payable within the current period. Bonds payable, mortgage notes payable, long term notes payable and pension obligations are examples of long term liabilities. This section discusses long term debt exposure from accounting and economic perspectives. First, we discuss the various accounting methods used for translation of long term liabilities including the pros and cons of the historical and current rate methods, and, having identified some shortcomings in each method, we suggest alternative procedures. In the second part we focus on the economics of long term debt exposure. Here, we relate the long term debt exposure to the exposure generated by the asset financed by the liability—a concept known as cover.

1. Accounting translation methods

Two basic accounting alternatives are available when treating long term debt. No loss or gain is recognized by translating the debt at historical rates, or a gain or loss is recognized at the time of the devaluation or revaluation through translation at current rate. The historical rate method mis-states the value of long term liabilities. Here, as long term debt does not change its value during a currency movement but retains its historical value, it is assumed not exposed. In reality, however, at some point in the future it must be repaid in a de- or revalued currency and the company will recognize a gain or loss. Thus, if long term debt is translated at historical rates, the balance sheet is distorted and the evaluation of gains or losses incurred is difficult. To illustrate, in the case of a depreciating currency, translating long term liabilities at historical rates creates a hidden reserve which can make a balance sheet misleading.

Under the current rate method it is assumed that long term monetary liabilities could theoretically be exchanged for the parent's currency through the foreign exchange market. They are considered vulnerable to exchange movements and are valued at the current rate. This valuation, therefore—if gains or losses are currently recognized—results in substantial swings in reported income if exchange rate changes are significant over the life of the debt. To illustrate, from a translation point of view, a long term debt of FC 100 million issued on 31/12/19X0 would impact the financial statements of a borrower as follows:

	FC	ER (PC/FC)	PC	FX gain/(loss)
31/12/19X0	100,000,000	1·0	100,000,000	—
31/12/19X1	100,000,000	0·9	90,000,000	10,000,000
31/12/19X2	100,000,000	1·1	110,000,000	(20,000,000)
31/12/19X3	100,000,000	1·0	100,000,000	10,000,000
31/12/19X4	100,000,000	1·0	100,000,000	0
			Net impact	PC 0

Although the net impact of the long term debt of FC 100 million over the four year period is nil, the company will report a gain of PC 10 million in 19X1, a loss of PC 20 million in 19X2, a gain of PC 10 million in 19X3, and zero gain/loss in 19X4, increasing or decreasing the owner's equity in line with currency fluctuations in each period.

The discussion indicates that, depending on the translation method used, long term debt can completely reverse the foreign exchange exposure of a company. For example, if the local currency devalues against the dollar, a leveraged firm reports a translation gain. Such a gain, however, reflects economic reality only where the devaluation clearly improves the international trading position of the subsidiary. Further, if the all-current translation method were used, a translation loss would be recorded, assuming the subsidiary is in a net asset position. Can one seriously say that a difference in translation method results in an economic loss in one case and an economic gain in the other?

Given the shortcomings of the current and historical rate methods when applied to long term liabilities, a number of alternatives have been suggested. These are all some variation of the current rate method where the balance sheet reflects the current value of the liability while the translation adjustment is either suspended in a deferred account, or charged to the profit and loss currently, or some combination of the two. The simplest variation of this approach is the current rate translation method with deferral of the translation gain or loss till the maturity of the obligation. In this case the periodic accruals are accumulated to a reserve account which is eliminated at maturity of the obligation. To illustrate, referring to the above example, the company would make the following entry in its books on 31/12/19X1:

Long term debt	10,000,000	
Deferred gain	10,000,000	

The successive entries in the deferral account would then be recorded as follows:

December 31, 19X1	+10,000,000
December 31, 19X2	−20,000,000
December 31, 19X3	+10,000,000
December 31, 19X4	0
Net impact	PC 0

In brief, instead of reporting accounting gains or losses in each period, the respective debits and credits are suspended in a reserve account till the maturity of the transaction. The swings in reported earnings that would have been recorded under the current rate are thus avoided; the mis-statement of the value of the liability that would have occurred under the historical rate method is avoided as well. This method, however, has a serious drawback when debt is issued in currencies that tend to move consistently in one direction—i.e. continuous appreciation or depreciation. For instance, long term liabilities denominated in a strong currency under this method would result in a deferral of all losses till the maturity of the instrument and their recognition at that time. Accordingly, when a currency has a definite and well established trend, the deferral of gains or losses results in one-off and often very large translation adjustment at maturity of the transaction.

Another variation of the approach attempts to remedy the above shortcoming by breaking down long term debt exposure into principal outstanding and interest expense. Under this approach, all foreign exchange gains and losses are charged to the statement as they occur; they are not, however, treated as foreign exchange gains or losses but as part of the interest expense. In other words, the translation adjustment here becomes an adjustment on interest cost. The rationale here is that borrowing costs in low interest currencies are likely to be increased by appreciation of the borrowed currency.

Finally, under yet another alternative, the translation adjustment is partly deferred and partly charged to the income statement. This approach may be appropriate for highly fluctuating currencies without a clearcut direction. Judgement has to be exercised as to the amount of the annual amortization, but normally it is pro-rated over the remaining life of the liability.

2. Concept of cover

Long term debt is ordinarily used by companies as a more or less permanent means of financing to increase the earnings available to stockholders. If a larger rate of return can be earned on the borrowed funds than is paid as interest, the excess will represent income to the stockholders. In many cases, such debt represents local borrowing to be repaid with local currency earned by the foreign subsidiary. For this reason such debt has the appearance of protecting the parent company from economic exposure. The protection of assets by liabilities denominated in the same currency is often referred to as the concept of cover. It is illustrated below within the context of financing of fixed assets.

Let us assume that a subsidiary of a multinational corporation borrows local currency to finance fixed assets. The rationale is that local operations will provide the cash flow necessary to repay loans as they come due. There is thus no economic exposure to currency translation for this debt. This is illustrated in Exhibit 1 with the following assumptions:

Transaction 1: On December 31, 19X0, the subsidiary borrows LC 1,000 to be repaid on December 31, 19X4, at 10% p.a. payable at the end of each year.[9] Translation gains/losses are assumed not to be taxable and no tax provisions are made for taxes. (The tax treatment of foreign exchange gains and losses on long term debt is discussed in detail in Chapter V.) The exchange rate moves as follows:

December 31, 19X0	LC 1 = PC 1
December 31, 19X1	LC 1 = PC 0·9
Transaction rate for year 19X1	LC 1 = PC 0·95

Exhibit 1—Subsidiary's debt in local currency

		Stated in PC at			PC impact analysis	
Exposure	Opening rate	Transaction rate	Closing rate	Operating variance	Translation gain/(loss)	Net impact
Principal (LC 1,000)	(1,000)	—	(900)	—	100	100
Interest (LC 100)	(100)	(95)	(90)	5	5	10
Exchange rate (PC/LC)	1·0	0·95	0·9			

As Exhibit 1 indicates, the subsidiary's debt of LC 1,000 results in a translation gain of PC 100 on December 31, 19X1. Concomitantly, the interest expense of LC 100 gives rise to a positive variance of PC 5 and translation gain of PC 5. The exposures generated by each of these components are conceptually identical to those discussed earlier and may be analyzed in the same manner. Specifically, the exposure of the principal outstanding may be viewed as a monetary liability, as discussed in Section B above; the interest expense may be analyzed as an income statement exposure (Section C above):

---

[9] In order to simplify the presentation we ignore premiums/discounts on capital market instruments.

Exposure	LC amount	Change in ER (PC/LC)	PC gain/(loss)
Principal outstanding	(1,000)	−10%	100
Interest expense	(100)	−10%	10

Transaction 2: On December 31, 19X0, the subsidiary purchases a fixed asset for LC 1,000. The asset has an estimated life of four years and expected salvage value of zero; depreciation is on a straight-line basis, i.e. LC 250 per year. The incremental rate of return on the asset is LC 450 per year.

Exhibit 2—Concept of cover

Year	Gross incremental revenues generated (1)	Depreciation of fixed asset (2)	Net income from fixed assets (3)=(1)−(2)	Interest expense on debt (4)	Net return (5)=(3)−(4)
19X1	450	(250)	200	(100)	100
19X2	450	(250)	200	(100)	100
19X3	450	(250)	200	(100)	100
19X4	450	(250)	200	(100)	100

Exhibit 2 indicates that the annual income of LC 200 on the fixed asset (column 3) more than offsets the annual interest expense of LC 100 on the debt (column 4), thereby generating net return of LC 100 (column 5) per annum. In other words, while part of the funds generated by the investment in the fixed asset is used to pay the interest expense on the debt, the higher return on the asset generates additional revenue to the stockholders. Also, it is worth noting that the cash flow of LC 1,000 generated by the annual depreciation charge of LC 250 is equal to the amount of principal due on December 31, 19X4.

Although there is no economic exposure in the above example, from an accounting perspective exposure may exist. For instance, under FASB–8 or the monetary/non-monetary method long term debt has to be translated at current rates of exchange while the fixed asset is at historical rates, thereby causing a short translation exposure of LC 1,000 at the beginning of the exposure period. In brief, the accounting impact does not necessarily reflect the underlying economics of the situation.

H. Economic exposure

If a firm is to properly manage a foreign exchange exposure generated by its operation, it must first properly identify that exposure. An ideal definition of exposure reflects the actual economic impact on the firm from a change in the exchange rate. As discussed in the first section of this chapter the accountants' need to apply hard and fast rules in order to maintain comparable financial statements may well be at odds with economic reality. Any decision to alter an exposure based on one of these conventions, may be far from having the intended affect.

An example[10] of this problem is an American firm, which prior to the French franc devaluation of 1969, rushed to reduce certain assets to avoid a potential translation loss of between $2 and 8 million. All of the French subsidiary's working balances were subsequently reduced to a minimum level. On a translation basis, this would appear to be a logical decision: reduce all French franc assets and increase French franc liabilities; yet at the same time this decision ignored other economic issues. In particular, it ignored the potential need for future working capital in order to take advantage of increased export sales due to a depreciated franc. This, in fact, did occur. An anticipated loss was turned into a real opportunity cost. The example emphasizes the need to identify better the real impact of exchange rate changes on a firm. Economic exposure provides a comprehensive and theoretical framework for analyzing exchange exposure. In order to properly analyze the impact of an exchange rate change on a firm's income, net worth or market value, one must consider the economic force which caused this exchange rate change and/or the economic force which will result from the rate change.

An analysis of economic exposure can best be framed in terms of two economic propositions:[11] Cassel's theory of Purchasing Power Parity (PPP) and Fisher's paradigm of interest rates (FT). Both of these theories deal with the interaction of prices in an open economy. PPP describes the relation between the domestic price of a foreign currency and the price levels of nonmonetary goods and

---

[10] Dufey, G., "Corporate Finance and Exchange Rate Variations", *Financial Management,* Summer 1972, p. 51.

[11] Aliber R., "Corporate Finance and Exchange Risk," unpublished monograph, University of Chicago, 1976.

services in separate economies, while the FT relates the domestic price of foreign currency to the price of financial claims in differing economies.

The main concept underlying PPP is that the equilibrium exchange rate between the two currencies is directly related to the differential inflation rate between the two economies. In equilibrium the external purchasing power of the domestic currency will be equilibrated to the internal purchasing power through the exchange rate. In equilibrium, the rate of change in the exchange rate between two currencies will equal the differential between the rates of change of the respective commodity price levels. If this proposition was valid on a continual basis, or at least on the basis of a determinable time lag, then in effect non-monetary assets denominated in a foreign currency would not be exposed to change in their real base currency value. Given a depreciation of the foreign subsidiary's exchange rate, the parent would be able to maintain the real base currency value of its foreign currency income stream because the decline in the base currency yield per foreign currency unit (depreciation) would be offset by a larger number of foreign currency units (inflation). On a pure translation basis there would be an apparent loss due to the exchange rate change, yet there would be no disclosed effect on the base currency value of the subsidiary's net income.

This concept is similarly applicable to monetary assets and liabilities through the Fisher proposition. In its original form the Fisher theory states that the nominal interest rate equals the real rate of interest plus the anticipated rate of price inflation. This may be referred to as Fisher Closed (FC) for it relates the current nominal rate of interest to the real rate plus the anticipated rate of price inflation in a closed economy. In an open economy this proposition, Fisher Open (FO) can be taken one step further to state that the domestic nominal interest rate equals the real domestic interest rate plus the anticipated change in the exchange rate.

Fisher Open states that in equilibrium, the differential interest rates on monetary instruments of similar risk and maturity will reflect the anticipated exchange rate between the two currencies. The logic of this theory is simple; no investor (borrower) is going to hold (borrow) one currency over another unless the expected change in exchange rates is fully compensated by the interest rate. The two nightmares every treasurer lives with are to be short in an appreciating currency and long in a depreciating currency. In a Fisherian world the treasurer can sleep at night for the long position will be compensated for by relatively higher interest yields while the short position will be compensated for by relatively lower interest charges. The operational significance of this proposition is again obvious; if this is a valid concept then there is no net impact on the expected value of the firm's income stream from holding a foreign currency denominated monetary asset or liability any expected change has.

Regardless of the empirical validity of these propositions, they provide a useful framework for analyzing a firm's economic exposure. Their utility is in the integration of an item's value in base currency and foreign currency. An accountant merely chooses which items are to be translated at the current rate (exposed) and which items are at the historic rate. The economist starts one step further back. He would first value the assets, liabilities and income streams in their local currency after an exchange rate change, and then translate them into the base currency at the current exchange rate. For the accountant's benefit, this would be the equivalent of applying the current rate method to current cost accounting statements. In this framework one cannot pass judgement on the exposure generated by a short term Swiss franc loan until one looks at the respective interest charge. This rate may in fact overestimate the appreciation of the franc, which in turn would result in an inordinately low effective interest rate relative to debt denominated in other currencies. Exchange rate gains and losses may now be analyzed in terms of deviations from these propositions. On an *ex ante* basis, exposure in nonmonetary assets can be framed in terms of the difference between the anticipated change in the local currency value of these assets and the anticipated change in the exchange rate. The *ex ante* exposure in monetary assets and liabilities is the difference between the anticipated exchange rate change and the differential interest rates.

This analysis is easily related to the forementioned transaction exposure. In order to calculate the exposure of foreign income streams in terms of the base currency, one must first calculate the local currency value of revenues and expenses. The impact of any exchange rate change on these flows will vary according to the economic circumstances:

- the proportion of output which is exported,
- the proportion of input which is imported,
- the adjustment of sensitivity of local prices to exchange rate changes,
- the potential for government to mitigate the above processes.

The significance of this method is that it avoids the straight-jacket effect of the accounting approach by first investigating the economic circumstances unique to each subsidiary before it translates these accounts into a base currency value.

52

The most clear-cut example of this approach is inventory, for it is the one item which spans the horizon across past, present, and future transactions. An accountant would classify inventory as either exposed or not, yet it is not such a black and white picture. There are several variables which will determine the exact degree of exposure. As stated above, this will primarily depend upon where the inventory is coming from and where it is being sold. On the supply side, a good part of which comes from a domestic source will be exposed to a much different extent than one which is imported. In the case of a depreciation, this will depend upon the inability of domestic suppliers to force the foreign source to absorb the depreciation. This, however, will depend upon the impact of the exchange rate change on the domestic price level, and the government's subsequent actions. The same parameters are applicable on the demand side. A good which is only sold domestically will have a much different price elasticity than a good which is sold in a world market. British Petroleum will be much more subject to the swings of the pound/dollar rate than will Cadbury Schweppes selling chocolate bars in Nigeria, yet both would have their inventories classified as exposed under the non-current/current method. The degree of exposure will also be contingent upon inventory turnover and the timing of exchange rate changes.

The message for the treasurer is to avoid the straight-jacket effect of accounting exposure. Instead, he should take a global perspective of the firm's international operations and analyze exposure in terms of the actual impact of exchange rate changes on the expected value of the firm's income stream. Before he takes the word of an accountant he must look at the corresponding change in the income statement. Exchange rates do not change by themselves. Thus, he must analyze the economic circumstances unique to each subsidiary. In general these circumstances are:

1. Where, and how, inputs are sourced;
2. Where, and how, the output is produced;
3. Where, and how, the output is sold;
4. Where, and how, these activities are financed.

Given the specifics of each subsidiary, this analysis may be further framed in terms of PPP and FO. While the empirical validity of these theorems remains questionable, they do provide a perspective for analyzing the real impact of exchange rate changes on the base currency value of expected income, because they emphasize the interrelation and offsetting nature of exchange rates and domestic prices. Analysis of exchange rate exposure must be followed through to the income statement in order to discern whether an exchange rate change will really increase the variability of the group's expected income. The only situation where accounting or translation gains and losses should be managed is where the firm perceives, and correctly perceives, that these differences affect the firm's stock price. While the existence of this problem is widely asserted in the business community, initial empirical evidence has not supported this behaviour.[12]

The significance of this issue is simply explained. Should a treasurer take a myopic view of exchange exposure and act to protect himself accordingly, he may in fact increase the variability of expected income by incurring unnecessary costs. One of the most dangerous aspects of accounting exposure is that gains and losses can be blatantly displayed in the financial statements, while the real cash costs may go undetected as they are hidden among the items of the income statement. See Chapter VIII for a detailed discussion of disclosure. The basis of any management strategy is a proper identification of exposure.

---

[12] FASB Research Report, December 1978.

CHAPTER III

Foreign exchange exposure management—asset/liability adjustments

A. Hedging policies

1. Introduction

In the preceding chapters, the building blocks for an effective foreign exchange management system have been discussed. This chapter discusses what actions should be taken to reduce or eliminate a corporation's risk to foreign currency exchange losses.

The term hedging is used to describe a variety of actions that may be taken to protect a company against the risks resulting from exposure to foreign currency exchange rate fluctuations. The cost of hedging, inherent in reducing foreign currency exposure, must be measured against the foreseen loss due to a given currency exchange rate change. This comparison must be a continuous process, since in every country both the cost of reducing exposure and the risks associated with maintaining an exposed position are constantly changing. Below we discuss corporate policies and strategies within the context of a systematic approach to making hedging decisions.

2. Hedging policies of corporations

When considering hedging policies to eliminate or reduce foreign exchange risk, a corporation must select one of the following: (1) never hedging, (2) always hedging, or (3) hedging selectively. Additionally, if selecting one of the latter two policies, a decision must be made whether to hedge on a before- or after-tax basis.

Never hedging: Corporations that select the never hedge policy remain open to foreign exchange risk. The rationale for such a policy is that exchange gains or losses in the long run will offset each other. The never hedge policy ignores the impact of foreign exchange fluctuations on material costs, local currency sales prices and interest rates. In addition, a blind eye to foreign exchange does not encourage management to incorporate the realities of foreign exchange into their everyday management decisions.

Few corporations with international operations follow this policy, as it has proved to be expensive in a number of currencies over the past decade.

Always hedging: A 100% hedge policy is similar to buying insurance without a discount; it can be very costly. Small companies, along with some large corporations, follow a 100% hedging policy on an after-tax cash flow basis. They follow this policy because they cannot afford to suffer the downside risk.

When a 100% hedging policy is used to hedge not only cash flows but also reported earnings the cash consequences of such a policy are often too expensive even for large corporations. The negative cash consequences result when a company tries to hedge the potential accounting exchange impact. Losses on hedging actions (e.g. forward contracts) are settled in cold cash while offsetting reported gains are merely accounting entries with no immediate cash flow impact.

In addition to the cash consequences of a 100% hedge policy, such a policy ignores the basis for economic decision making; risk versus reward. The policy does not compare the cost of hedging to the exchange loss risk. For the above reasons few large corporations have a 100% hedging policy.

Selective hedging: Corporations with a policy of hedging selectively cover individual currency exposures in line with anticipated currency movements. In other words, individual exposures are covered selectively when the currency risk exceeds the cost of hedging. Accordingly, corporations with the policy of hedging selectively usually have an active exposure management function. The currency manager constantly evaluates and reassesses the corporation's risk to currency fluctuations and the cost of hedging such risk. With this procedure comparing the exchange risk to the hedging cost the negative impact of foreign exchange fluctuations can be mitigated. The majority of international corporations follow a selective hedging policy.

Once a policy is established as to whether to always hedge, never hedge or hedge selectively, corporations with the latter two policies must decide whether to hedge on a before or after tax basis.

Before and after tax hedging: As currency exposures result in a variety of tax effects, corporations often have a policy of hedging on an after-tax basis. As discussed in Chapter V, Sections D and F, tax consequences often depend on the type of exposure and the hedging vehicle selected. Accordingly, if gains or losses on exposure are taxed at a rate different from the gains or losses on the hedging vehicle, the amount of the hedge must be adjusted to achieve tax neutrality. Examples of after-tax heading by forward contracts are provided in Chapter III.

3. Hedging strategies and decision rules

Most corporations find it difficult to respond to rapidly changing relationships between currencies even if they hedge selectively. More specifically, as the market's psychology and perception of risk change constantly, it is important for the treasurer to allow for a gradual adjustment of a corporation's currency exposure in line with the perceived degree of foreign exchange risk. It is thus important to quantify the currency risk inherent in the corporation's exposures. In other words, the purpose here is to provide a guide to determine whether and to what extent a corporation should hedge a given currency position with a forward exchange contract or other hedging alternative.

The degree of risk may be quantified as follows. The corporation develops forecasts for the currencies in which it has exposure. The choice of forecasters should include the full range of market participants. These exchange rate forecasts are then used to develop a probability range for the market at a future date. The mode, minimum and maximum are used to calculate the potential exchange gain or loss for each of the three scenarios. The potential foreign exchange impact for these three points is then compared to the cost of hedging the same currency exposure for the period in today's exchange markets. If the potential mode exchange loss is greater than the cost of the hedge, hedging a percentage of the currency exposure would be recommended. Exhibit 1 illustrates how this rule operates for both a net long and a net short exposed position.

Exhibit 1—Hedging decision rule

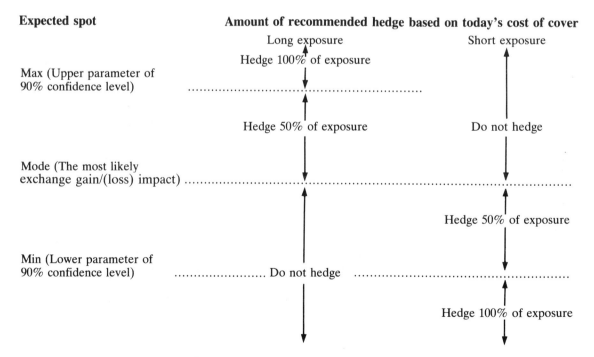

Expected spot

Amount of recommended hedge based on today's cost of cover

Long exposure   Short exposure

Hedge 100% of exposure

Max (Upper parameter of 90% confidence level)

Hedge 50% of exposure   Do not hedge

Mode (The most likely exchange gain/(loss) impact)

Hedge 50% of exposure

Min (Lower parameter of 90% confidence level)   Do not hedge

Hedge 100% of exposure

Do not hedge: If the cost of cover is more expensive than the mode (i.e. the most likely situation) the corporation should not hedge.

56

Hedge full exposure: If the cost of cover is less expensive than the most beneficial scenario—the 90% probability range (i.e. max for a long position; min for a short position) the corporation should take full cover.

Partial hedge: Finally, if today's cost of cover is less expensive than the most likely (mode) expected loss, but more expensive than the most beneficial scenario a hedge may be appropriate depending on the risk aversion of the corporation. The recommended percentages of the hedge may be adjusted upward or downward to reflect the risk aversion of the hedger.

To illustrate how the decision rule works let us assume that ABC is a U.S.-based company with a long sterling position of $10 million equivalent on December 31, 19X0. The spot exchange rate is $2·10, the cost of cover for one year is 2%, i.e. $200,000 and the 90% distribution of the one year sterling forecast is as follows:

Min: $1·70
Mode: $2·00
Max: $2·40

In this situation, the ABC company should hedge part of its sterling exposure, because the $0·2 million cost of hedge is less than the most likely expected loss of $0·48 million. See Chart 1.

Chart 1—Hedging decision rule

Exposure: $10.0 million long on December 31, 19X0.
Hedge cost: $0.2 million discount.

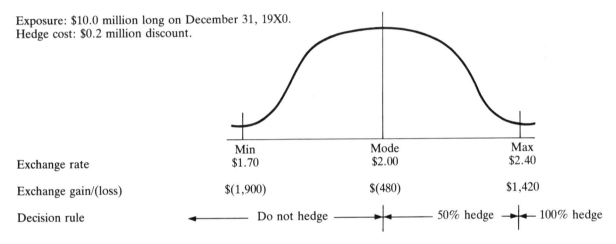

	Min	Mode	Max
Exchange rate	$1.70	$2.00	$2.40
Exchange gain/(loss)	$(1,900)	$(480)	$1,420
Decision rule	← Do not hedge →	← 50% hedge →	← 100% hedge

As shown in Exhibit 1, the hedging decision rule would recommend that the corporation hedge 50% or $5·0 million of its sterling exposure. This decision is arrived at by comparing the $0·2 million cost of hedging to the min, mode and max of the distribution curve. The $0·2 million cost is less than the mode's $0·48 million exchange loss, but not greater than the max's $1·4 million gain.

The hedging decision rule is meant only to be a guide for making decisions and is only as good as its data input. Should the exposure be incorrect or the forecasted exchange rates be non-representative, the decision rule may indicate incorrect hedging decisions. If the decision rule is used properly, however, it gives a corporation a useful guide to hedging decisions.

4. Hedging techniques

Once a decision has been made to hedge a corporation's foreign currency exposure, the corporation has a number of hedging alternatives from which to choose. The decision making process for determining specific hedging actions must be well defined, with responsibilities assigned and appropriate authority delegated. Decisions should be reached in a timely fashion and implemented at least cost.

Before deciding on a technique, however, the exposure managers should consider the following issues within the context of the discussion in Chapter V:

1. Length of time the hedge is desired;
2. The flexibility of the technique (i.e. can it be terminated, adjusted or rolled over);
3. Restriction imposed upon the operation as a result of the technique (i.e. covenants, collateral and guarantees); and
4. Exchange controls and regulations.

Once this process is completed, the exposure manager is ready to select the appropriate hedging vehicle. The hedging vehicles which are most commonly used are listed below:

1. Forward foreign exchange contracts.
2. Local currency borrowing.
3. Eurocurrency market and multicurrency lines of credit.
4. Balance sheet restructuring.
5. Foreign exchange reserve.
6. Parallel and back-to-back loan.
7. Currency swap.
8. Simulated loan.
9. Sales price adjustments.
10. Billing and invoicing currency.
11. Leading and lagging.
12. Parallel hedge.

Each of these vehicles and technique is described and analyzed below in the relevant sections of this and the following chapters.

B. The real cost of borrowing

Every liquidity decision a multinational corporation makes has foreign exchange exposure implications. The truth of this maxim, let alone its consequences, has been learned either first hand or vicariously over the past few years as companies have watched helplessly while home currency values of low coupon, strong currency debt have appreciated, sometimes enormously so. The trend of modern accountancy to publicize the balance sheet translation effects of foreign exchange reverses has induced many multinational corporations to evaluate very cautiously the foreign exchange risk implications of their decisions regarding the currencies which they borrow for medium and long term purposes. These companies often attempt, where possible, to match the currency of the debt to the currency of the asset. Where such matching is not feasible economically, or possible from the point of view of availability, they review carefully the magnitude, location and timing of any resulting mismatch, thereby to anticipate the exposure and liquidity consequences of their decisions. Among the factors they generally consider are the following:

(1) Will the earnings of the asset be in the currency of the debt?
(2) Would mismatching create an exposure large enough to produce material gains or losses should exchange parities change?
(3) Will the location of the foreign currency debt alleviate or exacerbate the potential loss from foreign exchange rate movements, e.g. will the local taxing entity permit deductibility of exchange losses on both interest and principal?
(4) Is the term of the foreign currency loan such that the long term accrual of a favourable interest rate differential more than offsets the potential for adverse currency realignments?

In short, companies have become more thorough in drawing their indifference curves while they consider the trade-offs inherent in mismatching their medium and long term assets, liabilities and flows.

1. Long and medium term debt

There is a simple formula for evaluating the coupons of two loans in two different currencies, when it is anticipated that the value of one currency will change with respect to the other during the term of the loan:

$$(1 + i_a)^n = (1 + i_b)^n \times \frac{\text{Spot 1}}{\text{Spot N}}$$

where: i_a is the p.a. coupon on debt in currency a
i_b is the p.a. coupon on debt in currency b
n is the term of the loan in years
Spot 1 is the cross rate on the first day of the loan
Spot N is the cross rate on the date both interest and principal are repaid.

One problem with this formula is that it does not forecast what the future spot rate will be.[1] In

---

[1] Another problem is that it does not compute taxes.

order to use the equation one generally solves for Spot N to determine the exchange rate at which the two loans will have identical costs:[2]

$$\text{Spot N} = \frac{(1 + i_b)^n \times \text{Spot 1}}{(1 + i_a)^n}$$

For corporations which are especially sensitive to the impact of disclosed balance sheet translation losses on their ability to raise capital, the choice of which currency to borrow is not influenced materially by such calculations. In these companies, a conscious decision is generally made to borrow the local currency, and often therefore to pay the higher of two alternative interest rates. In doing so, these firms implicitly assume that the gentle erosion of earnings due to higher interest expense is preferable to a large, highly visible, and often untimely deduction from reported earnings which may stem from balance sheet translation.

For those companies which place more emphasis on minimizing their worldwide interest costs, all that remains to do is to plug the coupon rates for currencies a and b into the formula and to play with different scenarios with respect to term, foreign exchange fluctuations, tax treatments, etc. In evaluating medium and long term debt alternatives, this is a simple matter as the terms and conditions of such loans are generally straightforward. However, in the money markets of the world's less robust currencies, medium and long term debt are often unavailable, and if one wishes to construct an indifference curve, one must use short term rates.

2. Shorter term borrowing

The problem is that domestic short term rates are not generally all that explicit in alerting the potential borrower to their all-in costs. To cite a familiar example, though in these times a somewhat endangered species, one need look no further than the working capital loans traditionally made by American banks at prime interest rates. Such loans have carried an understanding that the borrower would maintain compensating balances of 10% of the facility plus an additional 10% of the amount borrowed. Given this understanding regarding balance support, the true cost of borrowing is always more than the posted prime rate.

For example, if a company wishes to receive loan proceeds of $1 million, it must open a facility (F) in excess of that amount. It would then borrow 10% of that facility to leave as compensation with the lending bank, draw down the $1 million, and leave an additional 10% of the $1 million with the lender. However, as the compensating balances are themselves borrowed in the sense that they are not found money or without time value, additional balances must be financed to support them. Thus, the 10% compensating balances required to support the $1 million drawn equal 11·111% of the $1 million, or $111,111·11. Applying this multiplier effect to the balances required to support the facility (F), it is determined that in order to draw down $1 million,

$$F = F (0·111 . . .) + \$1,111,111·11$$
$$F (0·888 . . .) = \$1,111,111·11$$
$$F = \$1,250,000·00$$

the company open a facility of at least $1,250,000. Prime, under such circumstances, is always 125% of what it appears to be.

If all local money markets operated under the same ground rules, there would be no real problem. But market conditions vary enormously. In Australia, for example, it has been common for companies to think of their bank overdrafts as costing 12% per annum, the posted overdraft rate. In fact, many Australian overdraft facilities stipulate that the overdraft rate is charged on the amount of the facility which the borrower uses, and that a per annum facility fee, ranging from $\frac{1}{4}$% to $1\frac{1}{2}$% or more is charged on the unused portion. A company which is currently utilizing only A$1 million of an A$10 million facility pays 12% for the million and, say, 1% on the unused A$9 million, or A$210,000 in all. The true cost of the borrowing is 21%. It also means that incremental borrowings cost 11%.

In Mexico, it has been common for banks to lend to corporate borrowers on 180 day discounted notes bearing interest at 18% per annum and requiring balance support in the region of 10 to 30% of

---

[2] For those fortunate enough to have currency forecasts sufficiently reliable to use as data in long term corporate planning, the equation can be employed to optimize the term of the loan by solving for n:

$$n = \frac{\text{Log} \dfrac{\text{Spot 1}}{\text{Spot N}}}{\text{Log} \dfrac{(1 + i_a)}{(1 + i_b)}}$$

the borrowing. While it is quite common to hear companies talking about "borrowing at 18%", their all-in cost of funds is closer to 27%.

Borrow	MP 1,000
Deduct interest @ 18% p.a.	(90)
Deduct balances @ 20%	(200)
Receive	MP 710

$$\left[\frac{90}{710} + 1\right]^2 - 1 = \cdot269578\ldots$$

Thus, although rates may be reasonably explicit in the medium and long term markets, appearances in local credit markets can often be deceiving. Moreover, as corporate borrowers sharpen their pencils and as their bankers become more and more competitive, any number of variations on these existing themes may be negotiated. When one adds to this already confusing array of interest rates the factor of withholding tax on cross-border loans—and the consideration that some banks are willing to absorb these taxes for their borrowers—the need to analyze carefully one's alternatives becomes all the more apparent.

3. Example

Suppose an American multinational wishes to finance its Mexican subsidiary and has the choice of borrowing pesos locally at 27%, or Eurodollars at 8%, assuming the lending bank is willing to absorb the 21% Federal withholding tax. Using this formula, and substituting the known quantities of term, interest rates, and Spot 1, we see:

$$(1\cdot27)^{\frac{1}{2}} = (1\cdot08)^{\frac{1}{2}} \times \frac{\$0\cdot0439}{\text{Spot N}}$$

Spot N is therefore $0·0405; thus a 7·8% devaluation is an acceptable risk to the Mexican borrower of Eurodollars over the next 180 days, assuming that *interest and principal are repaid bullet fashion*, at the end of the loan.

If one assumes, for the moment, that interest rates in Mexico and the Eurodollar market will hold at their present levels, it might be useful to determine what an acceptable devaluation would be if the Eurodollar loan were for a year or more. If n is set equal to one year, Spot N becomes 3·73¢: if n is set equal to five years, Spot N becomes 1·95¢, etc. One must be careful to remember that models like these do not work particularly well under disaster conditions.

n (years)	Spot N	Acceptable devaluation %
$\frac{1}{2}$	$0·04048	7·783
1	$0·03733	14·961
$1\frac{1}{2}$	$0·03443	21·579
2	$0·03175	27·683
$2\frac{1}{2}$	$0·03046	30·612
3	$0·02699	38·502
$3\frac{1}{2}$	$0·02489	43·289
4	$0·02296	47·703
$4\frac{1}{2}$	$0·02117	51·773
5	$0·01952	55·527

If, after completing an analysis similar to the above, the prospective borrower decides that the risk of devaluation does not warrant paying the higher rate for pesos it is likely that he will proceed to borrow dollars. At this point it is useful to turn the formula around to calculate the highest Eurodollar rate the Mexican company would be willing to pay.

$$i_{USA} = n\sqrt{\frac{(1 + i_{MEX})^n}{\left(\frac{\text{Spot 1}}{\text{Spot N}}\right)} - 1}$$

or

$$\frac{(1\cdot27)}{\left(\frac{0\cdot0439}{0\cdot0400}\right)} - 1 = 15\cdot7175\ldots$$

This means that if the borrower expects a 4¢ peso at the end of one year, the Mexican borrower would be indifferent to paying 15·7% for one year Eurodollars. And, as one year Eurodollars can be

60

borrowed for approximately 8%, the Mexican borrower seems well advised to borrow dollars instead of pesos.

However, it is critical to remember, given the hypothesis that the peso may devalue to 4¢, that the all-in cost of the Eurodollars to the Mexican borrower is not 8%. The true, or risk affected cost, is given by the formula:

$$i_{MEX} = \sqrt[n]{(1 + i_{USA})^n \times \frac{Spot\ 1}{Spot\ N}} - 1$$

or, in our example:

$$i_{MEX} = 1\cdot08 \times \frac{\$0\cdot0439}{\$0\cdot0400} - 1 = 18\cdot53\%$$

Thus, any use of the funds yielding more than the risk affected cost (i.e. 18·53%) is a profitable peso use of the dollar funds.

It is this rate, 18·53%, which the Mexican company should use as its cost of funds in making interest sensitive operating decisions such as taking local suppliers' cash discounts. This risk affected rate should also be used in respect of making local currency investments, considering corporate leading and lagging opportunities, in computing local profit centre performance, and in any other corporate decision in which the Mexican company's cost of funds is a material consideration.

4. Conclusion

The lessons which corporate financial decision-makers have learned regarding funding weak currency assets with strong currency term debt can find broad useful applications in multinational corporations. The natural law relationship between international liquidity and foreign exchange exposure obtains in the short term considerations of overseas finance directors as well as in the medium and long term perspectives of corporate financial vice presidents. This relationship applies not only to major financing decisions and consolidated balance sheets prepared under FASB No. 8 guidelines, but to everything which multinational corporations do, from measuring the return on local short term portfolios to taking supplier's discounts to rationalizing the profit centre algorithms of foreign subsidiaries. Moreover, the application of this principle is, or should be, indivisible. Corporations which apply the natural laws of international finance only with respect to major financing decisions and which fail to use it to rationalize day-to-day liquidity activities, do so at their peril.

C. Eurocurrency market

The Euromarket is an external currency market where institutions accept or place deposits outside the jurisdiction of their respective national banking authorities. The result is that most Eurobanks are free of reserve requirements, administered interest rates or other controls that artificially increase their cost of funds. Interest rates on Euro-deposits correspond to the national interest rates for the currency, adjusted for the above factors. Yet, as foreign exchange and/or capital controls diminish the ability of funds to flow from the national banking system into the Euromarket and *vice-versa*, external rates may begin to move independently from domestic ones. Once severed from their national markets, Euro-rates reflect actual external supply/demand, speculative positions, etc.

There is a symmetry between various Eurocurrency interest rates and forward foreign exchange rates. For example, if a Eurodollar deposit pays 10% p.a. and the dollar discount on the yen is 7% for the same period, then the Euro-yen rate will equal approximately 3% p.a. If the Euro-yen was lower than 3%, say 2¼%, there would be an incentive to borrow Euro-yen, sell them for spot dollars to invest and simultaneously (swap) sell the dollars forward for yen to repay the borrowing. This activity would generate covered arbitrage profits which foreign exchange traders would be quick to exploit. Euro-deposit traders will take similar steps if they observe the cost of the swap moving to a point where borrowing in one currency and lending in another becomes profitable.

1. Hedging of exposures in the Eurocurrency markets

Hedging of exposure is usually thought of in the context of buying or selling a currency in the forward market. An alternative method, however, is available in the Eurocurrency market. This method may be used for hedging either transaction or translation exposure. The following example illustrates hedging of transaction exposure in the Eurocurrency market. More specifically, it compares the after-tax cost of not hedging a foreign currency receivable with hedging the receivable in the Eurocurrency market. In the example we assume that on 31/12/X0 the company has a receivable of FC 1,000 to be collected on 31/12/X1. The company is taxed at a rate of 40% on exchange gains/losses on both the exposure and the Eurocurrency deposit interest. Assuming that the foreign currency devalues from FC 1·0 = $1·0 to FC 1·0 = $0·75 at the beginning of the exposure period, Section A analyzes the company's data on an unhedged basis.

A. Exposure

	31/12/X0	31/12/X1
(1) Exposure (FC)	1,000	1,000
(2) Exchange rate ($/FC)	1·0	0·75
(3) Dollar equivalent; (1) × (2)	1,000	750
(4) Before-tax gain/(loss)		(250)
(5) Tax (40%)		100
(6) After-tax gain/(loss)		(150)

The above computations indicate that if the company did nothing the after-tax foreign exchange loss would be $150 (line 6). Sections B, C and D demonstrate how the exposure could be hedged by borrowing Euro-FC and investing the proceeds in Eurodollars. Forecasting a depreciation of the foreign currency, the company decides to borrow Euro-FC 1,000 @ 25% p.a. and invest the proceeds in a Eurodollar deposit @ 10% p.a.

B. Euro-FC borrowing

	31/12/X0	31/12/X1
(7) Amount borrowed	FC (1,000)	FC (1,000)
(8) Dollar equivalent: (7) × (2)	$ (1,000)	$ (750)
(9) Before-tax gain/(loss)		250
(10) After-tax gain/(loss)		$ 150
(11) Euro-FC interest cost @ 25%		FC (250)
(12) Before-tax interest cost: (2) × (11)		$ (187·5)
(13) After-tax interest cost		$ (112·5)

C. Euro-$ deposit

	31/12/X0	31/12/X1
(14) Amount invested	$ 1,000	$ 1,000
(15) Before-tax interest income	@ 10%	100
(16) After-tax interest income		60

D. Overall impact—$

		31/12/X1
(17) Before-tax FX gain/(loss): (4) + (9)		Ø
(18) After-tax FX gain/(loss): (6) + (10)		Ø
(19) Before-tax interest cost: (12) + (15)		(87·5)
(20) After-tax interest cost: (13) + (16)		(52·5)
(21) After-tax cash impact: (18) + (20)		(52·5)
(22) After-tax cash savings achieved by covering exposure: (6) − (21)		97·5

By utilizing the Eurocurrency market for hedging significant savings would occur if the FC depreciated against the dollar by more than the interest rate differential. In our case the net after-tax impact with a hedge is negative $52·5 (line 21) compared to a loss of $150 with an unhedged position (line 6). The net saving thus amounts to $97·5 (line 22).

2. Borrowing and investing in the Eurocurrency markets

The preceding discussion explained the symmetry between Eurocurrency and forward foreign exchange markets. Borrowing and investing unhedged in the Eurocurrency markets, however, can present significant opportunities if the forecast of the future spot rate is reasonably accurate. Within this context multinational corporations should consider borrowing via a multicurrency line of credit. This facility allows the treasurer to select the currency of denomination of the borrowing based upon his expectations regarding interest rate trends and currency movements. To illustrate, if a U.S. parent company has a long position in Deutschemarks and desires to finance its U.K. operations, the financing can be done in DM. With the Euro-DM loan the long DM position may be reduced or eliminated.

Borrowing Eurocurrencies, indeed, entails the risk that rate relationships will move contrary to expectations. For example, if Euro-yen can be borrowed for one year @ 9% p.a. vs. borrowing Eurodollars @ 15% p.a., a 6% p.a. interest saving is achieved if the dollar/yen exchange rate remains stable over the period examined. This saving would be wiped out if during the year the yen appreciated by more than 5·5%.[3]

---

[3] U.S. currency factor × U.S. interest rate = yen currency factor multiplied by ¥ interest rate = 1·0 . 1·15 = X . 1·09 ⇒ X = 1·05504; for explanation of formula, see below.

Alternatively, the breakeven yen/$ exchange rate for the borrowing decision is computed as follows:[4]

L = Local currency	U.S. $
F = Foreign currency	Japanese yen
I_L = Local borrowing rate	15% p.a.
I_F = Foreign borrowing rate	9% p.a.
P = Amount to be borrowed	$1 million
S = Spot exchange rate	Yen 250·00
X = Breakeven foreign exchange rate	Yen 236·96

$$(1) \quad \frac{FP \ (1 + I_F)}{X} = (1 + I_L)$$

$$(2) \quad \frac{Yen \ 250,000,000 \ (1 + 0·09)}{X} = \$1,000,000 \ (1 + 0·15)$$

$$(3) \quad \frac{Yen \ 272,500,000}{\$1,150,000} = Yen \ 236·956$$

In accounting terms this is presented as follows:

Exhibit 1—Breakeven exchange rate

	Exchange rate		$ Impact analysis	
	Opening rate	Closing rate	At opening rate	At closing rate
Exposure	**(1)**	**(2)**	**(3)**	**(4)**
(1) Principal of yen 250,000,000	250	236·95652	1,000,000	1,055,045·88
(2) Interest expense of yen 22,500,000	250	236·95652	90,000	94,954·12
(3) Net $ cost				1,150,000

Referring to Exhibit 1, line 1 analyzes the principal outstanding of yen 250,000,000 and its dollar equivalent of $1,055,045·88 (column 4). The interest expense of yen 22,500,000 is shown in line 2, with column 4 identifying its dollar equivalent of $94,954·12. The sum of the two dollar equivalents, i.e. $1,150,000 is the net dollar cost of the yen borrowing, as indicated on line 3. This cost is equivalent to the cost of borrowing $1,000,000 at the cost of 15% p.a.

Investing and borrowing on an unhedged basis can be systematized by means of a currency index. The currency index is based upon two factors: an interest rate factor and a currency factor. The interest rate factor reflects available Euro-rates and the currency factor is based upon the projected spot rates for the same maturity dates. If these two factors are multiplied, they yield an index which indicates the highest yield/lowest cost opportunities in the various Eurocurrencies. For example, assume a U.S. dollar based investor has the choice of investing in three Eurocurrencies for a year: $, LC and TC, yielding 10%, 25%, and 8% respectively. With the three currencies being at par at inception, he forecasts the following parity changes over the period: LC depreciation by 25% to LC = $0·75 and TC appreciation by 5% to TC = $1·05. Based upon these currency projections and yields, the investment/borrowing opportunities are ranked as follows.

TC currency index = TC interest factor × TC currency factor = (TC 1 × 1·08) × (TC 1 × 1·05) = 1·134
$ currency index = $ interest factor × $ currency factor = 1·10 × 1 = 1·10
LC currency index = LC interest factor × LC currency factor = (LC 1 × 1·25) × (LC 1 × 0·75) = 0·9375

Thus, based upon the investor's projections, TC would yield 13·4% as against investing in his home currency at 10%. Investing in Euro-LC at 25% would result in a net loss of more than 6%. This ranking would be reversed for borrowing decisions, with borrowing costs lowest in Euro-LC.[5]

This analysis for utilizing the Eurocurrency markets for hedging, investment and borrowing purposes is based upon the accuracy of projected spot rates. In some cases miscalculations or unforeseen events could reduce the accuracy of the projected results; reliance on the methods

---

[4] The formula for direct terms is: X (FP) $(1 + I_F) = LP (1 + I_L)$.
[5] This analysis could be expanded to include both domestic and Euro-rates over various maturities to derive the highest possible yield or lowest possible borrowing cost.

described above must therefore be balanced with the risk aversion of the hedger, investor or borrower.

D. Foreign exchange reserve

1. Introduction

The accounting profession shows a certain distrust of foreign exchange reserves. It is difficult to establish objective rules for them—rules which can be consistently adhered to, and which management cannot twist to iron out swings in earnings. Foreign reserves may be juggled arbitrarily, added to or depleted, not so much to hedge exposure as to smooth corporate profits. The accountants' concern is legitimate. But there is an element of arbitrariness with other types of reserves. In general the accounting profession insists that such reserves be provided in the name of conservatism, so as not to overstate reported profits. The same accounting logic should apply to foreign exchange reserves. In many cases, so-called translation losses are nothing more than adjustment to prior earnings—foreign earnings which were translated and consolidated at too high an exchange value because they could not be reserved against.

Take the receivables of a French subsidiary. When they are collected in francs there will not be any realized exchange loss, no matter what happens to the franc/dollar relationship. No cash loss will occur; and yet the U.S. parent of the French subsidiary will have to record a translation loss. What is really being recorded by the parent is an adjustment to the French franc profit on the sale which had previously been translated and consolidated with the parent's accounts under the implicit (and quite unrealistic) assumption that the exchange rate would not change. A receivable was also set up under this assumption, and now it and the former profit figure have to be altered. The lack of realism associated with this process has led some to conclude that translation gains and losses are nothing more than paper entries which can and should be ignored. Such an attitude is quite understandable. But translation gains and losses, being adjustments to prior reported foreign earnings, are as real as those earnings.

Since the prior earnings were used, in part, to determine dividends, stock values and executive bonuses, the subsequent adjustments to those earnings must also be considered and given equal, if belated, weight. It is not so much that translation gains and losses are unreal as it is that the translation and consolidation of prior earnings, in the absence of reserves and under the implicit assumption that exchange rates will not change, is a very unreal foundation on which to base dividends, stock prices and bonuses. In a very important sense, then, the lack of a reserve provision undermines the validity of consolidating foreign profits and the validity of using them for making a number of key decisions.

Most treasurers and managements have taken note of this situation and are doing something about it. They cannot unilaterally change the accountants' edict against reserves, but they can take action to hedge their balance sheets against translation loss. The large multinationals are increasingly adopting exchange policies which call for neutral foreign exchange positions. They reason that they are not in the foreign exchange business and they fear, quite rightly, that foreign exchange losses smack of speculation or, worse, bad management. Few are prepared to face their shareholders or analysts and explain why a material exchange loss is irrelevant and should be ignored. So they direct their treasurers to hedge where and when they can.

For the major convertible currencies hedging an exposed position is not too difficult, since an active forward exchange market exists by which to hedge. In addition it is possible in many countries to take on sufficient local borrowing to balance locally denominated assets with local liabilities, and to net out translation exposure. However, there are still some countries, most notably the underdeveloped ones, where local borrowing is either unavailable or prohibited by law to foreign subsidiaries, and where there is no forward exchange market outside the country. In these countries, where inflation is often rampant, a treasurer cannot hedge and remains in the uncomfortable position of consolidating local profits at too high a value, waiting unarmed for the inevitable devaluation loss. All he can do is hope that the loss, when it comes, will not be material to his firm's overall profits.

Reserves are the only means of protecting earnings in cases like these. Not only that, they are the only sensible method of accounting for local profits. Reserving a portion of those profits results in more objective and conservative accounting and obviates the later, otherwise inevitable need for profit adjustment. It seems ludicrous to call that adjustment, as we do now, a translation loss.

Reserves are not the answer to all exposure problems. Obviously, there are exposure situations where a real cash loss will be suffered if no hedging action is taken. For example, to forego hedging a future dividend payment out of a weak currency simply because a reserve exists, is clearly laying oneself open to a real cash loss. No treasurer is going to sit back and do nothing simply because he is protected by a foreign exchange reserve, any more than he does nothing to collect slow receivable accounts just because he has a bad debt reserve. Foreign exchange reserves give the treasurer the option to hedge or not to hedge, depending on his assessment of the exchange market and the cost of hedging. He need not be continually biased, as he now is, in favour of hedging, in order to avoid reporting a translation loss. Instead, he can take a more balanced view of the risks as weighed against the costs.

2. The cost of hedging

It is fundamental in considering whether to hedge or not to compute the cost of hedging properly. That cost is not, as some believe, the discount in the forward market. When one is hedging by rolling over forward contracts, the gain or loss on these contracts is taken out, but at the same time the contract matures and has to be rolled over. Correspondingly, the amount of the gain or loss depends not on the forward premium or discount at the time the contract was made but rather on the difference between the contract forward rate and the spot rate at the time the contract matures. What one gains or loses by such hedging activity is the difference between the forward and the spot rates in effect at the time the forwards mature and have to be rolled over.

One can therefore lose on hedging a strong currency, even though it always sells with a forward premium, whenever the premium understates the subsequent upward movement of the spot rate. One can gain on selling a weak currency forward, even though it is at a discount in the forward market, whenever that discount understates the subsequent downward movement of the spot rate. The forward discount or premium in the forward market is irrelevant for the purpose of determining cost. In fact it can be downright misleading, giving a contra-indication of cost. A treasurer has to be just as careful in determining the cost associated with local borrowing. It clearly makes no sense to argue that you have saved money by hedging, say, a Swiss franc exposure just because you have substituted low interest rate Swiss franc debt for Eurodollar debt. More has happened than a reduction in your interest expense; your exposure to the Swiss franc has also been reduced and you have given up the opportunity to gain on that Swiss franc exposure. The real cost of increased local borrowing, therefore, is the difference between the interest saving (or cost) and what would have been the exchange gain (or loss) on the exposed position.

3. Never hedging, or hedging selectively

An alternative to eliminating the costs associated with total hedging would be to take the opposite and never hedge. The problem with a policy of never hedging is that most companies are not prepared to accept the consequent losses. There is no assurance that history will repeat itself and that everything will turn out all right over the long run. Neither extreme—never hedging or always hedging—is viable. One exposes the company to too great a potential loss; the other costs too much over the long run. The only sensible approach is to hedge selectively. This involves taking a view of the market. It forces the treasurer, like it or not, to forecast the future course of exchange rates. He may have all the right reasons for his view of the market, carefully weigh the risks and the cost, and still be wrong. Unpredictable events, emotions which overwhelm a thin market, or a very slight error in timing are not his fault. But he will have got it wrong just the same.

The error which may show up in the next quarterly report as an exchange loss, requiring management explanation, haunts the treasurer as he makes his judgement on hedging. He is understandably biased towards incurring the costs required to protect his position, even though he suspects these costs will be sizeable. To do otherwise he argues would be speculative.

4. Using a foreign exchange reserve

The situation would be different if there were foreign exchange reserves which could be used to offset the impact of unpredictable forces in the foreign exchange market. The treasurer could effectively self-hedge and avoid paying a significant price to buy protection.

Reserving and hedging both have the same objective for the income statement—they smooth out adverse foreign exchange fluctuations. Hedging, however, is done in the market place, involves paying someone else to bear the risks, and, as we have already seen, can be very expensive. The accountant's rule against reserving does not prevent management from attempting to insulate its profits from the vagaries of the foreign exchange market; all it does is to make the attempt very expensive.

5. Reserve guidelines

The remaining question is whether reserve guidelines can be established on a basis objective enough for their adoption by the accounting profession. Most, if not all, multinational companies now know what their net world-wide exposure amounts to, as defined by their accountants. That known exposure level forms the basis on which an accrual for a foreign exchange reserve can be made.

The next question is the rate of accrual. Any number of approaches could be suggested but the easiest one that comes to mind is simply the average rate of change during the past, say, five years. The rate of change could be either positive or negative. When the rate is positive it would lead to accruing a reserve for a net negative exposure to a currency and *vice-versa*. The amount of accrual would be simply the average monthly rate of change for the currency during the past five years times the month ending world-wide net exposure. Naturally the net exposure would be calculated after including outstanding forward foreign exchange contracts.

If there were translation gains on a particular currency during the preceding month, they would be added to the reserve along with the monthly accruals. The amount of the reserve would be built up over time until it had reached a predetermined level. That level would also be based on the company's actual exposure as well as on the historical pattern of the currency involved.

One objective approach to determining a reserve level would be to stipulate that for any given month the reserve should be adequate to absorb any adverse loss, say, 95% of the time. Past experience can again be relied on as an indication of what percentage changes one can expect from particular currencies. Shown in Exhibit 1 are percentage limits within which selected currencies have fluctuated monthly between 1974 and 1978. (Statistically, the figures are twice the standard deviation of the percentage monthly change in the spot exchange rate.)

Exhibit 1—Volatility of selected currencies: 1974–78

	Percentage monthly change
Sterling	4·72
French franc	4·96
Deutschemark	5·36
Yen	3·50
Swiss franc	5·56

According to these figures, if one wanted a reserve adequate to absorb losses 95% of the time for a sterling exposure, one would set a maximum reserve level equal to 4·72% times one's exposure. Naturally such a reserve would not provide absolute security, but it should be sufficient for operating purposes. For some companies, it might be too high. For them a reserve able to handle losses two-thirds of the time would seem sufficient. They would cut the above percentages in half and remain protected for the level at which they desire protection. For example, assuming an exposed position of LC (500), the maximum reserve level might be set at LC 25 (equal to 5% × LC 500). Monthly accruals to the reserve up to this maximum level would be accumulated based on the average monthly depreciation of the local currency over the past five years. The maximum reserve level would be altered as the basic underlying exposure changed.

It can thus be seen that everything about the establishment, accrual, and level of a foreign exchange reserve can be based on facts, with the one exception of deciding the protection desired. This remains subject to management determination, as it should be. This does not mean that it is subject to management's whim. In the first place the protection level is explicitly set out; it is not a judgement for which there is no supporting detail. Second, a decision to change that level must be made explicit and open to challenge on audit. The reasons for change have to be related to exposure management, and have to make sense in that context.

Guidelines for foreign exchange reserves can be set up so that they are no different in kind from other types of reserves. This should alleviate the legitimate concern of the accounting profession, and make it possible for treasurers and managements to follow more sensible exchange exposure policies, saving their shareholders the cost now being incurred to over-protect exchange positions.

E. Parallel and back-to-back loans

Parallel loans and back-to-back loans involve two entities with headquarters in different countries, each having subsidiaries in the other's country, and each having mirror-image liquidity positions and financing requirements. For example, a U.S. parent company with a subsidiary in the U.K. may have surplus dollar liquidity or ready access to new dollar borrowings in the U.S. while its U.K. subsidiary needs additional sterling financing. Simultaneously, a U.K. parent company (or pension fund or investment trust) may have surplus sterling liquidity or access to new sterling borrowings in the U.K. and be seeking U.S. dollar financing for its U.S. subsidiary (or to support a portfolio investment).

A parallel loan transaction consists of a U.S. dollar loan from the U.S. parent company to the U.S. subsidiary of the U.K. parent, and a simultaneous sterling loan in an equivalent amount from the U.K. parent company to the U.K. subsidiary of the U.S. parent. This structure satisfies the respective financing objectives of both parties, while avoiding the exchange risks inherent in direct investment by each parent and higher costs of independent borrowing by each subsidiary. Under some circumstances, a parallel loan transaction may directly involve two or three business entities.

Parallel loans differ from back-to-back loans only in that parallel loans do not include a right of offset or cross-collateralization between loans, while back-to-back loans do include a right of offset. As the exchange control regulations of many countries prohibit rights of offset, parallel loans are more common than back-to-back loans.

Parallel loans have become an attractive overseas financing alternative for a number of reasons, some of which are equally relevant for both parallel loans and currency swaps. Interest in these transactions has developed principally as a result of the following factors:

1. **Blocked currency situations**
   Parallel loans provide a use for otherwise sterile cash balances.
2. **Unavailability of foreign loan capital**
   Funding from conventional sources in a foreign market may not be available for the term required or at a reasonable cost.
3. **Interest cost considerations**
   A multinational parent firm can reduce the cost of a foreign subsidiary's borrowings by lending another currency at a below-market interest rate to the subsidiary of a second multinational. The second multinational in turn reciprocates with a lower interest rate on its parallel loan, thus benefiting the first multinational's foreign subsidiary.
4. **Withholding taxes**
   Withholding taxes may increase the cost of intracompany cross-border lending in the absence of a double tax treaty.
5. **Weak markets**
   When a company's home country debt, equity, or property investment alternatives are not attractive, the company may wish to invest in a foreign market. Parallel loans allow companies to make such investments while eliminating their exchange risk.
6. **Exchange control regulations**
   Outright purchase of foreign currency may be prohibited by law or discouraged by high investment currency premiums.

Interest rates on the two parallel loans are usually set at a fixed rate corresponding to commercial rates prevailing for each currency at the time of closing and are subject to local governmental regulations. The spread between the two interest rates is subject to negotiation but would be a function of general interest rate levels in the two countries as well as the current equilibrium or disequilibrium in the market between providers of either currency.

Maturities generally range from six months to 10 years, depending on the currencies involved. Parallel loans are usually bullet loans for administrative simplicity, though some transactions may provide for interim amortization.

Parallel loans (as distinct from back-to-back loans) do not include a right of offset. If either counterparty considers the other's subsidiary less than creditworthy in its own right, specific security or a parent guarantee is usually negotiated. A topping up provision may also be included in order to keep the principal amounts outstanding in balance in the event that exchange rates move significantly during the life of the loans. However, such topping up does not as a legal matter decrease the credit risk entailed in a parallel loan transaction because as already observed, there is no right of offset. Prepayment provisions may be written to enable one party to prepay its loan without accelerating the other's payment.

A parallel loan transaction and a currency swap are quite similar techniques to achieve the same objectives. However, four main differences should be noted which might influence a company's choice between parallel loans or a currency swap:

1. Accountants differ on how parallel and back-to-back loans should be reported by the parent company on its balance sheet. Even if there exists a right of offset, some accountants feel that both loans should appear in the balance sheet rather than being treated as off-balance sheet items. Such treatment inflates the company's balance sheet, may produce adverse consequences under outstanding indentures and may therefore make a currency swap preferable.

2. In a parallel loan transaction, each borrower has an unambiguous tax-deductible interest expense and each lender taxable interest income. In a currency swap, the annual fee paid by one party to the other (representing the interest differential between the long term rates in the respective currencies) may or may not be tax-deductible depending upon local law. Either a parallel loan transaction or a currency swap might be preferable depending upon the tax position of each counterparty.
3. An implied right of offset often exists in the case of a currency swap, whereas no such right exists between parallel loans. If this right of offset is important as a credit matter, a currency swap or back-to-back loan might be preferable.
4. If one counterparty is a trust, its trust instrument may permit it to enter into a parallel loan but not to engage in a currency swap.

The transaction is presented in Exhibit 1.

Exhibit 1—Back-to-back or parallel loan

F. Currency swaps

A currency swap involves two corporate entities with headquarters in different countries, each having operations in the other's country and each having mirror-image liquidity positions and financing requirements. These entities then sell their respective currencies to each other, with an agreement to reverse the sale in the future by a forward exchange contract. For example, a U.S. parent company with a subsidiary operation in the U.K. may have surplus dollar liquidity or ready access to new dollar borrowings in the U.S. while its U.K. subsidiary operation needs additional sterling financing.

Simultaneously, a U.K. entity, such as a portfolio investor (major pension fund or investment trust) or industrial group with overseas expansion ambitions, may have excess sterling or a similar access to sterling borrowing and be seeking overseas investments. A currency swap provides a means by which both groups can satisfy their investment objectives while avoiding the exchange risk and higher costs of independent financing.

Currency swaps have become an attractive overseas financing alternative for a number of reasons, some of which are equally relevant for both currency swaps and parallel loans. Interest in these transactions has developed principally where swap transactions may provide a use for otherwise sterile balances and where funding from normal sources in the overseas market for support of a foreign subsidiary's operations or expansion may not be available for the term required or at a reasonable cost.

By using a swap transaction, a U.S. multinational parent firm could finance an overseas subsidiary's activities at a lower interest cost. For instance, it might finance at a 2% margin versus an approximate 5% differential if the firm were to invest its available dollars in the U.S. and borrow the foreign currency in the relevant local domestic markets.

When a company's home country equity, debt or property investment alternatives are not attractive, the company may wish to position itself in a foreign market. Currency swaps allow companies this freedom while eliminating their exchange risk. Currency swaps are also useful in the face of exchange control regulations where outright purchase of foreign currency may be prohibited by law or discouraged by high investment currency premiums.

To illustrate, here is a typical example of a currency swap, with the following companies involved:

- *U.S. Company Inc.*—a parent corporation located in the United States, which has access to dollars.

- *U.S. Company Ltd.*—a U.K. subsidiary of U.S. Company Inc. which needs sterling financing.
- *U.K. Company Ltd.*—a U.K. pension fund, investment trust or industrial company with access to sterling.
- *U.K. Company Inc.*—a U.S. subsidiary of U.K. Company Ltd. which needs U.S. dollar financing.

U.S. Company Inc. and U.K. Company Ltd. enter into a spot exchange transaction at current exchange rates (e.g. $1·72 = £1·00); U.S. Company Inc. thus buys £5,800,000 against payment of $10,000,000. Simultaneous with the spot exchange transaction, the same parties enter into a forward exchange agreement which will exactly reverse the swap made above at the same rate after 10 years.

U.S. Company Inc. immediately lends to its U.K. subsidiary the £5,800,000 purchased. The interest rate on this loan must conform to relevant exchange control and tax regulations of both countries. U.K. Company Ltd. also immediately lends to its subsidiary the dollars it received in the swap. As in the above case, an annual interest rate must be in accord with appropriate regulations.

U.S. Company Inc. pays U.K. Company Ltd. a negotiated annual fee in sterling approximating the interest differential between sterling and dollars of the same maturity (i.e. the interest differential between sterling and dollars if the transaction had been accomplished as a parallel loan). The tax status of this fee is subject to clarification by professional advisors. Ten years later, at the maturity date of the initial forward exchange agreement, the subsidiaries will repay or refinance the loans they received from their parent companies. With those loans repaid, the parent corporations will then re-exchange the swapped currencies at the exchange rate originally used.

The removal of exchange controls in the U.K. in the autumn of 1979 eliminated some of the reasons U.K. parties entered into currency swaps and back-to-back loans. On the other hand, certain U.K. investors continue to use this mechanism as a cheaper way to obtain long term fixed rate dollars. Needless to say, currency swaps are arranged in a variety of currencies for much the same reasons: a means to obtain long term fixed rate finance and a way to eliminate foreign exchange risk.

The transaction is illustrated graphically in Exhibit 1.

Exhibit 1—Currency swap with a bank intermediating

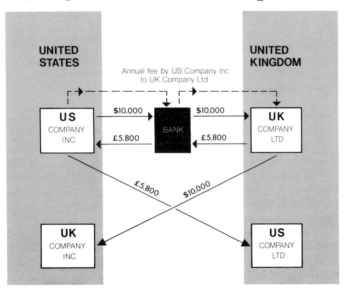

G. Simulated currency loans

A simulated currency loan is one in a given currency where the amount of repayment is expressed in terms of a second currency. The interest rate charged is based on the rate structure of the second currency. For example, a U.S. multinational company with a successful subsidiary in Spain may possess blocked Spanish pesetas, while a second U.S. multinational may be about to invest additional dollars into its Spanish subsidiary. A simulated dollar loan from the first subsidiary to the second would be denominated in pesetas, be repayable at maturity in pesetas in an amount equal to the original dollar equivalent of the loan and carry a negotiated interest rate at or near the dollar London Interbank Offered (LIBO) rate, payable in pesetas or dollars.

For administrative simplicity, simulated currency loans generally have bullet maturities (no amortization prior to final maturity) ranging from six months to 10 years depending on the currency. Although the lender assumes the credit risk, that risk can be supported by a guarantee issued by the borrower's parent company, or such other available security as is acceptable to the lender.

Consider, as an example, a typical transaction: on January 2, 1979, Company A agrees to lend Company B 400 million Spanish pesetas. On that date, the U.S. dollar equals 80 pesetas. The principal of the loan (400 million pesetas) is therefore equivalent to $5 million. The interest rate is negotiated at the dollar LIBO rate (7% per annum rather than the 15% per annum rate applicable to one year Spanish pesetas). This interest is payable in pesetas at maturity. The maturity date is January 2, 1984. On that date, Company B repays to Company A the equivalent of $5 million in pesetas. If on that date, the U.S. dollar equals 100 pesetas, Company B repays the original 400 million pesetas, an additional 100 million pesetas and the accrued interest in pesetas.

Simulated currency loans offer attractive opportunities to both lending and borrowing companies. To the lender, simulated currency loans convert an asset denominated in one currency into an asset denominated in a second currency. In the above example, peseta balances were effectively converted into a dollar receivable. A U.S. parent company finds this particularly attractive since it must report its earnings in dollars and its foreign exchange losses on a quarterly basis.

Simulated currency loans, like currency swaps and parallel loans, provide a use for otherwise sterile funds, and may in certain cases permit long term investment of these funds, an alternative that might not otherwise be available in the local money markets.

To the borrower, simulated currency loans have become an interesting overseas financial alternative. For instance, the second currency interest rate affixed to simulated currency loans may be lower than market rates. For example, the lender might loan pesetas at the dollar LIBO rate, where the borrowing company would normally pay a spread over LIBO to borrow real dollars rather than simulated dollars. In such a case, the simulated dollars are also cheap dollars. In any case, the interest rate is usually lower than interest rates on local funds and if there is no devaluation during the period of the loan, the borrowing company has obtained cheap pesetas.

In some cases, the borrower's parent company may not be able to fund its overseas subsidiary directly because withholding taxes may make intercompany cross-border financing prohibitively expensive in the absence of a double tax treaty. An intracountry, intercompany loan may be free of such cross-border withholding tax.

When a company injects new capital (debt or equity) into a foreign subsidiary, it runs the risk that repatriation of such capital might be restricted in the future. Simulated currency loans, like currency swaps and parallel loans, make supplement capital availability where governmental regulations limit borrowing from traditional financial intermediaries such as banks.

H. Balance sheet restructuring

The objective of a successful foreign exchange risk management is to incur the least cost in the way of losses due to currency fluctuation and direct costs paid to protect against these losses. One technique to achieve this objective is to restructure the balance sheet. That is to manipulate the balance sheet accounts in order to obtain a more desirable foreign exchange exposure position. Balance sheet restructuring implies that hedging decisions cannot be separated from financing decisions, where financing decisions include the management of net assets.

1. Relationship between financing and exposure

The interrelationship of exposure management and financing is characterized by the following: (1) exposure may be controlled by the choice between local and foreign currency financing; (2) decisions regarding the cost of financing are a function of comparative interest rates, degree of currency risk and expected exchange gain or loss; (3) cross-border trading and intercompany flows constitute a mechanism for shifting the location of borrowing from one money market to another, thereby shifting the incidence of currency exposure from one country to another; and (4) taxation of foreign exchange gains or losses may have an impact on the net cost of foreign versus local currency borrowing.

In order to quantify the impact of financing decisions on exposure, the balance sheet accounts are separated into revaluable and non-revaluable accounts. Revaluable accounts, e.g. cash, are those accounts affected by a currency fluctuation; non-revaluable accounts, e.g. property, plant and equipment, are not. Whether an account is revaluable or non-revaluable depends on the translation method used.

The revaluable accounts are further subdivided into decision and non-decision accounts. Revaluable decision accounts are those assets and liabilities about which a decision can be made either to meet financing requirements or protect against exchange losses. Notes and loans payable, cash and intercompany accounts may be considered revaluable decision accounts. Revaluable non-decision accounts are those assets and liabilities about which nothing can be done. For example, inventory and taxes payable may be considered revaluable non-decision accounts.

Exposure can then be defined as the sum of the revaluable decision accounts and the revaluable non-decision accounts. Accordingly, in order to achieve a balanced exposure (i.e. zero exposure), the revaluable decision accounts must equal the additive inverse of the revaluable non-decision accounts. Exposure can thus be reduced or eliminated by manoeuvring the revaluable decision accounts which are made up by the financing requirements of the subsidiary. There are numerous ways to manoeuvre these accounts. Financing may be obtained by borrowing local currency, third currency or the parent currency. Funds may also be obtained by intercompany financing, leading and lagging of trade payables or dividends.

Each type of financing has a cost associated with it. This cost is made up of two components: (1) the after-tax impact of exposure; and, (2) the after-tax effective interest cost. The financial accounting and cash impact are not always identical. For instance, interest costs are real charges and have both a cash and accounting implication while translation foreign exchange gains or losses have an accounting implication but not a cash implication. Therefore, a subsidiary might be considering all items with cash impacts while the parent might be concerned with cash and accounting items. These two components and their relevance for exposure management are discussed below.

Cost of foreign exchange fluctuations: One of the costs involved in the decision to protect exposure by balance sheet restructuring is the expected foreign exchange impact. That impact is a function of the amount and direction of a currency movement and should be expressed in percentage terms of the change from the base currency.

Financing cost: Another cost that must be considered in protecting exposure is the net cost of borrowing. The borrowing cost is the after-tax effective interest rate of the borrowing facility expressed as a percent per annum.

For *local currency financing* the nominal interest rate of the facility and/or existing interest rate structures are good indicators to compare relative costs of debt. Often, however, various terms in the loan agreement alter the nominal rate considerably. Some of these terms include a grace period for principal repayment, delayed interest payment, compensating balances or parent guarantee. The cost of financing should then comprise an effective rate which represents the actual financing cost. For example, if an overdraft facility has been extended at 10% for one year with compensating balances equivalent to 1%, and the tax rate is 40%, the annualized after-tax borrowing costs is 7% ($= 10\% \times 60\% + 1\%$).

The cost of *intercompany financing* is determined indirectly from the company doing the borrowing. To illustrate, if subsidiary A lags its payables to subsidiary B, subsidiary B is, in effect, financing subsidiary A. Subsidiary B might draw on its overdraft facilities; hence the cost of this financing facility is determined from the interest rate attached to subsidiary B's overdraft facility and its tax rate.

2. Net cost of decision

The key consideration in the decision making process are the company's objectives and strategies concerning exposure.

If a company covers assets in a weak currency so that exposure nets to zero, a policy of minimum risk is being pursued when no exchange losses or gains are allowed. If a company chooses to incur some exchange gains, a policy decision is needed as to the magnitude of the gain allowed. The range from a totally covered position to the point where the company could incur an after-tax exchange gain exactly equal to a potential after-tax exchange loss is defined as after-tax cover. An exchange gain beyond this point is defined as speculation.

For example, a company with a subsidiary in a net asset position in a weak currency might choose to remain exposed if the cost of hedging is more expensive than the cost of the currency fluctuation. Or the subsidiary with a choice of borrowing locally or borrowing the parent currency in the Euromarket at the same net cost might choose to borrow locally because the offset to exposure—from a consolidated viewpoint—is the full amount of the loan instead of the partial offset caused by taxation of the potential Euroborrowing transaction loss.

The *consolidated cost* (which computes the after-tax cost of the borrowing and the cost of the remaining exposure) is computed by the following equation:

$$\text{Cost} = c_1 \times F + c_2 \times \text{EXP}$$

Where

c_1 = effective after-tax cost of financing expressed as a decimal
c_2 = cost of exposure expressed as a decimal
EXP = currency exposure after-tax
F = financing amount.

For example, if the after-tax effective cost of borrowing \$1 million is 10%, the expected devaluation is 10% and the exposure is ·5 million after the borrowing, the net cost is 10% × (1 million) + 10% (·5 million) = ·15 million.

The *cost of the subsidiary* is computed by the same formula except that exposure (EXP) in the equation is a subsidiary exposure not a currency exposure.

3. Borrowing of local currency

Local currency borrowing includes a subsidiary borrowing from an external source in its own currency using notes, loans or overdrafts, usually of one year duration or less.

Assume subsidiary A has an account receivable of LC 1,000 when the exchange rate is LC 1 = PC 1 at 31/12/X0. The subsidiary has working capital requirements of LC 1,000 and borrows this amount at 10% per annum from an external source. On 31/03/X1, the local currency devalues by 10% to LC 1 = PC 0·9. Assume a 40% tax rate.

Cost to subsidiary: The *financing cost* for this type of borrowing is the effective interest rate, i.e. the nominal interest rate plus compensating balances. The decision process of whether or not to incur this debt over another financing instrument is made by comparing the effective cost of financing in the local currency *vs.* financing in another currency. The *exposure cost/benefit* for local currency financing, as far as the subsidiary is concerned is nil because the borrowing is denominated in the local currency. The *net cost* to the subsidiary is thus the after-tax effective interest expense $0·10 \times 0·6 \times \text{LC } 1,000 = \text{LC } 60$.

Consolidated cost: The *foreign exchange impact* of local currency borrowing is a function of the translation exposure. As exposure is defined as that amount such that when multiplied by the rate of dollars per foreign currency unit yields the foreign exchange gain or loss, the entire local currency borrowing becomes part of the exposure calculation. In this example, the exposure before the borrowing was LC 1,000 = PC 1,000. After the borrowing, assuming the proceeds are used for a non-exposed asset, the exposure is LC 1,000 – LC 1,000 = 0. There are, of course, no tax effects on translation exposure.

- The financing cost is the same after-tax effective interest expense as computed above.
- The net consolidated cost is the same as the financing cost because the exposure was reduced to zero. If there were no borrowing, the consolidated cost would have been the exchange loss of PC 100.

4. Borrowing of parent currency

Under discussion in this section is the borrowing of the parent currency in the external market by the local company. For example, a U.K. subsidiary of a U.S. parent might borrow U.S. dollars in the Euromarket. Assume subsidiary A has an account receivable of LC 1,000 when the exchange rate is LC 1 = PC 1 at 31/12/X0. This subsidiary has working capital requirements of LC 1,000 and borrows PC 1,000 at 5% per annum. On 31/03/X1, the local currency devalues to LC 1 = PC 0·9.

Before undertaking the PC 1,000 borrowing, subsidiary A had a balance sheet exposure of LC 1,000 = PC 1,000 arising from the net asset position. Had the PC borrowing not been transacted, upon a change in rates, the parent would have incurred a translation loss of PC 100. Borrowing 1,000 units of the parent currency does not change this position. When the rate changes from PC 1·0 to PC 0·9, the number of the parent currency units does not change as the parent currency remains at its original value.

Transaction exposure of subsidiary: Parent currency borrowing does, however, affect the transaction exposure. When the LC moves, it will take more or less LC units to repay the parent currency loan. Because it is a transaction, in most countries the gain is taxed or a tax deduction is received for the loss.

On a before tax basis, the transaction exposure is PC 1,000 which gives rise to a loss to the subsidiary of LC 111·11. On an after-tax basis, assuming that the exchange loss is tax deductible at the rate of 40% the after-tax loss is LC 66·67.

- The financing cost to the subsidiary is the after-tax effective interest rate adjusted for the currency change or $0.05 \ (1 - 0.4) \ (PC \ 1{,}000)/.9 = LC \ 33.3$. If there were no devaluation, the cost would be LC 30.
- The net cost to the subsidiary is LC 66·7 + LC 33·3 = LC 100

Translation exposure of parent: Parent currency borrowing also affects the translation exposure. After the loan is written up or down in the event of a local currency change, the account is translated to the parent currency. This translation results in a gain or loss to the parent. Using the previous example, the exposure giving rise to a gain of PC 100 is a short translation exposure of LC 1,000. There are no tax effects on translation exposure.

Consolidated exposure: In the above paragraphs, transaction and translation exposure are defined. If the two exposures are added, on a before-tax basis, they will always net to zero; on an after-tax basis, they will always net to the tax effect. In other words, pre-tax, the transaction loss (gain) of the subsidiary equals the translation gain (loss) of the parent; after-tax, only the tax deduction (credit) remains. In our case, the tax credit is PC 40.

- The financing cost from the consolidated point of view is PC 30 (LC 33·3 × 0·9).
- The net consolidated cost is PC 150 before-tax and PC 90 after-tax as computed by:
  Cost of PC borrowing (before-tax) = $0.05 \times 1{,}000 + 0.1 \times 1{,}000 = PC \ 150$
  Cost of PC borrowing (after-tax) $\ = 0.03 \times 1{,}000 + 0.1 \times 600 = PC \ 90$

5. The decision process

The net cost of the decision of several borrowing alternatives or remaining exposed can be computed and compared to choose the least cost strategy. For example, compare a local currency and parent currency borrowing of either PC 1,000 or LC 1,000 when the exchange rate is at par. Assume the effective borrowing rate of the parent currency is 5%, the local currency is 10%, the expected devaluation of the local currency *vis-à-vis* the parent currency is 10% and the exposure is LC 2,000. Tax rate is 40%. From the consolidated point of view, the costs are:

Cost of local borrowing before-tax = $.10 \times 1{,}000 + .10 \times 1{,}000 = 200$
Cost of local borrowing after-tax $\ = .06 \times 1{,}000 + .10 \times 1{,}000 = 160$
Cost of PC borrowing before-tax $\ = .05 \times 1{,}000 + .10 \times 2{,}000 = 250$
Cost of PC borrowing after-tax $\ = .03 \times 1{,}000 + .10 \times 1{,}600 = 190$

From the subsidiary's viewpoint, the costs are:

Cost of local borrowing before-tax = $.10 \times 1{,}000 = 100$
Cost of local borrowing after-tax $\ = .06 \times 1{,}000 = 60$
Cost of PC borrowing before-tax $\ = .05 \times 1{,}000 + .10 \times 1{,}000 = 150$
Cost of PC borrowing after-tax $\ = .03 \times 1{,}000 + .10 \times 600 = 90$

Despite the higher interest rate on the LC borrowing, the local currency borrowing is less costly before and after tax from the subsidiary's and consolidated points of view.

6. Other borrowing alternatives

The methodology outlined in the previous sections is applicable to third currency borrowing except that there are three currencies involved. The cost to the subsidiary and the consolidated cost depend on whether the local currency moves with respect to the parent currency and the third currency. From the subsidiary viewpoint the financing cost and transaction exposure costs are affected if the local currency and third currency move *vis-à-vis* each other. The consolidated cost is affected if either currency move against the parent currency. Both pre-tax and after-tax exposure are impacted by external third currency borrowing.

The methodology can also be applied to intercompany borrowing. Usually, the borrowing is denominated in the debtor, creditor or parent currency. If the parent is either the debtor or creditor (and the transaction is denominated in either the parent or local currency) only two currencies are involved. Otherwise three currencies must be considered. The financing cost to the borrowing subsidiary is the interest cost levied by the lender subsidiary or parent. The consolidated financing cost, is, however, the cost of borrowing these funds on the outside market. For example, assume subsidiary A in country A lends LC to subsidiary B in country B for 10% per annum but paid 8% for LC from a commercial lender. Subsidiary B's cost is 10% but the consolidated cost to the parent is only 8%. The interest rate between subsidiaries becomes a funds transfer.

In intersubsidiary transactions, the foreign exchange cost of the intercompany borrowing is borne by the subsidiary that has the payable or receivable denominated in a currency other than its own. There is no pre-tax foreign exchange cost, but there is an after-tax cost. If we assume that LC (in country A) revalues 10% *vis-à-vis* LC (in country B), subsidiary B (which has a payable) has to come up with more of its currency units to repay subsidiary A. Hence B bears the foreign exchange risk. This foreign exchange loss yields a tax credit. On a consolidated basis, the tax credit remains as the only cost contribution.

I. Other techniques and strategies

In addition to the hedging vehicles discussed above, there are many other techniques available for hedging exposure. This section discusses the following: price adjustments, leading and lagging, parallel hedges and billing and invoicing practices.

1. Sales price adjustments

The value of a corporation's foreign assets is contingent upon its future income stream. If this stream is reduced in terms of the parent currency, the value of the parent company's foreign investment is reduced. To illustrate, let us assume that a US company invests $1 million in France in order to produce 250 motorcycles per year. Each motorcycle is sold for $1,000 or Fr 5,000 at the time of the investment, i.e. a 25% pre-tax return on investment. If the French franc devalues from five to six francs per $1·00, the dollar pre-tax return drops from 25% to 20·8% thereby decreasing the value of the corporation's investment. This is illustrated as follows:

Pre-tax return on investment

	Fr	Exchange rate ($/Fr)	$
(1) Investment	5 million	0·2	1 million
Pre-devaluation results:			
(2) Pre-tax profit	1·25 million	0·2	250,000
(3) Pre-tax return (line 2/line 1)	25%		25%
Post-devaluation results:			
(4) Pre-tax profit	1·25 million	0·1667	208,375
(5) Pre-tax return (line 4/line 1)	25%		20·8%

In order to offset the decrease in the pre-tax profit, the local subsidiary has to increase its franc prices to Fr 6,000 to obtain a pre-tax profit of $1,000 for each motorcycle (Fr 6,000 × $0·1667).

Although usually appealing, the technique of increasing prices to offset exchange losses is not always a viable alternative for hedging. For instance, local manufacturers may continue to charge the current local market price for their goods thereby making those of foreign investors non-competitive. Even without local competition it is possible, depending on price elasticity of the product, that demand for the goods sold at a higher price will decrease. Finally, even if the above factors do not enter into play, price controls in some countries prohibit price increases.

2. Leading and lagging

This is defined as a planned acceleration or deceleration of payables and/or receivables. Leading and lagging has a value in short term balance sheet hedging as well as for longer term operational management. Leading and lagging is most efficiently pursued when inter-company flows are involved, as many of the problems can be avoided if both participants, the leader and the lagger, work to improve the return of the same company. If this is the case, the subsidiary which does not receive its payment on time will not alter its selling terms, begin legal action, or attempt to harm the slow payer's reputation.

In certain respects, leading and lagging uses the same concepts as a borrowing hedge. The subsidiary in the weak currency country borrows from its local bank, and then it pays its current and prepays its future intercompany payables. The subsidiary in the strong currency country converts and deposits its receipts from the weak currency country and delays paying its payables to the weaker currency subsidiaries. The result of this tactic is a decrease in net exposed assets in the weaker currency and a desired increase in the net exposed assets in the stronger currency.

Leading and lagging are usually implemented on a continuous basis rather than in response to a sudden shift in exchange rates. This requires an appraisal of both the exchange rate and the interest rates in the two countries. For example, it may be that the interest on a local currency investment may more than compensate for any depreciation of the currency, thus making the investment more attractive than a dollar investment.

An example of this interest rate/exchange rate decision is as follows:

- The U.S. parent company has an intercompany payable of LC 1,000 to its subsidiary on December 31, 19X0, when the exchange rate is $1·00 = LC 1·00;
- The parent company has the option of leading or lagging its payment to the subsidiary;
- The parent can earn 10% if it invests the $1,000 in the U.S. while the going interest rate for the Euro-LC investments is 5%;
- The breakeven exchange rate (x) is computed as follows:

$$\$1,000 \times (1 + 10\%) = (LC\ 1,000) \times (1 + 5\%) \times X$$

$$\$1,100 = \$1,050X$$

$$\frac{1,100}{1,050} = X$$

$$\$1·048 = X$$

According to the above calculation, the parent company should be indifferent between a local currency or a dollar investment if the exchange rate at the end of 19X1 is LC 1·0 = $1·048. If the dollar were expected to be stronger (e.g. $·95/LC), then the return on the local currency investment would fall to $997·50; the parent company should lag its payment to the subsidiary in order to take advantage of the higher return on the dollar investment. If the local currency is expected to appreciate to more than $1·048/LC, then leading of the intercompany payable becomes desirable.

3. Parallel hedge

A parallel hedge, sometimes called a cover by proxy, involves subsidiaries in two countries with closely related or linked currencies. The Dutch guilder and the Deutschemark are currencies that have been used by corporations in a parallel hedge situation; in the past they have moved in tandem against the dollar. For example, if a corporation is short marks and long guilders, a parallel hedge exists since, in theory, gains in one currency should be offset by losses in the other. This is illustrated in the table below, where on December 31, 19X0 the Dutch subsidiary has a long translation exposure of Dfl 4,061 (line 1) when the guilder exchange rate is $0·4071 and the German subsidiary a short translation exposure of DM 4,205 (line 5) when the mark rate is $0·4240.

	31/12/X0	31/12/X1	
(1) Exposure (Dfl)	4,061	4,061	
(2) Exchange rate ($/Dfl)	0·4071	0·4020	
(3) $ equivalents	1,653	1,632·5	
(4) FX gain/(loss) before tax		(20·5)	(20·5)
(5) Exposure (DM)	(4,205)	(4,205)	
(6) Exchange rate ($/DM)	0·4240	0·42	
(7) $ equivalents	(1,783)	(1,766)	
(8) FX gain/(loss) before tax		17	17·0
(9) Net impact			($3·5)

In the above example, if both currencies decline in parallel against the dollar the net impact is small. In our case the translation loss of $20·5 on the long guilder exposure (line 4) is almost entirely offset by the translation gain of $17 on the short mark exposure (line 8), yielding a net loss of $3·5.

The major advantage of parallel hedging, therefore, is that there is no cash cost associated with its use. The primary risk in a parallel hedge, though, is that exchange rates will move contrary to expectations and that a loss in one currency will not be offset by a gain in the other.

4. Use of billing and invoicing currency

When a corporation negotiates a sale or a purchase contract, the currency of denomination can dramatically affect a corporation's foreign currency exposure. With regard to sales, a corporation should always seek to invoice its customers in a strong currency. For example, a U.S. corporation has a choice to invoice a customer for a computer in Brazilian cruzeiro, Swiss francs or U.S. dollars for the equivalent of $100. If the cruzeiro is expected to depreciate against the Swiss franc, the corporation should invoice its customer in Swiss francs. Often, however, a corporation does not have the option to choose the currency. In such cases the relative strength of the invoicing currency and the cost of hedging the currency must be taken into consideration to determine the sales price.

When a corporation negotiates a purchase contract, the currency of payment can affect the corporation's foreign currency exposure. For example, if a corporation buys its products in a strong currency country and sells them in a weak currency country, it runs the risk of being priced out of the weak currency market—an experience that Volkswagen faced during the 1970s. To avoid this problem, the manufacturing or purchase of goods should take place in the market where the final product is sold. This strategy insures the company's profit margins.

CHAPTER IV

Foreign exchange exposure management—forward contracts

Introduction

Recourse to the forward foreign currency markets has grown in use and importance as a means by which a corporation can insulate its earnings and cash flows from currency movements. But before deciding whether to hedge or not, the financial manager should know precisely what is being hedged, and what the consequences of his actions will be. This chapter discusses how the various types of currency exposures may be hedged in the forward markets.

A. Translation exposure of parent

If a forward contract is intended to be a hedge of a foreign currency exposed net asset or net liability position, gains or losses should be accrued for accounting purposes in each accounting period based on the spot exchange rates at the beginning and end of the accounting period. Before taxes, the foreign exchange gain or loss on the exposed position is exactly offset by the gain or loss on the forward contract if the contract is for the same amount of local currency units as the underlying exposure. If taxes are taken into account, the amount of forward contract may be increased to the amount of the foreign currency exposure multiplied by the reciprocal of (1 minus the tax rate). This formula applies when the unrealized gain or loss on the exposure is not taxed, but the gain or loss on the contract is. The original discount or premium on the contract should be accounted for separately and amortized to income over the life of the contract.

The accounting treatment, cash impact and economic implications of a translation exposure and an offsetting hedge contract are shown in Exhibit 1 with the following assumptions:

- A U.S. multinational company's subsidiary in Country A has a net liability exposure of 1,000 local currency units (LC) on 31/12/X0. This exposure remains unchanged throughout the accounting period. The translation rate on 31/12/X0 is LC1·00 = $1·00. The tax rate for the U.S. parent is 40%.
- On December 31, 19X0, the U.S. parent projects a substantial appreciation of the local currency over the next year, and buys forward LC1,666·67 to cover its balance sheet exposure on an after-tax basis, for delivery on January 1, 19X2, at $1·05.

The exchange rate moves as follows:

    30/6/X1   LC1·00 = $1·05
    1/12/X1   LC1·00 = $1·15
    1/1/X2   LC1·00 = $1·15

The subsidiary's exposure data and the parent's forward contract data are shown in the first column of Exhibit 1. The remaining columns in this exhibit show the results for the first and second halves of 19X1 (Columns 2 and 3), and the cumulative impact of currency fluctuations on cash, income and taxes in 19X1 (Column 4).

Going down the lines of data in Exhibit 1, the first seven lines concern the balance sheet exposure data and the related foreign exchange translation gains or losses. For instance, if on June 30, 19X1, the exchange rate changed to $1·05, a foreign exchange loss of $50 would flow through to consolidated net income, since $1,050 instead of the original $1,000 would be needed to repay the liability of LC1,000. This loss, as line 6 shows, is not tax deductible in the foreign country and is assumed not to reduce taxes in the United States.

On the forward contract data (lines 8 to 14), the foreign exchange gain or loss is computed in accordance with paragraph 25 of FASB-8. Line 9 identifies the amount to be bought forward if the exposure is to be fully hedged on an after-tax basis.

Exhibit 1—Accounting treatment and cash impact

Balance sheet exposure		First half of 19X1	Second half of 19X1	Cumulative for 19X1
(1) Date	31/12/X0	30/6/X1	31/12/X1	
(2) Exposure (LC)	(1,000)	(1,000)	(1,000)	
(3) Exchange rate ($/LC)	1·00	1·05	1·15	
(4) $ equivalents	(1,000)	(1,050)	(1,150)	
(5) FX gain/(loss) before tax		(50)	(100)	(150)
(6) Tax (0%)		0	0	0
(7) FX gain/(loss) after tax; lines (5) + (6)		(50)	(100)	(150)
Forward contract				
(8) Date	31/12/X0	30/6/X1	31/12/X1	
(9) Amount bought (LC)	1,666·67	1,666·67	1,666·67	
(10) Spot ($/LC)	1·00	1·05	1·15	
(11) $ value of contract	1,666·67	1,750	1,916·67	
(12) FX gain/(loss) before tax		83·33	166·67	250
(13) Tax (40%)		(33·33)	(66·67)	(100)
(14) FX gain/(loss) after tax		50	100	150
FASB-8 gain/loss				
(15) FX gain/(loss) reported (FASB-8) lines (5) + (12)		33·33	66·67	100
(16) Increase (decrease) in net income (before premium) lines (15) + (6) + (13)		0	0	0
Income and cash impact				
(17) Premium to be amortized ($)*		(41·67)	(41·66)	(83·33)
(18) Tax (40%)		16·67	16·66	33·33
(19) Decrease in after-tax income; lines (16) + (17) + (18)		(25)	(25)	(50)
(20) Total cash flow from forward contract (14) + (19)—at maturity		25	75	100
(21) Total increase (decrease) in net income (16) + (19)		(25)	(25)	(50)
(22) Total economic impact (implied cash flow) lines (7) + (20)		(25)	(25)	(50)

* Premium to be amortized = (spot at start of contract — forward rate) × LC amount bought = (1 − 1·05) × 1,666·67 = $83·33.

Line 15 shows the total reported FASB-8 foreign exchange gain. This is the sum of the foreign exchange loss on the net exposed liability position of LC1,000 and the before-tax foreign exchange gain on the forward contract. Line 16 shows the after-tax foreign exchange gain or loss, which is the reported FASB-8 foreign exchange gain net of the appropriate tax expense resulting from the forward contract gain. If the after-tax exposure is perfectly hedged, line 16 should be zero, as it is in the table.

Lines 17 to 21 identify some of the cash and net after-tax income implications of foreign currency exposures and related hedge contracts. It is worth noting that the reported foreign exchange gain or loss on a hedge contract does not include the premium/discount accounting entries. A decrease of $83·33 (line 17—cumulative) in before-tax income, which would occur from amortization of the premium, would not be classified as part of the foreign exchange gain or loss on the forward contract. The cash impact of hedging is another consideration (line 20), and the table indicates that the after-tax cash gain is $100. (Should the exchange rate on Dec. 31, 19X1, be $0·95, then the cash cost of hedging a net exposed liability of LC1,000 would be $100; in the absence of a hedge there would be no cash cost and a $50 foreign exchange gain.)

Finally, the overall economic impact of hedging strategies is computed (line 22). This figure is derived by adding the after-tax foreign exchange gain or loss on the exposure (i.e. the paper gain or loss) and the cash impact of hedging, under the assumption that as exchange rates change, net monetary (exposed) assets abroad are worth more or fewer dollars. To illustrate, if the Deutsche-mark suffered another 1923 style depreciation, it would take just a few dollars to liquidate net liabilities in that currency; hence, the term economic gain or loss. In this context, the economic loss with coverage (line 22) is the same as the total decrease in net income (line 21).

In the light of the above analysis one can select an appropriate strategy depending on the company objectives. Should the objective be to minimize earnings-per-share fluctuations, one would cover, and the decrease in after-tax income would be $50 (line 19—cumulative). On the other hand, should the objective be to minimize cash outlays, accepting the risk of earnings-per-share fluctuations, one should not cover. In this case, the after-tax (no tax) effect of the foreign exchange loss would be $150 (line 7, cumulative) with no cash outflow. In other words, the risk factor is much larger when the exposure is not covered, in that the earnings-per-share could suffer much more under no cover than with cover. It is worth noting that, by entering into a forward contract, an after-tax loss of $50 (premium of $83·33 minus the tax credit of $33·33) has been guaranteed regardless of what happens to the exchange rate. This is because the effect on the balance sheet exposure and the after-tax hedge will always net to zero if the hedge is properly structured on an after-tax basis.

To show the accounting treatment of hedge contracts in greater detail, using the data in Exhibit 1, we should note that the three components used in evaluating a hedge forward contract—the FASB-8 gain or loss, the premium or discount, and the cash impact—always add together on both before-tax and after-tax bases. In other words, if only two are known, the third can easily be derived (see Exhibit 2).

Exhibit 2—Components of the forward contract

(1) FX gain (FASB-8) = (spot at maturity − spot at start of contract) × amount of LC
bought = $(1·15–1) × 1,666·67$ =

	$250·00
Tax 40%	(100·00)
After-tax gain	$150·00

(2) Premium to amortize = (forward rate − spot at inception of contract) × amount
of LC bought $(1·05–1) × 1,666·67$ =

	(83·33)
Tax 40%	33·33
After-tax loss	($50·00)

(3) Cash impact = (spot at maturity − contract rate) × amount of LC bought
= $(1·15 − 1·05) × 1,666·67$ =

	$166·67
Tax 40%	(66·67)
Cash gain (3) = (1) + (2)	$100·00

Broadly speaking, the cash effect of a hedge forward contract is the sum of the FASB-8 gain or loss and the amortization of the premium/discount, again before and after taxes.

B. Transaction exposure of parent

This section considers the hedging of transaction exposure of the parent. Here exposure arises when the parent has on its books assets or liabilities whose monetary value is denominated in currencies other than its own. Transaction exposure and a related forward contract are thus from an accounting viewpoint treated within the parameters of Paragraph 25 of FASB-8—the same as in the case of translation exposure.

Nevertheless, as the underlying exposures in the two cases differ, their cash and tax impacts will differ as well. Transaction exposures normally have a direct cash and tax impact on the trading entity whereas translation exposures may not affect cash flows and/or taxes. In other words the overall cash impact in the case of a covered transaction exposure is the sum of the cash impacts of (1) the transaction exposure and (2) the related forward contract. (In the case of a covered translation exposure only the forward contract impacts cash flows.) Similarly, the after-tax transaction exposure differs from the after-tax translation exposure in that the former has normally a tax effect whereas the latter does not; the reported gains and losses and the overall cash impact are not identical in the two cases.

1. Assumptions

The accounting treatment and cash impact of a foreign exchange exposure and offsetting hedge contract are shown in Exhibit 1 with the following assumptions:

—A U.S. multinational company books a payable of 1,666·67 foreign currency units (FC) on 31/12/X0. The payable is due on 31/12/X1. The translation rate on 31/12/X0 is FC 1·00 = $1·00. The tax rate for the U.S. parent is 40% and is assumed to apply to gains and losses on both the transaction and the forward contract.

—On December 31, 19X0, the U.S. parent projects a substantial appreciation of the foreign currency over the next year, and buys forward FC 1,666·67 to cover its exposure on an after-tax basis for delivery on January 1, 19X2, at $1·05. The exchange rate moves as follows:

$$
\begin{array}{ll}
30/6/X1 & \text{FC } 1·00 = \$1·05 \\
31/12/X1 & \text{FC } 1·00 = \$1·15 \\
1/1/X2 & \text{FC } 1·00 = \$1·15
\end{array}
$$

The exposure and forward contract data are shown in the first column of Exhibit 1. The remaining columns in this table show the results for the first and second halves of 19X1 (columns 2 and 3), and the cumulative impact of currency fluctuations on cash, income and taxes in 19X1 (column 4).

2. Treatment

The first seven lines of the table concern the exposure data and the related foreign exchange transaction gains or losses. On the forward contract data (lines 8 to 14), the foreign exchange gain or loss is computed in accordance with FASB-8.

Line 15 shows the total reported FASB-8 foreign exchange gain. This is the sum of the before-tax foreign exchange loss on the net exposed liability of FC 1,666·67 and the before-tax foreign exchange gain on the forward contract. Line 16 shows the after-tax foreign exchange gain or loss, which is the reported FASB-8 foreign exchange gain net of the appropriate tax impacts of the transaction exposure and the forward contract. If the after-tax exposure is perfectly hedged, line 16 should be zero, as it is in the table.

Lines 17 to 22 identify the cash and net after-tax income implications of a foreign currency exposure and a related hedge contract. It is worth noting that the reported foreign exchange gain or loss on a hedge contract does not include the premium/discount accounting entries. A decrease of $50·00 (line 19—cumulative) in after-tax income, which would occur from amortization of the premium, would not be classified as part of the foreign exchange gain or loss on the forward contract. Line 20 identifies the total decrease in after-tax income, which in this case is identical to the after-tax premium expense of $50·00.

The cash impact of hedging transactions is another consideration. Cash flows in this will be affected by both the transaction and the forward contract. Accordingly, as the after-tax cash loss resulting from the settlement of the liability is $150 (line 7) and the cash gain resulting from the closing of the forward contract is $100 (line 21), the overall cash loss is $50 (line 22). This cash loss is identical to the total decrease in net income (line 22), which, in turn, is identical to the after-tax premium expense (line 19). The overall cost of hedging a transaction is thus the premium/discount expense/revenue.

Exhibit 1—Accounting treatment and cash impact

Exposure		First half of 19X1	Second half of 19X1	Cumulative for 19X1
(1) Date	31/12/X0	30/06/X1	31/12/X1	
(2) Exposure (FC)	(1,666·67)	(1,666·67)	(1,666·67)	
(3) Exchange rate ($/FC)	1·00	1·05	1·15	
(4) $ equivalents	(1,666·67)	(1,750·00)	(1,916·67)	
(5) FX gain/(loss) before tax		(83·33)	(166·67)	(250·00)
(6) Tax (40%)		33·33	66·67	100·00
(7) FX gain/(loss) after tax; lines (5) + (6)		(50·00)	(100)	(150·00)
Forward contract				
(8) Date	31/12/X0	30/06/X1	31/12/X1	
(9) Amount brought	1,666·67	1,666·67	1,666·67	
(10) Spot ($/FC)	1·00	1·05	1·15	
(11) $ Value of contract	1,666·67	1,750·00	1,916·67	
(12) FX gain/(loss before tax)		83·33	166·67	250
(13) Tax (40%)		(33·33)	(66·67)	(100)
(14) FX gain/(loss after tax)		50	100	150
FASB 8 gain/loss				
(15) FX gain/(loss) before tax (5) + (12)		0	0	0
(16) FX gain/(loss) after tax (7) + (14)		0	0	0

	30/06/X1	31/12/X1	Cumulative
Income and cash impact			
(17) Premium to be amortized ($)*	(41·67)	(41·66)	(83·33)
(18) Tax (40%)	16·67	16·66	33·33
(19) Decrease in after-tax income			
(17) + (18)	(25)	(25)	(50)
(20) Total increase (decrease) in			
net income (16) + (19)	(25)	(25)	(50)
(21) Total cash flow from forward			
contract (14) + (19)—at maturity	25	75	100
(22) Overall cash gain/(loss)			
(7) + (21)—at maturity			(50)

* Premium to be amortized = (spot at start of contract − forward rate) × FC amount bought = (1–1·05) × 1,666·67 = $83·33

C. Hedging subsidiary's transactions

Subsidiaries' transactions with third parties denominated in third currencies may be protected in the forward markets by either the subsidiary, the parent or both entities simultaneously. The manner in which the exposure is protected depends on corporate objectives in the area of exposure management and the degree of centralization of the exposure management function. This section analyzes the impact of two techniques available to hedge a subsidiary's third currency exposure. The first is the subsidiary's hedge of its transaction exposure within the framework of a decentralized exposure management function; the second is the parent's after-tax hedge of the after-tax consolidated exposure as it relates to centralized exposure management. In each situation we identify the impact of the exposure and the related hedge on the subsidiary and the consolidated entity in terms of foreign exchange, net income and cash impacts.

1. Subsidiary's hedge of transaction exposure

This definition is appropriate for a decentralized exposure management function as the transaction exposure exists from the subsidiary's viewpoint and gives rise to foreign exchange gain or loss on the subsidiary's books.

In the following example we assume that a German subsidiary has a £10,000 receivable from a third party on its books on 31/12/X0, collectable on 31/03/X1. Anticipating a depreciation of sterling against the Deutschemark, the subsidiary covers its exposure by selling £10,000 against DM @ DM 2·95. The exchange rate moves as follows:

$$31/12/X0 \quad £1 = DM \ 3 \ = PC \ 1·5$$
$$31/03/X1 \quad £1 = DM \ 2·9 = PC \ 1·595$$

Impact on subsidiary: The subsidiary's exposure data are presented in Section A of Exhibit 1 and indicate an after-tax loss of DM 600 (line 6). The data pertaining to the subsidiary's forward contract are shown in Section B, identifying an after-tax gain of DM 600 (line 11) and discount expense of DM 300, resulting in a cash inflow of DM 300 (line 15) on the contract. Section C combines the subsidiary's exposure and forward contract data, indicating zero foreign exchange gain/loss (line 17) and a net cash outflow of DM 300 (line 19). The net cash outflow is the sum of the exposure and forward contract gains and losses and is identical to the subsidiary's discount expense of DM 300. The hedging cost to the subsidiary is thus the after-tax discount expense, as the foreign exchange gains and losses on the exposure and the contract offset each other (line 17).

Exhibit 1—Subsidiary's hedge

A. Subsidiary: exposure	31/12/X0	31/03/X1
(1) Exposure (£)	10,000	10,000
(2) ER (DM/£)	3·0	2·9
(3) DM equivalent	30,000	29,000
(4) FX gain/(loss) B.T.		(1,000)
(5) Tax (40%)		400
(6) Cash and FX gain/(loss) A.T.		(600)

	31/12/X0	31/03/X1
B. Subsidiary: forward contract		
(7) Amount sold (£)	(10,000)	(10,000)
(8) DM equivalent; (2) × (7)	(30,000)	(29,000)
(9) FX gain/(loss) B.T.		1,000
(10) Tax (40%)		(400)
(11) FX gain/(loss) A.T.		600
(12) Discount expense B.T.*		(500)
(13) Tax (40%)		200
(14) Discount expense A.T.		(300)
(15) Cash impact A.T.**		300
C. Subsidiary: consolidated		
(16) FX gain/(loss) B.T.; (4) + (9)		0
(17) FX gain/(loss) A.T.; (6) + (11)		0
(18) Net income A.T.; (14) + (17)		(300)
(19) Cash impact A.T.; (6) + (15)		(300)
D. Parent and subsidiary consolidated		
(20) Exposure (DM)	30,000	30,000
(21) ER (PC/DM)	0·5	0·55
(22) PC equivalent	15,000	16,500
(23) FX gain/(loss)		1,500
(24) PC equivalent of discount expense B.T.; (12) × (21)		(275)
(25) PC equivalent of tax; (13) × (21)		110
(26) PC equivalent of discount expense A.T.; (24) + (25)		(165)
(27) Net income A.T.; (23) + (26)		1,335

* Discount to be amortized = (forward rate − spot at inception) × amount of £ sold = (2·95 − 3·0) × £10,000 = <u>(DM 500)</u>

** Cash impact of forward contract A.T. = (forward rate − spot at maturity) × amount of £ sold × (1 − tax rate) = (2·95 − 2·90) × 10,000 × 0·6 = <u>DM 300</u>

The consolidated after-tax impact is analyzed in Section D of the exhibit. Here, as line 20 indicates, by selling sterling against mark, the subsidiary has eliminated the £ exposure but has, at the same time, created a long DM exposure for the consolidated entity as follows:

Item	Parent and subsidiary consolidated
(1) Transaction exposure	£10,000
(2) Forward contract	
a. £ sold	(£10,000)
b. DM purchased	DM 30,000
(3) Net exposure	
a. £ (1) + (2a)	£0
b. DM (2b)	DM 30,000

The exposure of DM 30,000 results in a gain of PC 1,500 for the consolidated entity (line 23), which is assumed not to be taxable in the home country. Finally, the net impact on consolidation is shown on line 27, indicating an increase of PC 1,335 in net income, which is the sum of the translation gain of PC 1,500 on the contract and the PC 165 equivalent of the subsidiary's discount expense on the forward contract.

2. Parent's after-tax hedge

After-tax exposure definition is appropriate for a centralized exposure management function. Here, the parent enters into forward contracts with the objective of neutralizing the consolidated after-tax impact of the subsidiary's exposures. The impact of the exposure on the subsidiary, however, is not taken into account by the parent's hedge.

In the example presented in Exhibit 2, we assume that the only exposure on the subsidiary's books on 31/12/X0 is an account receivable of TC 1,000. The subsidiary's tax rate on foreign exchange gains and losses is 40% while gains and losses on forward contracts undertaken by the parent are taxed at the rate of 30%. Finally, we assume that the parent projects a decline of both, LC and TC, against the parent currency and sells both in the forward market. The exchange rate moves as follows:

$$31/12/X0 \quad TC\ 1 = LC\ 1 = PC\ 1$$
$$31/03/X1 \quad TC\ 1 = PC\ 0{\cdot}8$$
$$LC\ 1 = PC\ 0{\cdot}9$$
$$TC\ 1 = LC\ 0{\cdot}8889$$

Exhibit 2—Parent's after-tax hedge

	31/12/X0	31/03/X1
A. Subsidiary: exposure		
(1) Exposure (TC)	TC 1,000	TC 1,000
(2) ER (LC/TC)	1·0	0·8889
(3) LC equivalent	1,000	888·89
(4) FX gain/(loss)—B.T.		(111·11)
(5) Tax 40%		44·44
(6) FX gain/(loss)—A.T.		(66·67)
B. Consolidated exposure		
(7) Exposure (TC)	TC 1,000	TC 1,000
(8) ER (PC/TC)	1·0	0·8
(9) PC equivalent	1,000	800
(10) FX gain/(loss) B.T.		(200)
(11) ER (PC/LC)	1·0	0·9
(12) PC equivalent of tax; (5) × (11)		40
(13) FX gain/(loss) A.T.; (10) + (12)		(160)
C. Parent: forward contract #1 (LC)		
(14) Amount sold (LC)	(571·43)	(571·43)
(15) PC equivalent; (14) × (11)	(571·43)	(514·29)
(16) FX gain/(loss) B.T.		57·14
(17) Tax (30%)		(17·14)
(18) FX gain/(loss) A.T.		40
D. Parent: forward contract #2 (TC)		
(19) Amount sold (TC)	(857·14)	(857·14)
(20) PC equivalent; (19) × (8)	(857·14)	(685·71)
(21) FX gain/(loss) B.T.		171·43
(22) Tax (30%)		(51·43)
(23) FX gain/(loss) A.T.		120
E. Consolidated exposure and forward contracts		
(24) FX gain/(loss) B.T.; (10) + (16) + (21)		28·57
(25) FX gain/(loss) A.T.; (13) + (18) + (23)		0

Impact of balance sheet exposure: Section A of the exhibit presents the subsidiary's exposure data and the resulting foreign exchange loss of LC 66·67 (line 6). The consolidated exposure figures are shown in Section B, showing a negative impact of PC 160 (line 13).

Forward contracts: In order to neutralize this impact, the parent has to enter into two forward contracts: one to cover the LC tax component of the subsidiary's transaction exposure and the other to cover the TC after-tax exposure. (See Chapter II, Section B for exposure components.)

- Forward contract #1 (LC)—Section C: As 40% of the subsidiary's exposure constitutes a tax event in LC terms, this amount is exposed to the PC/LC exchange rate movements. Accordingly, to cover the tax exposure of LC 400, the parent sells LC 571·43 (line 14), computed as follows:

> LC tax exposure = LC 400 (40% of exposure)
> Amount of LC after-tax hedge = LC tax exposure/(1 − tax rate on forward contract) = 400/(1—0·3) = <u>LC 571·43</u>

This contract results in an after-tax gain of PC 40 (line 18).

- Forward contract #2 (TC)—Section D: As 60% of the subsidiary's exposure maintains its value in TC terms, it is exposed to the PC/TC exchange rate movements. To cover the after-tax exposure of TC 600, the parent sells TC 857·14 (line 19) forward, computed as follows:

TC after-tax exposure = TC 600 (60% of exposure)

Amount of TC after-tax hedge = TC after-tax exposure/$(1 -$ tax rate on forward contract) = $600/1(1 - 0.3) =$ TC 857·14

The second contract results in a gain of PC 120 (line 23).

Consolidated after-tax exposure and forward contracts data—Section E: The after-tax loss of PC 160 (line 13) on exposure is perfectly offset by the after-tax gains of PC 40 on the LC contract (line 18) and PC 120 on the TC contract (line 23). The cost of this protection to the parent, though not presented in our example, would be the discount expense on the forward sale of each of the two currencies against the parent currency. That cost would be accounted for in conformity with Paragraph 25 of FASB-8.

Conclusions

Each of the two strategies for hedging third currency exposures of a subsidiary meets certain objectives while creating other concerns for one of the entities involved. More specifically, the subsidiary's hedge eliminates the subsidiary's sterling transaction exposure while creating new mark exposure for the consolidated entity. The parent's after-tax hedge, on the other hand, eliminates the consolidated currency exposures but is of no help to the subsidiary. These conflicts are inherent in the management of third currency exposures and are discussed and quantified further in Chapter VII, Section C.

D. Intercompany flows

From an exposure management point of view intercompany flows are frequently analyzed as translation, transaction or consolidated after tax exposures. Accordingly, depending on the definition selected, intercompany flows may be hedged by various strategies in the forward markets. In this section we analyze two such strategies: (1) the subsidiary's hedge of the transaction component of the exposure and, (2) the parent's after-tax hedge of the consolidated after-tax exposure.[1]

In order to simplify the presentation, throughout the section we use an identical example of an intercompany exposure denominated in the parent currency where on December 31, 19X0 a subsidiary owes PC 10,000 to the parent, payable on March 31, 19X1. The exchange rate assumptions are identical throughout the section as well and for convenience are summarized below:

Date	Spot rate	3 months forward rate
31/12/X0	LC 1 = PC 1	LC 1 = PC 0·95 (PC 1 = LC 1·0526)
31/3/X1	LC 1 = PC 0·9	____

1. Subsidiary's hedge

As discussed in Chapter II, intercompany transaction exposure exists for the entity whose transaction is denominated in a currency other than its own. Referring to our example, if the intercompany payable on the subsidiary's books is denominated in the parent currency it is exposed because at maturity the subsidiary will have to use more LC units if the PC appreciates or less LC units if the PC depreciates. The parent has no transaction exposure in this situation, since its receivable is denominated in its own currency.

Assuming that the subsidiary anticipates an appreciation of the parent currency, it covers its short exposure of PC 10,000 by buying PC 10,000 @ LC 1·0526 in the forward market. The relevant data for this situation is presented below:

Intercompany exposure denominated in PC: subsidiary's hedge

Intercompany exposure

(1) Subsidiary: PC intercompany payable	(10,000)
(2) Parent: PC intercompany receivable	10,000
(3) Net intercompany exposure	0

---

[1] The hedges discussed herein are accounted for as paragraph 25 hedges under FASB-8, where gains or losses are accrued in each accounting period based on the spot exchange rates at the beginning and end of the accounting period. The discount or premium on the contract is accounted for separately and is amortized to income over the life of the contract. If these hedges were accounted for under Paragraph 26 of FASB-8, the *net* impact of the contract would be identical at maturity, though the accounting treatment throughout the period would differ.

Forward contract

(4) Subsidiary: PC amount bought   10,000
(5) Subsidiary: LC amount sold   (10,000)

By purchasing PC 10,000 in the forward market (line 4), the subsidiary effectively eliminated its short transaction exposure of PC 10,000 (line 1). By selling the local currency forward against the parent currency, it has, however, created a short LC exposure for the consolidated entity. The originally neutral consolidated position has thus been altered and a short exposure of LC 10,000 created (line 5).

This situation is analyzed further in Exhibit 1. The subsidiary's exposure data are shown in Section A, and line 6 identifies an after-tax loss of LC 666·67. The data related to the forward contact undertaken by the subsidiary are analyzed in Section B, indicating an after-tax foreign exchange gain of LC 666·67 (line 11), an after-tax premium expense of LC 315·79 (line 14), and net after-tax income of LC 350·88 (line 16). The subsidiary's combined data are presented in Section C and indicate no foreign exchange gain or loss either before or after-tax and a net after-tax income impact of negative LC 315·79 (line 19) which is identical to the after-tax premium expense (line 14). The subsidiary's net cost of covering is thus the after-tax premium expense. Finally, the after-tax consolidation in the home country (Section D) identifies a foreign exchange gain of PC 1,000 (line 23) and net positive after-tax income impact of PC 715·79 (line 27) on a negative consolidated exposure of LC 10,000 (line 20).

Exhibit 1—Subsidiary's hedge

	31/12/X0	31/03/X1
A. Subsidiary: exposure		
(1) Exposure (PC)	(10,000)	(10,000)
(2) ER (LC/PC)	1·0	1·11111
(3) LC equivalent (1) × (2)	(10,000)	(11,111·11)
(4) FX gain/(loss) B.T.		(1,111·11)
(5) Tax (40%)		444·44
(6) FX gain/(loss) A.T.		(666·67)
B. Subsidiary: forward contract		
(7) Amount bought (PC)	10,000	10,000
(8) LC equivalent; (2) × (7)	10,000	11,111·11
(9) FX gain/(loss) B.T.		1,111·11
(10) Tax (40%)		(444·44)
(11) FX gain/(loss) A.T.		666·67
(12) Premium expense B.T.*		(526·32)
(13) Tax (40%)		210·53
(14) Premium expense A.T.		(315·79)
(15) Net income B.T.; (9) + (12)		584·79
(16) Net income A.T.; (11) + (14)		350·88
C. Subsidiary: combined data		
(17) FX gain/(loss) B.T.; (4) + (9)		0
(18) FX gain/(loss) A.T.; (6) + (11)		0
(19) Net income A.T. (6) + (16)		(315·79)
D. Consolidation after-tax in home country		
(20) Exposure (LC amount sold)	(10,000)	(10,000)
(21) ER (PC/LC)	1·0	0·9
(22) PC equivalent (20) × (21)	(10,000)	(9,000)
(23) FX gain/(loss) B.T. (9) × (21)**		1,000
(24) PC equivalent of premium B.T.; (12) × (21)		(473·69)
(25) PC equivalent of tax; (13) × (21)		189·48
(26) PC equivalent of premium A.T.; (24) + (25)		(284·21)
(27) Net income A.T.; (23) + (26)		715·79

* Premium expense to be amortized = (spot at inception − forward rate) × PC amount bought = $(1·0 − 1·0526315) × 10,000$ = (LC 526·315)
** FX gain of PC 1,000 is assumed not to be taxable

From the consolidated point of view, the impact on net after-tax income is the sum of the translation gain due to the short LC 10,000 exposure, i.e. PC 1,000 (line 23) and the PC equivalent of the subsidiary's after-tax premium expense of PC 284·21 (line 26). The net after-tax consolidated income is thus affected positively by PC 715·79.

2. Parent's hedge: after-tax consolidated exposure

As discussed in Chapter II, after-tax intercompany exposure is an issue primarily for the consolidated entity because the tax effects of transaction gains or losses of the subsidiary are reflected in the consolidated results.

Returning to the example of an intercompany payable of PC 10,000 due by the subsidiary to the parent and assuming that foreign exchange gains or losses on the subsidiary's transactions are taxed at a rate of 40% while gains or losses on forward contracts undertaken by the parent are taxed at a

Exhibit 2—After-tax hedge by parent

B. Consolidation: exposure

(7) Exposure (LC)	0	0
(8) FX gain/(loss) B.T.		0
(9) ER (PC/LC)	1·0	0·9
(10) PC equivalent of tax; (5) × (9)		400
(11) FX gain/(loss) A.T.; (8) + (10)		400

C. Parent: forward contract

(12) Amount bought (LC)	5,714·29	5,714·29
(13) PC equivalent; (9) × (12)	5,714·29	5,142·86
(14) FX gain/(loss) B.T.		(571·43)
(15) Tax (30%)		171·43
(16) FX gain/(loss) A.T.		(400)
(17) Discount revenue B.T.*		285·71
(18) Tax (30%)		(85·71)
(19) Discount revenue A.T.		200
(20) Net income; B.T. (14) + (17)		(285·71)
(21) Net income; A.T. (16) + (19)		(200)

D. Consolidation: exposure and forward contract

(22) FX gain/(loss) B.T.; (8) + (14)		(571·43)
(23) FX gain/(loss) A.T.; (11) + (16)		0
(24) Net income A.T.; (23) + (19)		200

* Discount revenue = (spot at inception − forward rate) × LC amount bought = (1·0 − 0·95) × LC 5,714·29 = 0·05 × 5,714·29 = PC 285·71

rate of 30%, the relevant data are presented and analyzed in Exhibit 2. The subsidiary's exposure in data is identical to that in the previous example and indicates an after-tax loss of LC 666·67 (line 6). The consolidated exposure data in Section B indicates an after-tax gain of PC 400 (line 11) which is due to the short tax exposure of LC 4,000, computed as follows:

$$LC \text{ tax exposure} = LC \text{ exposure} \times \text{subsidiary's tax rate} = (LC\ 10{,}000) \times 0.4 = \underline{(LC\ 4{,}000)}$$

The after-tax exposure of negative LC 4,000 indicates that a strengthening local currency would result in an increased tax liability for the consolidated entity while a weakening local currency would decrease the tax liability in PC terms upon consolidation.

Section C pertains to the forward contract undertaken by the parent. In order to protect against a potential negative after-tax impact on consolidated results if the LC appreciated, the parent buys forward LC 5,714·29 to offset the short tax exposure of LC 4,000. The appropriate amount of the parent's after-tax hedge is computed as follows:

$$\text{Amount of after-tax hedge} = LC \text{ tax exposure} \div (1 - \text{tax rate on forward contract gain/loss})$$
$$= LC\ 4{,}000 \div 0.7 = \underline{LC\ 5{,}714 \cdot 29}$$

Finally, the consolidated after-tax results are presented in Section D. As line 23 indicates, the after-tax foreign exchange impact is nil with an after-tax hedge. A before-tax exchange loss, however, is reported in this situation as the parent went long LC 5,714·29 in a weakening currency.

Conclusions

This section discussed and analyzed hedging of transaction and after-tax consolidated exposures as embodied in intercompany flows. The analysis indicates that each individual strategy eliminates the foreign exchange impact of only one of the two entities involved. More specifically, the decentralized hedge eliminates the transaction exposure of the subsidiary but leaves the translation component of the exposure uncovered for the consolidated entity. The centralized hedge, on the other hand, eliminates the consolidated after-tax exposure while ignoring the transaction exposure of the subsidiary. These conflicts are inherent in the management of intercompany flows and are directly related to corporate objectives of exposure management and to the issue of centralization vs. decentralization of the exposure management function.

How can these conflicts be resolved? What actions should the treasurer take to eliminate exposure for both the subsidiary and the consolidated entity? A coordinated hedge resolves the conflict and provides cover at both levels. More specifically, under this approach each entity covers exposure as computed at its own level. In our case this would be accomplished by the subsidiary's hedge of the transaction component of the exposure accompanied by the parent's hedge of the translation component of the exposure, where the parent would buy forward an appropriate after-tax amount to eliminate the short translation exposure of LC 10,000. With both components of the exposure covered, any potential foreign exchange impact at either the subsidiary or consolidated level is eliminated and a perfect hedge achieved. (See Chapter VII, Section B.)

E. Dividend exposure

Anticipated or declared dividends from foreign subsidiaries are exposed to foreign exchange fluctuations as are any other exposed monetary assets. This is because the value of the dividend in terms of the parent currency changes in line with the exchange rate change between the local and the parent currency.

A dividend exposure, however, differs from other current monetary exposures in several respects. First, as a dividend distribution results in a switch from the local currency into the parent currency, exposure exists only until the time of the dividend distribution. Second, whereas translation gains or losses on earnings considered to be reinvested are assumed to have no tax effect upon consolidation, gains or losses on earnings earmarked for dividend distribution may have tax effects. Finally, dividend remittances are frequently subject to a withholding tax which, in effect, reduces the amount of the dividend distribution. These differences may affect the maturity and the amount of a hedge if compared to a hedge of a translation exposure as discussed in Section A above.

1. Assumptions

The accounting treatment, tax implications and cash impact of a dividend exposure and an offsetting forward contract are demonstrated with the following assumptions.

- A multinational company's subsidiary in country A has a net asset exposure of LC 1,000 on 31/12/X0. This exposure is assumed to be earmarked for dividend distribution on 31/3/X1. The tax rate of the parent is 40%.
- On 31/12/X0, the parent projects a depreciation of the LC over the next quarter and sells forward LC 1,000 to cover the dividend exposure, for delivery on 31/3/X1, @ PC 0·97.
- On 28/2/X1, the subsidiary declares a dividend of LC 1,000, and books a dividend payable of the same amount. The dividend payable does not reduce the exposure, since it is offset by a dividend receivable booked by the parent. What is exposed is the net asset of the subsidiary (e.g. cash) earmarked for dividend distribution.
- On 31/3/X1, the subsidiary remits LC 1,000 to the parent. Given a withholding tax of 15% on dividend remittances, LC 850 is received by the parent. The withholding tax, however, does not reduce the exposure as demonstrated by and explained in connection with Exhibit 2.
- The spot exchange rate moves as follows:
31/12/X0	LC 1·00 = PC 1·00
28/02/X1	LC 1·00 = PC 0·93
31/03/X1	LC 1·00 = PC 0·90

2. Treatment

The exposure and forward contract data are shown in the first column of Exhibit 1. The remaining columns in this table show the results upon the declaration of the dividend (column 2), the remittance of the dividend (column 3) and the cumulative impact of exchange rate fluctuations on foreign exchange gain/loss, net income and cash (column 4).

The first six lines provide the data for the dividend exposure, and show a cumulative loss of PC 100 before-tax and PC 60 after-tax. Lines 7 to 13 concern the forward contract, and indicate cumulative foreign exchange gains of PC 100 and PC 60 before and after-tax respectively. The discount expense amounts to PC 30 before-tax and PC 18 after-tax.

Exhibit 1—Hedging of dividend exposure

Dividend exposure	31/12/X0	28/02/X1	31/03/X1	Cumulative
(1) Exposure (LC)	1,000	1,000	1,000	
(2) ER (PC/LC)	1·0	0·93	0·90	
(3) PC equivalent	1,000	930	900	
(4) FX gain/(loss) B.T.		(70)	(30)	(100)
(5) Tax (40%)		28	12	40
(6) FX gain/(loss) A.T.		(42)	(18)	(60)
Forward contract				
(7) Amount sold (LC)	(1,000)	(1,000)	(1,000)	
(8) PC equivalent; (7) × (2)	(1,000)	(930)	(900)	
(9) FX gain/(loss) B.T.		70	30	100
(10) Tax (40%)		(28)	(12)	(40)
(11) FX gain/(loss) A.T.		42	18	60
(12) Discount expense B.T.*		(20)	(10)	(30)
(13) Discount expense A.T.		(12)	(6)	(18)
Consolidated after-tax impact				
(14) FX gain/(loss); (6) + (11)		0	0	0
(15) Net income; (13) + (14)		(12)	(6)	(18)
(16) Cash impact at maturity**				(18)

* Discount to be amortized = (spot at start of contract − forward rate) × LC amount sold = $(1·00 − 0·97) × 1,000 = (PC\ 30)$.

** Cash impact at maturity = (Cash gain/loss on exposure + cash gain/loss on forward contract) × (1 − tax rate) = {[exposure × (spot at maturity − spot at inception)] + [Amount sold × (spot at maturity − forward rate)]} × (1 − tax rate) = {[1,000 (0·9 − 1·0)] + [−1,000 × (0·9 − 0·97)]} × (1 − 0·4) = (−100 + 70) × 0·6 = −PC 18

The total impact of the exposure and the contract is shown in lines 14 to 16. As both the exposure and the contract are valued on the spot-to-spot basis and the tax applicable to the related gain/loss is identical for both, the total foreign exchange impact is nil (line 14). Net income and cash are impacted negatively by PC 18 (lines 15 to 16 cumulative). The negative impact of PC 18 is identical to the after-tax discount expense on the LC (line 13), and, accordingly, the cost of covering the dividend exposure is the after-tax discount expense.

3. Tax considerations

If a corporate treasurer intends to hedge the dividend remittance, he should take into account the related tax implications. Whereas the above example ignores the withholding tax on the dividend and assumes the same tax rate on foreign exchange gains/losses on exposure and the forward contract, in real life additional tax considerations should be taken into account.

1. Withholding tax

Assuming a 15% withholding tax on the dividend, the parent receives LC 850 as a dividend while the remaining LC 150 is used to pay the withholding tax. It should be noted that in order for the parent to fully protect its cash position, it must hedge the full LC 1,000 and not just the LC 850 net dividend.

Exhibit 2—Hedging of dividend exposure: Impact of withholding tax

Item:	LC 1 = PC 1 No hedge Tax	LC 1 = PC 1 No hedge Cash	LC 1 = PC 0·9 100% hedge Tax	LC 1 = PC 0·9 100% hedge Cash	LC 1 = PC 0·9 85% hedge Tax	LC 1 = PC 0·9 85% hedge Cash
Dividend received	850	850	765	765	765	765
Withholding tax (15%)	150		135		135	
FX gain/(loss) on contract	—		100	100	85	85
Total taxable/cash income	1,000		1,000		985	
U.S. tax (48%)	(480)		(480)		(472·80)	
Less foreign tax credit	150		135		135	
U.S. tax due	(330)	(330)	(345)	(345)	(337·80)	(337·80)
Cash income A.T.		PC 520		PC 520		PC 512·20

88

Exhibit 2 indicates that a 100% hedge of the dividend with local currency devaluation has the same net impact as no hedge with a stable local currency.

2. Taxation of FX gains/losses

In the above example we assumed that the dividend income and the gain realized on the contract are taxed at the same rate. In reality, however, these separate income components may be taxed at different rates. Under such circumstances if the treasurer wants to protect the after-tax dividend exposure he should first compute the after-tax exposure and then determine the amount of the after-tax hedge. If these amounts are correctly computed, the after-tax gain or loss should net to zero. Assuming a 48% tax rate on foreign exchange gains/losses on the dividend exposure and a 10% tax rate on the forward contract gains and losses, the after-tax exposure of LC 520 and the amount of the after-tax hedge against that exposure are computed as follows:

- After-tax exposure = before-tax exposure × (1 − tax rate on FX gains/losses on exposure) = LC 1,000 × (1 − 0·48) = LC 520
- Amount of after-tax hedge = After-tax exposure ÷ (1 − tax rate on FX gains/losses on forward contracts) = LC 520 ÷ (1 − 0·1) = LC 577·78

The impact of the after-tax hedge is analyzed in Exhibit 3.

Exhibit 3—Hedging of dividend exposure: Impact of after-tax hedge

Dividend exposure	31/12/X0	31/03/X1
(1) Exposure (LC)	1,000	1,000
(2) ER (PC/LC)	1·0	0·9
(3) PC equivalent	1,000	900
(4) FX gain/(loss) B.T.		(100)
(5) FX gain/(loss) A.T.		(52)
Forward contract		
(6) Amount sold (LC)	(577·78)	(577·78)
(7) PC equivalent; (2) × (6)	(577·78)	(520)
(8) FX gain/(loss) B.T.		57·78
(9) FX gain/(loss) A.T.		52
Consolidated		
(10) FX gain/(loss) B.T.		(42·22)
(11) FX gain/(loss) A.T.		0

As lines 10 and 11 in the exhibit indicate, the treasurer has succeeded in achieving a zero after-tax foreign exchange impact. The before-tax impact on reported income, however, has not been neutralized, and a foreign exchange loss of PC 42·22 is reported.

F. Commitment exposure

A forward contract is treated as a hedge of a commitment if three conditions are met. They are laid down in Paragraph 27 of FASB-8. The conditions are: (a) the life of the forward contract extends from the foreign currency commitment date to the expected transaction date or a later date; (b) the forward contract is denominated in the same currency as the foreign currency commitment (a condition revised in December 1977 by Paragraph 13 of FASB 20); and (c) the foreign currency commitment is firm and uncancellable.

Commitment exposure generally begins at the time a purchase contract is issued or a sales contract is accepted, but accounting recognition of the commitment is delayed until the transaction date, which is the date on which the purchase or sale is recorded in the accounting records in conformity with generally accepted accounting principles. (Some commitments do not involve purchases or sales; for example, the transaction dates under a lease are the dates on which individual lease payments come due.)

Since no accounting recognition is given to the commitment or the exchange rate fluctuations during the commitment period, FASB-8 states that no separate recognition be given to the gain or loss on the covering forward contract during that period. Instead, any gain or loss on the forward contract is included in the measurement of the related transaction on the transaction date. From that time, i.e. after the transaction is recorded, the covering forward contract will have to be accounted for as a hedge contract, with any gain or loss on the forward contract offsetting the loss or gain on the balance sheet exposure after the transaction date.

The premium or discount on the forward contract should be accounted for separately; it must be amortized (recognized) over the life of the contract, but the portion amortizable during the commitment period may be included in the measurement of the related transaction—i.e. as an adjustment of the cost of the inventory purchased.

1. Assumptions

The accounting treatment, cash impact and tax implications of a foreign exchange commitment exposure and an offsetting forward contract are shown in the Exhibit 1, with the following assumptions:

- A U.S. company commits itself on December 31, 19X0 (commitment date) to purchase inventory in local currency for LC 1,666·67 on June 30, 19X1 (date at which it takes delivery of the inventory and therefore the transaction date) payable on December 31, 19X1. The tax rate for the U.S. company is 40% (tax effects are discussed further below).
- Projecting an appreciation of the LC, the company enters into a 12-month forward contract on December 31, 19X0 to buy LC 1,666·67 at $1·05.
- The exchange rate moves as follows:
  31/12/X0 LC 1·00 = $1·00
  30/6/X1 LC 1·00 = $1·05
  31/12/X1 LC 1·00 = $1·15
- The company chooses not to include the contract premium relating to the commitment period in the measure of the dollar basis of the inventory.

The exposure data and the forward contract data are shown in the first column of the table. The remaining columns show the results for the first and second halves of 19X1 (columns two and three), and the cumulative impact of foreign exchange fluctuations on cash, income, taxes and inventory in 19X1 (column four).

The first sub-group concerns the balance sheet exposure data (lines one to seven, inclusive). As the first column shows, the commitment of LC 1,666·67 is the equivalent of $1,666·67 on December 31, 19X0. On June 30, 19X1 the commitment, although unchanged in LC terms, has increased to the equivalent of $1,750·00, as the LC has appreciated in value from $1·00 to $1·05 (column two). Since the commitment is an off-balance sheet item, no foreign exchange loss on the contractual liability would be recognized or reported by the company under U.S. accounting principles.

On June 30, 19X1 (transaction date) the inventory is delivered and an account payable of $1,750·00 (LC 1,666·67 times $1·05) is recorded in the books. When the debt comes due on December 31, 19X1, the payable is translatable at the prevailing exchange rate of $1·15 and is the equivalent of $1,916·67. Accordingly, a foreign exchange loss (on the payable) of $166·67 ($1,916·67 minus $1,750·00) is recognized by the company, in part mitigated by a tax credit of $66·67, resulting in an after-tax loss of $100·00.

Lines 8 to 14 inclusive concern the forward contract data. As the first column shows, the amount of LC 1,666·67 purchased forward is the equivalent of $1,666·67 on December 31, 19X0. On June 30, 19X1 (column two) the contract is worth $1,750·00 (LC 1·00 = $1·05) but no foreign exchange gain is recognized or reported, consistent with the non-recognition of the foreign exchange loss on the commitment during the first half of 19X1. (On the transaction date the unrecognized gain of $83·33 on the forward contract will be included in the dollar measure of the inventory purchased.) From July 1, 19X1 to December 31, 19X1, i.e. after the transaction is recorded, the forward contract must be accounted for as a hedge of balance sheet exposed position, as described earlier in this chapter.

Line 15 shows the total reported foreign exchange gain or loss under FASB-8. This is the sum of the before-tax foreign exchange loss on the net exposed liability position of LC 1,666·67 and the before-tax foreign exchange gain on the forward contract. Line 16 shows the after-tax foreign exchange gain or loss, which is the reported FASB-8 foreign exchange gain or loss, net of the appropriate tax credit or expense, resulting from the balance sheet exposure loss and the forward contract gain (the same tax rate is assumed for both transactions; see the last two paragraphs below). If the exposure is properly hedged on an after-tax basis, line 16 should be zero, as it is in Exhibit 1.

2. The cash implications

Lines 17 to 20 inclusive identify some of the net after-tax income and cash implications of commitment exposures and related commitment forward contracts. It should be noted that the reported foreign exchange gain or loss on the forward contract does not include the premium or discount accounting entries. The decrease of $83·33 (line 17, last column) in before-tax income,

Exhibit 1—Accounting treatment and cash impact of a commitment situation

The contract premium relating to the commitment period is not included in the measure of the dollar basis of the inventory.

		First half of 19X1	Second half of 19X1	Cumulative for 19X1
Exposure				
(1) Date	31/12/X0	30/06/X1	31/12/X1	
(2) Exposure (local currency)	(1,666·67)	(1,666·67)	(1,666·67)	
(3) Exchange rate ($/LC)	1·00	1·05	1·15	
(4) $ equivalents	(1,666·67)	(1,750·00)	(1,916·67)	
(5) FX gain/(loss) before tax			(166·67)	(166·67)
(6) Tax (40%)			66·67	66·67
(7) FX gain/(loss) after tax; lines (5) + (6)			(100·00)	(100·00)
Forward contract				
(8) Date	31/12/X0	30/06/X1	31/12/X1	
(9) Amount bought (LC)	1,666·67	1,666·67	1,666·67	
(10) Spot ($/LC)	1·00	1·05	1·15	
(11) $ value of contract	1,666·67	1,750·00	1,916·67	
(12) FX gain/(loss) before tax			166·67	166·67
(13) Tax (40%)			(66·67)	(66·67)
(14) FX gain/(loss) after tax			100·00	100·00
FASB-8 gain/loss				
(15) FX gain/(loss) before tax (5) + (12)		0	0	0
(16) FX gain/(loss) after tax (7) + (14)		0	0	0
Income and cash impact				
(17) Premium to be amortized ($)*		(41·67)	(41·66)	(83·33)
(18) Tax (40%)		16·67	16·66	33·33
(19) Decrease in after-tax income; lines (16) + (17) + (18)		(25·00)	(25·00)	(50·00)
(20) Total cash flow from forward contract (14) + (19) + (24) + (25)—at maturity				100·00
Inventory				
(21) LC value		1,666·67		
(22) Spot ($/LC)		1·05		
(23) $ value		1,750·00		
(24) FX gain on forward contract during commitment period		83·33		83·33
(25) Deferred tax (40%)		(33·33)		(33·33)
(26) Decrease $ value of inventory		(83·33)		
(27) Book ($) value of inventory (23) + (26)		1,666·67	1,666·67	
(28) Total decrease in after-tax income (7) + (14) + (19)				(50·00)

* Premium to be amortized = (spot at start of contract − forward rate) × LC amount bought = (1·00 − 1·05) × 1,666·67 = $83·33.

which would occur from the amortization of the premium, would not be classified as part of the foreign exchange gain or loss on the forward contract. The cash impact of the forward contract is another consideration (line 20), and the table indicates that the after-tax cash gain (on the contract) is $100·00.

The impact of the above transactions on the inventory is analyzed in lines 21 to 27, inclusive. When the inventory is received on June 30, 19X1 (column two), it is valued at LC 1,666·67, which, translated into dollars at the June 30 exchange rate of LC 1·00 = $1·05, is $1,750·00 (line 23). The dollar value of the inventory must then be adjusted to reflect the foreign exchange gain on the forward contract during the commitment period, i.e. $83·33 (line 24). The book value of the inventory as of June 30, 19X1 is therefore $1,666·67 (line 27), precisely the cost (spot rate) prevailing on December 31, 19X0 when the inventory was purchased (commitment date). The deferred tax of $33·33 (due to the foreign exchange gain of $83·33 on the forward contract during the commitment period—line 25) will subsequently be charged to income when the inventory is sold.

As a result of all the transactions, total after-tax income will decrease by $50·00 (line 28, last column), which is the sum of the after-tax loss on the balance sheet exposure (line 7), the reported after-tax gain on the commitment contract (line 14) and the after-tax premium expense over the life of the forward contract (line 19). The decrease in the reported after-tax income is thus equal to the after-tax premium expense (line 19, last column).

FASB-20 amends FASB-8 to provide for after-tax hedging of a commitment and illustrates the rather complex rules laid down for the situation where after-tax hedging of a commitment is applicable and is undertaken. An after-tax hedge should be based on after-tax exposure. A commitment is most likely to be hedged in an import or export situation where only the domestic tax laws apply and the after-tax hedge (the after-tax exposure divided by one less the tax rate) will equal the before-tax exposure except when different tax rates apply to the results of the transaction and to the results of the forward contract. When a portion of a forward contract is intended to provide a hedge on an after-tax basis, a gain or loss pertaining thereto, to the extent that that portion is in excess of the related commitment (none in the case of the import or export situation described in the preceding sentence), shall be deferred and shall be offset (literally) against the related tax effects when they are recognized, i.e., that portion of the gain or loss on the forward contract is credited or charged to tax expense for accounting purposes.

The hedging calculations in the preceding paragraph are illustrated by the import example used in this section. The company imports inventory costing LC 1,666·67, establishing a before-tax FASB-8 exposure (short) of that amount. A 40% tax rate is assumed applicable to the exchange difference on the exposure (whether it is considered for tax purposes to be an exchange gain or loss, or an adjustment of inventory cost and therefore ultimately of cost of sales), so the after-tax exposure is LC 1,000·00 (LC 1,666·67 times one minus the tax rate or LC 1,666·67 times 0·60). A 40% tax rate is assumed applicable to the gain/loss on the forward contract. The after-tax hedge is therefore LC 1,000·00 divided by one minus the tax rate or LC 1,000·00/·60 or LC 1,666·67 and the company should enter into a forward contract to buy (go long) the latter amount if it wishes to hedge its before-tax FASB-8 exposure of the same amount.

G. Speculative contracts

Forward foreign exchange contracts that are neither standard hedges nor hedges of commitments as defined by FASB-8 are treated as speculative. The word should not be taken literally. Speculative contracts are quite frequently used by U.S.-based corporations for hedging their foreign exchange exposures not defined as exposures by FASB-8. Speculative contracts exist where a monetary asset or liability is not being protected or where there is no firm and uncancellable purchase (expenditure) or sales commitment. FASB-8 defines as speculative forward contracts entered into as hedges against inventories (inventories are a non-monetary asset) or intercompany flows (no FASB-8 exchange gain or loss arises on intercompany flows).

Under FASB-8, speculative contracts are the easiest to account for. The reported foreign exchange gain or loss on an outstanding speculative contract is the difference between the contract rate and the current forward rate to the maturity of the existing contract, i.e. the current market quote for a contract which would offset the existing contract for its remaining term. Premiums or discounts are not accounted for separately on this category of forward contracts.

Exhibit 1—Accounting treatment and cash impact of a speculative forward contract

Forward contract		First half of 19X1	Second half of 19X1	Cumulative for 19X1
(1) Date	31/12/X0	30/6/X1	31/12/X1	
(2) Amount bought (LC)	1,666·67	1,666·67	1,666·67	
(3) Forward contract rate ($/LC)	1·05	1·05	1·05	
(4) Forward rate to maturity ($/LC)	1·05	1·10	1·15	
(5) Value of contract if sold: (2) × (4) (in $)	1,750·00	1,833·33	1,916·67	
(6) FX gain/(loss) before tax (FASB-8)		83·33	83·34	166·67
(7) Tax (40%)		(33·33)	(33·34)	(66·67)
(8) FX gain/(loss) after tax: (6)–(7)		50·00	50·00	100·00

Cash flows				
(9) Spot ($/LC)			1·15	
(10) Amount received ($): (9) × (2)			1,916·67	
(11) Amount paid ($): (3) × (2)			1,750·00	
(12) Cash gain/(loss) before tax: (10)–(11)			166·67	166·67
(13) Tax (40%)			(66·67)	(66·67)
(14) Cash gain/(loss) after tax: (12)–(13)			100·00	100·00

1. Assumptions

The accounting treatment, cash impact and tax implications of a speculative forward contract are presented in Exhibit 1, with the following assumptions:

- Expecting an appreciation of the local currency, a U.S company enters into a 12 month forward contract on December 31, 19X0, to buy forward LC 1,666·67 @ $1·05. The tax rate for the U.S. company is 40%.
- The exchange rates (spot and forward) move as follows:

	Spot rate	Forward rate to maturity
31/12/X0	LC 1·00 = $1·00	$1·05
30/6/X1	LC 1·00 = $1·05	$1·10
31/12/X1	LC 1·00 = $1·15	$1·15

The forward contract data are shown in column one. The remaining columns in the table show the results for the first and second halves of 19X1 (columns two and three), and the cumulative impact of foreign exchange fluctuations on cash, income and taxes in 19X1 (column four).

The first eight lines concern the income impact of the foreign exchange forward contract. As the first column shows, the purchased amount of LC 1,666·67 is equivalent to $1,750·00, which is the amount of LC bought multiplied by the forward contract rate. This purchased amount of LC 1,666·67 can (by definition) be sold to the same maturity for $1,750·00 (line five). Accordingly, no foreign exchange gain/loss exists on December 31, 19X0. On June 30, 19X1, the forward rate on the LC has increased (from $1·05 to $1·10), and the forward contract could now be reversed to the same maturity for $1,833·33. The reported foreign exchange gain at that date is consequently $83·33.

2. Cash flows

This FASB-8 foreign exchange gain will incur a tax expense of $33·33 (line 7) to result in a net gain of $50·00. When the contract matures on December 31, 19X1, a foreign exchange gain of $83·34 will be recorded in line with the movement of the forward rate from $1·10 to $1·15 (the spot rate at maturity equals the forward rate to maturity). This gain will again incur a tax expense of $33·34, resulting in a net gain of $50·00 during the second half of 19X1. Accordingly, a cumulative foreign exchange gain (on the contract) of $166·67 is recognized by the company along with tax expense of $66·67, resulting in an after-tax gain of $100·00.

The next six lines of the table (9 to 14 inclusive) concern the actual cash flows. The company contracted to pay $1,750·00 for LC 1,666·67 it purchased on December 31, 19X0 @ $1·05 (line 11). This same amount of LC 1,666·67 concomitantly will be sold for $1,916·67 at the prevailing spot rate at maturity on December 31, 19X1 of $1·15 (line 10). The difference between the dollar amounts received ($1,916·67) and paid ($1,750·00) is the before-tax cash gain of $166·67 (line 12). A tax expense of $66·67 will reduce this gain to $100·00, which is the same amount as reported in the income statement (line 8—cumulative).

Exhibit 2—Summary of reporting methods

		Hedge			Type of contract Speculative			Commitment	
Item		Before tax	Tax	After tax	Before tax	Tax	After tax	Before tax	Tax	After tax
(1) Exposure loss		(150)	0	(150)	—	—	—	(166·67)	66·67	(100)
(2) Fwd contract gain		250	(100)	150	166·67	(66·67)	100	166·67	(66·67)	100
(3) FASB-8 gain/(loss):	:									
(1) + (2)		100	(100)	0	166·67	(66·67)	100	0	0	0
(4) Premium expense		(83·33)	33·33	(50)	—	—	—	(83·33)	33·33	(50)
(5) Inventory*		—	—	—	—	—	—	83·33	(33·33)	50
(6) Cash impact of fwd contract:										
(2) + (4) + (5)		166·67	(66·67)	100	166·67	(66·67)	100	166·67	(66·67)	100
(7) Total income:										
(1) + (2) + (4)		16·67	(66·67)	(50)	166·67	(66·67)	100	(83·33)	33·33	(50)

* Effect on income deferred until inventory is sold.

3. Summary

As Exhibit 2 indicates, the cash impact is the same regardless of how the forward contract is classified under FASB-8 (line six). The reported income (line seven) in the three situations varies because the underlying exposures (transactions) vary. In the case of the *hedge* contract, the after-tax loss on the exposure is perfectly offset by an after-tax gain on the contract. In the *commitment* situation, the after-tax loss on the balance sheet exposure also is perfectly offset by the after-tax gain on the forward contract after the end of the commitment period; an opportunity loss (not recognized for accounting purposes) on the unrecorded payable has occurred during the commitment period and the foreign exchange gain on the forward contract during that period is credited to the inventory account. Finally, in the case of a *speculative* contract, no underlying transaction (exposure) is considered to exist and the after-tax cash and income impacts are the same. In the final analysis, the key difference between the three types of forward contracts is the manner of reporting them under FASB-8.

H. Long term forward contracts

The long term forward contract provides a tailored opportunity to obtain foreign exchange cover where no established foreign exchange market exists. Companies entering into such an agreement typically have exposures which mirror each other and are therefore equally motivated to lock in a future exchange rate.

A long term forward contract may be made directly between two companies or with a bank acting as principal in the middle. Structuring the transaction directly may marginally improve the pricing for the parties, but may also increase the credit risk, negotiating time and resulting legal costs and, most important, may reduce the flexibility and the potential for anonymity. For example, when two companies enter into an intercompany forward contract directly, they are each obliged to evaluate the other party's long term credit and to subsequently assume the credit risk. Even in those cases where both companies are of exceptional quality and financial soundness, many companies believe the savings in spread do not justify the risk. They prefer to let the banks who are in the business of making credit evaluations act as principal between the parties. Many banks have developed standardized documents which may be used with only slight modification. Thus, it is not necessary for two sets of lawyers to develop the necessary legal documentation from scratch for what may appear to them to be an unusual transaction.

One of the most important advantages of the bank-intermediated forward contract, however, is structural flexibility. Each counterparty in a bank intermediated transaction may be able to realize a different structure, and thereby achieve different objectives with regard to legal, tax or accounting benefits that might otherwise have been unobtainable. For instance, a bank might book a currency swap with one counterparty, and a forward contract with the other counterparty, thereby satisfying each party's need for a different structure. Such flexibility ultimately broadens the range of potential counterparties available to any specific client, and correspondingly increases the probability of closing a successful transaction. Furthermore, a direct contract usually obligates both parties for the entire term of the contract, whereas a bank-intermediated forward contract may be structured to allow for early termination by one party without obligation to the other.

Intercompany forward contracts enable companies to hedge potential foreign currency accounting and funds flow exposures. Interest in these transactions has developed principally as a result of the following factors:

1. Foreign currency funding requirements
Corporations wishing to borrow abroad in foreign currencies very often find that they cannot command as fine a rate in foreign markets as they could at home. By combining an intercompany forward sale of foreign currency with a home currency borrowing, they achieve the effect of having borrowed the foreign currency at a finer rate than would have been available in the foreign borrowing market.

2. Foreign currency receivables, payables and debt
The volatility of exchange rates over the last decade has motivated many companies to seek to lock in their costs or profits relating to cross border flows in terms of their reporting currency.

3. FASB No. 8 accounting regulations
Forward contracts provide U.S. companies with a means of effectively fixing the foreign currency denominated net asset or liability position to dollars during the period of the agreement for U.S. reporting purposes.

Forward contracts have been used effectively in each one of these areas. Below are three examples which describe how either a corporate or government entity has used a forward contract to resolve the funding or exposure problems outlined above:

1. Foreign currency funding
Recently a U.S. subsidiary of a German company reviewed the financing alternatives available in the U.S. market. The most attractive offer received was a 7 year borrowing at a $12\frac{3}{4}\%$ p.a. cost. The parent company, on the other hand, could borrow Deutschemarks at 8% p.a. in Germany and lend the funds to its subsidiary which in turn could buy Deutschemarks forward at a cost of $4\frac{1}{8}\%$ p.a. The overall cost of "dollar" borrowing was thereby reduced by $\frac{5}{8}\%$ p.a.

2. Hedging foreign currency
A company bought capital equipment from France which was financed in French francs for a 10 year period when the exchange rate was Ffr/$ 4·50. Although the rate of interest was attractive, the company was faced with increasing costs as the franc appreciated in value. The company determined to seek to cover this exposure and was able to arrange to buy forward French francs in amounts equal to the principal and interest due under its borrowing for an average rate of Ffr/$ 4·50.

3. FASB No. 8 accounting regulations
A major U.S. multinational recently found itself with an increasing long net asset position in an exotic currency where no forward foreign exchange market exists. Although the currency had been strong, the company felt uncomfortable with the size of its long position and had exhausted all apparent possibilities for shortening it. However, there were also several companies which had payments to make into the country on a regular basis. A hedging agreement was reached between the two companies whereby the first company sold forward the currency to the second. At the maturity of the contract, it was agreed that the foreign currency would not be delivered but only the gain or loss in U.S. dollars would be received or paid. The first company was thereby able to fix the dollar value of its net asset position and the second was able to lock in the U.S. dollar cost of its payables.

The cost of entering into such contracts depends upon a number of factors. These would include the long term interest rate differentials if they exist, the general availability of counterparties and their appetite for entering into the contract, and the need by one side or the other for a speedy turnaround time. In addition, a fee is normally charged by the entity arranging the transaction and is typically a certain percentage of the amount involved.

CHAPTER V

Other elements of exposure management

A. Introduction

Chapter II investigated the most complex parameter of exposure management, that of the measurement and definition of exposure. Any pure accounting measurement and definition of exposure mandated by accounting standards boards is a common parameter faced by all corporations. But as Chapter II has demonstrated the corporation ultimately can delineate a number of exposure definitions.

Chapter V examines three additional parameters of exposure management: the currency outlook, taxation, and exchange rules and regulations. All must be taken into account by the exposure manager before protective actions are pursued because each affects the nature, cost, magnitude and time horizon of those actions as well as the situs of the hedge. Chapters III and IV discussed how these exposures can be hedged.

1. Currency forecasting

I have maintained for many years that exchange rate forecasting is the least desirable part of our business. A corporate treasurer cannot survive without forecasts; yet, he recognizes that the accuracy of currency forecasts is by no means guaranteed. Really, currency forecasting is just a higher-order restatement of the interest rate outlook problem vividly familiar to domestic financial managers.

A corporation can formulate its own forecasts or purchase them from outside experts in a variety of formats and time horizons, produced by judgemental, econometric, and other techniques; yet as our perceptions of risk change continuously, the forecasts become obsolete as soon as the ink is dry.[1] When, however, we do find a forecaster with a better than average track record, his forecasts are frequently in a format (e.g. quarterly) which does not satisfy the dynamic needs to protect cash flows embodied in transactions, the essence of short run exposure management.

The bottom line of currency forecasting, as Professor Levich underscores in the following section, is not the accuracy of the forecast itself but the profitability of the decision taken in conjunction with the forecast. Even the technical side of forecasting cannot escape this bottom-line criterion. Those who have used the various technical forecasts (e.g. momentum, congestion, trend change, head-and-shoulder formation, oscillation, and the atomic-inverto line) know that the proprietary technology of one technical expert just as frequently yields a recommendation in conflict with another's.

2. Taxation

While currency forecasting is the most treacherous parameter of exposure management, international taxation is one of the most complicated and least understood subjects in exposure management. The importance of taxes cannot be overstated, because once a corporation has passed the first hurdle of defining and measuring its exposures, taxes become a factor in the decision of when to hedge, how much to hedge, for what maturity, where to lodge hedging actions, whether to compensate forward contracts before maturity, and where to settle forward contracts.

The many dimensions of taxes facing exposure managers are examined in detail by Messrs. Hammer, Schwarz, Costello and Brenner, four distinguished experts in the field. Those dimensions are too numerous to cover. Only a few words of caution are advised to the reader: do not forget that financial accounting and tax accounting are distinctly different; always remember to

---

[1] In addition to Professor Levich's excellent contribution herein, the reader is referred to "Corporate Uses of Foreign Exchange Forecasts", by Jeffrey C. Donahue, which originally appeared in *Euromoney*, June, 1976. A revision was printed in *The Management of Foreign Exchange Risk*, edited by Richard Ensor and Boris Antl, published by Euromoney Publications, London, 1978.

distinguish between tax consequences of gains and losses arising from exposures and tax consequences of gains and losses arising from protective actions.

3. Exchange rules and regulations

In the early days of our discipline, exposure managers would check with the exchange regulations and controls experts to see if their proposed currency protection measures were within the law. Today, the proliferation of rules and controls makes us first check with the experts to see if anything can be done at all.

Exchange controls and regulations have a profound effect on the practice of exposure management because by inhibiting protective actions they force us to more thoroughly evaluate foreign investment decisions in light of sourcing, selling, pricing and financing alternatives. This strikes at the heart of long run, or strategic, exposure management. Concomitantly, of all the parameters of foreign exchange exposure management, controls and regulations come closest to the tail wagging the dog, as any managing director of a Brazilian subsidiary will testify.

B. Use and evaluation of foreign exchange forecasts

1. Introduction

With over 150 countries in the world and nearly as many currencies, it would be extremely fortuitous if national economic policies and developments were so well coordinated that exchange rate changes were not required to maintain international equilibrium. The post World War II era reflects a varied history of exchange rate behaviour. For most industrial countries, infrequent exchange rate changes of moderate magnitude characterize the pegged exchange rate regime under the Bretton Woods system. Since the early 1970s, the exchange rates for most industrial countries *vis-à-vis* the U.S. dollar have been determined in a flexible exchange rate regime dominated largely by private free market trading with occasional, if not substantial, official intervention. As a consequence, the behaviour of these exchange rates over the last few years has reflected a higher frequency of relatively small price changes. Over time, however, the cumulative price change for several currencies has been substantial.

Exhibit 1 presents a history of the level of exchange rates during the 1970s. The cumulative decline in the value of the U.S. dollar *vis-à-vis* the Swiss franc, Deutschemark and Japanese yen are striking during this period. Evidence on recent exchange rate volatility suggests that it is not unusual for an exchange rate to change by 0·5% in a single day; changes in excess of 1·0% are also not uncommon.

The experience for less developed countries is somewhat different. Many less developed countries have elected to maintain a pegged exchange rate *vis-à-vis* their major trading partner, and so the exchange rate may be unchanged for long stretches of time. For other less developed countries extremely high and persistent inflation is an important feature of the economic environment. As a consequence, many of these countries utilize a crawling peg system, so that the exchange rate changes by a large amount at regular intervals.

It is important to note that for exchange rate volatility to be a matter of concern, two conditions must be met. First, the exchange rate changes must correspond to real changes. The data in Exhibit 1 are nominal changes. If the Purchasing Power Parity (PPP) theory and Fisher Effect theory are valid, then the real exchange rate is constant over time and the real interest rate is equal across countries.[2] In this case, nominal exchange rate changes do not have real consequences. Second, the exchange rate changes must not be fully anticipated by the market. If the exchange rate changes described in Exhibit 1 were fully anticipated, then investors with knowledge of the future could not earn unusual profits and uninformed investors would still be able to transact at fair market prices.

In practice, most nominal exchange rate changes correspond to real exchange rate changes (especially in the short run) and a high percentage of exchange rate change is unanticipated.[3] This suggests that investors and managers who possess superior forecasts of exchange rates can make investments and managerial decisions which produce results that are superior to those based on naive forecasts or strategies.

For the multinational firm, exchange rate forecasts play a role in a wide variety of decisions. Obviously, any foreign borrowing or investment decision requires a forecast of future exchange

---

[2] For a discussion of these two important relationships, see Aliber and Stickney (1975) and Aliber (1978).

[3] Recent evidence on the purchasing power parity is summarized in McKinnon (1979, Chapter 6). Empirical results reported by Bilson (1979), Levich (1979), Longworth (1979), and Tryon (1979) suggests that the forward premium (a variable commonly felt to reflect exchange rate expectations) explains only a small fraction of exchange rate changes.

Exhibit 1—Exchange rates against the dollar

Rates per U.S. cent

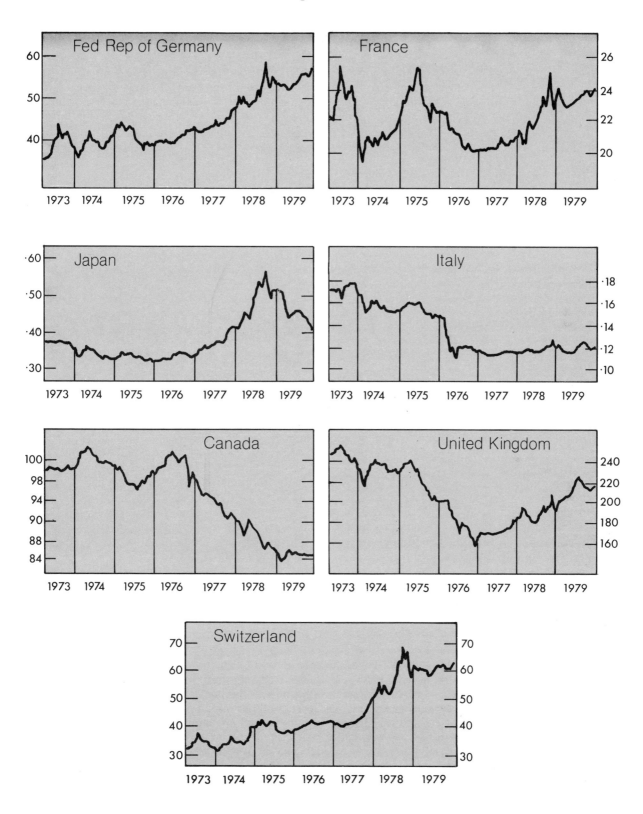

Source: Euromoney

rates so that future foreign cash flows can be converted into units of domestic currency and a comparable domestic cost of funds or return on investment can be computed. A currency forecast is generally required for the firm to manage its currency exposure that results from current and planned holdings of foreign currency.[4] Currency forecasts can play a role in marketing, specifically with respect to pricing decisions. Suppose a Japanese automobile which sells for 1,200,000 yen in Japan is priced at $6,000 in the United States when the exchange rate stands at 200 yen/$. If the yen appreciates to 180 yen/$, each U.S. auto sale will earn only $6,000 × 180 yen/$ = 1,080,000 yen. The Japanese firm is now worse off and it is clear that its decision to raise U.S. prices will depend upon many factors including the future yen/$ exchange rate. From this example we can also see that assessing subsidiary performance will also require exchange rate projections.[5] Finally, exchange rate forecasts may be valuable for long range or strategic planning. If the real exchange rate is expected to change the U.S. firm can maximize its dollar profits (revenues-costs) by incurring costs in those countries where the currency has depreciated below its PPP level (so that the real value of production costs is lower) and by earning revenues in those countries where the currency has appreciated above its PPP level (so that the real value of revenues is higher).

Below in Section 2, we detail some of the sources of exchange rate forecasts and their characteristics. A discussion of the evaluation of currency forecasts is presented in Section 3. Further issues in forecast evaluation and conclusions are presented in Section 4.

2. The foreign exchange forecasting industry

As we indicated previously, recent exchange rate changes have been large, frequent and, for the most part, unanticipated. Under these conditions, the opportunities for gains or losses resulting from exposure to foreign exchange risk are enhanced greatly. The demand for foreign exchange forecasts has increased to exploit these opportunities.

There are three primary sources of forecasts: (1) specialized foreign exchange forecasting companies, (2) currency traders and advisory units within international banks, and (3) forecasts based on market determined prices. Point (3) suggests the popular notion that a consensus market forecast of the future spot rate is available simply by observing market prices. Under a strict set of assumptions, it can be demonstrated that today's forward rate represents all investor expectations and it is the best available forecast of the future spot rate.[6] If these conditions are met, then many multinational firms would view the forward rate as a very attractive forecast to use—first, because it represents the collective wisdom of many well-informed, profit-seeking traders; second, because the forward rate will be revised quickly as new information becomes available; and third, because the forward rate is a very inexpensive forecast to use. However, there are three counter-arguments against the forward rate as in ideal predictor—first, the forward rate may be influenced by official intervention; second, the forward rate may reflect a risk premium as well as exchange rate expectations (much the same as an interest rate can include a liquidity or risk premium); and third, expectations themselves may be weakly held or very imprecise. This final point suggests that the forward rate prediction may be very inaccurate, even though it is unlikely that investor expectations will be wrong consistently. The forecasting accuracy of the forward rate is an extremely important question, but one that remains unsettled given the empirical research to date.[7]

Forecasting companies are another major source of exchange rate predictions. There are two broad categories of companies— first, those with an horizon of one to eight or more quarters ahead, and second, those with a very short run, day-to-day horizon. Within the first category, we can classify companies as using either an econometric or judgemental approach.[8] The econometric forecasts very often are based on a single equation regression model.[9]

For example, the company could use the equation

$$\%S = a_0 + a_1 (\%M_{US} - \%M_G) + a_2 (\%IP_{US} - \%IP_G) + a_3 (i_{US} - i_G)$$

where $\%S$ = per cent change in $/DM exchange rate.

         $\%M_{US}$ = per cent change in U.S. money supply.

         $\%M_G$ = per cent change in German money supply.

         $\%IP_{US}$ = per cent change in U.S. industrial production.

---

[4] An exposure management model that does not require precise exchange rate forecasts is described in Kohlhagen (1978).

[5] Methods for evaluating the performance of foreign subsidiaries are discussed in Lessard and Lorange (1977).

[6] The practical meaning of the expressions "best available forecast" is not unambiguous. For example, it might refer to a forecast whose errors (a) have the lowest average value, (b) have the lowest average squared value, and (c) are serially uncorrelated; but we could desire that other criteria are met.

[7] The empirical evidence on this issue is reviewed in Levich (1978, 1979).

[8] Bayesian statisticians will recognize that this classification is arbitrary. The decision to accept one forecasting equation and reject all others clearly involves judgement.

[9] Other techniques are multiple equation regression models and factor analysis.

$\%\text{IP}_G$ = per cent change in German industrial production.
i_{US} = one year interest rate on U.S. dollar asset.
i_G = one year interest rate on German DM asset.
a_0, a_1, a_2, a_3 = parameters estimated from historical data.

The company then predicts (either using judgement or another equation) the required right-hand-side variables and computes its forecast for the per cent change in the $/DM exchange rate. The prediction could be a point estimate (e.g. the expected exchange rate for December 31, 1980) or a period average forecast (e.g. the average exchange rate for the fourth quarter of 1980) depending on the time dimension of the right-hand-side variables.

In addition some forecasting companies report their equations or make them available to users with an interactive computer programme. In either case, the user can compute a new exchange rate forecast based on different assumptions for predicted values of the right-hand-side variables. This allows the user to explore the sensitivity of the forecasting equation and, for example, to calculate the minimum and maximum exchange rates that are expected. The forecasting company may also report diagnostic checks on the equation which suggest how much confidence a user might have in the equation.[10]

Other forecasting companies follow a more judgemental approach. Some may consider econometric estimates of important (and quantifiable) variables (e.g. the money supply, trade balance, inflation rate, etc.). However, economic factors that are difficult to quantify (e.g. currency expectations, changes in capital controls or tax policy) along with other factors (e.g. political elections and appointments) are also considered. All of these factors are combined in some unspecified way to determine a forecast.

Some forecasting companies specialize in very short run forecasts. These so-called technical or momentum services advise their customers primarily on the direction of exchange rate movements in the very short term and, correspondingly, whether customers should hold long or short positions in particular currencies. These directional forecasts are typically based on a statistical analysis of recent exchange rate behaviour. Judgement may, however, play an equally large role.

A final source of currency forecasts, advisory services within international banks and their currency traders, are similar in many ways to our other sources. Bank advisory services tend to prefer a judgemental approach to forecasting although most banks have access to econometric estimates of many input variables. Bank advisory services generally forecast over a range of one-quarter to eight quarters. If clients desire a prediction for the very short run, the bank's currency trader may be called on although banks are clearly not in the business of publishing these short-run forecasts.

3. Evaluating foreign exchange forecasts

How can we evaluate and choose among alternative foreign exchange forecasts? As in other similar problems (such as evaluating the performance of mutual fund managers or of individual subsidiaries or profit centres within the firm), evaluating foreign exchange forecasting performance is a tricky procedure. Basically, we need to establish a standard of performance and then to calculate how a forecast compares to the standard. There are two general approaches for analyzing forecasting performance. The first concentrates on the forecast error. Forecast error = Forecasted exchange rate − actual exchange rate) and its various statistical properties. One desirable property of a forecast is that its forecast errors be small. However, even this simple criterion needs qualification. For example, assume that today's forward rate is $2·00 and two alternative forecasts of the future spot rate are $S_1 = \$1·99$ and $S_2 = \$2·08$. If the actual spot rate turns out to be $2·02, the forecast error associated with S_1 (−$·03) is smaller than the forecast error associated with S_2 (+$·06). However, forecast S_2 is superior because it leads investors to take long and profitable forward positions in sterling—i.e. forecast S_2 leads to a correct decision. As a further qualification, suppose that a third forecast, $S_3 = \$2·14$, also exists. Even though its forecast error is +$·12, it does not follow that this forecast is twice as bad as forecast S_2. If, for example, the firm is remitting a dividend from its U.K. subsidiary to its U.S. parent and the firm is considering an all-or-nothing hedging decision, it will make the same decision using either S_2 or S_3 as a guide, and so there is no additional cost associated with S_3's larger forecast error. On the other hand, forecast S_3 may be more than twice as bad as forecast S_2. If the firm is considering investing a variable amount in U.K. bonds, based on the substantial appreciation predicted by S_3 the firm may invest 10 times as much in the U.K. as it would based on forecast S_2. As a consequence, the firm foregoes other profitable investments; these opportunity costs of using S_3 may exceed twice the cost of using S_2. Therefore we

---

[10] This may be important if we want to separate the company's skill in selecting the proper set of variables and estimating their regression coefficients from the company's skill in predicting the future values of the right-hand-side variables.

conclude that there is no simple relationship between the magnitude of forecast errors and the cost of forecast errors for investors.

If we ignore the magnitude of forecast errors, we can evaluate a forecast by calculating the fraction of periods where the forecast correctly predicts only the direction of exchange rate movement. We can define direction relative to the current forward rate or some other decision variable (e.g. the forward rate plus a risk premium). For instance, in our earlier example, S_2 and S_3 were correct forecasts (relative to the forward rate), while S_1 was incorrect. If the fraction of correct forecasts is unusually high, then we can conclude that the forecasting service has expertise.

Exhibit 2—Hypothetical data on forward rates, forecasts and speculative profits (U.S. cents)

Month	Forecast	Forward rate	Future spot rate	Profit	Cumulative profit	Cumulative profit (with perfect information)	Ratio (6)/(7)
(1)	(2)	(3)	(4)	(5)	(6)	(7)	(8)
1	49	50	53	−3	−3	3	−1·00
2	53	52	54	2	−1	5	−0·20
3	50	51	53	−2	−3	7	−0·43
4	51	52	53	−1	−4	8	−0·50
5	53	52	56	4	0	12	0·00
6	56	55	58	3	3	15	0·20
7	58	57	58	1	4	16	0·25
8	57	59	56	3	7	19	0·37
9	57	58	60	−2	5	21	0·24
10	61	60	64	4	9	25	0·36
11	64	63	65	2	11	27	0·41
12	66	65	62	−3	8	30	0·27
13	66	67	64	3	11	33	0·33
14	64	63	63	0	11	33	0·33
15	60	61	60	1	12	34	0·35
16	61	60	62	2	14	36	0·39
17	60	58	58	0	14	36	0·39
18	59	60	57	3	17	39	0·44
19	55	56	55	1	18	40	0·45
20	58	57	58	1	19	41	0·46

A numerical example will help to illustrate the above procedure. Consider the hypothetical set of forecasts, forward rates and spot rates presented in Exhibit 2. In this sample of 20 observations, there are 15 correct forecasts, or a 75% track record. Is this an unusually good track record that demonstrates expertise or is it simply the result of a sequence of lucky guesses? The question is analogous to another basic statistics problem: if a fair coin is tossed 20 times, what is the probability that it will land on heads 15 or more times? The answer is that this event would occur with roughly 1% probability.[11] There are two ways to interpret this track record.

(1) The forecaster does not have any special expertise in picking the direction of currency movements. A one-in-a-hundred event happened—the forecaster guessed correctly on 15 of 20 trials.
(2) The forecaster does have special expertise. His track record for picking the direction of currency movements correctly is close to 75%, significantly greater than 50%, which would result from simply guessing.

In this case, we would probably pick interpretation (2). The track record appears too high to be the likely result of just guessing.

The second general approach for evaluating forecasting performance is to calculate the stream of returns that an investor could earn by following the forecast. We would conclude that the advisory service has expertise and that the forecasts are useful if the stream of investment returns (adjusting for risk) is high relative to alternative investments. Again, this straight forward evaluation procedure raises two difficult questions.

First, how does an investor translate a set of currency forecasts into a set of investment decisions?

---

[11] The exact test is a binomial probability test that the fraction $p = r$ successes/n forecasts is significantly larger than 0·5. See Levich (1980).

The investor recognizes that forecasts are seldom perfect. If the forward rate stands at $2·00, the investor may not be willing to buy forward contracts unless the forecast is $2·02, $2·06, or perhaps higher. Furthermore, the investor is free to increase the number of forward contracts he purchases as his expected profits, and the confidence in those profits, increases. The issues are often handled by assuming that the investor uses the forecast to determine a lump-sum investment rather than an investment which increases with the expected returns predicted by the forecast or which decreases with the expected variance of returns.

The second difficult question is how we should measure the risk associated with currency investment. This calculation is necessary so that we can determine if the return on currency investment is high relative to the risk incurred. Since the measurement of this risk factor is somewhat controversial,[12] many analyses will simply compare the returns from selective currency investments based on a forecast with returns from (a) always holding U.S. dollar assets, or (b) always holding foreign currency assets. These latter alternatives correspond to the (a) always hedge foreign exchange risk strategy and (b) never hedge foreign exchange risk strategy which are simple rules-of-thumb for comparison. Another investment strategy is the hypothetical set of currency investments that would have been made with perfect information about future exchange rate changes. According to this performance criterion we compare the actual profits based on the currency forecast with potential profits under perfect information. If this ratio is high, we conclude that the advisory service has expertise and that the forecasts are useful.[13]

The data in Exhibit 2 present the stream of profits earned by trading (i.e. buying or selling) one forward contract following the advice of the forecast. Our interest is whether this sequence of profits is unusually large relative to risk or relative to other investment opportunities. Total profits for the 20 month period are $0·19. Based on an average forward contract price of $0·578, the return is 33% for the 20-month period or about 20% per year. This return is in addition to the risk-free rate[14] but clearly these profits are not risk-free.[15] There are speculative losses in five months and the ratio of actual to perfect information profits varies between $-1·0$ in the initial period to $0·46$ in month 20. If we view this investment in a portfolio context, however, we would want to compare the risk and return properties of column (5) with the risk and return properties of alternative investments. Without further assumption about these alternative investments, we cannot conclude whether the stream of profits in the exhibit is unusually high.

The above approaches have not dealt adequately with the issue of foreign exchange risk. This is not because the riskiness in a stream of currency investment returns is unimportant, but rather that there is no theoretically sound and operational technique for measuring this risk. The result is that if we find an advisory service whose forecasts can guide us to a 5%, 10% or 20% annual return on investment, we cannot conclude that these results are superior or inferior to alternative investment opportunities unless we take account of risk.

4. Further issues in the evaluation of foreign exchange forecasts

The analysis of foreign exchange forecasts involves a number of operational difficulties that are important to mention. First, there may be a considerable time lag between producing a forecast and making it available to users. This time lag would be most harmful to our assessment of a short run (say, one month) forecast. Second, published forecasts are sometimes updated by subsequent oral advice from the forecasters. If this new advice is correct and ahead of market price changes it will lead to large profits and we should upgrade our evaluation of the service. However, the new advice may be wrong or lag changing market prices. Third, forecasting services charge different amounts for their services. We should expect that a service that charges $75,000 per year is considerably more accurate than a bank service which passes along its forecasts free of charge.

There are also two more technical issues that should be raised. First, most techniques for

---

[12] The basis of the controversy is whether foreign exchange risk is non-diversifiable (a systematic risk with which we associate a risk premium) or diversifiable (a non-systematic risk not associated with a risk premium).

[13] Comparing actual profits with perfect information profits is based on the assumption that the probability of correct prediction and the distribution of speculative returns are constant over time. When these assumptions are not met, our calculation can give misleading results. For example, suppose a forecasting service provides incorrect forecasts in nine consecutive periods, however in each period the loss is small ($·01 per contract). In period ten the service correctly predicts a large exchange rate change ($·41). The ratio of actual profits ($·32) to potential profits ($·50) is high (64%) and we might therefore conclude that the service has expertise. However, the probability of correct advise in any period has been low (10%) and significantly worse than guessing. An investor might still conclude that the service is useful since although it cannot predict small exchange rate changes it can predict the large ones.

[14] This is because interest earning U.S. Treasury bills can be used as collateral on currency futures markets such as the International Monetary Market in Chicago.

[15] The risks are naturally greater if the forward contracts are purchased on margin. For example, assuming a 6% or less margin, the investor would have a total loss in month one.

performance evaluation implicitly assume that the forward rate is the best publicly available source of exchange rate expectations. In Section 2 we argued that this need not be correct. In this case, we expect that advisory services should forecast better than the forward rate; and furthermore, their ability to do this does not indicate unusual forecasting expertise or profit opportunities.

Second, most forecasting services and most methods for evaluating forecasting performance totally ignore portfolio considerations. For example, one advisory service may use a single equation model which is similar for many currencies. If the service makes a bad forecast for one currency it is likely to be wrong on every currency. This is a very risky situation. A second advisory service may assign a country specialist to forecast each individual currency. If these specialists forecast independently, it is unlikely that they will all be right (or wrong) at the same time. This structure of forecast errors reduces risk for the user.

5. Conclusions

We have briefly considered some of the uses for foreign exchange forecasts as well as the general techniques for producing these forecasts. There are two general techniques for evaluating forecasting performance—the first is a statistical analysis of forecast errors, the second is an analysis of the profit opportunities available to forecast users. As we illustrated, both of these techniques require careful interpretation to avoid misleading results. If the analyst is willing to make some simplifying assumption—such as an interest only in the direction of the forecast and not its magnitude—then a number of simple statistical tests are valid for assessing forecasting performance. Two major problems remain with any assessment of forecasting performance—first, the assumption that the forward rate is the best publicly available forecast and second, the assumption that the forecasts are generated independently. If these assumptions are not satisfied, then the standard techniques that we outlined will overestimate the returns and underestimate the risks of using currency forecasts.

C. International corporate taxation—a framework

1. Issues and concepts

A. Classical *v.* integrated tax systems

Virtually every country of the world subscribing to the legal concept of private ownership of property recognizes a corporation as an entity legally distinct and separate from its owners, the shareholders. The corporate entity, as a juridical person, carries its own rights, privileges and obligations, including the fact that it is a separate and distinct taxpayer. In many of these countries, there exists a system of full taxation at the corporate level combined with full taxation at the shareholder level with respect to corporate distributions. Such a system, referred to as the classical system, gives rise to full economic double taxation (as opposed to legal or juridical double taxation). Minimal relief, if any, is granted at the shareholder level to take into account corporate taxes paid. In other words, the conduit theory, i.e. that the corporation is nothing more than the aggregate of its shareholders and thus has no tax-paying ability beyond that of its shareholders, is ignored. As a consequence of the notion that a corporation is a distinct juridical person separate from its shareholders, profits generated by it are subjected to corporate income tax. All net income is so taxable, whether retained or distributed, and, if distributed, whether distributed to residents of the distributing corporation's country of residence or domicile or to non-residents thereof.

One general exception to this rule should be noted. If the dividend recipient is a domestic corporation, most classical system countries provide for relief in the form of an intercorporate dividend exemption, either in whole or in part. The rationale is to avoid *double corporate* tax, since the earnings have yet to flow to the ultimate individual investor. Not providing such an intercorporate dividend exemption could, under some circumstances, lead to multiple taxation of corporate earnings, not merely double taxation. Nonetheless, even with the intercorporate dividend exemption, when the income finally reaches the individual shareholder, it will be fully taxed again (a second time) at the appropriate individual rates.

If the recipient shareholder is a resident of the distributing corporation's country of residence or domicile, he will be subjected to full individual income taxation on that income without regard to the corporate tax paid by the distributing corporation. If, on the other hand, the individual recipient is a nonresident, he will *not* be subject to the source country's regular individual income tax system, but rather will be subjected to a flat rate tax regime, the rate to be determined by statute of the source country, subject to reduction by tax treaty. In either case, however, the result is to subject corporate earnings to double taxation.

In recent years, several countries have mitigated the incidence of full economic double taxation through some form of corporate-shareholder integration. The development of this relief concept has taken two forms, with some countries providing relief directly at the corporate level, through a so-called split rate system, and others at the shareholder level, through an imputation credit mechanism.

Under the split rate system, the corporate income tax rate for profits retained in the corporation is higher than on profits distributed to shareholders under the theory that dividends will be subject to the graduated individual income tax rates in the hands of the shareholders. This approach, in essence, effects integration at the corporate level. Countries having adopted this system include Austria, Finland, Germany, Japan and Norway. Austria, Germany and Japan achieve their objective through the application of a higher statutory rate of tax to undistributed income than to distributed income; for example, Germany's statute provides for a rate of 56% on undistributed earnings with a 36% rate applied to distributed earnings. On the other hand, Finland and Norway have approached the problem of integration at the corporate level by permitting a deduction for dividends paid, which, in effect, provides for a reduced rate of tax on distributed earnings.

Under the imputation system, the shareholder is allowed a credit upon the receipt of a dividend for all (full imputation) or part (partial imputation) of the domestic corporate taxes paid on the corporation's income. The U.K., after a brief experience with the classical system (1965–1973), has reverted to an imputation system. France adopted it in 1965, Canada in 1972, Germany in 1977 and other Common Market countries have adopted it (e.g., Belgium, Italy and Ireland) or plan to do so. While imputation systems of various countries may have broadly similar consequences for domestic shareholders with respect to domestic income, there are many variations among them in their relationship to foreign investors and foreign investment. For example, most imputation systems do *not* grant a credit to non-resident shareholders, although these shareholders are generally taxed at flat withholding rates. The U.S., in particular, has had difficulties in accommodating its tax treaty negotiating posture to these systems. Before the signing of the new U.S.–U.K. treaty, only one major country, France, had concluded a treaty protocol with the U.S. incorporating the imputation credit, but only for U.S. portfolio investors (less than 10%). The discriminatory aspects of these systems have been stumbling blocks to the renegotiation of important tax treaties with France, Canada and Germany.

B. **Deferral *v.* accrual methods of taxing foreign subsidiaries**

As previously mentioned, virtually every country recognizes the corporation as an entity separate and apart from its shareholders. Therefore, if a domestic corporation forms a subsidiary in another country to carry on its foreign operations, that foreign subsidiary's income is not normally subject to taxation in the parent's home country until such time as it distributes a dividend to the parent company. This repatriation basis of taxation of foreign subsidiary earnings by the parent's country has come to be known as the deferral privilege, because the parent company is considered to be in a position to defer payment of home country tax until it receives a dividend. This is indeed a cash-flow advantage if the foreign tax rate is lower than the home country tax rate, because it enables a foreign subsidiary to use its earnings in foreign operations without the necessity of bringing them back to the parent's country in the form of taxable dividends. However, the advantages of deferral are somewhat reduced in practice by the fact that foreign subsidiaries will generally pay income tax in the source country and these taxes are often equal to or higher than those in the home country.

Nonetheless, the U.S., Canada, Germany, Japan and France have enacted legislation in recent years to curb what they perceived to be abuses of the deferral privilege. In general, the effect of such legislation is to subject certain tax haven income of foreign subsidiaries to taxation at home (to the parent) on an accrual basis, without regard to whether the income is repatriated to the parent. Although there have been recent proposals in the U.S. for a complete termination of deferral (in effect, a foreign corporation would be treated as a branch), adoption of such legislation at the present time appears doubtful.

C. **Trading *v.* capital income**

Another distinguishing feature among tax systems is the treatment of trading and capital income. Some countries tax all forms of income in the same manner. However, many countries distinguish between income arising from capital transactions and trading income. *Trading income* arises from the conduct of the company's ordinary business operations. This income is generally taxed at regular (ordinary) corporate rates with deduction allowed for all expenses associated with earning this income. By contrast, income arising from *capital transactions* is sometimes taxed at lower rates with a few related deductions. Other countries exempt capital gains income entirely.

D. **Timing considerations**

Differences are also encountered in the *timing of gain or loss recognition*. Some countries allow for monetary correction, or the recognition of unrealized gain or loss, arising from the adjustment of unsettled foreign currency account balances to the prevailing applicable exchange rates of the home country. Other countries, e.g. the U.S., require a closed transaction for recognition of gain or loss. A closed transaction generally requires repayment.

2. Tax systems of countries

A. Methods of taxing foreign income

There is general agreement among countries that their tax systems should not discriminate against international trade and investment. If some semblance of neutrality between domestic and foreign investment is to be achieved, international double taxation must in practice be avoided. Countries have, over the years, developed different ways of avoiding international double taxation. The two most common methods used are territorial limitations, whereby the home country or capital exporting country excludes foreign income from its tax base entirely, and secondly, the worldwide taxation of repatriated earnings with a foreign tax credit given in the home country. The latter method is used by the U.S. and the U.K., for example, and seems to be the method which many countries are adopting. These two systems are discussed below.

B. Territorial approach

Countries employing a territorial system of taxation *tax only those profits derived within their borders* and exempt all foreign source direct investment income. This means that income derived from foreign branches (permanent establishments) and foreign affiliates are not subject to home country taxation. Most countries which have adopted a territorial (exemption) system apply it only where the direct investment income is subjected to income tax, at least in principle, in the source country. Interest and royalty income from foreign affiliates, as well as portfolio investment income, remain subject to home country taxation.

C. Global approach, with foreign tax credit or foreign tax deduction

Countries employing a global system *subject to tax all income, irrespective of source*. The system generally relieves double taxation through the provision of a credit against the domestic home country tax liability for income tax paid in the source country. The credit is generally limited to the amount of tax that would have otherwise been paid in the home country with respect to the foreign source income.

The result of a credit system is to tax income earned abroad at the higher of the domestic or foreign effective rates. Thus, if the foreign effective rate of tax is equal to or greater than the domestic rate, no additional tax will be paid in the home country; however, if the foreign effective rate is lower than the domestic rate, the home country will ultimately receive in tax revenues the differential between the two rates.

Since the foreign tax credit limitation is computed by comparing a corporation's foreign source income with its total, worldwide income, determining the source of income (and, in some cases, deductions) is extremely important.

Some countries employing the global system grant only a deduction for foreign income taxes paid. Since a deduction provides only partial relief from double taxation, unlike the territorial and credit approaches, these countries' tax systems contain a bias against foreign investment.

3. Income tax treaties

The concepts described in Section 2 above constitute unilateral relief measures aimed at avoiding international double taxation. However, *such measures are often inadequate for several reasons*. First, many countries tax corporations on the *basis of residence and great variation exists* among such countries as to the definition of residence. Thus, a corporation may find itself regarded as resident in more than one country, each country taxing resident corporations on their worldwide income.

Secondly, double taxation can also arise when a home country *corporation conducts its foreign operations through foreign subsidiaries*. The source country will tax the income as earned and will also levy a withholding tax upon remittance of profits to the parent. Some countries also impose withholding taxes on distributions or deemed distributions of branch profits, in effect treating the branch as a separate entity. The combination of corporate and withholding taxes can be well in excess of the rate charged in the home country, so unilateral relief in the form of a foreign tax credit may be inadequate. And unilateral relief may be refused because, for example, of the different sourcing concepts applied in various countries.

Finally, although many countries have similar concepts of taxable income determination, application of these concepts can often produce conflicting results. A common example is the

106

intercorporate transfer pricing area where pricing adjustments made by the revenue authorities of a particular country may not necessarily be acceptable to the authorities of the other country.

Income tax treaties are generally designed to grant relief in the following ways:

1. Residence is clearly defined to avoid jurisdictional overlap;
2. A treaty may provide that profits will be taxed in only one (e.g. the source) country;
3. A treaty may provide that a foreign corporation will not be subject to taxes on profits derived within the source country unless the corporation maintains a permanent establishment therein;
4. A treaty often provides for reduced (or zero) rates of withholding tax on remittances of dividends, interest, royalties and other items to the other country;
5. A treaty often provides for taxation by the source country with a credit in the home country for any taxes paid.

D. Taxation of foreign exchange gains and losses

1. Taxation of foreign source income in the U.S.

A. General

Under the U.S. approach, the place of incorporation of an entity is the cornerstone. If a corporation is organized under the laws of one of the states, it becomes subjected to U.S. tax on its worldwide income, i.e. unlimited tax liability. (If it is not U.S. incorporated, its liability is determined by reference to income from U.S. sources and U.S. connected activities.)

Foreign source income of a U.S. corporation, whether derived from foreign sales or investment activities generated by its U.S. offices or conducted abroad from a foreign branch office, is taxed currently. However, foreign income earned by a foreign subsidiary of a U.S. corporation is not normally taxed until it is received by the U.S. corporation, usually in the form of a dividend. The dividend is subject to the full corporate taxation, with a *direct* credit allowable for foreign withholding taxes, as well as *indirect* credit for underlying corporate income taxes imposed on the foreign affiliate, if the U.S. corporation owns at least 10% of the shares of the foreign corporation. This credit is also available for foreign income taxes paid by second and third-tier subsidiaries on income distributed up the chain to the U.S. corporation. The rules for computing the indirect credit are discussed below.

In certain cases, the income of a foreign subsidiary is taxed to its U.S. parent on an accrual basis (i.e. on a current basis whether or not repatriated). This results from application of the Subpart F provisions of the Internal Revenue Code, pursuant to which the undistributed income of a "controlled foreign corporation", i.e. a corporation of which more than 50% of the stock is owned by U.S. shareholders (each owning at least 10% of the stock) is included in the taxable income of the U.S. shareholders. Subpart F was designed to eliminate the earning and accumulation of profits by U.S. shareholders in tax haven jurisdictions for the primary purpose of avoiding income taxation.

Only certain categories of income earned by a controlled foreign corporation are deemed to be tax haven income, taxable under Subpart F. This would include most items of passive income (i.e. dividends, interest, royalties, capital gains, etc.) as well as certain types of sales and service income. Similar rules exist in Canada, Germany and most recently, Japan. Where Subpart F applies, foreign tax credit relief is available to U.S. shareholders as if the income had actually been distributed. The rules for computing the Subpart F credit are discussed in Section 2.E.

As noted, a foreign corporation carrying on operations outside the U.S. may do so either through a branch or a separate subsidiary corporation. A branch usually connotes the establishment of a foreign office, but can also be established through the mere sending of employees or agents abroad from time to time. Many European countries, for example, require that branches of foreign corporations be registered with the local authorities but the formalities involved are generally not as extensive as setting up a subsidiary. A foreign subsidiary may in appearances be no different from a branch, but it becomes a separate legal entity when its parent has complied with the formalities of local law. These generally include the filing of a corporate charter (analogous to the requirements for certificate of incorporation and bylaws in the U.S.) with a government notary, registration of the company in the official commercial register, and the issuance of shares of stock.

There are several types of corporations that may be formed under foreign law and there is generally flexibility as to the characteristics that may be assigned to a particular entity. The Brazilian *limitada*, for example, may sometimes have the characteristics of both a branch and a subsidiary. The distinction is an important one since branch profits are currently taxable in the U.S. to the parent company but a subsidiary's earnings are generally not taxable until repatriated in the form of dividends (known as the deferral privilege). The Internal Revenue Service has rules that in determining whether a foreign entity qualifies as a corporation for U.S. tax purposes, U.S. corporate concepts will be applied. Thus, the *limitada* will qualify as a subsidiary if it has limited liability, a perpetual life, and freely transferable shares.

B. Foreign tax credit

The *direct* foreign tax credit is calculated on a worldwide basis by aggregating all foreign income taxes paid or accrued. The portion of this total that may be offset against the U.S. tax liability on a corporation's worldwide income is limited using the following computation:

(*a*) Compute the corporation's foreign source taxable income. This is the sum of the foreign source gross income less all direct and indirect expenses incurred in producing such income, including an appropriate portion of general expenses not specifically related to earning foreign income.

(*b*) Compute the corporation's total taxable income. This figure is the tax base on which the U.S. tax is imposed.

(*c*) Divide (*a*) by (*b*) and multiply the quotient by the U.S. tax.

(*d*) Reduce the U.S. tax to the lower of (*c*) or the total foreign income taxes paid or accured.

Example: Assume a taxpayer has total taxable income of $200 of which $100 is from foreign sources. A foreign tax of $60 is imposed on the foreign income and a U.S. tax (before credit) of $92 (46% times $200) is imposed on the total taxable income.

The maximum foreign tax credit (FTC) is as follows:

$$\frac{\$100}{\$200} \times \$92 = \$46$$

The allowable foreign tax credit is $46 (the foreign tax credit limitation) since this is smaller than the amount of foreign taxes actually paid or accrued. In effect, relief is granted up to the amount of the U.S. tax that would have been paid on the net foreign income, in the absence of a credit ($46 in this case).

As can be seen from the example, the effect of the foreign tax credit provisions is to limit the combined U.S. and foreign tax on foreign source income to the higher of the two effective tax rates. If the foreign effective tax rate is lower than the U.S. rate (before credit), some U.S. tax will be due. If, on the other hand, the foreign effective tax rate is higher, no U.S. tax will be payable on the foreign source income.

In the above example, taxable income has already been divided between foreign and domestic sources. In practice, however, it will be necessary to first source each item of gross income according to special rules provided in IRC Section 861. To determine foreign source taxable income, it is then necessary to apportion or allocate all expenses, losses and other deductions to each item of gross income pursuant to detailed rules found in Reg. Sec. 1.861-8. Corporate managements, in an effort to increase foreign tax credits, attempt to structure transactions so that any resulting income or gain will be sourced outside the U.S. and any resulting loss will be allocated to U.S. sources, thereby increasing the numerator of the FTC limitation fraction.

Prior to the Tax Reform Act of 1976, the source of income on transfers of property or assets was fixed in the location where title passed. Since most foreign currency transactions could be effected through a foreign bank, it was viewed as relatively simple to source gains on the sale of foreign exchange contracts outside the U.S., while sourcing loss contracts in the U.S.

Since the 1976 TRA, gain which is treated as ordinary income will follow the old rules; however, gains which are characterized as capital gains are subject to a completely new regime of sourcing rules. Capital gains will generally be domestic source regardless of where the transaction is closed (i.e. title is passed), unless a foreign tax of at least 10% is incurred on the gain. Losses (including exchange losses) must now be allocated or apportioned between foreign and domestic sources according to the 1.861-8 regulations applicable to expenses generally.

2. Taxation of foreign exchange gains and losses

Under the general rules of taxation in the U.S., all items entering into the computation of taxable income must be stated in terms of U.S. dollars. Therefore, an exchange gain or loss is registered by a U.S. corporation when a foreign currency is devalued or revalued in terms of dollars and the firm has unpaid accounts due to, or owing from, a foreign entity. These might consist of foreign currency receivables and payables for inventory or services, amounts due in foreign currency on loans to affiliates and amounts owing in foreign currency on borrowings from banks. The tax questions which arise on such transactions include: whether exchange gains are taxable as ordinary income or capital gains; whether exchange losses are deductible as ordinary or capital losses; and when is the gain or loss recognized, i.e. must there be a closed transaction before recognition?

The U.S., like most other major industrialized countries, has not established clear cut rules for transactional gains and losses involving foreign currency. The basic rule which has emerged from the quagmire of cases and rulings is that foreign currency is to be treated as *property* or as a *commodity* and that exchange gains and losses are computed separately from the underlying transaction. This is known as the "separate transactions" theory. Another evolving rule is that characterization of the exchange gain or loss as *capital* or *ordinary* generally depends on the basic character of the underlying transaction. Therefore, ordinary gain or loss will result where the underlying transaction is an integral part of the taxpayer's trade or business.

The difference between the principles of tax accounting and those of financial accounting provide still more problems for corporate management. For example, balance sheet items will often be revalued for financial statement purposes, while for purposes of taxation, where the separate transaction theory governs, revaluations are not generally recognized (with certain exceptions to be noted below).

Yet another crucial question is whether the exchange gain or loss should be sourced inside or outside the U.S. The answer to this question is particularly important for compliance with the foreign tax credit regulations under Section 861 of the Internal Revenue Code.

A. Specific transactions

Discussed below are typical areas in which the tax impact of exchange fluctuations must be routinely considered.

1. *Import transactions*

The weight of judicial authority dealing with exchange gains and losses in connection with payables resulting from the importation of goods follows the separate transactions theory. Under this approach, inventory is translated at the exchange rate in effect at the date of purchase. Accounts payable are translated at the same rate, with no recognition of gain or loss as long as the account remains unsettled. Foreign exchange gain or loss is recognized as ordinary gain or loss when the account is finally closed by repayment, since the original transaction was an ordinary income transaction.

> *Illustration:* On November 1, U.S. Corporation X buys 1,000 widgets from a U.K. manufacturer on credit (either from the seller or through a bank or by means of other credit facilities) for £1 per widget at a time when the exchange rate is £1 = $3. The purchase price is due in 90 days (January 29) and is payable in pounds sterling. The U.S. company records this inventory at $3,000 (1,000 × $3), the date-of-purchase exchange rate, and sets up an accounts payable in the same amount. The pound is subsequently devalued so that on December 31, the rate is £1 = $2·50. X has an unrealized foreign exchange gain of $500 ($3,000 payable less $2,500 now required to effect payment), but no gain is recognized. On January 29, X settles its account when the rate is £1 = $2, exchanging $2,000 for £1,000. Under the separate transactions theory, X realizes a $1,000 gain, taxable as ordinary income.

It should be noted that fluctuations in exchange rates create foreign exchange problems only when the goods are purchased or sold on credit and a foreign currency is used as the medium of exchange. Suppose that a U.S. corporation buys goods from Country Z and pays for them at the time of purchase. A devaluation of Country Z's currency will have no effect on the transaction since there are no amounts payable at the time of devaluation. Similarly, in cases where a U.S. corporation buys goods from Country Z on credit and the terms of payment are in dollars, a devaluation of Country Z's currency will have no effect on the U.S. corporation since it has to pay the same amount of dollars as before the devaluation.

The importation by a U.S. company of fixed depreciable assets, instead of inventory, will generate similar treatment under the "separate transactions" theory if the purchase is to be paid for in a foreign currency. The item will be entered in the fixed-asset accounts of the U.S. corporation at the dollar equivalent of the foreign currency cost on the purchase date and, at settlement, the exchange gain or loss will be recognized as an item of ordinary income or loss. The Internal Revenue Service adopted this position in *Revenue Ruling* 78–281. Here a U.S. corporation borrowed foreign currency to purchase an asset for its business operations. The IRS held that the basis of the asset became fixed at the time of purchase and should not be adjusted by subsequent currency fluctuations. It also stated that each instalment payment on the loan constituted a separate taxable transaction. As regards the nature of the gain to the taxpayer on repayments of the bank loan, the gain was held to be ordinary since the credit transaction was incidental to the taxpayer's business (see further discussion of *Revenue Ruling* 78–281 below).

2. *Exportion of goods*

The same principles apply to export transactions giving rise to foreign currency receivables. The amount receivable for the goods is included in the U.S. taxpayer's sales income at the exchange rate in effect at the time of sale. Differences to the sales income originally recorded caused by upward or downward revaluations of the currency unit against the dollar will be regarded as ordinary income or ordinary losses, as the case may be, when the currency is converted at the time the transaction is closed. As is the case with foreign currency payables, no tax consequence would result from a change in exchange rate if payments were either received before devaluation or specified in dollars.

3. *Interest payments and royalty remittances*

When a U.S. company accrues interest or royalties due from a foreign corporation and the amount is payable in foreign currency, a change in exchange rates will give rise to exchange gain or loss. A number of earlier rulings provided that unpaid amounts due to an accrual basis taxpayer should be translated at the year-end rate. However, this position is a departure from the separate transactions theory and its current validity seems doubtful. The better view would be to follow the court decisions dealing with the purchase and sale of goods, and to translate the income at each accrual date and recognize the gain or loss when the transaction is closed by payment and conversion into dollars (under the separate transactions theory).

4. *Accounts receivable and payable to an affiliated company*

The separate transactions theory applies equally well to intercompany transactions. If the balance arises from an ordinary business transaction, the settlement in foreign currency will result in ordinary gain or loss; alternatively, where the balance arises from a capital asset transaction, the settlement will result in capital gain or loss.

In the case of intercompany transactions, it becomes extremely important to properly document (formalize) intercompany loans in order to avoid their recharacterization as equity by the IRS. This may result, for example, where the borrowing affiliate has a high debt-equity ratio (i.e. is thinly capitalized) or where the funds are advanced under circumstances which indicate the absence of a *bona fide* loan (e.g. lack of fixed maturity date, contingency as to repayment, etc.). If the IRS recharacterizes the underlying transaction as capital in nature, it is also likely that it will characterize any exchange loss on repayment of the debt as a capital loss.

5. *Long term debt payable in a foreign currency*

The tax treatment of gains and losses resulting from the repayment of loans denominated in foreign currency has been the subject of considerable jurisprudence, with many cases appearing to be distinguishable from the others on their own particular facts. Nonetheless, the trend seems to be towards the separate transactions method. This position was followed by the IRS in *Revenue Ruling* 78–281 (see above page 109) involving a U.S. corporation which operated an equipment rental business abroad and had borrowed local currency from a foreign bank to finance the purchase of a rental machine. The loan was repayable in five annual instalments. Immediately after the purchase and execution of the rental agreement with a third party, the foreign country devalued its currency by 20% against the dollar. The IRS relied on the *Willard Helburn* case in holding that the accounting basis of the machine is the dollar equivalent of the foreign currency cost of the machine, translated at the time of purchase; no basis adjustments are permitted thereafter because of currency fluctuations. The ruling further held that the taxpayer will recognize ordinary gain or loss on each annual payment to the bank measured by the difference between the original U.S. dollar value of that portion of the loan principal which is discharged and the U.S. dollar value of the foreign currency used to make repayment as converted on the date such payment is made.

The separate transaction approach was also applied to a long term loan, unconnected with the purchase of goods, in *KVP Sutherland Paper Co.* This case involved an exchange gain on the repayment of Canadian notes. The gain was held to be ordinary income since the notes fell within a part of Section 1232(a)(1) of the Internal Revenue Code that denies the benefits of capital gains rates otherwise extended by that provision to bonds issued before January 1, 1955. In 1943, KVP Sutherland spent over C$9 million to purchase a Canadian paper mill. In 1946, when the mill was ready for production, KVP Sutherland transferred the assets to a newly formed Canadian subsidiary, KVP Ltd., in exchange for shares and notes payable in Canadian dollars. KVP Sutherland also loaned its subsidiary an additional C$6 million, also in exchange for notes. The notes were later repaid partly in Canadian dollars and partly by credit in Canadian dollars to the intercompany account. The court treated the intercompany credits, a procedure used to avoid bank conversion fees, as if they were actual payment in Canadian dollars followed by conversion into U.S. dollars. The notes themselves were held for more than six months before they were repaid, but the Canadian dollars received for them were immediately converted into U.S. dollars at the then current rate of exchange. However, before the notes were repaid, the Canadian dollar appreciated *vis-à-vis* the U.S. dollar. KVP reported the resulting gain as long term capital gain in its tax returns, but the Internal Revenue Service argued in court that the gain was taxable as ordinary income on the ground that no sale or exchange was involved.

The court focused on the issues of characterization and timing: Was the gain long term capital gain, short term capital gain or ordinary income? Was the gain realized at the time of receipt of the Canadian dollars or at the time of conversion into U.S. dollars? The court held that there were three separate transactions, each of which was a taxable event:

1. *The acquisition and transfer of the Canadian property and Canadian dollars in exchange for the notes in 1946.* The basis of the notes was the cost in U.S. dollars at the exchange rate prevailing at the time of purchase of Canadian dollars in the case of the Canadian property transferred. The court indicated that the loan to the subsidiary would have produced taxable gain if the Canadian currency had appreciated between the time the Canadian dollars were purchased and the time they were lent to the subsidiaries.
2. *Repayment of the notes in Canadian dollars.* There KVP realized a gain measured by the difference between the Canadian dollars received, translated at the exchange rate in effect at the time of repayment, and the cost basis in the notes. Since the notes were issued before 1955 they were not within the scope of Section 1232(a)(1) and their retirement did not constitute the sale or exchange of a capital asset. Therefore, the gain realized was ordinary income (although perhaps under Section 1232 today the gain might have been treated as a capital gain).
3. *Conversion of Canadian currency into U.S. dollars.* Since the Canadian currency had not been held for more than six months, any exchange gain realized in this transaction was a short term capital gain.

6. *Foreign currency as an asset*

Most cases treat foreign currency not as money but as an *asset* which may be held for investment purposes. Under this theory, holding foreign currency and later converting it to U.S. dollars may result in a capital gain or loss. In 1970, the Court of Claims applied this theory in the *Gillin* case. Here the taxpayer, John A. Gillin, borrowed a total of $260,000 in Canadian currency against promissory notes bearing standard interest rates, and immediately converted the funds into U.S. dollars. The taxpayer used the money for personal and investment purposes (not regular business purposes). Gillin, who repaid the loans by buying Canadian currency with U.S. dollars at a lower rate, was then charged by IRS with a taxable exchange gain of $19,510. Gillin petitioned the court for a complete rebate of his taxes. He also petitioned that if he were not allowed full rebate, he should be subject to the lower long term capital gains tax rate, since he held the notes for over six months and these notes should qualify as long term rather than short term capital assets.

Noting the speculative nature of Gillin's Canadian loan transactions and the rapidity with which the taxpayer had converted the borrowed Canadian dollars into U.S. dollars, the Court of Claims held that the exchange profit realized by Gillin constituted ordinary income from the discharge of indebtedness for less than the amount owed.

This approach of treating foreign currency as an asset is, in effect, an extension of the separate transactions theory discussed above.

7. *Hedging transactions*

A company engaged in international operations will often wish to protect itself against risks arising from fluctuations in the value of foreign currencies. Moreover, since the promulgation of FASB No. 8, effective for years beginning in 1976, many U.S multinationals have routinely hedged against the financial statement translation exposure inherent in their foreign currency denominated foreign branch and subsidiary assets by entering into forward exchange contracts. FASB No. 8 is the accounting rule that requires a U.S. corporate parent to translate the value of its foreign currency denominated net assets, for consolidated financial statement purposes, at current exchange rates and to include in its consolidated income statement an exchange gain or loss to reflect an intervening change in exchange rates from the end of the prior period. By hedging against the exposed net asset position (current assets less current liabilities) of its foreign branches and subsidiaries, the multinational seeks to offset, on an anticipated after-tax basis, the negative impact that volatile currency fluctuations could have on its financial statements, including its earnings per share.

Although a currency devaluation has immediate financial statement impact, a FASB-8 gain or loss has no significance for U.S. tax purposes. This is because U.S. tax rules require a settled or closed transaction before gain or loss is recognized. The type of risk the U.S. parent company seeks to protect against here is translation exposure. A second type of risk, referred to as transaction exposure, relates to future transactions in foreign currency, including receivables and payables arising from credit sales of goods and services and dividends and royalties from a foreign subsidiary.

The forward exchange contract is the most common form of hedge but other methods are also used. The most difficult tax questions that arise in connection with these transactions concern the timing of the resulting gain or loss; whether the gain or loss should be characterized as capital or ordinary; and the sourcing of the gain or loss as domestic or foreign. A review of the various hedging techniques and a detailed discussion of the related tax consequences are presented in Sections E and F below.

8. *Foreign construction projects: commitment exposure*

A U.S. owner of a fixed price, foreign construction project payable in a foreign currency can freeze its U.S. dollar cost by entering into a forward exchange contract to purchase the foreign currency required at a fixed price at a fixed date or dates in the future. The tax consequences of this form of hedge is discussed in detail in Chapter IV, Section F "Commitment Exposure".

B. **Translation of subsidiaries' financial statements**

U.S. accounting rules under FASB 8 require a U.S. parent to translate balances representing cash and amounts receivable or payable that are denominated in a foreign currency (including such balances of its foreign subsidiaries) at the current (period-end) exchange rate for consolidated financial statement purposes and to include in its consolidated income statement an exchange gain or loss to reflect an intervening change in exchange rates from the end of the prior period. For tax purposes, however, consolidation of a foreign subsidiary with its U.S. parent is not permitted, and the FASB 8 gains or losses have no significance for tax purposes. Instead, translation of the earnings of a foreign corporation is required only upon the happening of one of two taxable events. First, when the subsidiary distributes a dividend to its parent, the subsidiary's earnings and profits must be translated to U.S. dollars for purposes of computing the indirect foreign tax credit. Under this method, exchange gain or loss is not recognized for tax purposes until realized through remittances to the U.S. (see C below). The second event is the recognition by the parent of income under Subpart F. Under the Subpart F translation method, the earnings and profits of the foreign subsidiary are relevant for purposes of limiting the amount of Subpart F income which is recognized and for calculating the indirect credit under Section 960 and are translated at an average rate of exchange for the period during which the income was realized (see E below). While the Subpart F method is similar to the foreign currency financial statement translation method, there are differences between the two methods. These differences are discussed below in connection with long term debt, fixed assets and inventory.

Long term debt is translated at the year-end exchange rate for FASB 8 purposes but at historical rates for Subpart F translation purposes, i.e. the rate of exchange at the time the liability was incurred. The result is the current recognition of exchange gain or loss for financial accounting purposes but not for tax accounting purposes.

Fixed assets and related depreciation expense are recorded at historical dollar costs for both accounting and tax purposes. However, accelerated methods of tax depreciation which are not recognized for financial accounting purposes can result in timing differences between tax and accounting income; these differences require the recording of a deferred income tax liability, which is also translated at historical rates for FASB 8 purposes although these rates relate to the time of provision of the deferred income taxes rather than to the acquisition of the related fixed assets.

Additional differences between tax and accounting income also arise on disposal of a fixed asset, when the asset and the related accumulated depreciation account are removed from the books and any related balance remaining in the deferred tax account is reversed.

Inventory is also translated at historical rates for book and tax purposes. The effect of historical rate translation is to defer recognition of foreign exchange gains and losses until the inventory is sold. The extent of deferral may vary depending on whether the LIFO or FIFO method of inventory is used. Since, under a LIFO method, the inventory on hand is treated as having been acquired earliest in time, this method has the effect of prolonging deferral of foreign exchange gains or losses; by contrast, the inventory on hand under a FIFO system treats the earliest acquired goods as those sold during the period, producing a more limited deferral period.

C. **Dividends received from a foreign subsidiary**

When a U.S. parent receives dividend distributions from a foreign subsidiary, the dividend plus any withholding tax are translated into U.S. currency at the exchange rate in effect on the dividend payment date. An indirect or "deemed paid" foreign tax credit is granted to a U.S. corporation receiving a dividend from a foreign corporation in which it owns 10% or more of the voting stock. This is in effect a credit for the foreign taxes actually paid by the distributing corporation on the income from which the distribution is made. The amount of the deemed paid credit is derived from a formula which uses "earnings and profits" (which is foreign income less foreign income taxes), foreign income taxes and dividend(s), as follows:

$$\frac{\text{dividend}}{\text{earnings \& profits}} \times \text{foreign income tax}$$

Where the foreign corporation keeps its books in foreign currency, the earnings and profits, foreign taxes and the dividend are all converted into dollars using the exchange rate prevailing at the date the dividend is paid. Where the foreign corporation keeps its books in dollars, the foreign taxes have already been converted at the rate of exchange existing when the taxes were paid, whereas the dividend will be converted at the exchange rate prevailing at the time of the dividend payment. Under either method, no exchange gain or loss is reflected in income or in the foreign tax credit.

D. Earnings of foreign branches

Two methods are described in rulings for the translation of foreign branch assets and earnings into dollars when branch accounts are kept in foreign currency.

Under the "net-worth" or "balance-sheet" method, branch profit and loss is computed solely by reference to opening and closing balance sheets. A balance sheet is prepared at the end of each year. Monetary assets (e.g. current assets, receivables and liabilities) are translated into dollars at the year-end rate. Non-monetary assets (e.g. property, plant and equipment) are translated at historic rates (i.e. the exchange rates prevailing at the time the assets were acquired). Remittances are translated at the actual rate of conversion when remitted. Branch profit for the year is the difference between opening and closing net worth, less remittances for the year.

The second method is referred to as the "profit and loss" method. Under this method, a profit and loss statement is prepared in foreign currency and any remittances made during the year are deducted therefrom and converted at the payment date rate. The remaining profit is translated at the year-end rate.

The effect of the net-worth method is to recognize currently gain or loss, as yet unrealized, from changes in the exchange rate with respect to capital in foreign currency. Under the profit-and-loss method, recognition of exchange gain or loss is postponed until the capital is returned to the U.S. The profit-and-loss method may be more desirable where it is necessary to identify separately transactions which produce capital gains and loss or if there is income from more than one source which must be segregated.

Whether income is computed on the net-worth method or the profit-and-loss method, the foreign tax on branch earnings will be translated at the same rate. A cash-basis taxpayer must use the exchange rate in effect on the date of payment; an accrual-method taxpayer must initially convert the foreign taxes at the exchange rate in effect on the last day of the taxable year. If the rate of exchange on the date the foreign taxes are eventually paid differs from the year-end-rate used for accrual purposes, the credit previously taken must be adjusted to reflect the payment-date rate. A refund of a foreign tax for which a credit has previously been claimed is converted at the rate in effect on the date of refund rather than the date of the original assessment.

E. Subpart F

When the foreign tax credit relates to Subpart F income inclusions, the foreign taxes and the dividend income are converted at the exchange rate existing when the dividend was paid or deemed paid. However, the earnings and profits and the distribution therefrom, solely for purposes of computing the portion of total taxes which is deemed paid under Section 960, are converted, under a complex set of rules, at the average rate of exchange prevailing during the period such income was realized by the foreign corporation.

3. Tax exposure and foreign exchange exposure management

A company engaged in international operations will often wish to protect itself against risks arising from fluctuations in the value of foreign currencies *vis-à-vis* the U.S. dollar. The corporate planner must always operate on the basis of after-tax exposure in order to achieve this result, and thus tax considerations are very significant. Exposure management is made more difficult by the fact that hedging activity can produce a wide variety of tax consequences, particularly from one country to the next. Problems arise because the applicable tax rules are often unclear and tax consequences may be difficult to predict. For example, exchange gains in a particular country may be fully taxable but exchange losses nondeductible. In another country, an exchange gain could, in certain circumstances, go untaxed.

In the U.S., tax consequences often depend on the hedging vehicle selected and the manner in which the transaction is eventually settled. Section F considers the various hedging tools and their tax implications.

Hedging of exposure on after-tax basis

Translation exposure: Where a U.S. parent enters into a forward exchange contract to protect the translated financial statement value of a foreign branch or subsidiary for consolidation purposes, the parent must tax effect the hedging transaction in recognition of the fact that generally no offsetting tax loss will result from a purely financial statement devaluation. If the parent anticipates the settlement of the foreign exchange contract to result in a capital gain, on which a 28% tax would be due, the amount of the hedge must be approximately 140% (1/1 − ·28) of the exposed position. Any foreign taxes imposed on the gain must also be taken into consideration.

Transaction exposure: Where a specific transaction is the subject of the hedge, it is first necessary to calculate the amount of after-tax exposure on the transaction. It will then be necessary to protect this exposure with a hedging transaction, again on an after-tax basis. It should be noted that the rate of tax on the hedging transaction will not always be the same as the tax treatment of the underlying transaction.

Example: A U.S. company accrues a royalty receivable of $100,000 from its German subsidiary, payable in marks (say DM 50,000). Since this income will be taxable to the U.S. parent at a 46% rate, the after-tax exposure is $54,000. Thus a 10% devaluation of the DM *vis-à-vis* the dollar will mean an after-tax loss to the U.S. parent of $5,400. If the parent's treasurer feels it can sustain capital gain treatment on a DM hedge (even though the hedge is related to an item of ordinary income), the amount of DM he must sell forward to fully protect its position can be computed as follows:

$$\$54,000 \times \frac{1}{1 - ·28} = \$75,000 \text{ or DM } 37,500$$

The net economic impact of a 10% devaluation may be summarized as follows:

Cash expected DM 50,000 @ $2		$100,000
Tax @ 46%		46,000
Net	A	$54,000
Amount received: DM 50,000 @ $1·80		$90,000
Tax @ 46%		41,000
Net	B	$48,600
Economic loss (A − B)	C	$5,400
DM sold forward: DM 37,500 @ $2		$75,000
Value of DM 37,500 at closing (37,500 @ $1·80)		67,500
Foreign exchange gain		$7,500
Tax @ 28%		2,100
Economic gain	D	$5,400

Since C and D offset each other, the taxpayer will have fully hedged the transaction by selling forward only DM 37,500 rather than the full DM 50,000 receivable. Of course, if the foreign exchange gain is taxed at ordinary rates, the full DM 50,000 must be sold forward in order to provide full protection.

The chapter which follows describes the more common hedging vehicles and their associated tax consequences.

E. Objectives of hedging—a tax perspective

Introduction

The previous section has outlined the taxation of foreign exchange gains and losses within the United States. This section will apply those general principles to forward exchange contracts,

114

back-to-back loans and currency swaps. Particular emphasis will be given to the characterization and sourcing of exchange rate gains and losses recognized in hedging transactions.

1. Fundamentals

A. The objective of hedging

In minimizing foreign exchange exposure risks the focus of the financial manager is directed towards hedging, presumably with tax neutrality. Neutrality, which by definition includes the tax system's non-interference in economic decision making, is a desired goal because it avoids tax induced economic distortions and risk. This focus principally involves consideration of United States tax laws.

The theory of tax neutrality is that as a planning matter the after-tax position of the hedger and its affiliates should be unaffected by the foreign exchange exposure and the hedge taken as a whole. To this extent, the financial manager's concern is the predictability of result. There may be opportunities, however, to take advantage of a tax benefit on closing a hedge after the risk of exposure has matured, nor is a financial manager precluded from taking a tax return position that is more favourable than under the concept of tax neutrality. For example, on closing the hedge a corporation may be able to generate capital gain rather than ordinary income. Similarly, for the purpose of increasing the foreign tax credit, a corporation may generate foreign source income or minimize foreign source deductions.

B. Types of exposure

Hedging transactions are entered into to protect against two types of exposure, translation exposure and transaction exposure. For the United States parent's own operations, foreign exchange rate gains and losses on transactions in foreign currencies are generally taken into account for tax purposes. However, there is generally no United States tax consequence arising from translation exposure of a foreign subsidiary's financial statements regardless of the type of exposure. There are tax consequences for the parent only upon the declaration of dividends or some other remittance, such as liquidation, unless the income of the foreign subsidiary is constructively taxable to the parent under Subpart F (Sections 951–964) of the Internal Revenue Code (hereinafter "Code"). A foreign subsidiary may have exposure in currencies other than the local currency, namely, the parent and third currencies. With respect to those, the foreign subsidiary may experience exchange rate gain or loss, and may be taxed in its own jurisdiction on any gain or receive a tax benefit upon any loss. With respect to the local currency, an exchange rate fluctuation will produce no tax consequences for the foreign subsidiary. The parent corporation, however, will have local currency translation exposure in the foreign subsidiary against which it may wish to hedge.

C. Methods of tax hedging

In general, hedging against an exposure might normally take one of three forms: the acquisition of a forward exchange contract, a back-to-back (or parallel) loan, or a currency swap. Of these three approaches, the most common is the purchase of a forward exchange contract.

2. Tax considerations upon entering into hedging

A. General

Upon entering into a hedging transaction, a financial manager will have to consider a number of tax factors:

1. The characterization of the gain or loss (*Corn Products*),
2. Holding period requirements, including possible application of short sales rules,
3. Realization (or timing) of gain or loss,
4. The source of the gain or loss—foreign or domestic,
5. "Effectively connected" income,
6. Local tax considerations,
7. Relationship between tax considerations and types of exposure.

Before considering the significance of these factors to a particular type of hedge, a brief statement regarding their general application should be helpful.

B. Characterization of gain or loss

Capital gain treatment occurs if there is a sale or exchange of a capital asset. Both elements are required. If the asset is not a capital asset, either because of a statutory exclusion (e.g. inventory) or the application of *Corn Products*, or if the asset is disposed of in a fashion other than by sale or exchange, the transaction will produce ordinary income or loss.

In effect, the *Corn Products* rule is a judicial expansion of the statutory exclusions from the definition of capital asset as set forth in Section 1221 of the Code. In *Corn Products* the taxpayer, a manufacturer of corn products, purchased corn futures in order to protect itself against an increase in the price of spot corn, its major raw material. The Supreme Court held that profits arising from the sale of the corn futures were ordinary income, not capital gain as contended by the taxpayer.

The Court accepted the findings of the lower courts that the corn futures were vitally important to the taxpayer's business thus constituting an integral part of its business. While the Court acknowledged that the corn futures did not specifically come within the statutory exclusions to the definition of a capital asset, it nonetheless concluded that Congress had intended that profits and losses arising from the everyday operation of a business should be treated as ordinary income, or loss, not capital gain or loss. Following *Corn Products*, the Internal Revenue Service has taken the position that property is an "integral part" of a taxpayer's business if "a directly measurable benefit" is derived from the property, i.e. "if a sufficient and direct relationship to the taxpayer's ordinary and operating aspects of its business is shown."

An important qualification to the *Corn Products* doctrine has developed in recent years, with which the Internal Revenue Service has acquiesced in Revenue Ruling 78–94. In *W. W. Windle Company*, the Tax Court held that even if the predominant motive for entering into a transaction is to protect a business activity, the transaction will nevertheless give rise to capital gain or loss if there is a substantial investment motive. The presence of a substantial investment motive depends upon all the facts and circumstances, and the mere projection of profitability does not *per se* establish an investment motive.

C. Holding period

Capital gains and losses may be either long term or short term, depending upon the period the asset is held. (If *Corn Products* applies, there is no capital asset, and consequently the holding period is irrelevant.) The general rule that an asset must be held more than one year to qualify for long term capital gain treatment admits to a shorter holding period (i.e. more than six months) for certain commodities transactions subject to the rules of a board of trade or commodity exchange. If the hedging contract is purchased upon an exchange, this shorter period may apply. However, regardless of whether the more than six month or 12 month rule is applicable, the holding period may be subject to the short sale rules of Code Section 1233.

Short sale rules: The short sale rules are designed to prevent manipulation of the holding period requirements for long term treatment. Although the term short sale is not defined in the Code or Regulations, it is generally regarded as a sale of borrowed property and subsequent repayment with substantially identical property. Under Section 1233(a) of the Code, gain or loss realized on a short sale is capital gain or loss if the property used to close the short sale is a capital asset in the hands of the taxpayer. The holding period requirements depend upon the applicability of Sections 1233(b) and 1233(d) of the Code.

Section 1233(b) provides that if a taxpayer enters into a short sale and on the date of the short sale has held for less than 12 months property "substantially identical" to that sold short, or if there is acquired such "substantially identical" property between the date of the contract and the date the contract is closed, i.e. the date the property is delivered, any gain realized on the sale is short term. Section 1233(d) provides a comparable remedial rule with respect to short sales which result in an economic loss to the taxpayer. In such case, the loss will be long term if the taxpayer has held "substantially identical" property for more than 12 months on the date of the short sale, regardless of the holding period of the property actually used to close the short sale.

While property for purposes of Sections 1233(b) and 1233(d) is narrowly defined, including therein only stocks, securities, and commodity futures, it appears that foreign currency futures are commodity futures for these purposes since foreign currency is generally accepted as a commodity *vis-à-vis* a United States dollar denominated taxpayer. Also, since foreign currency is a commodity, the more than six month holding period applicable to commodities subject to the rules of an exchange probably should be used for purposes of Sections 1233(b) and (d), rather than the general 12 month rule. Finally, even if a foreign currency future is property for Section 1233 purposes, Section 1233(g) provides that the short sale rules do not apply in the case of a "hedging" transaction in commodity futures. As will be seen, the application of these short sale rules is important because they may transform what would otherwise be a long term capital gain into a short term capital gain.

D. Realization (or timing) of gain or loss

While accounting treatment often requires the accrual of unrealized exchange gains or losses, the

116

basic tax rule is that no gain or loss is realized until a transaction is closed. A closed transaction giving rise to realization occurs when there is a sale, exchange, or other disposition of the foreign currency or contract involved. For example, if a taxpayer enters into a forward sale contract, it would not realize any gain or loss until the contractual obligation was fulfilled or otherwise satisfied. Similarly, if a taxpayer enters into a forward purchase contract, it would not realize gain or loss until the disposition of the contract or the currency, i.e. the mere acquisition of the foreign currency upon maturity of the contract would not be a taxable event. Further, in the case of either a forward purchase or sale contract, the mere acquisition of an off-setting contract does not produce a taxable event.

Even if there is a realization event in a foreign subsidiary, for United States tax purposes, realization is not taken into account unless the income is constructively includible in the United States parent's income under Subpart F of the Code.

E. The source of gain or loss—foreign or domestic

A taxable transaction will generate either foreign or domestic source income/gain or loss. In most instances, it is preferable to have an ordinary domestic source loss, and a capital foreign source gain. The source of gains and losses is determined under Sections 861–863 of the Internal Revenue Code and the Regulations thereunder. As a tax planning matter, more flexibility is available in sourcing gains than in sourcing losses. Conceptually, the source rules for gains rely upon the application of mechanical tests such as the passage of title, while the rules for sourcing losses are cost accounting rules, which require that a loss or expense be related to a class of income.

The principal significance of the sourcing rules is that for the foreign tax credit limitation computation, the taxpayer's foreign source taxable income relates directly to the amount of foreign tax which may be claimed as a credit. That is, the smaller the amount of foreign source taxable income, the smaller the foreign tax credit generally will be. If there is an inability to utilize fully foreign tax credits on a current basis, hedging of foreign exchange exposure may, with proper planning, constitute a technique for absorption of these credits.

Recently promulgated Treasury Regulation Section 861–8 will generally cause more expenses/losses to be allocated to foreign source income, thereby decreasing the foreign tax credit. In addition, Code Section 904 recharacterizes foreign source capital gain of a United States taxpayer as domestic source capital gain unless the gain was subject to a 10% foreign income tax (subject to three minor exceptions), which may also decrease the foreign tax credit.

F. Effectively connected income

A foreign corporation is taxed at the regular United States income tax rates with respect to income which is effectively connected with a United States trade or business. If a foreign subsidiary were to enter into a hedging contract with a United States bank, there are circumstances under which it might have effectively connected income.

G. Local tax considerations

If the hedging will occur outside the United States, consideration must be given to the tax laws of the local jurisdiction. No generalizations can be made about the tax laws of foreign nations. However, general considerations might include the tax treatment of exchange gains and losses, hedging costs and the tax status of a particular subsidiary, e.g. a loss subsidiary that could absorb exchange gains. See also below, Section F. 1.D "Which legal entity should enter the forward contract".

H. Relationship between tax considerations and types of exposure

This sub-section attempts to develop each of the foregoing points to provide the financial manager with some tax insight into determining how to construct his hedge.

With respect to certain of the above rules, it will not be material for tax purposes whether the exposure hedged against is a translation or a transaction exposure. However, the fact that an exposure is a transaction rather than a translation exposure could determine whether a hedging transaction gives rise to ordinary income or capital gain, whether the short sale rules apply, or whether certain income is Subpart F income. While for tax purposes, the issues will probably not be cast in these terms, i.e. transaction *vs.* translation exposure, it is possible that distinctions will be drawn within each of these categories. And, in general, the type of exposure against which the taxpayer is hedging may impact upon the tax consequences of the hedge.

3. Interrelationships among tax rules

While for purposes of analysis and elaboration these various factors will be discussed separately in some detail, the financial manager, upon entering into a forward exchange contract, will have to consider the interrelationship among the various tax rules. For example, if *Corn Products* applies, the manner in which the contract is settled will have no effect upon characterization (although it could affect the source of the gain or loss), whereas if *Corn Products* is inapplicable, the manner of settlement could determine whether the transaction produces ordinary income or capital gain. Similarly, if *Corn Products* is inapplicable, any gain realized on the sale of a capital asset (either the foreign currency itself or the underlying contract) in a foreign country, which would ordinarily produce a foreign source gain, will be subject to recharacterization as domestic source gain for purposes of computation of the foreign tax credit, unless the gain is subject to a 10% foreign income tax (but not for other tax purposes); however, if *Corn Products* is applicable, there is no provision for recharacterizing the source of the gain. Also, the financial manager should be aware if a hedged position in foreign currency moves in an unanticipated direction producing a loss on the hedge, a capital loss can often be converted into an ordinary loss. However, there may be far less control over whether the loss is foreign or domestic source. The relative significance to be given to the sourcing and characterization of income will require a consideration of the overall tax posture, with particular emphasis being placed upon the foreign tax credit position.

In determining where to place a hedge, it should be recognized that having the hedge placed by a foreign subsidiary will often (subject to the application of Subpart F) enable the United States parent to defer realization of income for United States purposes. However, local tax consequences, if any, must be taken into account. Similarly, the decision to enter into a contract on an exchange or through a financial institution may affect the holding period, the computation of Subpart F income, and the determination of whether a trade or business is effectively connected to the United States. With respect to closing a contract, the mode of settlement may be determinative with respect to the computation of the holding period, subject however, to the possible application of the short sale rules and the *Corn Products* doctrine.

While these examples by no means provide an exhaustive statement of the interrelationships among the various tax provisions that may be relevant in determining how and where to place a hedge, they are illustrative of the type of tax considerations which the financial manager should have in mind when considering entering into a hedging contract. If the opportunity is available to choose among various hedging techniques, a similar type of analysis would be required for each technique, although other provisions of the Code, such as the Section 482 allocation provisions, would also have to be considered.

4. Application of *Corn Products* doctrine to hedging transactions

A. General

As indicated previously, foreign currency (except in the case of a dealer in foreign exchange, who may treat it as inventory), is generally a capital asset, and so also is a forward contract in foreign currency. Consequently, a transaction involving either of these assets will usually produce capital gain or loss unless *Corn Products* applies.

B. Clarification of the technical application of *Corn Products* to foreign currency hedging

The *Corn Products* doctrine was applied to a forward sale of foreign currency in *Wool Distributing Corporation*, in which the taxpayer sold foreign currency short to protect against a devaluation in its inventory. That case, which involved a relatively straight forward application of *Corn Products* in finding the absence of a capital asset, is of limited utility to most multinational corporations. Two recent Tax Court cases, however, are of considerable significance.

C. IFF

In *International Flavors & Fragrances* ("IFF") (1974), the parent and its foreign subsidiaries were engaged in the manufacture and distribution of flavouring extracts. In order to offset any losses which might be sustained by the translation exposure of its foreign subsidiaries in the event of devaluation of sterling, the parent entered into a sterling forward sale contract. After the pound was devalued, but before the delivery date, the parent sold the contract at a profit. The Tax Court viewed the sale of the forward contract as an ordinary income related transaction which constituted a "hedge" against the risk of future losses of income. Thus, relying on *Corn Products* it held that the gain on the forward contract was ordinary income.

In reaching this conclusion, the Court defined IFF's exposure by collapsing the corporate separateness of parent and subsidiary, so that exposure to the subsidiary was exposure to the parent. This analysis was inconsistent with a long line of cases which had strictly recognized the separateness of the stockholder/corporation relationship.

After the government abandoned its reliance on the *Corn Products* doctrine, the Second Circuit

Court of Appeals reversed and remanded the case to the Tax Court to decide the factual question of whether the purported sale of the contract was a sale of property or whether the transaction with the buyer was really a disguised principal/agent relationship. Presumably the government abandoned *Corn Products* on appeal because such a rationale had never been applied in a case where a hedging operation was entered into by one corporation as a protection against a potential translation loss of another corporation, and such an application would have involved a long standing impermissible piercing of the corporate veil.

D. **Hoover**

In *Hoover Co.* the Tax Court held that, for a hedging transaction to be regarded as "a *bona fide* hedge" (a concept closely related to, in fact virtually indistinguishable from, the *Corn Products* doctrine), it must be entered into as "a means of protecting ordinary operating profits realized in the day-to-day operation of the business enterprise". Applying this standard, the Tax Court concluded that the foreign currency hedging transactions entered into by a parent to offset anticipated exchange losses of a foreign subsidiary did not constitute *bona fide* hedging transactions. Of particular relevance was the Tax Court's rejection of the taxpayer's argument that since it was not engaged in speculation, it must have been engaged in *bona fide* hedging:

> "These transactions . . . more clearly represented a wise investment technique to offset 'poor' financial image for petitioner as a whole. Thus, we are unwilling to convert a wise investment technique into a 'hedge' because of lack of speculation."

E. **Practical applications of the clarified *Corn Products* doctrine**

What a financial manager regards as a hedging transaction in a financial sense may not constitute a *bona fide* hedge or *Corn Products* transaction for federal income tax purposes. In light of *Hoover* and *Windle*, courts will have to determine whether there was a substantial investment motive, namely, whether the purpose of the hedge was the protection of the parent's or the subsidiary's day to day operating profits.

This determination would appear to be factual in nature, and may require careful documentation. While it is not certain that motive is solely determinative, a court should choose to rely upon subjective (and possibly self-serving) rather than objective evidence, and such documentation will be useful in characterizing a transaction. This is essentially all the tax planning that can be done with respect to anticipating the application of *Corn Products*. Should a financial manager determine that *Corn Products* will otherwise be applicable to a proposed hedge (i.e. hedging of a parent's transactional exposure), the doctrine may be avoided by having another member of the affiliated group enter into the hedge. However, the financial manager will be limited by those elements which in fact resulted in the decision to hedge in the first instance.

F. **Effect of *IFF* and *Hoover***

If a parent decides directly to hedge against the FASB 8 exposure of its subsidiary, it probably cannot, after *Hoover*, bring itself within *Corn Products* by any planning technique, although it may still obtain an ordinary loss upon settlement of the contract by compensation, discussed infra at pp. 121–2. One possible exception may exist with respect to international banking. In a 1979 Private Letter Ruling, the Internal Revenue Service indicated that *Corn Products* applied where a banking corporation hedged against the FASB 8 exposure of its subsidiaries. The ruling was published before *Hoover* was decided, and it may no longer represent the Service's ruling position. It should also be noted that where the hedge is entered into to protect the exposure of a foreign branch as distinguished from a subsidiary, *Corn Products* will be fully applicable.

F.1. **Taxation of forward contracts and other hedging techniques**

A. **Introduction**

A forward exchange contract calls for delivery at a future date of a specified amount of foreign currency against dollar payment at an exchange rate fixed at the time the contract is made. On the settlement date foreign currency is required to be delivered, typically constructively by means of a credit against the obligor's account. However, it is also possible to settle the contract prior to maturity by entering into an offsetting contractual obligation, selling the underlying contract or obtaining a release from the obligee for payment.

The tax consequences of a forward contract depend upon where and the manner in which the contract is settled. The treatment of forward sales and forward purchase contracts is basically the same except when the contract is performed in accordance with its terms.

B. Forward sales contracts

1. General

If the financial manager enters into a forward sale contract in a context in which *Corn Products* is inapplicable, and the currency is devalued as anticipated producing a gain, presumably there would be a preference to have the gain taxed as long term capital gain. However, there are two difficulties in achieving this goal: the possible applicability of the short sales rules and finding an asset satisfying the more than twelve month (or six months, if applicable) holding period requirement. Generally, if the contract has a maturity exceeding the required holding period, both of these considerations suggest that the contract should be settled by selling the contract itself rather than by performing the contract or entering into an offsetting obligation (see p. 121, *infra*). If ordinary treatment is desired, the contract should be compensated.

2. Performance of forward sale contract

If the contract is held to maturity and performed by delivery of the foreign currency by definition the sale is completed. In many cases, delivery under the contract will produce short term capital gain, either because of the short sale rules or inability to satisfy the relevant holding period requirements with respect to the delivered currency.

Application of short sale rules

The Tax Court in *Hoover Co.* held that the short sale rules are generally applicable to foreign currency transactions, although the Court of Claims in another recent (1979) case, *American Home Products Corp.*, declined to pass upon the issue. The operative term under Section 1233 is "substantially identical" property. In *Hoover*, the Tax Court indicated that "the Section 1233(b) and (d) rules might not apply where a taxpayer sold a commodity short (a forward sale contract) but acquired not a commodity purchase future but the actual currency to close the short sale". However, in *American Home Products*, the Court of Claims indicated that the currency might be "substantially identical" property. The regulations also indicate that two different currencies would not be considered substantially identical property unless they were "generally through custom of the trade used as hedges for each other."

Assuming that foreign currency is not "substantially identical" to a forward contract, the actual holding period of the currency will determine whether the gain is long or short term. In most cases, however, it will not be feasible to acquire the foreign currency sufficiently early to satisfy the 12 month holding period requirement (or six month period, if applicable).

Source

Generally the gain will be sourced where the title passage to the currency takes place. However, two patterns need to be distinguished. First, the actual foreign currency can be delivered by the taxpayer, thus allowing considerable flexibility in sourcing gain. Alternatively, if the delivery is made by having a bank in the foreign jurisdiction credit the foreign currency account of the purchaser, the actual transfer of title occurs within a foreign country's banking system, and will produce foreign source income. However, unless *Corn Products* applies in either fact pattern, the gain will probably be recharacterized as domestic source, since it is unlikely that the United States parent will be subject to a tax of at least 10% by a foreign jurisdiction.

3. Offsetting the forward sale contract

As an alternative to performance in accordance with its terms, the contract can be offset by a forward purchase contract. In *Hoover*, the court noted that "the most common method of settling a forward sale contract has traditionally been to enter into a purchase contract and to offset the contractual obligations to sell and purchase. Offset of the contractual obligation by the seller has been held to be delivery under the sale contract . . . satisfying the sale or exchange requirement on the date the contract is settled." It is likely that the short sale rules of 1233 would apply in computing the holding period, unless the offsetting contract is (1) entered into by a different member of the affiliated group, or (2) has a maturity date in a month different from the original obligation. Thus, a contract to sell DM 100,000 in December is not identical to a contract to purchase DM 100,000 in January.

Source

The gain or loss should probably be sourced in the same manner that it would have been had the contract actually been performed in accordance with its terms. The difficulty is that, since there is a constructive delivery, it is unclear where the delivery occurs. Assuming that *Corn Products* is inapplicable, the sourcing question becomes moot if the transaction is not subject to a 10% tax by a foreign jurisdiction.

4. Sale of forward sale contract

Because of the practical difficulty in obtaining long term capital gain on a forward sales contract performed at maturity, a common technique for obtaining this result is selling the contract prior to maturity. The Service, however, has challenged this approach either by characterizing the sale as a "sham" or by characterizing the purchaser as an "agent". As a tax planning technique, the purchaser of the forward sale contract should be unrelated to the seller, the contract should be sold without recourse, the risk of losses should be transferred at a time when some future risk remains and the documentation should establish that the purchaser is not acting as agent for the seller.

Application of short sale rules

In *American Home Products Corp.*, the Service argued unsuccessfully that the short sale rules should apply to a mere sale of a forward sale contract. The Service's theory was that such a sale was analogous to the assignment of a contract to sell stock when issued, which the legislative history of Section 1233 indicated should be treated as a short sale. Although the court refused to apply the short sale rules to the sale, it indicated that a regulation treating a sale of a forward contract as a short sale might be valid. If such a regulation were promulgated, however, it would almost certainly be challenged (perhaps successfully) as being in conflict with the statute. In any event, since the sale of a forward contract will generally produce long term capital gain (if the contract has been held for more than 12 months), it can be expected that the Service will pursue this short sale argument or some other theory (e.g. the sale is equivalent to a direct delivery of the foreign currency), particularly since careful tax planning will make it difficult for a sale to be attacked as a sham.

Source

If the contract is sold abroad the gain will be foreign source. If, however, the sale is made by the United States parent and is not subject to a 10% tax by a foreign jurisdiction the gain will be recharacterized as domestic source unless *Corn Products* applies.

5. Compensation

It would appear to be well settled law that if, prior to the maturity date, the contract is cancelled or a release is obtained with the payment of appropriate compensation, the disposition would not be treated as a sale or exchange, and the transaction will produce ordinary gain or loss. For purposes of this discussion, the terms cancellation and release can be regarded as synonymous meaning simply a discharge by the obligee under the contract of the obligor's required performance in exchange for payment. While some commentators believe that this analysis is merely a formal one and fails to give due regard to the essential economic similarity between different modes of disposition, the issue is not one of substance over form, since it is quite permissible for a taxpayer to select one of a number of possible ways to close a transaction.

Mechanics of compensation

The mechanics of the settlement transaction are very important. What a financial manager regards as compensation may in fact be an offsetting purchase or sale. The notation on the contracts is not determinative, nor is the intention of the parties. While the tax law may provide flexibility in characterizing the gain or loss upon settlement of a forward exchange contract, the particular form of settlement that is advantageous must in fact be utilized.

Source

Some commentators believe that the loss upon compensation of a forward sale contract should be sourced in the country in which the contract was compensated, but support for that position is nonexistent. First, even if a loss were to be sourced in the same manner as a gain would have been, there is no clear rule for sourcing a compensation gain. The general tenor of Section 863 of the Code suggests that an approach based upon a grouping of contacts be employed, but there is no firm authority for this analysis. Second, if the loss is sourced under the 861–8 sourcing rules for losses, there is some question whether the compensation of a futures contract constitutes a loss on the sale, exchange or "other disposition" of a capital asset under Regulation Section 1.861-8(e)(7), although presumably it would be. Third, there may be a question as to what class of income such asset ordinarily generates. In the case of the United States multinational who enters into a number of hedging contracts, it may be necessary to apportion the loss *pro rata* between foreign and domestic source loss in the same proportion that gains from gross income outside of the United States and gross income within the United States respectively bear to the class of gross income.

C. Forward purchase contracts

1. Performance of forward purchase contract

Generally, the tax treatment is the same as previously discussed for a forward sale contract. The only exception is in the case of the actual receipt of the foreign currency.

With respect to receipt under a forward purchase contract, two analyses have been suggested. One view (perhaps the correct one) regards the receipt of foreign currency in the same manner as the purchase of any other commodity, namely: it is not a taxable event; the basis in the commodity is equal to the contract price; and the holding period begins on the contract date of the purchase contract. An alternative analysis views the receipt of the foreign currency as a taxable event, producing gain or loss measured with reference to the difference between the contract exchange rate and the exchange rate on the settlement date. There are no cases or rulings in this area, and this issue may be regarded by some as unsettled.

Holding period

Assuming that performance is not a taxable event it will be easier to obtain long term capital gain treatment under a forward purchase than a forward sale contract, because the holding period begins with the date of the purchase contract. If there is a substantial gain on a forward purchase contract, but the maturity date occurs prior to satisfying the requisite holding period, it may be advantageous to take delivery of the currency. Assuming that Section 1233 is inapplicable, it may be possible to deposit the foreign currency with a banking institution until long term capital gain can be realized.

Source

If the receipt of the foreign currency is a taxable event, the source rules discussed above (see p. 121) should be equally relevant here.

2. Offsetting the forward purchase contract

The tax treatment is the same as for the offsetting of a forward sale contract.

3. Sale of forward purchase contract

Although the treatment is the same for the sale of a forward purchase or forward sale contract, it might be easier to persuade a court that a forward purchase contract had been actually sold. Because Code Section 1223(8) tacks the holding period of the contract to the currency purchased, there would be no potential for manipulation of the holding period requirement.

4. Compensation

The character of the gain or loss is ordinary, because the sale or exchange requirement cannot be satisfied.

D. Which legal entity should enter into the forward contract

1. General

For federal tax purposes, there is no general rule requiring the aggregation of exchange rate gains and losses within the group. Because the United States parent will be taxed differently than its foreign subsidiaries, and since each foreign subsidiary may in turn be subject to taxation both by the jurisdiction in which it is located or some other foreign jurisdiction, careful consideration must be given to which entity should enter into the transaction.

2. Foreign tax credit

An important consideration in determining where to enter into a hedging transaction is the effective utilization of foreign tax credits. Many United States multinationals have credits available in excess of the foreign tax credit limitations. Consequently, if the gain from a hedging transaction is foreign source gain, the effect may be to receive a portion of the gain tax free under the shelter of the credits which would not otherwise be utilized.

3. Flexibility

It is probably far simpler for a foreign subsidiary to engage in forward exchange contracts without concern for United States income tax consequences. For example, a foreign subsidiary generally is not subject to the limitations provided for in Section 904.

By way of contrast, while it might be possible for a United States parent to obtain a foreign source long term capital gain by selling a contract outside of the United States in a jurisdiction that taxed the transaction at a 10% rate, it will be difficult to locate such a jurisdiction.

4. **Certainty of tax consequences**

One of the most important goals in hedging is predictability. To the extent that the absorption of foreign tax credits is not an important consideration, the most predictable (and favourable) after tax hedge would appear to be the hedge by a United States parent of a subsidiary's exposure compensating the contract where there is a loss and selling the contract where there is a gain. The relevant tax rules in jurisdictions other than the United States are for the most part unclear with tax consequences difficult to predict. While the development of the United States federal tax law in this area is still relatively slight, there is sufficient certainty to allow for effective tax planning.

5. **The hedging affiliate**

One general approach for achieving tax neutrality, the starting point of this discussion, would be to have the affiliated group's overall accounting (as distinguished from economic) exposure hedged through a hedging affiliate incorporated and engaging in the hedging activities exclusively in a jurisdiction in which there would be no local tax consequences of a hedging contract (e.g. Bahamas) and in which there would be no United States Subpart F consequences to the United States parent. Whether the latter result can be obtained is a matter of some controversy, and depends upon how literally the Subpart F provisions of the Code are read. One component of Subpart F income is foreign personal holding company income, which includes "gains from futures transactions in any commodity on or subject to the rules of a board of trade or commodity exchange". At present, a taxpayer can enter into a hedging contract either privately through a bank or on an exchange, with the former being the far more common practice. While the latter presumably would produce foreign personal holding company Subpart F income, with respect to the former, it seems clear that these futures transactions would not be governed by the rules of any board of trade or commodity exchange.

In a 1977 Private Letter Ruling, the Internal Revenue Service indicated that foreign currency futures traded upon the Chicago mercantile exchange were commodities for purposes of determining whether a trade or business is carried on in the United States under Code Section 864. If, therefore, a taxpayer determines that it wishes to hedge by a forward contract through a foreign subsidiary but wishes to avoid having any effectively connected income, it should enter into the hedge abroad.

However, even aside from the possibility of effectively connected income or Subpart F income, such a hedging affiliate may not be the ideal sole solution to every problem of tax neutrality. For example, as is not uncommon, it might be advantageous and administratively convenient for a subsidiary to hedge its own FC exposure, and have the hedging affiliate hedge against the parent's overall net currency exposure after taking into account local hedging.

F.2. **Back-to-back loans**

A. **Introduction**

1. **Definition of back-to-back loan**

In a typical back-to-back loan, a United States parent lends dollars to an unrelated foreign corporation or United States subsidiary of such foreign corporation, and simultaneously borrows an equivalent amount of foreign currency based upon current rates. Each lender charges interest to the other, based upon prevailing lending rates in the United States and in the relevant foreign jurisdiction, (see Chapter III, Section E). There are two separate loan agreements, two separate gross interest rates, and the loans are reported as a liability on each borrower's balance sheet.

2. **Overview**

While the same tax considerations that apply to forward contracts are equally applicable to back-to-back loans, the different structure of the transaction introduces additional considerations for the financial manager. There are special rules for certain interest income and interest expenses, as well as the possibility of varying the tax consequences depending upon whether the loan to the foreign subsidiary is denominated as an open account or by an evidence of indebtedness. The tax consequences may also depend upon whether the transaction is a two-party transaction or a multiparty transaction, although the Service may seek to re-characterize a multiparty transaction as a two party transaction.

3. General considerations

The United States income tax rules that are applicable to a back-to-back loan transaction may vary depending upon whether it is a two, three or four party transaction. For example, most tax questions relating to exchange rate gains and losses can be avoided if the transaction is structured as a three or four party back-to-back loan, rather than a two party transaction, since it is only in the two party transaction that the United States parent borrows foreign currency.

4. United States parent as conduit

The fact that these exchange rate issues can be avoided by varying the form of the transaction raises a question for tax purposes as to the true substance of the transaction. That is, if the foreign subsidiary of the United States corporation could borrow the money directly from the United States subsidiary of a foreign corporation, but instead it chooses to have its parent borrow the foreign currency, and then it in turn reborrows from the parent, the Internal Revenue Service may take the position that the parent is merely a conduit in the transaction, despite its form. This issue is particularly likely to be raised where the parent enters into the transaction to generate foreign source interest income. One means of forestalling such a challenge would be to provide that, in the event of a default by the United States parent, the third party to the transaction would have no rights over against the foreign subsidiary.

5. Evidence of indebtedness/open account

If the foreign currency received by the United States parent in a back-to-back loan is to be re-loaned to a foreign subsidiary the financial manager must determine whether the loan should be an open account or whether there should be an evidence of indebtedness.

Section 1232 of the Code provides that the amounts received by the holder of an evidence of indebtedness upon its retirement shall be treated as amounts received in exchange therefore, i.e. subject to capital gains treatment. Therefore, if a corporation makes a loan in a weak currency, it would be preferable to structure the transaction as an open advance rather than in the form of a note, since the exchange rate loss on the payment of a loan is an ordinary loss, while any amount received on repayment of a note would be capital. The reverse strategy should be employed in a strong currency. The holding period for these purposes would be the length of time that the evidence of indebtedness was held. (There is no holding period for an open advance.) However, even if the taxpayer employs an evidence of indebtedness, the transaction would still produce ordinary income or loss if the particular circumstances of the loan required the application of the *Corn Products* doctrine. Assuming that *Corn Products* is inapplicable, the holding period for determining gain or loss may depend upon the short sale rules of Section 1233.

B. Repayment of loan by the foreign subsidiary

1. General

The principal consideration upon the repayment of a loan by a foreign subsidiary is the sourcing of the exchange rate gain or loss.

2. Source of loss upon repayment of loan by foreign subsidiary

The source of an exchange rate loss upon repayment of the loan by the foreign subsidiary may depend upon the applicability of *Corn Products*. If it applies, the exchange rate loss might be sourced where the underlying transaction occurred, on the theory that the transaction should be regarded as integrated. Alternatively, the source of the loss could be related to the interest income, in which case the source of the loss is the situs of the debtor.

3. Source of gain upon repayment of loan by foreign subsidiary

With respect to the repayment of a loan, some commentators take the position that any repayment in a foreign currency, if done other than through physical delivery of the currency, is deemed to take place in a foreign jurisdiction because of the usual mechanics of settlement. In addition, it could be argued that gain on repayment of the loan is foreign source because the interest income thereon would be foreign source. However, if there is an evidence of indebtedness the gain may be recharacterized as domestic source under Section 904 unless it is subject to a 10% tax in the foreign jurisdiction, or unless *Corn Products* applies.

4. Source of gain or loss upon sale of evidence of indebtedness

The gain may be sourced differently than the loss. If the note is interest bearing any exchange rate gain on its sale in the United States would be domestic source but any exchange rate loss would be foreign.

C. Repayment of loan by United States parent

1. General

Section 1232 does not apply to debtors. Thus it is immaterial whether there is an open account or an evidence of indebtedness. Exchange rate gain or loss on the repayment of the foreign currency by the United States parent will be capital unless *Corn Products* applies.

2. Realization

The leading case (*Gillin*) held that the repayment of a foreign currency obligation is a taxable event. However, if a parent lends currency to its foreign subsidiary and if the loan remains open and is denominated in the same currency, there may be no taxable event when the parent repays its obligation (*Goodrich*).

3. Source of loss upon repayment of loan by United States parent

The loss could be treated as an interest expense, i.e. the cost of borrowing money in a strong currency jurisdiction. It has also been suggested that the loss be treated as a Section 165 loss or a Section 162 business expense. The effect of such a characterization is that the taxpayer may be permitted to trace the use of the foreign currency whereas the tracing of interest expenses is generally prohibited by the 861–8 regulations.

4. Source of gain upon repayment of loan by United States parent

The gain could be sourced where the creditor is paid. However, the taxpayer should be concerned about the possibility that the Service will argue that foreign currency is a capital asset, that it was sold or exchanged to repay the debt, and that consequently the gain will be recharacterized as domestic source. In addition, if the repayment of the loan is in effect a short sale, then the repayment of the foreign currency usually will be a foreign delivery generating foreign source income unless the actual delivery takes place in the United States. Once again, however, even if there is foreign delivery, the taxpayer runs the risk that the gain will be recharacterized as domestic source under Section 904. However, the gain will not be subject to recharacterization as domestic source if *Corn Products* applies.

D. Other tax considerations

1. Foreign tax credit on foreign source interest income

In addition to the foreign currency exchange rate issues, there may be withholding tax considerations although in many instances this will be covered by treaty. Also the transaction will generate intervening interest income which will be foreign source. However, the United States parent will be required pursuant to Section 904, to calculate separately foreign tax credits on interest income, unless the taxpayer falls within one of the three statutory exceptions—(a) interest derived from a transaction directly related to the active conduct of a trade or business in the foreign country; (b) interest derived from the conduct of banking; and (c) interest received from a corporation in which the United States taxpayer owns, directly or indirectly, at least 10% interest in the voting stock. If a separate calculation of interest is required, the total foreign tax credit may be reduced.

2. Interest expense

In addition to the interest income derived from a back-to-back loan, there is an interest expense. Pursuant to the 861–8 regulations*, this expense will be allocated between all the taxpayer's foreign and domestic source income, and will reduce, in part, the foreign source income generated by the transaction. However, there is a possibility that both interest income and interest expense could be treated as rental income and rental expense.

3. Section 482

If the United States parent loans the proceeds of the loan to its foreign subsidiary, it will be subject to the Section 482 allocation rules. These rules require that interest be charged on loans or advances made by one member of a controlled group to another member of the group. If the parent is regularly engaged in the business of making loans, an arm's length interest rate should be charged. If the parent is not in the business of loaning money or making advances, either an arm's length rate based on all the facts and circumstances or a safe haven rate (6–8% rate) is acceptable. The regulations also provide, with reference to back-to-back loans, that if the parent obtained the loan

---

* The Internal Revenue Service proposed regulations in February, 1980, pursuant to which foreign corporations (including banks) which have United States income "effectively connected" with the conduct of a United States trade or business would allocate their interest expense in accordance to special rules.

at the "situs" of the subsidiary, the arm's length rate which must be charged is the rate actually paid by the parent plus any costs or deductions incurred in obtaining the loan. Section 482 issues may also arise with respect to the performance of services by the United States parent for the foreign subsidiary, e.g. guaranteeing the loan in a three party transaction, or obtaining a loan under favourable conditions because of credit standing. There, too, the basic rule is that an arm's length charge for the services must be made.

F.3. **Currency swap**

A. **General**

A currency swap is a current exchange of two currencies and an agreement to re-exchange these currencies after a set period of time. The initial exchange of currencies is made at the current spot rate, and the same currency rate is used for the subsequent exchange, regardless of intervening exchange rate fluctuation. There is only a single agreement, and a single exchange differential fee, which should probably be characterized as a net interest rate. Such a swap offers an automatic hedge against foreign exchange translation risk by eliminating at the outset any possibility of exchange rate gain or loss. The tax problems presented by a currency swap can be analyzed if the transaction is broken down into its two component parts.

B. **Characterization as sale or loan**

The first leg of the transaction for tax purposes is the purchase of foreign currency from an unrelated party, usually either the United States subsidiary of a foreign corporation or a foreign corporation. The primary issue presented is whether the transaction is actually a purchase of currency or is more accurately characterized as a borrowing of the currency. There is no authority directly on point, but there are certain cases and rulings involving municipal bonds that provide a close analogy.

In one case, *Citizens National Bank of Waco* v. *United States*, a national bank had entered into an agreement with a long time customer to acquire municipal bonds owned by that customer. The transfer price was fixed at the par value of the bonds, plus interest. As part of the overall agreement and without any additional charge, the customer gave the bank the right to put the bonds back to it.

As this transaction was analyzed by the Internal Revenue Service, the bank had not purchased the bonds and therefore was not entitled to treat as tax free the income from the bonds. Rather, the bank had loaned money to its customer and received in return the bonds as security for the loan. The bank, however, in arguing that the transaction was a purchase, emphasized the fact the customer had no right to compel resale of the bonds to itself. The court found for the bank, and cited the following factors, among others, in holding that a *bona fide* sale had occurred:

1. The seller did not have the right to require re-transfer of the bonds by the buyer to itself.
2. The buyer was free to hold the bonds to maturity or sell to third parties at any time.
3. The form of the transaction was a purchase rather than a loan and elements typical of debt obligations, such as a fixed maturity date and default provisions, were not present.
4. Book entries of both parties treated the transactions as a purchase/sale rather than a loan.
5. Evidence of the intent of the parties indicated that a purchase/sale had occurred.
6. There was a single isolated transaction, rather than a series of transactions.

Another important factor, not cited in the case but relied upon in Revenue Ruling 74–27, is the equivalence of the sale price of the bonds to the fair market value of the bonds. The basic proposition is that parties selling and purchasing at arm's length would set the price at fair market value, whereas a lender and a borrower arranging security for a loan presumably would not be concerned with the exact equivalence of the value of the collateral and the amount of the loan.

When a court cites a number of factors in its deliberative process it is hazardous to predict how a future case will be decided when the factors are not identical. The problem is further bifurcated when one must resort to reasoning by analogy. Further, the decision of the Supreme Court in 1978 in *Frank Lyon Company* v. *United States* suggests that, if certain conditions are satisfied, then, at least in transactions involving more than two parties, the allocation of rights and duties effectuated by the parties should be honoured. However, the breadth and potential ramifications of the *Lyon* case are still uncertain, and financial managers should probably not rely upon it. In any event, it does appear that a factor that is accorded particular significance by both the courts and the Service is the presence of a mandatory buy-back provision. Such a provision, especially if self executing (as in the case of a currency swap) as opposed to being discretionary, is regarded as indicative of a loan, because the borrower retains the risk of loss and the benefit of potential gain in the property pledged as collateral. As applied to a currency swap situation, the taxpayer "purchasing" foreign currency and "selling" dollars to an unrelated third party will receive back the dollars at the termination of the agreements. In effect, therefore, it may be regarded as borrowing foreign currency from the unrelated third party, and pledging dollars as collateral for the loan, since it will bear both the risk of loss and the possibility of gain with respect to the dollars.

As stated previously, there is no clear cut answer as to the characterization of the transaction. While the transaction may meet some of the requirements taken into account by the *Waco* court (*viz*—the book treatment of the transaction, the intention of the parties, the equivalency of the currencies exchanged), the better view would be that the transaction is a borrowing.

However, as a practical matter it may well be that the Service will not seek to re-characterize the transaction. If the transaction is treated as a purchase there is some question whether the exchange differential fee is deductible currently or should be capitalized. But if the transaction is a borrowing of property, the exchange fee is almost certainly deductible, either as an interest expense or a rental payment.

C. Tax consequences of characterization as a sale or loan

If the currency swap is a purchase, then there will be a capital gain treatment upon repayment (assuming that *Corn Products* is inapplicable). However, if the swap is characterized as a loan, then the parent might realize ordinary income upon repayment, on a cancellation of indebtedness theory under the *Gillin* case. Nevertheless, there is considerable support for the position that the transaction should produce capital gain treatment. It is an accepted principle that the conversion of foreign currency to dollars is a sale or exchange. Thus, at the time the two currencies are re-exchanged, the sale and exchange requirement should be deemed satisfied.

If the currency swap is regarded as a purchase, it will probably be regarded for tax purposes as a purchase at spot, with the simultaneous acquisition of a forward sale position. If the currency swap is so characterized, then the rules and strategies applicable to forward sales contracts generally will be equally applicable here. Similarly, if the acquisition of the foreign currency is regarded as a borrowing, then the tax rules applicable to back-to-back loans become relevant.

D. Currency swap and back-to-back loans distinguished

Even if a currency swap were treated as a back-to-back loan, it is not certain that the tax results would be precisely the same. The use of a net interest payment as compared to two gross interest payments may produce a different result with respect to sourcing. In the former instance (assuming that the exchange differential fee is regarded as interest), the payment by the United States parent is an interest expense to be apportioned between foreign and domestic source income. In the latter case, the transaction gives rise to both a gain and a loss, and the results in the two transactions will not be equivalent with respect to source, because the interest expense will not generally be netted against a particular class of income for tax purposes. While this result is troubling, it appears to be a literal application of the law.

This result could generally be avoided if the net interest expense were regarded as a rental expense. Since interest is the cost or forbearance for the use of money, and foreign currency is not money for United States tax purposes, the amount paid for the use of foreign currency may technically be rent paid for the use of property. Also, if the payment is regarded as rent, then the source of this expense will depend upon the manner in which the foreign currency is used, i.e. to produce domestic or foreign source income.

F.4. Comparison of tax consequences of hedging techniques

A. Introduction

The United States federal system of taxation does not really favour one type of hedging arrangement over another.

B. Characterization

The *Corn Products* doctrine applies to all types of hedging transactions.

C. Realization

There is little possibility of deferral under any hedging technique. Under a forward purchase contract, the currency can be received and there will be no taxable event. It may also be possible to extend by renegotiation the maturity date of a forward contract, although such renegotiation may be regarded as a compensation and the entrance into a new contract—a taxable event. Generally, however, gain or loss will be realized when the contract is settled. If the financial manager enters into a back-to-back loan there will be two taxable events: the repayment of the loan to the United States company, and the repayment of the loan by the United States company. (Under the separate transaction theory, there could be a third taxable event, if there is any exchange rate fluctuation between the time the currency was first borrowed and the time it was relent.) Similarly, with respect to a currency swap there are generally two taxable events, with a possibility of a third.

D. Sourcing

In a three party or four party back-to-back loan transaction, there will be no exchange rate gains and losses. If a purpose for entering into the back-to-back loan is to generate foreign source income, this advantage is negated. In a currency swap or a back-to-back loan, the source of the expense incurred in obtaining the use of the foreign currency may depend upon whether the expense is characterized as interest or rent. In general, the present state of uncertainty with regard to the source of gains or losses on foreign exchange transactions makes it difficult to compare hedging techniques in this area.

E. Certainty of result

At the present time, the most predictable results can probably be obtained through forward exchange contracts. First, simply in terms of the development of the law, there is more case law with respect to forward exchange contracts than either back-to-back loans or currency swaps, although *KVP Sutherland* discusses a transaction similar in structure to a currency swap. Second, both back-to-back loans and currency swaps raise serious questions of substance over form, about which it is difficult to make any predictions. That is, while the tax consequences of either of these transactions can be computed with a fair degree of certainty if they are taxed according to their form, it is difficult to determine whether, for tax purposes, the form will be recognized. In a two party back-to-back loan, in form the United States parent is both a borrower and a lender, but in substance it may be regarded by either the Service or the courts as a conduit. Similarly, in a currency swap, it may be a close question whether the transaction is a sale or a loan, and the precise terms of the agreements may have to be closely considered to make the determination.

F. Flexibility in settlement after risk of exposure has matured

In a back-to-back loan or currency swap, there should be no net exchange rate gain or loss. Nevertheless, neutrality will not necessarily be achieved if the exchange rate gain and loss are not sourced in the same manner. However, because of a lack of authority with respect to sourcing exchange rate gains it is difficult to know what flexibility is available in recharacterizing the source of gain. In contrast, in a forward exchange contract, the rules for sourcing gain on the sale of a capital asset (i.e. the foreign currency or the forward contract) are clear. While there is less certainty with respect to compensating a contract, it will be an unusual case in which a contract is compensated to generate ordinary income.

Similarly, with respect to characterization, a forward exchange contract may afford greater flexibility. If there is an exchange rate loss, it will be ordinary if the contract is compensated. However, in a back-to-back loan, if an open account is used, it may be difficult to obtain capital gain treatment. If an evidence of indebtedness is employed, it should be possible to transform a capital loss to an ordinary loss by compensation, unless the amount received is deemed received upon retirement of the indebtedness. However, such an approach would be inconsistent with the separate transaction theory.

G. Foreign exchange regulations and controls

A country's regulatory environment can determine the nature and degree of foreign exchange exposure and which hedging procedures and strategies may be used to minimize this exposure. Legislation imposed by governments to regulate transfers for trade and investment purposes include foreign exchange controls and foreign investment laws. This legislation governs not only inward transfers by non-residents, but also transfers abroad by residents, including individuals and foreign or domestically controlled companies.

Exchange controls are the most comprehensive set of regulations impacting exposure management. These laws must be consulted to ensure that hedging strategies are not in violation of regulations, inasmuch as the controls govern both current (commercial, invisible, and financial payments) and long term capital transfers for financing or direct investment. (Since commercial payments or receipts are more easily documented than financial or capital payments, commercial transfers are normally less heavily regulated.) Exchange controls also may regulate forward markets, foreign currency accounts, and establish whether a country's exchange rate system is fixed, floating or two-tier.

Foreign investment laws are another important category of legislation impacting foreign exchange exposure. They establish the framework and structure under which capital may enter a country for direct investment. They also may specify remittance and repatriation limits which have a direct impact on minimizing exposure.

Although developed nations may resort to exchange controls and investment restrictions during periods of balance of payments difficulties, such legislation is more prevalent in developing nations. Countries are constantly amending legislation as the overall economic climate improves or deteriorates. A company must therefore always keep current on regulatory changes to determine the impact on corporate operations.

Although not specifically implemented to regulate or control international transfers, accounting, tax, and wage and price control legislation must be considered when evaluating foreign exchange exposure management policies and strategies. Withholding taxes may make foreign borrowing or dividend transfers unattractive exposure management techniques. Accounting legislation may require a company to allocate a percentage of profits to reserves prior to declaring dividends. Wage and price controls may affect a company's dividend policy by limiting dividend declarations to a percentage increase over the prior year. The impact of accounting, tax and wage and price control legislation on exposure is more thoroughly discussed in other sections of this book.

1. Import/export regulations

Trade regulations affect exposure management in several ways. They can determine exposure by defining currency of billing for commercial transactions. Depending on whether a currency is weak or strong, a company may prefer to lead or lag payments. The ability to do so would be defined in exchange control laws. Credit terms or the length of time payments may be outstanding is key in setting up parameters for exposure. Exports generate foreign exchange while imports drain a country's reserves. Therefore, import regulations are normally more restrictive than those applicable to exports. The severity and complexity of control must be considered prior to trading with a country.

A. Import credit terms and mechanisms

Exchange control laws normally establish credit terms and other conditions to ensure that import payments are *bona fide* and to control currency speculation. This may restrict exposure management options by not permitting the cash manager to make payments at will.

Credit terms granted to importers normally may not exceed customary commercial practice. For instance, foodstuffs are normally imported on cash or 30 day terms while capital goods sometimes may be imported on extended credit terms of up to 10 years. If a country is experiencing balance of payments shortages, sight payments for goods may be required even though this is not in line with commercial practice. This mechanism restricts imports by increasing the buyer's cost. Conversely, a supplier may be required to grant extended credit terms. Of primary importance in the ability to lead and lag intercompany payments is whether a company may make or delay advance payment for imports. This prepayment may not be permitted or may be restricted to a certain percentage of the total import payment or to select categories of goods, primarily special order or capital equipment imports.

To recoup extended financing costs, the supplier can often charge interest on supplier's credit. Such interest is normally only permitted on payments exceeding normal commercial practice, at a rate either in line with interest rates in the supplier's country, or else at rates specified by the central bank. Withholding tax is normally applied to the interest payment.

The cost of importing may also be affected by how payments must be made. If payment must be in foreign currency, regardless of the currency of billing on the invoice, then the exchange risk is borne by the importer. This may increase the cost of an import if the purchaser is in a country with a depreciating currency. The cost of the instrument, i.e. letter of credit, or draft, may also influence the cost of a transaction. In most cases, an exporter will want to ship on a letter of credit basis, while an importer would request open account or draft terms. In some instances, a country may require letter of credit payments for goods. This tends to discourage imports because of letter of credit costs, and also assists the central bank in ensuring that foreign exchange is available to service its import bill during coming months.

B. **Import controls**

Import controls are usually effected by ban, import license, prior deposit or import tariff. The initial way to control import payment outflows is not to permit goods to enter the country. Governments may thus ban certain imports altogether. Prohibited imports normally comprise luxury items since central banks would prefer to preserve foreign exchange to pay for more essential raw materials. They may also be those that compete with domestically produced goods and create what is considered to be undue competition for local manufacturers. Bans normally are imposed selectively, remain in effect for relatively short periods of time, and prevent foreign exchange outflows for specified items.

An import license is not as restrictive as a ban, but it also is used to control certain imports. Under the licensing system, a company must obtain approval, normally on a case-by-case basis for each import. Approval may be granted selectively based on a company's prior year's level of imports, proven need for a product, or value of the product to a nation's economy. If an import license is required and is not obtained within the specified period set by exchange regulations, normally the central bank will not permit payments to be remitted abroad. In certain countries, exchange licenses are also required prior to making payments. In this instance, an import license or permit is normally a prerequisite to obtaining the exchange license.

Also effective in discouraging imports, is the prior deposit. This requires that a percentage of the import value be lodged in a non-interest bearing account with the central bank generally at the time of obtaining the import license. The deposit substantially increases the cost of the import. The funds may either be released to the borrower for payment of the import, or else held for a fixed period of time. In addition, the importer may be required to lodge separate deposits against the opening of letters of credit, or else be required to close foreign exchange contracts for import payments at the time of obtaining a license. These regulations all serve to increase the cost of the transaction and must be considered when organizing intercompany trade.

While not an exchange control *per se*, tariffs can be used to also restrict imports. Working together with the exchange control authorities, customs can impose high duties on goods whose entry the government wishes to discourage.

When the import control system is extensive, when licensing exists, and the approval framework is well-structured, any abrogation of controls can lead to nonpayment or extremely delayed payment. If an import license specifies payment to be made on a certain date for shipments made on a certain date, the exporter must be certain that all documents are in order and received by the importer in sufficient time to permit him to remit payments. Remittance of payments past specified payment periods is often difficult and may be refused. It can always be the purvey of the central bank that payments, particularly intercompany payments, were not remitted on a timely basis for currency speculation reasons.

C. **Export controls**

Regulations governing exports are less restrictive. They are applied to ensure that the central bank receives foreign currency payments and to prevent speculation and the export of vital goods. These regulations normally define exposure for the company in a given currency.

Exports may be subject to licensing. The license states the credit terms which may be granted by the exporter. If the exporter does not abide by these terms he may not be able to ship to a specific customer at a later date, or else he may be liable for punitive action. In many countries, foreign currency proceeds from exports must be converted into local currency either immediately or within a certain time period. Often exporters may only maintain foreign currency accounts from export proceeds (either domestically or abroad) if the funds are used immediately for import payments.

Countries also can have export incentive programmes. These can vary; however, they may consist of a more favourable exchange rate for export conversions, tax incentives and low interest loan programmes. All of these must be considered in the light of possible reduction of exchange exposure.

2. **Ownership control and capital structure**

If import regulations are overly restrictive, companies may consider direct investment abroad to preserve market share. Direct foreign investment gives rise to exchange exposure and adds complexity to exposure management.

Foreign exchange exposure management can be facilitated considerably if a company has maximum management control and correctly handles the capital structure of a subsidiary. However, exchange control and foreign investment legislation often set the percentage of permitted foreign ownership or control in a company and determine how a direct foreign investment must be structured.

A. Ownership control

Foreign investment regulations normally differ by sector. Often direct investment is not permitted in the financial and natural resource sectors or in areas of national interest such as publishing and television. If permitted, foreign investment may then only be on a minority interest basis or through participation in service contracts. Legislation applying to the manufacturing sector varies according to the level of technology and the degree of capital intensity within the industrial sector. Generally a greater degree of foreign ownership control is permitted in the high technology and capital intensive industries.

To help improve a country's economic base, joint ownership or joint venture agreements for new companies may be required. As in the Andean Common Market countries, a company may also be required to distribute a percentage of a wholly foreign owned company to nationals within a given time span. To encourage local ownership in a company, legislation may make domestic borrowing or daily operations more restrictive for the wholly owned foreign company. This affects exposure by possibly forcing companies to fund overseas.

Although not included in the foreign investment law, some countries may require employee representation on the Board of Directors of a company. Local ownership or labour participation on the Board may affect a firm's management by the foreign parent in that the Board may try to limit dividend payments abroad or promote other financial policies that benefit the host country.

B. Capital structure

Foreign investment and/or exchange control legislation defines the types of foreign inflows that will be accepted for direct investment purposes. When domestic capital is scarce, capital for investment must be brought in from abroad either in the form of funds, equipment or technology. This then becomes the registered foreign capital base upon which future dividend remittances are calculated and against which repatriation limits are established in the case of disinvestment. This capital base may only be increased by reinvesting profits or bringing in additional foreign capital or equipment. This affects exposure by, in some cases, not permitting the parent to freely withdraw funds from a country to reduce its position in a currency. It also affects exposure by forcing a parent to inject foreign capital for investment as opposed to permitting it to use locally borrowed or generated currency.

3. Traditional exposure management techniques

The principal means of managing foreign exchange exposure is by balancing local assets and liabilities. While the nature of exposure, the currency outlook, and the cost of hedging will all be factors in selecting a hedging technique, foreign exchange and investment laws will determine whether a particular technique is feasible. Exposure management may be accomplished by changes in local assets or liabilities. This may occur in a number of ways including: dividend remittances, service payments, foreign lending or investment, domestic or foreign borrowing, capital repatriation, leading and lagging and forward sales and/or purchases of currencies.

A. Dividend remittances

Although legislation may provide for curtailment of dividend remittances in times of balance of payments difficulties, in actuality, few countries have exercised this option. Central banks and governments do not wish to totally discourage foreign investment, but rather to ensure that foreign investment contributes to domestic economic and industrial development. As a result, many developing countries in particular set limits on the amount of dividends that may be remitted abroad annually. Usually the percentage of profits that may be remitted is based on registered foreign capital.

In developed nations, controls on dividends are generally not part of investment or exchange control laws but may be included in wage and price controls. In times of economic crisis, a number of developed countries have restricted dividends to a percentage of company capital or to a percentage over the prior year's declaration. Dividend declarations may also be restricted by allocation of a certain percentage of profits to a legal reserve prior to any dividend declaration.

Taxes may also affect dividend remittances. In some countries, high withholding taxes may restrict dividends, although rates may be reduced under tax treaties with another country. In other countries, progressively higher penalty taxes are applied to dividends over certain limits.

B. Royalty and other service payments

Royalty, management fees and other service payments provide another means of reducing exposure and repatriating investments. Such transfers are often subject to control and licensing to ensure that these mechanisms are not solely employed to circumvent dividend controls. Frequently, royalties and related payments are prohibited to affiliates if a subsidiary is majority foreign owned unless an arm's length transaction can be proven. If permitted, royalties and related fees normally may not exceed a set percentage based on either sales or income.

C. Lending abroad

A subsidiary can also reduce local currency assets by lending abroad. This generally requires prior approval. Normally, only downstream loans from a parent to a subsidiary or else loans which benefit the balance of payments of the lender's country are approved. Upstream loans from a subsidiary to a parent are generally prohibited unless the parent company can document a need for the funds and also prove that the loan does not represent an indirect dividend payment. Lending domestically to related or unrelated firms is usually permitted. Therefore, some companies can achieve external lending by arranging the types of currency swaps or parallel loans described later in this section.

D. Portfolio investment regulations

If external lending is prohibited, purchase of foreign securities may provide another avenue for reducing local assets. Regulations governing foreign portfolio investments are generally restrictive and are greatly influenced by the country's currency situation. If the currency is stable, investment regulations may be more liberal. In some instances, purchase of foreign securities by residents is permitted only upon lodging a deposit with the central bank equal to a percentage of the investment. The percentage ownership of total equity in a foreign company is normally limited and investment in money market instruments is generally not permitted. It is normally easier for non-resident companies to purchase domestic securities in a country even though percentage ownership requirements may be established. Non-residents may be prohibited from holding money market instruments.

E. Foreign currency accounts

Local assets may also be reduced by placing excess funds in foreign currency accounts either domestically or abroad. In many countries, residents must obtain prior approval in order to hold foreign currency accounts. Approval is only granted if there is a proven need for accounts such as faciliating import or export payments. Often, non-residents must also obtain approval to hold local currency accounts in a country. Here again, approval is granted only if there is a genuine need to hold accounts. Since transfers into those accounts are often considered speculative, strong currency countries may discourage flows into non-resident accounts because of the resultant upward pressure on the exchange rate and the concomittant disequilibrium in the market and economy. Occasionally countries have discouraged non-resident bank accounts by forcing banks to lodge excessive reserves or deposits against the funds (ranging up to 100% in some instances), or else have placed commission charges on accounts.

F. Leading and lagging

Companies may lead or lag intercompany, commercial or other payments as a means of managing exchange exposure. For instance, subsidiaries may pay intercompany accounts in advance or delay collecting intercompany accounts to reduce assets in depreciation prone currencies. Conversely, they may delay paying intercompany accounts or collect them in advance to increase assets denominated in strong currencies. In most countries the flexibility to lead or lag commercial payments is limited by the credit or payment terms as stated in foreign exchange controls. Leading and lagging of financial payments is more restricted and may be altogether prohibited. Normally financial payments must occur as stipulated by the central bank when authorizing the initial transaction. Here again financial payments receive greater scrutiny because of their tendency to be considered speculative.

G. Capital repatriation

Repatriation of capital may also be used to reduce local exposure. The ability to do so depends on the restrictiveness of regulations governing repatriation. In some instances, capital may have to remain in a country for a specific number of years before repatriation may begin, or repayment must occur in a fixed percentage over a period of years. If partial repatriation occurs due to sale of a division or certain assets, the company must take care to structure the transaction as a sale on the part of the parent rather than on the part of the subsidiary, or repatriation of sales proceeds may not be permitted. Finally, in some countries, withholding taxes will have an impact on capital repatriation. If gains result from the sale of an investment, normal withholding tax is applied.

H. Domestic borrowing

Often the degree of foreign ownership determines a foreign subsidiary's ability to obtain domestic financing from banks. In certain developing countries, companies with foreign ownership may only obtain local bank financing equal to a percentage of paid-in capital or some other ratio, or they may only be eligible for short term borrowings, or financing for imports. Foreign controlled firms are normally not permitted to obtain domestic long term financing for capital expenditures. Such funding must usually be contributed by the foreign parent, and not deplete limited domestic long term capital resources. Moreover, banks may only be able to lend a certain percentage of their portfolio to foreign controlled companies.

When firms are unable to borrow domestically from financial institutions, they may be able to obtain loans from another company. Such borrowing in most instances is more freely permitted than borrowing from financial institutions. In some countries, however, domestic borrowing between companies is not permitted because companies may not act as financial intermediaries. In some cases, a company may place funds on deposit with a domestic financial institution for on-lending to another company at market or negotiated rates depending on the country involved.

I. External borrowing

External borrowing by resident firms is often restricted. Although foreign loan inflows have an immediate positive impact on a country's overall balance of payments, loan repayments and interest payments will result in a drain on foreign exchange reserves. Excessive foreign borrowing puts pressure on the monetary supply and inflation. In some cases, foreign borrowing by resident companies is monitored by requiring prior approval for all incoming foreign loans. Generally, when a domestic borrowing requires a parent guarantee, the loan is treated as a foreign loan and also requires approval. This is because the loan would be repaid by the parent company if the local subsidiary defaulted.

In instances where approval is required for foreign borrowing, commercial financing requirements are most easily approved. Normally approval for financial loans is granted on a case-by-case basis. In general, documentation is required to show the purpose of the borrowing. Restrictions may be placed as to maturity and amounts, with long term financings of five years or longer more readily approved. Foreign loans from banks, affiliates other than parent companies, or unrelated companies are accorded equal treatment under exchange control. Long term loans from parent companies may be granted more liberal treatment because they are often considered a form of direct investment.

J. Forward cover regulations

The forward exchange market may offer an alternative to balance sheet hedging techniques discussed above. Generally, the forward purchase or sale of foreign currencies is permitted to cover commercial transactions for tenors in line with normal commercial practice. Regulations are more restrictive with regard to forward cover for either financial transactions or balance sheet positions.

4. Innovative hedging techniques

A number of sophisticated techniques have evolved to facilitate exposure management, particularly in countries where there is no forward market or where especially tough exchange control regulations make standard hedging practice difficult. These include netting, currency swaps, parallel loans and reinvoicing centres.

A. Netting

Netting is the offsetting of claims and liabilities between two or more organizations with only the net credit balance transferred across borders. Bilateral netting occurs between two companies while multilateral netting takes place between three or more companies. Netting may involve only trade transactions or financial transactions or a combination of the two. Most commonly netting involves the offsetting of intercompany accounts although third parties might be involved. For the most part bilateral netting of trade transactions is either freely permitted under exchange control regulations or approval is granted when required. In almost all cases, multilateral netting requires prior approval which is generally only granted for trade transactions. Netting of financial or financial *vs.* trade transactions is not readily permitted.

B. Parallel loans and swaps

Back-to-back, parallel loans and currency swaps provide another means of obtaining domestic financing if regulations or economic considerations restrict access to local credit. They also allow companies with excess cash in a country with dividend limits access to funds for temporary use elsewhere. From an exchange control point of view, back-to-back and parallel loans are more feasible because they are often considered domestic transactions and thus do not come under strict exchange control purvey. (See Chapter III, Sections E and F.)

C. Reinvoicing centres

Another vehicle for managing as well as centralizing exchange exposure is the reinvoicing company. Under this technique, a manufacturer's exports are sold to the reinvoicing company which in turn reinvoices the overseas customer. Foreign exchange exposure is thus transferred to the books of the reinvoicing company. Such companies are specifically located in countries where exchange controls do not exist. As a result, forward markets may be used or foreign currency accounts held. In addition, other hedging strategies may be undertaken that might not be permitted in the country where the manufacturing entity is located.

5. Conclusions

Regulations in a country are constantly changing; companies must therefore be sure that they are current on the exchange control or investment regulations which impact operations. There are several ways in which a company may keep itself informed of regulatory changes, utilizing both primary and secondary sources. A number of weekly, monthly, and annual publications exist which provide information on exchange control and foreign legislation including the IMF's *Annual Report of Arrangements and Exchange Restrictions*. For the most part, these publications are geared to a broad audience. Thus, the information provided is general and often does not answer a company's specific questions. In addition, the publications only report the regulations and rarely indicate when laws differ from practice. The information contained in secondary sources should always be checked. Legislation may be inaccurately reported, and since regulations are often revised, the studies may already be out of date by the time they are received.

Companies can depend on their foreign subsidiaries to provide them with regulatory information. There are advantages and disadvantages in using corporate networks. General managers are in a position to obtain information first hand from central banks or relevant government agencies or obtain copies of the legislation. However, they may overlook exchange control or investment changes because they are heavily involved with other operational problems. Finally, a subsidiary may have a bias when reporting information back to headquarters. Companies may also rely on banks, accountants, and attorneys to assist them in obtaining information about regulations and controls. These professional organizations are impartial, rely on primary sources, and generally have the expertise to correctly interpret regulations in their respective fields.

CHAPTER VI

Policies, objectives and strategies

A. Strategy on long term foreign exchange exposure management[1]

1. Introduction

The purpose of long term foreign exchange management is not to cover a given foreign exchange exposure through dealings on the forward markets but to minimize and, if possible, eliminate such exposures before they become critical and therefore too costly to cover. A long term approach differs from conventional approaches in three important respects:

A. Longer time horizon

Accepted current methods of covering foreign exchange risks normally use a time horizon of three to six months. However, because of production and investment commitments, foreign exchange risks may actually arise as much as five years before they are reflected in the accounting system. With a three to six month time horizon, therefore, coverage operations will often come too late. Once a currency is under serious pressure, the forward coverage costs become exorbitant, frequently exceeding the probable foreign exchange loss.

Take the example of, say, a Japanese auto manufacturer. As Exhibit 1 shows, the company produces a car in January for export to the United States and sells it in April for $3,000, which it will collect three months later, in July. This company's accounting system would identify a foreign exchange exposure only during the three months when the figure of $3,000 in accounts receivables would appear on its books. Losses due to a devaluation of the dollar between January and April would, for accounting purposes, be defined as losses on regular transactions, not as foreign exchange losses.

Exhibit 1—Foreign exchange risk must be identified early

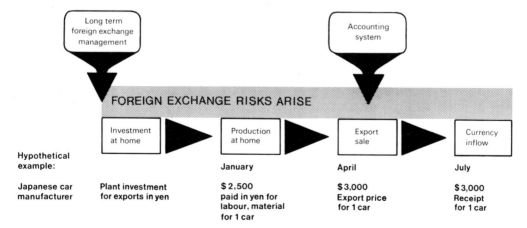

Yet that is exactly what they are, because the company committed itself in January to the export sale. To have risked the loss of its U.S. markets by stopping its exports or to have raised its final selling price in line with the devaluation would not have been realistic options. In effect, the company was locked into the exposure at least from the time the car came off the assembly line.

Indeed, the company actually incurred exchange risks considerably earlier—from the point at which it invested in production facilities to supply foreign markets. In fact, domestic facilities that supply foreign markets commonly entail a much greater risk than do foreign facilities, since material and labour cannot be paid for in the same currency for which the products are sold. The point seems obvious, yet few companies even consider covering such risks when they invest at home.

Thus, the first key characteristic of a longer term approach to foreign exchange management is that it does not rely on the accounting system. Risks are "managed" from the time the investments are made until the final receipts from sales of the product are received.

B. Dynamic orientation

To identify the foreign exchange exposure, it is not enough, as some companies have recognized, simply to compare foreign assets and liabilities (however defined) on a particular date—whether by the current or noncurrent method or the monetary or nonmonetary method. Rather, the *flows* of foreign currencies arising from transactions affecting these assets and liabilities over an appropriate period of time must be considered.

For example, if an Italian company has assets of 10 million French francs that mature in two years and liabilities of 10 million French francs that mature in one year, its franc assets and liabilities are exactly in balance. But foreign exchange risks still exist in both years, since there will be an outflow of 10 million francs in one year and an inflow of 10 million francs in the next. If the franc is revalued in the first year and devalued in the second, the company will have incurred exchange losses on both its assets and its liabilities.

Many assets and liabilities translate into currency flows over time, and it is the difference between inflows and outflows that define a company's exposure in any given period. Thus, the dynamic of time is a second vital characteristic of proper foreign exchange management.

C. Preservation of earnings

Finally, under the new approach the financial manager's objective concerning foreign exchange management is entirely different. Rather than seeking to minimize *reported* foreign exchange losses, he tries to preserve the earning power of the company as a whole through exchange rate fluctuations. For example, suppose a U.S. company has to repay a loan of 10 million French francs in 1978 and expects export sales to France of 10 million francs during the same year. Only the liability, not the expected income, will be shown on the books. Assuming that the export estimates are reliable, it should not be necessary to cover that loan, since the export receipts can be used to repay it. In other words, there is no foreign exchange risk if the export sales are realized.

Yet from an accounting point of view, the financial manager is still in an awkward position. If the franc should revalue by 10% his liabilities will result in an accounting loss of 1 million francs, while the increased dollar value of the French sales receipts will be identified not as foreign exchange gains, but as additional profit on regular transactions.

If, therefore, the financial manager merely wants to safeguard the interest of his own department, he will make sure to cover the 10 million franc liability, even if his expected export receipts from France are 10 million francs or considerably more. If he is to protect the earning power of the company as a whole, however, he needs to take a more systematic approach, which can only be implemented with fuller understanding and support on the part of top management.

2. Systematic steps

Recently a few large companies have successfully put into practice this more fundamental approach to foreign exchange management. While their programmes differ in detail, they all include the same three basic steps:

A. Estimate net exposures

Net exposure is the difference between estimated inflows and outflows of a foreign currency over a specified period or periods—not only those already known or contracted (from maturing receivables and payables, loan repayments, and interest and dividend payments), but also those that are expected or can reasonably be foreseen on the basis of the company's short and long term plans (from forecasted export sales, material purchases from abroad, planned investments in other countries, capital issues in other currencies, and equity increases in foreign subsidiaries).

To calculate the overall net exposure, the parent and each subsidiary estimate their expected inflows and outflows of each currency for the period or periods in question. Rather than allowing each subsidiary to cover its risks on its own, with attendant high coverage costs, management then consolidates all these estimates for the corporation as a whole. Instead of imposing this step as a requirement, companies with partially decentralized financial management have found it possible to achieve central control of foreign exchange exposure by giving subsidiaries concrete incentives to cover their risks only with the parent.

For a manufacturing company, the time horizon for estimating net exposure might be five years, broken down into cumulative 30 day, 60 day and 90 day estimates; six month, nine month, and 12 month estimates; two year, three year, and four year estimates, and estimates for all flows after five years. The periods cited are arbitrary, but the principle involved is simple: a series of staged forecasts for successively longer time periods, up to some reasonable limit. Obviously, a higher degree of precision is both possible and desirable for the first year; for subsequent years, rough estimates suffice.

Since inflows and outflows of any given currency may be subject to significant uncertainties, it is also helpful to consider the probable upper and lower limits of variation from the projected values in estimating net exposures. The object is to develop an approximate picture of net exposure positions in the major currencies involved, so that the company can move early to reduce its exposure through decisions on currency denominations, maturities of loans, repayment schedules, and the like.

Logically, then, the impact a given decision (for example, on a plant investment or a long term purchase contract) will have on the company's net exposure becomes an important input to that decision. Currently, foreign exchange risks associated with investment projects are specific—if at all—only for the individual projects, but what is important is the extent to which each investment will increase or decrease the overall net exposure of the company.

For example, in analyzing alternative production sites for one of its major components, one American company discovered that building a plant in West Germany instead of in the United States would substantially reduce its overall net exposure over the next five years. The DM inflow from the company's present exports of finished products to Germany would in fact then be offset by the DM payments for investment outlays in Germany and the subsequent purchase of components by the U.S. plants. Had the project been evaluated by itself, building the plant in Germany would have appeared, on the basis of foreign exchange risk, much less desirable than building it in the United States.

There are many other factors a company has to consider besides foreign exchange risks when it makes its final investment decisions. For instance, product market strategies, raw material supplies, availability of qualified personnel, differences in the investment climate of various countries, and regulations concerning profit and capital transfers may be far more important considerations than the risks associated with possible fluctuations in foreign exchange rates. Only the combined assessment of all these factors and their probable influence on the company's future profitability will lead to sound investment decisions.

B. Estimate range of exchange rates

As William D. Serfass has pointed out, the pursuit of speculative profits on the foreign exchange markets is a pastime about as rewarding as Russian roulette for corporate money managers.[2] Informed guesses of the likely range (not necessarily direction) of long term future exchange rate movements do, however, serve a vital purpose: that of providing a rough idea of the range of possible gains or losses that may result, given a particular net exposure.

To take an obvious example, a U.S. company ought to be less concerned about its exposure in Canadian dollars than, say, half the same exposure in English pounds. By computing the upper and lower limits of the probable gains or losses, the financial manager can predict and possibly forestall threats to a company's financial health arising from excessive exposure in volatile currencies.

Over the shorter term (three to six months), these same estimates provide a necessary basis for weighing the cost of forward coverage against the risks of leaving the net exposure uncovered. Note that it may at times be preferable to accept these risks. Since the costs of coverage are primarily determined by the differences in short term interest rates among countries, rather than by expectations concerning exchange rate movements, coverage may be attractive at some times, yet prohibitively costly at others.

Of course, specific exchange rate movements are difficult if not impossible to predict, but a company can at least reduce its undesirable net exposure positions well in advance, decreasing its vulnerability to exchange rate swings.

C. Cover risks

Having highlighted its principal future foreign exchange risks, the company can now devise means of coverage. Basically these reduce to two techniques:
1. Buying or selling particular currencies on the forward market to cover estimated net exposures in those currencies at particular future periods.

---

[2] William D. Serfass, "You Can't Outguess the Foreign Exchange Markets", HBR, March–April 1976, p. 134.

Exhibit 2—How a European company reduced its net exposure

'Net exposure' before coverage operation

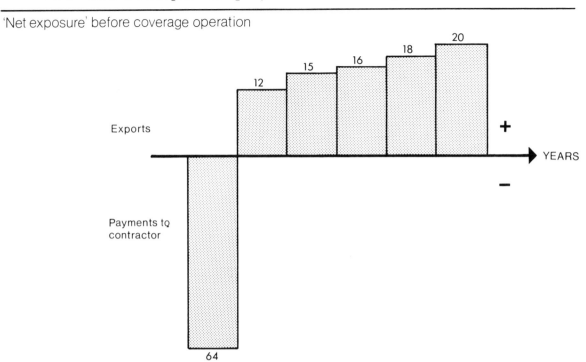

Coverage operation
Currency loan of 50 at 8% p.a. interest
20% p.a. repayments

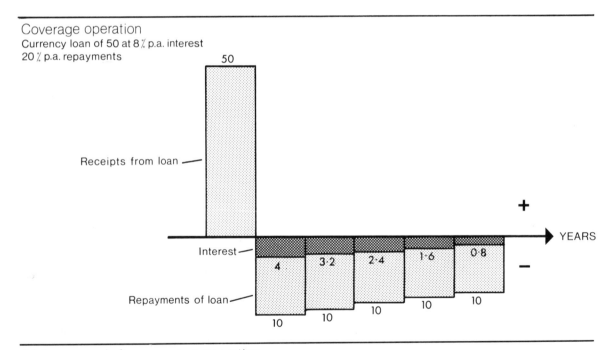

'Net exposure' after coverage operation

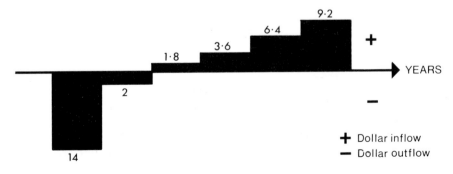

+ Dollar inflow
− Dollar outflow

2. Influencing individual components of expected currency inflows or outflows so as to reduce or eliminate estimated net exposures. This may mean changing the company's financial plans, such as by substituting a loan in another currency for a local loan, or its operating plans, such as by reducing exports to a certain country, purchasing more material from abroad, or expanding or curtailing capital investment in a particular country.

Since the forward market is essentially confined to short term (up to 12 months) contracts, longer term foreign exchange risks can usually be reduced only by changing the net exposure—and this frequently has the advantage of enabling the company to avoid undertaking large scale coverage operations in the forward market.

For example, a European chemical company bought a large factory from an American contractor for $64 million, agreeing to pay for it in U.S. dollars. A large outflow of dollars was in prospect for the first year, followed by increasing inflows of dollars from sharply rising exports. Covering the risk of the resulting net exposure during the first two years would have been extremely costly.

However, the company found that it could significantly reduce this net exposure by reducing its local bank loan and negotiating a loan of $50 million with a foreign bank. The proceeds of the loan were used for paying the U.S. contractor, while interest and loan repayments helped to offset the risks of dollar-denominated exports, as shown in Exhibit 2. This operation entailed no additional costs; indeed, the interest rate on the dollar loan at that time was slightly lower than on the local capital market. And because the loan was carried on the books of a foreign subsidiary that was subject to a higher tax rate, income taxes could also be reduced.

As a rule, the chief financial executive will wish to explore the choices available to him for altering the net exposure without affecting basic strategic or operating decisions. Should it appear that serious imbalances in net exposures will persist after available financial measures have been exhausted, top management might even consider revising its operating plans accordingly.

Though the ability of the financial manager to influence operating plans is generally limited, it is one of his major responsibilities to identify and highlight the foreign exchange risks associated with existing operating plans, so that these risks are properly entered into the overall evaluation of alternative strategies and plans.

3. Management system

Systems embodying the concept of foreign exchange management I have described in this section will inevitably differ from company to company in terms of organization and in the degree of computerization involved. Their principal elements can, however, be seen in the system (shown in Exhibit 3) that is being successfully used by a large international company. With this system, the company's financial managers go through the following cycle:

Long term financial plans—Based on the operating plans of the divisions, the parent and subsidiaries develop long term financial plans for five years. As part of the cash flow projection, the subsidiaries also submit their estimates of major foreign currency flows above a certain level, which is deliberately set high because of the enormous uncertainty involved. This confines the planning work to significant flows and avoids burdening the smaller subsidiaries with unnecessary paperwork.

Those in corporate finance consolidate all currency flows of the subsidiaries and the parent company, netting out the intercompany flows to derive the net exposure in each major currency for the total corporation.

Analysis of capital, tax, and regulatory outlook—With the support of the larger foreign subsidiaries, the corporate finance staff analyzes trends of major capital and foreign exchange markets to identify interest rate differentials between various capital markets, and estimates the upper and lower limits of possible exchange rate movements. For many currencies the estimated ranges will be very wide, signalling high risk if significant differences between currency inflows and outflows are anticipated.

Since financing and coverage decisions are subject to tax and legal regulations and constraints on capital and profit transfers, such constraints are carefully analyzed for each country, taking possible changes into account.

Sensitivity analysis—A sensitivity analysis model is used to calculate the effects of different rates of devaluation or revaluation on the profitability of the corporation and to test the impact of uncertainties in the estimates of each component of the net exposure. This model also shows the balance sheet and P & L statements for the total corporation, the parent, and each subsidiary for five years, highlighting the change in earnings after taxes due to exchange rate movements as well as foreign exchange losses or gains as defined by the accounting system. Corporate management can

139

Exhibit 3—System for foreign exchange management

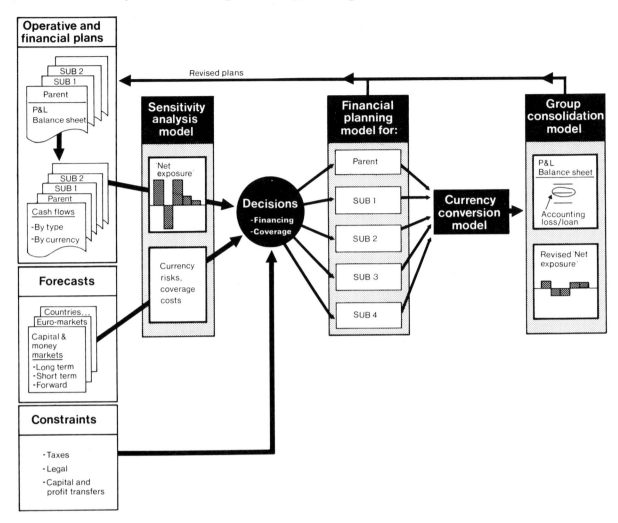

quickly see which subsidiaries are highly vulnerable to foreign exchange risks and how taxes and the degree of self-financing will be affected in each subsidiary if no specific counter measures are taken.

Coverage decisions—Having identified the major areas of foreign exchange risk, the corporate finance staff proceeds to develop measures for reducing the net exposure in particular currencies and years. Because they are highly interdependent, coverage and financing measures have to be worked out simultaneously and integrated into the financial plans of the corporation. All measures are thoroughly discussed with the subsidiaries affected and checked against legal and tax regulations or restrictions.

Adjustments of financial plans—The individual measures are then integrated into the financial plans of the parent and the subsidiaries. Adjustments are calculated with a financial planning model in local currencies and discussed with local management.

Currency conversion and group consolidation—The financial plans of the individual subsidiaries are converted from local currency into the home currency of the parent, using a currency conversion model. The plans are then consolidated on the basis of standard accounting rules for the total corporation with the aid of a group consolidation model. At the same time, the net exposure is recalculated for all major currencies to reflect the changes due to the coverage decisions. If the net exposure turns out to be still too high in certain currencies or periods, another round of adjustments is necessary.

In practice, the company has found this system to be a powerful tool to avoid excessive foreign exchange losses. Experience suggests, however, that such a system can be useful only if it is applied by imaginative financial managers who see beyond the boundaries of their organizational units.

140

B. The dynamic nature of exposure management

A dynamic approach to determining foreign exchange exposure based on cash flow concepts can be a powerful analytical tool for the corporate treasurer and financial executive. However, the ability to relate that exposure to accounting results is an essential ingredient in such an approach. An effective system of exposure management must include the capability of establishing the relationship which exists between two accounting concepts:

1. The change which an exchange rate fluctuation brings to the operating segments of an earnings statement, i.e. the measurement of variances hidden from the reader of conventionally prepared financial statements; and,
2. The disclosed translation gain/loss reported for an accounting period.

The controversy as to whether exposure management should focus on minimizing the translation gain/loss or whether it should concern itself with the broader effect on financial results can be attributed, in large part, to the fact that the variances in operating income are seldom quantified. Although the variances and the translation adjustment have a common cause—an exchange rate change—the user of financial statements is often unaware that the operating variances exist. A further point is that certain historic rate accounting rules create timing distortions which add to the difficulty of explaining the relationship which exists between these concepts.

The need to reconcile exposure concepts based on cash flow with financial accounting results cannot be blamed entirely on a particular set of accounting rules (such as FASB–8). Certain aspects of the Statement Number 8 (the inventory rules in particular) unduly complicate the reconciliation process. No set of accounting rules, however, has yet addressed itself to how the total impact of exchange rate fluctuations can be meaningfully presented to a reader of financial statements.

Cash flow based exposure assumes that a current, or beginning, balance sheet is only the starting point of the exposure computation. Transactions involving cash flows (inflows or outflows of cash denominated in a foreign currency, and also changes in other assets or liabilities) which occur within the period chosen for analysis (exposure period) will change the amount exposed in a particular foreign currency. Their inclusion in the exposure picture makes it possible to evaluate to what extent, and in what manner, financial results will be altered by a change in exchange rate.

The example represents the framework of an actual exposure management model stripped of some of the additional transactional complexity which would arise in a real situation.

The example involves exposures in a local currency (LC) arising out of a single manufacturing subsidiary. Third country currencies are excluded only to simplify the example, as are dollar denominated assets and liabilities. An exposure period has been chosen (a quarter) and the facts have been laid out (Exhibit 1) in such a way that the reader can quickly trace each transaction to the exposure computation and, thence, to the dollar (assumed to be the reporting currency of the parent) translated income statement.

The treasurer has correctly determined that at the beginning of the quarter he has a short exposure of LC 500 (line 5). Forecasting a gradual decline (rightly) of the LC over the next quarter, he feels quite comfortable and anticipates a translation gain by the end of the quarter. The picture which emerges from the impact analysis section of the exhibit is, however, a different one. It shows a reduction in accounting earnings of $30 (line 16). On a short exposure? Using the concept of dynamic exposure based on the cash flow of the subsidiary we are able to explain why.

1. The opening balance sheet

It is simple to determine the net asset/liability position as of the first day of the exposure period and to trace its impact on the translation gain/loss. The example assumes an excess of liabilities over assets denominated in LC and translated at current rates of exchange. This opening excess liability position of LC 500 accounts for a translation gain of $50 (translate LC 500 at $1·00, then at $0·90 and compare the results—line 5).

Inventory is excluded from the beginning position only because the complexity that the historic rate rule brings to the problem makes it more convenient to include the exposure it represents as part of the cost of sales (see below). Inventory belongs here if the current exchange rates are used to value it.

Most exposure management approaches exclude fixed assets and related depreciation from exposure. The use of historic exchange rates to record fixed assets and more particularly their relatively long useful life justifies such an approach. This, however, is a simplification. If, for example, we assume a decline in the value of the LC over the life of a depreciable asset, it becomes apparent that two unwelcome distortions occur:

141

1. Since the fixed assets have a frozen dollar value, the translation losses which would have resulted from the downward revaluation (in dollar terms) of the original cash investment are avoided.
2. The depreciation charge (in dollar terms) is artificially high by comparison to all other income statement categories. This is the equivalent of a negative operating variance in dollar terms.

Over the life of the asset (1) and (2) will offset each other. Within each accounting period, however, there will be timing distortions. If due weight is given to (2), it is no longer quite so clear that fixed assets should be excluded from exposure.

Exhibit 1—Reconciliation of cash flow based exposure and financial statement impact

Foreign manufacturing subsidiary reporting in local currency (LC). LC declines in value against the dollar (assumed to be the reporting currency of the parent) from LC 1·00 = $1·00 at the beginning of the exposure period to LC 1·00 = $0·90 at the end. Transactions occurring during the period are recorded at LC 1·00 = $0·95.

Local currency data

Balance sheet at beginning of exposure period
1. Cash, accounts receivable, etc	LC 500
2. Inventory	See below
3. Fixed assets	Not included in exposure
4. Liabilities	(1,000)
5. Beginning exposed position	LC (500)

Earnings for the exposure period
6. Sales		LC 1,000
7A. Opening inventory	LC (500)*	
7B. Cost of production	(500)†	
7C. Closing inventory	500†	
7D. Cost of sales		(500)*
8. Expenses		(200)
9. Income tax (33·3%)		(100)
10. Net income		LC 200

Other cash flows
11. Dividend distributed during period (LC)	(100)

Exposure (in $ at beginning rate)

Beginning exposed position	$(500)
Sales	$1,000
Cost of production	(500)†
Inventory	500
Expenses	(200)
Income tax	(100)
Dividend distributed	$(100)
12A. Ending exposed position	$100
12B. Impact of rate change from $1 to $0·90 applied to long exposure Loss	$(10)
13A. Amount of dividend being long exposure up to date of distribution	$100
13B. Impact of rate change from $1 to $0·95 (rate at distribution). Loss	$(5)
Impact based on exposure data	$(15)

Impact analysis and reconciliation

	Actual	Variances	Trans- lation gains/loss
Translation gain			$50
Sales	$950	$(50)	$(50)
Cost of production	NA	NA	25†
Cost of sales	(540)	(40)*	NA
Expenses	(190)	10	10
Income tax	(95)	5	5
Operating income	$125	$(75)	$40
Translation gain			5
14. Net translation gain		45	$45
15. Net income	$170		
16. Combined impact of variances and translation gain			$(30)
Elimination of timing differences:			
17. Deferred gain in beginning inventory			40*
18. Deferred loss in closing inventory			(25)†
19. Impact after eliminating timing distortions			$(15)

Notes:
* Opening inventory has a historic $ value ($540) based on an assumed rate of $1·08. On a simplified FIFO basis, this entire inventory is transferred to current cost of sales. The deferred amount ($40) penalizes the profit margin.

† Closing inventory is made up of current period production. Since the average exchange rate was $0·95, this becomes the historic rate for closing inventory: a book value of $475. If the inventory had been valued at the closing rate, it would have been stated at $450. The freezing results in a translation gain of $25 and an equivalent deferral of loss to the next period.

2. Sales and expenses

Each item of revenue creates an asset denominated in LC (translatable into dollars at the current rate) and each expense a current rate liability (or a reduction of a current rate asset). From the first day of the exposure period, the exposed position inherited from the beginning balance sheet is, therefore, subject to change. If the exchange rate moves during the period, each transaction responsible for a change in exposure influences the determination of the translation gain/loss for the period. A rate movement will also increase or decrease the dollar equivalent of reported sales or expenses. Just like a variance in a cost accounting environment, however, this increase or decrease is generally not identified as part of financial reporting.

Given sales of LC 1,000, operating expenses of LC 200 (cost of sales will be considered separately), and income tax expense of LC 100, these transactions will result in a build-up of current rate assets of LC 700 by the end of the period. It is, therefore, perfectly legitimate for the corporate treasurer to regard this cash flow as part of the exposure for the period. On the basis that the LC will have depreciated by 10% by the end of the quarter he can expect a negative impact on the translated dollar statements of $70 (translate LC 700 at $1·00, then at $0·90 and compare the results). Where is the $70 to be found? It may impact operating earnings, or the translation gain/loss adjustment, or both.

If the exchange rate changed on the last day of the period, all sales and expenses will be stated at the $1·00 rate, as will the assets and liabilities created by those transactions. The entire impact of the rate decline to $0·90 will be accounted for as part of the translation adjustment since the assets and liabilities will have to be restated at the closing rate.

If the rate changed on the first day sales, expenses and income tax will be stated in dollars at the $0·90 rate. The $70 decline in dollar income will be buried out of sight; an undisclosed operating variance. There will be no translation loss since the rate used to book the assets and liabilities created by the sales and expenses will be identical to the closing rate.

A more common result is that the $70 impact is distributed between the translation adjustment and the undisclosed operating effect. In the reconciliation section of the exhibit the impact is shown as being distributed equally in the case of sales (two negative $50 effects—line 6), expenses (two positive $10 effects—line 8), and income tax (two positive $5 effects—line 9). This is because the rate of $0·95 which is used to record transactions that occur during the exposure period happens to be halfway between the opening and closing rates for the period.

The allocation of the impact between the variance and translation segments of the earnings statement has a mere cosmetic effect. A reconciliation between the accounting cosmetics and the cash flow based exposure figures, however, is necessary if the latter are to be relied upon and understood by management.

3. Cost of sales and inventories

If inventories are translated at current rates of exchange and if cost of sales is stated in dollars by using the same average rate as for sales and other expenses, the impact of a rate change can be analyzed in exactly the same way as in the preceding section—and again distributed between the translation gain/loss and operating variance.

The accounting rules under which cost of sales is computed by reference to the historic dollar cost of the inventory deemed to have been sold is a complicating factor in the analysis. This deceptively simple rule influences accounting earnings in two ways:

1. The cost of sales for an accounting period is generally determined by reference to the exchange rate values of the preceding period. This is true where inventories built up in the preceding period are deemed to be consumed currently (as they would be under FIFO accounting rules). Line 7(D) of the example assumes that inventory inherited from the preceding period was booked at a historic exchange rate of $1·08. The dollar equivalent cost of sales for the period is therefore penalized by the fact that LC 500 are transferred from a historic rate asset (inventory) valued at $540. The penalty is measured by comparison with what the value of the LC 500 would have been using the rate of exchange as of the beginning of the exposure period ($500): an undisclosed negative variance of $40.[3]

   Since sales for the period are recorded at the $0·95 average rate, the result of the carry over of inventory with a historic exchange value is a misleading decrease in the operating gross profit margin (from 50% to 43%) when the earnings statement is translated into dollars. As none of this affects the translation gain/loss, the reader of conventional financial statements is none the wiser.

2. When inventory is acquired or produced, the dollar value of that inventory is fixed. In our example the LC 500 spent during the period on building up inventory will, to the extent that the inventory so purchased and produced is unsold at the end of the period, have a frozen dollar value (LC 500 at the average rate of $0·95, or $475). The result is that when the LC is declining against the dollar, a translation loss is avoided (the loss would have been the difference between the LC 500 inventory recorded at the historic $0·95 average rate and the same amount stated at the period-end current rate of $0·90, or $25). Unlike in (1) above only the translation adjustment is affected.

Again, the user of financial statements has, generally, no way of understanding the deceptive swing of the inventory impact between the income statement categories of translation gain/loss and operating variance. The final impact is that the net earnings of the period after translation adjustment have been affected by timing differences of $15 as follows:

---

[3] The rule that inventory is carried at the lower cost or market (in terms of dollars) may, if the LC is declining, require a writedown. It is assumed here that no such writedown is required.

1. Deferral from prior period to current period due to historic rate valuation of beginning inventory — ($40)
2. Deferral from current period to future period due to historic rate valuation of closing inventory — $25

Net timing difference — ($15)

How does the corporate treasurer keep track of exposure when applying a dynamic approach to cost of sales and inventory transactions? The inventory itself—LC 500 in the example—is considered to be part of the exposure in much the same way as a cash or receivable position is treated as being exposed. The cash outflow required to build up the closing inventory—also LC 500 in the example—is also taken into account. In our example these two figures offset each other so that the net impact is neutral (lines 7B and 7C in exposure section).

The reconciliation section bears this out. Cost of sales reflects a negative variance of $40; the translation adjustment, however, is positively affected by $25. If this timing difference is identified and reversed out for the purposes of management analysis the effect is neutral (lines 17 and 18).

4. Dividend exposure

A dividend distribution is a switch from LC into dollars. If the distribution occurs before the end of the exposure period, it is a LC cash outflow which reduces the exposure as of the end of the period. Unfortunately, it complicates the exposure computation since, prior to the distribution, the LC was at risk in the form of a long position. Hence, the need to look at two exposure figures: one as of at the end of the period, and another representing the LC switch into dollars as of the date of the distribution.

The example assumes the dividend (LC 100) is distributed before the end of the quarter at a time when the exchange rate is $0·95.

Dollar proceeds of distribution	$95
Dollar value of LC 100 at period-end if transaction had not occurred	$90
Financial statement impact—translation gain	$5

Assuming that the treasurer wants to protect the subsidiary's overall exposure—fearing a depreciation of the LC during the quarter—what actions may he logically take on the first day of the quarter to offset the impact on dollar net earnings of a change in value of the LC during the quarter?

If the corporate treasurer is concerned with protecting the dollar value of the dividend and knows when the LC 100 will be distributed he can, as a first step, sell forward the dividend amount to the date of distribution. The long exposed position as of the end of the first quarter (line 12A) is LC 100 (or $100 converted into dollars using the initial rate of exchange). As a second step this amount—assuming a before-tax hedge—can be sold forward 90 days. (Note that no account was taken of the beginning exposed position (line 5).)

Exhibit 2—Impact of hedging

Financial statements		Totals
Decrease in operating earnings (variance)	$(75)	
Net translation gain	45	
Combined impact of variance and translation gain—line 16	$(30)	
Elimination of timing difference due to historic rate value of inventory	15	
Impact after eliminating timing distortions —line 19	$(15)	$(15)
Forward contracts		
1. LC 100 sold forward 90 days		
Dollar proceeds at $1·00 contract rate	$100	
Cost of purchasing LC 100 at maturity at $0·90	(90)	
Gain	$10	$10
2. LC 100 sold forward to dividend date		
Dollar proceeds at $1·00 contract rate	$100	
Cost of purchasing LC 100 at distribution date—assumed rate of $0·95	(95)	
Gain	$5	$5
Overall impact		$0

Ignoring premiums/discounts on the forward contracts, the outcome of these actions is shown in Exhibit 2.

As the exhibit indicates, the gains of $15 on the two forward contracts exactly offset the $15 negative impact on the financial statements. Despite an exact match, however, an obvious problem remains. The gain of $15 on the forward contracts must now be added to the translation gain of $45. The cosmetic impact is now that the financial statements reflect a translation gain of $60. The large negative variance and the timing distortion are, of course, generally not disclosed. By the same token, should the LC move against the treasurer's expectations and appreciate by 10%, a pre-hedge translation loss of $45 would appear. The forward contracts would, to the treasurer's embarrassment, increase the translation loss to $60. His need for the reconciliation method presented in the example would be even greater.

The paradox is that the corporate treasurer who has made a correct determination by analyzing the overall impact of his exposure must now cope with a larger translation gain or loss than would have been the case had he not taken action. The problem becomes acute when it is realized that there are still many treasurers who operate under guidelines from management which have as a primary goal the minimization of translation adjustments. In such an environment a treasurer faced with the facts presented in the example might have entered into a forward purchase with a view to protecting the beginning short balance sheet exposure. Based on our assumption of a fall in the value of the LC, such action would have had an unfavourable impact on the bottom line. At the same time it would have borne no relationship whatever to the total financial impact of the exchange rate change. It might even be argued by some that such action had a speculative flavour.

The authors believe that there are still too many cases where hedging decisions are being made without regard to the operating impacts which are hidden from the view of the reader of financial statements. Having the correct information does not, unfortunately, facilitate the decision making. It can, however, avoid situations where hedges are being entered into in the wrong direction simply because it is conceptually easier to deal with only the translation adjustment which is the visible aspect of the problem.

C. Foreign exchange risk management

1. Introduction

A treasurer has essentially three tasks in relation to foreign exchange. He must forecast exchange rates, decide on an optimal hedging policy and choose the least-cost method of covering the relevant risk. This section concentrates on the second of these questions, that of determining whether and how much to hedge or speculate.

To penetrate this cloudy issue, it is helpful to proceed from the general to the operational. Corporate treasurers and their bankers may be pleased or disappointed by the proposition that an optimal hedging policy may not exist at all and, if it does, cannot be specified accurately given the present state of the economic art. We set forth the reasons for this statement in Part 2. Having sown this seed of doubt, one may nevertheless propose a practical and potentially implementable approach which also is free of some of the conceptual problems which beset current practice.

To this end one must distinguish between exchange risk on the one hand and exposure to exchange risk on the other. In Part 3, we point out that individual investors and corporate managers may define exchange risk differently. The definition one chooses depends on the objective of the hedging decision problem, but in any case should take account of uncertainty regarding the future exchange rate. Exposure, by way of distinction, should measure a company's sensitivity to future exchange rate changes. Numerous kinds of exposure can be defined. Corporate treasurers speak of translation, transaction, operational, economic and, possibly, commitment exposures to mention but a few. Part 4 employs a comprehensive numerical example which demonstrates for the first time how most of these various kinds of exposure can be linked. In a consistent framework, they turn out to be components of a decomposition of some global exposure, the definition of which depends on the firm's determination of the quantity to be protected from exchange rate variations. Part 5 discusses briefly the implementation of an exchange risk management programme using the proposed approach.

2. Is there an optimal hedging strategy?

A financial decision can be optimal only in relation to some objective. Many practitioners choose among alternative investments by comparing the present values of their future cash flows. In so doing, they have adopted as their target the improvement of the market values of the firm's outstanding securities. Academics call this value maximization. We first show why hedging exchange risk may have little importance if this is the firm's aim. Subsequently, we discuss the conditions, and the possibility of other goals, which can make hedging matter.

Consider a firm faced with the decision whether or not to hedge a given foreign currency exposure for a given future date. The payments that the firm will be able to make to its suppliers of funds on that date will be equal to the payments it could make in the absence of a forward contract plus the gain or loss on the contract.[4] When the principle known as value additivity (or, synonymously, the law of conservation of investment value) holds, the present market value of the outstanding securities of the firm with the forward contract will be equal to the present market value of the contract plus the value of an otherwise identical firm without the contract.[5]

Note, however, that if we ignore transactions costs or bankruptcy risks the value of the forward exchange contract *at the instant at which it is initiated* is equal to zero. No money changes hands between the contracting parties. When no investment is required for the purchase of a financial asset, its initial price must be zero regardless of its future payoff.[6] It follows then that the present value of the firm with the contract is equal to the value of the firm without the contract. Consequently, the firm cannot plan, *ex ante*, to use the hedging decision to increase the market value of its securities. In other words, no optimal hedging decision exists when the objective is value maximization, regardless of whether the firm or its assets are exposed, if market conditions are such that value additivity prevails.

There are three major reasons for questioning whether financial markets are sufficiently perfect for value additivity to hold. These are the existence of taxes, the possibility that individuals do not have access to the forward exchange markets on the same terms as firms, and the possibility of costly bankruptcy.

The regulations regarding the taxation of exchange gains and losses, particularly on forward contracts, are not wholly clear. However, to the extent that hedging can serve to reduce taxes or more properly, to increase after-tax cash flows, forward exchange contracting can affect the value of the firm. This introduces the theoretical possibility that an optimal hedging rule may exist, though none has ever been computed.

When individual investors' access to the forward exchange market is restricted, it becomes possible in principle for unrestricted firms to undertake forward exchange transactions on their behalf which, again, can potentially increase their market values. The possibility that the forward exchange market is thus segmented does not, however, necessarily produce a value-maximizing hedging decision for any single firm.[7] Investors care about the global exposure of their purchasing power to exchange risk. If they hold widely diversified portfolios, they will not be concerned about which firm hedges but rather that all firms together do so. Each firm's decision is indeterminate.

Bankruptcy costs are the third imperfection which may make hedging matter for value maximization. These costs are not fully understood. However, to the extent that they exist, a forward exchange contract which reduces the market's perception of a firm's probability of bankruptcy will reduce also the present value of these costs and thereby raise the value of the firm.

How imperfect are the capital and exchange markets? Conditions in actual financial markets undoubtedly depart from those required for value additivity strictly to hold. The trouble is that in order to design a value maximizing hedge a manager must identify the exact nature, magnitude and direction of the imperfections. This cannot be done, using present techniques, with any precision. Empirical tests for the existence of segmentation, for example, have been inconclusive.[8] No direct tests of the effects of firms' hedging activities on their stock prices have been performed. Other, indirect, evidence suggests these effects are probably minor.[9] Even if a value-maximizing hedging

---

[4] Let $_tF_T$ = the forward rate set at time t for maturity T and S_T = the (future) spot exchange rate which will prevail at T. The gain or loss on the contract is $(_tF_T - S_T)C$, where C is the amount of the contract.

[5] According to value additivity, the present value of a future (certain or uncertain) cash flow which is itself the sum of two distinct future payments is equal to the sum of the values of the two payments taken separately. Value additivity will generally hold under the same conditions which produce Modigliani and Miller's famous propositions about the irrelevance of financial decisions. Modigliani, F. and M. Miller, "The Cost of Capital, Corporation Finance and the Theory of Investment," *American Economic Review*, June 1958.

[6] Obviously, the forward contract acquires a non zero value immediately after the instant at which it is initiated that, at its expiration, is equal to $(_0F_T - S_T)C$. At the instant of contracting, however, the forward exchange rate is set at the level where the buyer and seller find it mutually advantageous to agree on a future exchange without current payment by either party to the other for services rendered or to be rendered. And a contract which costs nothing is worth nothing.

[7] See also, M. Adler and B. Dumas, "Optimal International Acquisitions," *Journal of Finance*, March 1975.

[8] See B. H. Solnik, "The International Pricing of Risk: An Empirical Investigation of the World Capital Market Structure", and, especially, the "Comment" on Solnik by B. A. Wallingford, both in the *Journal of Finance*, May 1974, 365–378, and 392–395.

[9] See for example, S. M. Robbins and R. B. Stobaugh, *Money in the Multinational Enterprise* (New York, N.Y. Basic Books, 1973). In Chapter 7 the authors report their sense that firms which hedge do approximately as well as firms which do not. Further, a recent FASB study found the introduction of FASB–8 to have no effect on firms' stock prices. See

strategy exists owing to considerations such as those above it will generally be hard accurately to compute its size and timing or to measure its impact.

In short, corporate treasurers are best advised to assume for the time being that their hedging activities will not have detectable effects on the prices of their firms' securities. Value maximization alone is a weak basis for justifying foreign exchange hedging. This does not mean that they should abjure forward exchange transactions altogether but rather that they should not, perhaps, seek to do so optimally.

Few practitioners, in fact, believe that value maximization should be a firm's only objective. At a given value managers may, according to this view, exercise their preferences. For example, they may aim to reduce the probability of default or of cash inadequacy so as to avoid abdicating control in favour of creditors. This objective can be served by a policy of minimizing the variability of cash flows given the firm's planned level of expected returns. Covering exchange risks can help in this context. Alternatively, executives may sometimes usefully take open, long or short, positions in foreign currencies (i.e. speculate) on behalf of the stockholders. When managers have better information, based on superior analysis or inside information, their beliefs as to future exchange rates may well diverge from the market's. Speculation in these circumstances will be profitable and can increase the value of the firm, but only later.[10]

Introducing either of these two objectives permits a policy of covering exchange risks to be viewed as an important component of programmes to manage and control financial risks and increase profits. While neither facilitates the determination of a single optimal hedging or speculative strategy, the former, especially, leads to practical and implementable decision procedures. These are discussed in Part 4. In the meantime, we turn to the matter of defining and distinguishing exchange risk and exposure.

3. What is exchange risk?

A currency is not risky because a devaluation is highly likely. If the devaluation were certain, there would be no risk at all. A weak, devaluation prone currency can be less risky than a strong currency. A strong currency does not become risky because it has been used to denominate a firm's liabilities.

Exchange risk should be related to the uncertainty of the future exchange rate. Uncertainty or risk is a matter of the unanticipated deviation of the exchange rate from its expected or most probable value. This risk can be important independently of whether either of these anticipated central values lies above or below its present level. Borrowing from statistics, riskiness can be associated with the variance since this measure summarizes the deviations of a variable around its expected (i.e. mean) level. The question is, what is the relevant variable?

It is possible to define exchange risk differently depending upon whether one takes the point of view of individual investors and/or allows a firm to serve some interest other than theirs. Individuals are rationally concerned with the uncertainty of their real purchasing power. Firms may be less. Let us consider each.

Take, for example, the returns on a riskless Japanese bond as seen by a representative U.S. investor. The nominally certain yen rate of return is $R_¥$. The uncertain future dollar/yen exchange rate is S: the current rate, for simplicity, is one. The uncertain future U.S. price deflator is I_{US}: the current deflator is one. The nominal rate of return on the yen bond in dollar terms is uncertain and equal to $R_¥S$. For the U.S. investor the story does not, however, stop here. What concerns him are his real returns which in this case are measured by $R_¥SI_{US}$. Multiplying $R_¥$ by the product of the exchange rate times the U.S. price index renders the yen return in constant dollars. The exchange risk or, better, the monetary uncertainty associated with the yen, is properly defined in this case as the variance of SI_{US}, i.e. $Var(SI_{US})$. This is the risk of a gain or loss in the purchasing power of a U.S. investor who owns a nominally fixed amount of yen.

The main difficulty with this definition is its subjective nature. In principle, exchange or currency risk is measured for each individual relative to a price index of his own consumption mix. For a representative Japanese investor the real return on the yen bond is $R_¥I_¥$, where $I_¥$ is the Japanese consumer price index. The U.S. and Japanese investors will view the riskiness of the bond differently when $R_¥I_¥$ is not equal to $R_¥SI_{US}$. This will be so in the typical case where purchasing power parity (PPP) does not hold, i.e. whenever exchange rates do not vary exactly with changes in

---

Dukes, Roland E., An Empirical Investigation of the Effects of FASB Statement No. 8 on Security Returns Behavior (FASB, December, 1978).

[10] The prices of the firm's securities will not immediately be affected since they are set according to the market's anticipations. Later, once the results are revealed, the market will acknowledge the firm's consistent success with a stock-price increase. This approach raises delicate issues of motivating, evaluating and remunerating the foreign exchange managers who do not transact in their own name.

price indices so that a given sum of money buys different amounts of the U.S. and Japanese consumption baskets. In such a setting exchange risk is an ambiguous concept.[11] The ambiguity is removed when investors everywhere share the same tastes, i.e. use the same deflator.

The choice of the correct currency risk definition for firms depends on their assumed objective. When the firm's goal is to undertake forward exchange transactions on behalf of investors who, for some reason, cannot do so themselves, it should adopt their objective. Currency risk should then be defined, as above, in terms of real purcasing power uncertainty, i.e. as Var(SI). However, purchasing power considerations matter less when the firm covers exchange risk with the purpose of reducing default risk and avoiding costly bankruptcy. Define bankruptcy as the condition where the future market value of the common stock is zero. It then matters little whether value is measured in real or nominal terms, for the bankruptcy condition will simultaneously be met by both. In this case, exchange risk can reasonably be defined nominally, as Var(S), without the intervention of a purchasing power index.

The use of Var(S) as the exchange risk measure has also been justified on the grounds that foreign exchange managers have little reason to be concerned with purchasing power variations. Their performance is generally evaluated nominally in the firm's currency of accounting on the basis of accounts rendered, for example, in current dollars. The basis for this claim will disappear, however, if and when price level adjustments are incorporated into firms' accounting statements for reporting and internal control. Further, lest the nominal definition seem superior, one should note that its use introduces ambiguity of a different kind. Its magnitude depends critically on which currency is chosen as numeraire. The variance of the dollar/yen exchange rate is not equal to the variance of the yen/dollar rate. (Technically, $\text{Var}(S) \neq \text{Var}(1/S)$). This problem does not arise when the monetary risk of every currency is measured relative to a common price deflator.

So much for defining exchange risk. Doing so has one main purpose, that of determining what we mean by a hedge. Hedging is not a question of avoiding a (possibly certain) loss. Rather, it is a matter of avoiding risk, i.e. the unanticipated deviations of some future price both above and below its anticipated future level. A perfect exchange risk hedge is therefore a transaction which renders the future price (of any asset or the firm) independent of the future exchange rate. A special case is a forward contract which effectively predetermines and sets constant the future reference currency value of a foreign currency position. These notions are useful below.

4. Exchange—risk exposure

A. Problems of definition

Let us now turn to the question of exposure as distinct from exchange risk. It is well to keep in mind that whereas exposure, whether of an asset or the firm as a whole, can exist and be defined, it will not matter if, following Part 2, no optimal hedge exists. In the case, forward exchange transactions need not be linked to any exposed quantity except for reasons other than value maximization.

A concept of exposure should express the sensitivity of the firm to exchange rate changes. More precisely, exposure should ideally measure the sensitivity of the market price of the firm's securities *at a specific future date* to the concomitant variation in the exchange rate on that date. This might be termed economic exposure. We emphasize the dated nature of the definition for two reasons. One is that forward exchange contracts are dated instruments: they can only protect an exposure with the same given maturity. To hedge an exposure for more than one period requires more than one contract. The second is to emphasize that exposure itself is dated. The exposure of a firm or an asset for a horizon six months ahead may be greater or smaller than the exposure a year ahead.

To state an ideal definition of economic exposure is to reveal immediately its practical limitations. One must initially decide whether the targeted future market value is to be measured in current or constant dollars, depending on the firm's objective. Exposure will vary according to this choice. More important, to implement such a definition requires in principle that one know (the probability distributions of) all the variables which can affect the firm's future market value, including the firm's own future operating and financial decisions, in order to isolate those variations which are due to the exchange rate from those due to other causes. Having established a list of all the risks to which the firm is subject, one must determine simultaneously its exposure to each one individually. With a

---

[11] This does not mean that exchange risk should be defined in terms of deviations from PPP. Quite to the contrary, such deviations play no role in any individual's measure of her own purchasing power uncertainty which for a U.S. investor is measured by $\text{Var}(SI_{US})$ without reference to $I_{\yen}$. Consequently, accounting treatments which decompose exchange gains and losses into components one of which is associated with PPP are unlikely to provide stockholders with useful information. Cf. H. E. Wyman, "Analysis of Gains and Losses from Foreign Monetary Items: An Application of Purchasing Power Parity Concepts," *The Accounting Review,* July 1976.

complete description of the firm's risks in hand, the way is then open for the design of a programme of global risk management which takes account of the links between the risks and the battery of financial hedging instruments at the firm's command. Unfortunately, there is little hope that this analysis can be performed exactly. Economic theory falls short of the synthesis of micro- and macro-economic modelling required to be able to associate specific market values of the firm and their probabilities with alternative future values of the exchange rate. The ideal definition, for the time being, is beyond practical reach.

What we can propose is a practical approximation, based on accounting conventions, which can also usefully be combined with simulation techniques (see Part 5). Since one cannot know the determinants of the firm's future market value, we propose to define exposure as the *variation in the nominal accounting book value of the equity as the exchange rate varies across its possible values at a single point in future time*.[12] A perfect hedge, that is a forward exchange transaction which renders the future book value of equity independent of changes in the future exchange rate, is possible with this definition if value moves linearly with exchange rates.

Despite their conceptual shortcomings, computations based on this definition will be an improvement over current accounting practice. What should matter for risk management is to be able to compare what will be gained or lost given an exchange rate change with what would be gained or lost without it. This involves looking to the future and comparing the value of the firm's equity associated with each possible level of the exchange rate to what that value would be were the exchange rate to remain constant. Our proposed procedure, illustrated below, facilitates such comparisons which are impossible with generally accepted accounting methods. These typically do not compare several instantaneously possible outcomes but rather report the one which actually materializes and match it with the one which occurred before. The *ex post* gain or loss is the difference between the two. Significantly, it is generally impossible to design in advance a forward exchange transaction which will perfectly hedge a gain or loss so defined.[13]

A second kind of benefit also emerges from our approach. Treasurers have long since recognized that the notion of translation exposure does not fully comprehend the potential impact of exchange rate changes on their firms. To aid in the management and control of exchange risk they have devised additional kinds of exposures. These include transaction exposure and operational or economic exposure.[14] Practitioners have been uneasily aware that the relationships among these various exposure concepts are imperfectly understood and have tended to view them as alternative objects for hedging transactions. Some firms, for example, undertake as a policy to ignore their translation exposures and hedge only their transaction exposures. Such policies may be ill-conceived. The example presented below shows that the various kinds of exposure are linked. In fact, once one accepts the notion of global exposure, defined above as the future comovement of net worth at book with the exchange rate, it can be decomposed into components which accord with reasonable definitions of the other kinds of exposure. Our method, in short, enables treasurers to fit their hedging strategies to a well-defined objective.

B. Numerical example

The firm in our example is headquartered in France.[15] It has a 100%-owned production affiliate in the United States which exports half its output to France. Exhibit 1 sets forth the affiliate's beginning balance sheet and, in the margin, the assumptions used throughout. For simplicity, we assume only two states of nature: one in which the exchange rate remains constant and a second in which the French franc (Ffr) devalues by 10%, from $0·25/Ffr to $0·225/Ffr, on July 1. Additional possibilities can easily be handled by computerized simulation. Exhibits 2 to 5 present pro-forma income statements and balance sheets under the alternative assumptions of devaluation and no devaluation. Exhibits 2 and 3 are in US$ while Exhibits 4 and 5 are translated into Ffr according to FASB–8 conventions.

---

[12] The approximation is crude for several reasons. First, the market value of fixed assets differs from their value at original cost. Replacement cost accounting would only partially improve the approximation. The market value of the firm reflects not only the liquidation values or replacement costs of the assets but also a premium reflecting the firm's possible monopoly rents from the sales produced by the assets, its access to future investment opportunities and the quality of its management. Second, long term debt is booked at redemption value minus unamortized premium rather than market value. Our main justification is that changes in the book-value of the equity can affect investors' estimates of the probability of future bankruptcy.

[13] A forward contract can be designed to avoid only the anticipated gain or loss which only by coincidence will equal the actual outcome. Any unanticipated deviation of the actual from the expected outcome cannot be hedged.

[14] Transaction exposure was baptized in print by R. K. Ankrom, "Top Level Approach to Foreign Exchange Management," *Harvard Business Review*, July–August, 1974. Economic and/or operational exposures are widely discussed but do not seem to have a single, generally accepted definition.

[15] We chose to locate the headquarters in France so as to be able to illustrate accounting issues without having to deal with any of the intricacies associated with the U.S. tax treatment of foreign source income and foreign exchange gains and losses. These are not taxed in France.

Exhibit 1—Beginning balance sheet

Assets	$US	Ffr	Ffr	$US	Liabilities
Cash	2,400	9,600	14,400	3,600	U.S. bank debt
A/R	3,600	14,400	14,400	3,600	Ffr long term debt
Inventory	4,800	19,200	38,400	9,600	Common stock
Fixed assets	6,000	24,000			
	16,800	67,200	67,200	16,800	

Notes and assumptions

1. Taxes due = taxes paid. For simplicity, no deferred tax accounts are created.
2. Suppliers are paid immediately.
3. Proceeds from sales are collected six months following the sales.
4. All sales are invoiced in $US. Half the output is exported to France.
5. Costs of raw materials and wages are 50% variable and 50% fixed.
6. Administrative costs are fixed.
7. Inventories are valued by the FIFO method at historical cost.
8. Inventory $(t+1)$ = Inventory (t) + (Dir. Lab. + Raw Mat. + Pl. Ohd) − CGS
   $6,000 \quad\quad = \$4,800 \quad\quad + (\$6,000 \quad\quad\quad\quad + \$1,200) \quad - \$6,000$
   where Pl. Ohd is plant overheads and CGS is cost of goods sold.
9. Target inventory in the absence of devaluation = prior year's cost of sales.
10. Production takes place entirely in the U.S.
11. Cost of goods sold includes $1,200 of plant overhead and depreciation.
12. U.S. corporate tax rate is 48%.
13. Interest payments are made on 12/31 of each year.
14. A 1% devaluation in the French franc would result in a decline of 1·8% in the volume of sales in France during the following six months.
15. On July 1, the Ffr devalues from $0·25/Ffr to $0·225/Ffr.
16. U.S. production is then reduced exactly in proportion to the change in sales.

Exhibit 2—Pro-forma income statement, with and without devaluation

Item	US$ With	US$ Without
Sales:		
U.S. 1st half	2,700	2,700
France 1st half	2,700	2,700
U.S. 2nd half	2,700	2,700
France 2nd half	2,160[1]	2,700
Cost of goods sold (CGS)	5,700[2]	6,000
Selling, general & admin. exp.	1,800	1,800
Interest:		
U.S. Bank	200	200
Ffr debt	180[3]	200
Earnings before tax (EBT)	2,380	2,600
Exchange gain on Ffr debt	360[4]	0
U.S. taxes:		
on EBT	1,142·4[5]	1,248
on exch. gain	172·8[6]	0
Net income after tax:		
Before FX-gain	1,237·6	1,352
FX-gain A.T.	187·2[7]	
	1,424·8	

Exhibit 3—Pro-forma balance sheet, with and without devaluation (US$)

Assets	With	Without	With	Without	Liabilities
Cash	2,054·8	1,952	3,600·0	3,600	U.S. bank debt
A/R:					
U.S.	2,700·0	2,700	3,240·0[10]	3,600	Ffr long term debt
France	2,160·0[1]	2,700	1,237·6	1,352	Ret. E. (W/O FX-gain)
Inventory	6,150·0[8]	6,000	187·2[7]	0	Exchange gain
Fixed assets	4,800·0	4,800	9,600·0	9,600	Common stock
Total assets	17,864·8	18,152	17,864·8	18,152	Total liabilities

150

Notes to Exhibits 2 and 3

[1] $2,160 = 2,700 [1 - (1 \cdot 8) (0 \cdot 111)]$: 2nd-half sales to France fall by 20%.

[2] The FIFO rule guarantees that 2nd-half sales are made entirely from inventory produced prior to June 30, and are therefore valued at 1st-half unit costs. Total 2nd-half sales decline by 10%. Hence, cost of goods sold $= \$3,000$ $(1 + 0 \cdot 9) = \$5,700$.

[3] $\$180 = (800Ffr) (\$0 \cdot 225/Ffr)$.

[4] $\$360 = \$3,600 - \$3,240 =$ Pre-tax translation gain on Ffr debt.

[5] $\$1,142 \cdot 4 = (0 \cdot 48) (\$2,380)$.

[6] $\$172 \cdot 8 = (0 \cdot 48) (360)$. Tax expense = tax due. The tax on the exchange gain on Ffr debt is expensed immediately rather than deferred until the gain is realized at the maturity of the debt. Alternatively, assume that the Ffr debt is retired on 12/31.

[7] $\$187 \cdot 2 = (0 \cdot 52) (\$360)$.

[8] Inventory T-accounts, with and without devaluation:

With			**Without**		
Beg. bal.	4,800		Beg. bal.	4,800	
Depr. & ohd.	600	3,000 CGS	Depr. & ohd.	1,200	6,000 CGS
R.M. & wages	3,000		R.M. & wages	6,000	
6/30 bal.	5,400		End bal.	6,000	
Depr. & ohd.	600	2,700 CGS			
R.M. & wages	2,850[9]				
End bal.	$6,150				

[9] $\$2,850 = 1,500 + 1,500 (0 \cdot 9)$; Raw materials and wages decline by 5% since they are 50% fixed and 50% variable.

[10] $\$3,240 = (14,400Ffr) (\$0 \cdot 225/Ffr)$; $\$3,600 = (14,400Ffr) (\$0 \cdot 25/Ffr)$.

Global exposure is easy to compute. One simply calculates the end-of-period balance sheets with and without devaluation. The difference in the net worths between the two states of nature is then the total exchange gain or loss. The total exposure is simply the gain or loss divided by the exchange rate change. For the dollar accounts, the exposure is given by (see Exhibit 3).

$$\frac{1,237 \cdot 6 + 187 \cdot 2 - 1,352}{0 \cdot 225 - 0 \cdot 25} = \frac{72 \cdot 8}{-0 \cdot 025} = -2,912 \text{ Ffr}$$

For the Ffr accounts, the exposure to the dollar, from Exhibit 5, is

$$\frac{5,265 \cdot 78 + 1,733 \cdot 33 - 5,408}{\dfrac{1}{0 \cdot 225} - \dfrac{1}{0 \cdot 25}} = (1,591 \cdot 11) (2 \cdot 25) = \$3,580$$

The reader will notice that the exposure to dollars is not the translated value of the exposure to French francs.

Exhibit 4—Pro-forma income statement, with and without devaluation

Item	French francs	
	With	**Without**
Sales:		
U.S., 1st half	10,800·00	10,800·00
France, 1st half	10,800·00	10,800·00
U.S., 2nd half	12,000·00[1]	10,800·00
France, 2nd half	9,600·00[2]	10,800·00
Cost of goods sold (CGS)	22,800·00[3]	24,000·00
Selling, general & admin. (SGA)	7,600·00[4]	7,200·00
Interest:		
U.S. bank	888·89[5]	800·00
Ffr debt	800·00[6]	800·00
Earnings before U.S. tax	11,111·11	10,400·00
U.S. taxes:		
on EBT	5,077·33[7]	4,992·00
on $ exch. gain	768·00[8]	5,408·00
	5,265·78	

Exhibit 5—Pro-forma balance sheet, with and without devaluation (French francs)

Assets	With	Without	With	Without	Liabilities
Cash	9,132·44	7,808·00	16,000·00[10]	14,400·00	U.S. bank debt
A/R:					
U.S.	12,000·00[1]	10,800·00	14,400·00	14,400·00	Ffr long term debt
France	9,600·00[2]	10,800·00	5,265·78	5,408·00	Ret. E. (W/O FX-gain)
Inventory	25,866·67[9]	24,000·00	1,733·33	0	Exchange gain
Fixed assets	19,200·00	19,200·00	38,400·00	38,400·00	Common stock
Total assets	75,799·11	72,608·00	75,799·11	72,608·00	Total liabilities

Notes to Exhibits 4 and 5

1. $12{,}000 \text{ Ffr} = \$2{,}700/(0{\cdot}225\$/\text{Ffr})$.
2. $9{,}600\text{Ffr} = \$2{,}160/(0{\cdot}225\$/\text{Ffr})$.
3. $22{,}800\text{Ffr} = \$5{,}700/(0{\cdot}25\$/\text{Ffr})$, since goods sold in the second half are produced in the first.
4. $7{,}600\text{Ffr} = \$900/(0{\cdot}25\$/\text{Ffr}) + \$900/(0{\cdot}225\$/\text{Ffr})$.
5. $888{\cdot}89\text{Ffr} = \$200/(0{\cdot}225\$/\text{Ffr})$.
6. $800{\cdot}00\text{Ffr} = \$180/(0{\cdot}225\$/\text{Ffr})$.
7. $5{,}077{\cdot}33\text{Ffr} = \$1{,}142{\cdot}4/(0{\cdot}225\$/\text{Ffr})$.
8. $768{\cdot}00\text{Ffr} = \$172{\cdot}8/(0{\cdot}225\$/\text{Ffr})$.
9. Translation of inventory (see footnote 8 to Exhibit 3).

	US$	FX-rate	Ffr
Beginning balance	4,800	1/0·25	19,200·00
+Raw materials & wages	3,000	1/0·25	12,000·00
	2,850	1/0·225	12,666·67
+Depreciation & overhead	1,200	1/0·25	4,800·00
−Cost of goods sold	5,700	1/0·25	22,800·00
=Ending balance	6,150	Avg.	25,866·67

10. $16{,}000\text{Ffr} = \$3{,}600/(0{\cdot}225\$/\text{Ffr})$

The interpretation of these values is particularly direct and intuitive. They represent the amount of the forward contract that the firm should take out if it wanted complete protection, i.e. if it aimed to render the book value of its net worth independent of any exchange rate change. To see this, consider the exposure to the French franc. Suppose the firm shorts francs, i.e. takes a contract to deliver 2,912 Ffr at a forward rate of F $US/Ffr on 12/31. We can then compare the stockholders' equity in the two states.

	Without devaluation	With 10% devaluation
Value of net worth (Exhibit 3)	$10,952	$11,024·80
Proceeds of forward contract	$-(F - 0{\cdot}25)2{,}912$	$(0{\cdot}225 - F)2{,}912$
Total value of net worth	$\$11{,}680 - (2{,}912)F$	$\$11{,}680 - (2{,}912)F$

Clearly the book values of net worth are equal in the two states of nature regardless of the actual value of the forward rate.[16] The comparison for the Ffr accounts is symmetrical.

Let us now turn to the decomposition. Exhibits 6 and 7 provide the requisite breakdowns for the $US accounts while Exhibits 8 and 9 refer to the Ffr statements. We first compare Exhibits 6 and 8 which set forth the FASB–8 translation exposures and gains and losses.

Since inventories in the example are all valued at historical cost, the FASB–8 translation exposures are respectively equal to the net monetary assets in each currency. These exposures cannot be read off the beginning balance sheet (Exhibit 1). Translation exposure involves the net monetary assets in existence *at the future moment of the exchange rate change*. This definition of translation exposure is not the product of our example but rather emerges directly from the conventional accounting calculation of the translation gain or loss. *Ex post*, this is equal to the exposure, so defined, times the exchange rate change.[17] In Exhibit 6, the translation gain is computed after tax to give effect to the U.S. regulations. Taxes are omitted in Exhibit 8 because translation gains and losses are not taxed in France.

---

16. This comparison is particularly simple since gains and losses on forward contracts are not taxed in France. Were the firm a U.S. citizen, as a first approximation one would have to gross up the hedge, i.e. take out a contract equal to (2912/0·52) Ffr. However, it is by no means certain that gains and losses on forward contracts will be considered as ordinary income. In addition, even though such contracts will not ordinarily be deemed to give rise to foreign source income, one should in principle keep in mind that the decision to hedge may affect decisions about remissions of, say, dividends. Additional tax consideration would then enter the picture.

17. The main but largely unmentioned difficulty with the conventional notion of translation exposure is that in the planning context, it involves a future quantity which cannot be known exactly in advance and cannot therefore be perfectly hedged. See also footnote 13.

Exhibit 6—Analysis of the FASB–8 translation gain in the US$ accounts

Ffr cash balance on July 1	0
Ffr A/R on July 1	0
Ffr long term debt	−14,400
French franc exposure	−14,400

After U.S.-tax translation gain

$$(1-0\cdot48)(-14{,}400)(0\cdot225 - 0\cdot25) = (0\cdot52)(\$360) = \$187\cdot2$$

Exhibit 7—Analysis of the variation in income before exchange gains or losses in the US$ accounts (Exhibit 2)

1. Income variation to be explained: $1,237\cdot6 - 1,352 = \$-114\cdot40$
2. Analysis:
   - (A) Transaction gain on nominal flows:
     - Interest on Ffr debt: $\qquad -800\text{Ffr} (0\cdot225 - 0\cdot25) = \underline{\$20\cdot00}$
   - (B) Gain or losses on changes in operations:
     - Variation in sales volume: $\qquad \$4{,}860 - \$5{,}400 = -\$540\cdot00$
     - Variation in cost of goods sold: $\qquad \$2{,}700 - \$3{,}000 = -\$(300\cdot00)$
     - Associated variation in U.S. taxes: $\qquad \$1{,}142\cdot4 - \$1{,}248 = -\$(105\cdot60)$
     - Total operations gain = $\underline{\$(134\cdot40)}$
   - (C) Reconciliation: $\$(134\cdot4) + \$20\cdot00 = \$-114\cdot40$

Exhibit 8—Analysis of the FASB–8 translation gain in the French franc accounts

Cash on July 1	$2,100·00
A/R: on July 1	+$5,400·00
U.S. bank debt	−$3,600·00
Dollar exposure	$3,900·00

Translation exchange gain $= (\$3{,}900\cdot00)\,(1/0\cdot225 - 1/0\cdot25) = 1{,}733\cdot33\text{Ffr}$.

Exhibit 9—Analysis of the variation in income before exchange gains or losses in the Ffr accounts (Exhibit 4)

1. Income variation to be explained: $5,265\cdot78 - 5,408 = -142\cdot22\text{Ffr}$.
2. Analysis:
   - (A) Transaction gains and losses on nominal flow:
     - Interest on U.S. bank debt: $\qquad \$-200(1/0\cdot225 - 1/0\cdot25) = -88\cdot89\text{Ffr}$
     - SGA, 2nd half: $\qquad \$-900(1/0\cdot225 - 1/0\cdot25) = -400\cdot00\text{Ffr}$
     - U.S. taxes, payable 12/31: $\qquad \$-1{,}315\cdot2(1/0\cdot225 - 1/0\cdot25) = -584\cdot43\text{Ffr}$
     - Sales, 2nd half: $\qquad \$4{,}860\cdot0(1/0\cdot225 - 1/0\cdot25) = 2{,}160\cdot00\text{Ffr}$
     - Total trasactions gain: $\qquad \$2{,}444\cdot8(1/0\cdot225 - 1/0\cdot25) = \underline{1{,}086\cdot58\text{Ffr}}$
   - (B) Gain or loss on changes in operations:
     - Variation in sales volume: $\qquad (-\$540)(4) = -2{,}160\cdot0\text{Ffr}$
     - Variation in cost of goods sold: $\qquad -(-\$300)(4) = 1{,}200\cdot0\text{Ffr}$
     - Variation in U.S. tax: $\qquad -(\$172\cdot8 - \$105\cdot6)(4) = -268\cdot8\text{Ffr}$
     - Total operations gain: $\qquad \underline{-1{,}228\cdot8\text{Ffr}}$
   - (C) Reconciliation: $\qquad 1{,}086\cdot58 - 1{,}228\cdot8 = -142\cdot22\text{Ffr}$.

While translation exposure is a component of global exposure, the two are not equal. The former does not exhaust the impact of exchange rate variations on the firm. Exhibits 2 and 3 reveal that there exists a change in $US net worth, *excluding translation gains,* equal to $\$1.237\cdot6 - \$1,352 = -\$114\cdot4$. Exhibits 4 and 5 show a comparable difference in the Ffr accounts, of $5,625\cdot78\text{Ffr} - 5,480\text{Ffr} = -142\cdot22\text{Ffr}$. These variations each have two further components, analysed in Exhibits 7 and 9 respectively.

The first is a transaction gain or loss incurred in connection with planned nominal flows between July 1 and December 31. This calculation assumes that the exchange rate change is permanent and not exactly compensated by a simultaneous inverse change in the firm's product prices.[18] The

---

[18] Here we confront a question often posed by practitioners. How should exposures or gains and losses be estimated in advance when exchange rates are variable and can move up or down? The answer is that if successive percentage exchange rate changes are serially uncorrelated i.e. if they follow a martingale as approximately they appear to do empirically, it is correct to suppose that the last shift within the forecasting horizon is permanent and will not be systematically counteracted by a jump in the reverse direction. In this case, the current spot or forward exchange rates will be highly inaccurate predictors of the future spot rate.

relevant nominal flows in Exhibits 7 and 9 are, in line with the net-worth objective, those which affect profits: interest payments, selling, general and administrative expenses, U.S. tax payments and additions to accounts receivable (equal to 2nd-half sales). The sum of these items is a measure of transaction exposure which, multiplied by the exchange rate change, produces the associated gain or loss. In the dollar accounts, the exposed flows are those denominated in French francs. The only Ffr denominated flow is interest on the Ffr debt, of 800Ffr. The transaction gain in Exhibit 7 is therefore $20. In the Ffr accounts, the exposed flows are those denominated in $US. The transaction gain in Exhibit 9 is 1,086·58Ffr and is equal to the total transaction exposure, $2,444·80, times the exchange rate change.

The second component of the variation in profit, net of translation gains or losses, is due to the change in the volume of operations owing to the devaluation. These consist of the reduction in sales and in cost of goods sold and the associated change in taxes. Such gains and losses are listed in Exhibits 7 and 9 under the heading, "operations gains". While they are similar to what most writers have called gains or losses due to economic exposure, we prefer to reserve that label for what we have so far termed global exposure. The calculation of operating gains in the dollar accounts seems clear. Its counterpart in Exhibit 9 deserves comment on two counts. Notice first that all the relevant variations are translated at the no-devaluation exchange rate, 4Ffr/$: this emerges from a decomposition principle known to every accountant.[19] Second, the relevant change in taxes from the French viewpoint is the net of the reduction due to lower pre-tax profits, $-\$105·6$, which is more than offset by the U.S. tax on the (realized) translation gain, $\$172·8$.

It is clear, therefore, that the global exposure cannot be accounted for by the translation and transaction exposures alone. One must, in addition, take account of the operations exposures. It is the last three together which add up to the total. Thus, in the dollar accounts, the change in net worth is $72·8 which in turn is equal to $187·2 + $20 - $134·4. In the Ffr accounts, similarly, the change in net worth is $1,591·11 = 1,733·33 + 1,086·58 - 1,228·80$. If one accepts the change in net worth as the objective for hedging, it will be a mistake to ignore any of its three constituents.

Some treasurers may be disturbed that the concept of transactions exposure which emerges from our decomposition does not exactly coincide with common practice which is based on cash flows. The reason is that we have chosen as the objective the change in net worth. To obtain a decomposition in which transaction exposure is associated with cash flows rather than with income-related nominal flows one must choose as the objective the change in the cash balance. This proposition is illustrated in Exhibits 10, 11 and 12. The price of letting the definition of transactions exposure accord with current conventions is that translation exposure is no longer given by the FASB–8 definition. It must be defined in terms of the translation gain or loss on the cash balance alone. Similarly, the concept of operations gains or losses must be rendered in terms of cash flows.

We see no particular benefit to taking this latter approach. In the context of bankruptcy risk reduction, changes in future net worth seem a more acceptable focus for managerial attention than changes in the future cash balance. Others may differ. We are merely suggesting that, given any such choice of the object to be protected from exchange rate changes, it is possible to produce a consistent decomposition the components of which may be reasonably identified with the kinds of exposures bandied about in common parlance. Consistency may be a virtue especially when it comes to decentralizing the function of exchange risk management.

Exhibit 10—Cash T-accounts, with and without devaluation

With devaluation				Without devaluation			
Beg. bal.	$2,400	$900	SGA	Beg. bal.	$2,400	$900	SGA
Collections	$3,600	$3,000	Purchases	Collections	$3,600	$3,000	Purchases
6/30 bal.	$2,100			6/30 bal.	$2,100		
Collections	$5,400	$900	SGA	Collections	$5,400	$900	SGA
		$2,850	Purchases			$3,000	Purchases
		$200	U.S. interest			$200	U.S. interest
		$180	Ffr interest			$200	Ffr interest
		$1,315·2	U.S. taxes			$1,248	U.S. taxes
12/31 bal.	$2,054·8			12/31 bal.	$1,952		

---

[19] Consider the difference between the translated value of an account in the state s, M_sS_s and its value in the reference state, M_oS_o. Then $M_sS_s - M_oS_o = M_s\Delta S - \Delta M \cdot S_o$. In a sense, the transaction gain corresponds to $M_s\Delta S$ and the operations gain to $\Delta M \cdot S_o$.

Exhibit 11—Analysis of the variation in the cash account in the U.S.$ statements

1. Cash balance variation to be explained: $2,054\cdot8 - \$1,952 = $ $\underline{\underline{\$102\cdot80}}$
2. Analysis:
   - A. Translation gain or loss on Ffr cash balance $\underline{\underline{\$0\cdot00}}$
   - B. Transaction gain or loss on Ffr cash flows
     Ffr interest payment: $-800\text{Ffr} (0\cdot225 - 0\cdot25) = $ $\underline{\underline{\$20\cdot00}}$
   - C. Cash balance changes due to changes in operations
Variation in sales collections:	$\$5,400 - \$5,400 = $	$\$0\cdot00$
Variation in purchases:	$-(\$2,850 - \$3,000) = $	$\$150\cdot00$
Variation in U.S. taxes:	$-(\$1,315\cdot2 - \$1,248) = $	$\$(67\cdot20)$
Total operations gain	$\$82\cdot80 + \$20\cdot00 = \$102\cdot80 = $	$\underline{\underline{\$82\cdot80}}$
   - D. Reconciliation:

Exhibit 12—Analysis of the variation in the cash balance in the Ffr statements

1. Cash balance variation to be explained:
   $$(2,054\cdot8)(1/0\cdot225) - (\$1,952)(1/0\cdot25) = 9,132\cdot44 - 7,808 = \underline{\underline{1,324\cdot44\text{Ffr}}}$$
2. Analysis:
   A. Translation gain or loss on cash balance at 6/30:
   $$2,100(1/0\cdot225 - 1/0\cdot25) = \quad 933\cdot33\text{Ffr}$$
   B. Transaction gain or loss on U.S.$ cash flows in 2nd half

Sales collections, 2nd half:	$\$5,400(1/0\cdot225 - 1/0\cdot25) = $	$2,400\cdot00\text{Ffr}$
Purchases, 2nd half:	$-\$2,850(1/0\cdot225 - 1/0\cdot25) = $	$-1,266\cdot67\text{Ffr}$
SGA expenses, 2nd half:	$-\$900(1/0\cdot225 - 1/0\cdot25) = $	$-400\cdot00\text{Ffr}$
U.S.$ interest payment:	$-\$200(1/0\cdot225 - 1/0\cdot25) = $	$-88\cdot89\text{Ffr}$
U.S. tax payments:	$-\$1,315\cdot2(1/0\cdot225 - 1/0\cdot25) = $	$-584\cdot53\text{Ffr}$
Total transactions gain:	$\$134\cdot8(1/0\cdot225 - 1/0\cdot25) = $	$59\cdot91\text{Ffr}$

   C. Cash balance changes due to changes in operations

Variation of sales collections:	$(\$5,400 - \$5,400)(1/0\cdot25) = $	$0\cdot00\text{Ffr}$
Variation of purchases:	$-(\$2,850 - \$3,000)(1/0\cdot25) = $	$600\cdot00\text{Ffr}$
Variation of taxes:	$-(\$1,315\cdot2 - \$1,248)(1/0\cdot25) = $	$-268\cdot80\text{Ffr}$
Total operation gain:	$\$82\cdot8(1/0\cdot25) = $	$331\cdot20\text{Ffr}$

   D. Reconciliation: $933\cdot33 + 59\cdot91 + 331\cdot20 = $ $1,324\cdot44\text{Fr}$

C. Further implications of the definition and of the example

Whatever the quantity chosen as the target to be protected by hedging, the management of total exposure depends on forecasts which take the economic determinants of the firm's future position into account. Our simplified example points to some of these: the extent of the firm's international activities; the price elasticity of demand for its products; competitors' reactions to its pricing decisions; the variable-fixed cost structure; and the currency composition of its nominal assets and liabilities. If global exposure, however measured, depends on such factors so also must the component exposures. Economic exposure, in this view, is not something which can be identified separately. This is the result of linking all exposed quantities to future values at a point in time.

More important, we have been able to conduct the entire discussion so far without reference to the exposure of individual assets or the need for any distinction between the degrees of exposure of physical and nominal assets. To be sure, the notion that only monetary assets are exposed underlies the construction of the FASB-8 translation exposure. But a different accounting convention could just as easily have been accommodated. It is clear both in our choice of objective and from the example that exposure, if it is relevant of all, is a matter of the *sensitivity of the firm as a whole to exchange rate changes*. It cannot be measured by summing up the individual exposures of the various physical and nominal assets and liabilities. To do so would be to ignore the firm's own future decisions which, the example shows, must be taken into account.

To adopt an exposure definition based on the value of the firm as a whole implies that all the firm's nominal and physical assets, liabilities and activities may well be exposed. Even if the assets and liabilities are not the firm may be. These points enable us to confront two academic arguments which have appeared recently.[20]

---

[20] See R. Z. Aliber and C. P. Stickney, "Accounting Measures of Foreign Exchange Exposure: the Long and Short of It", *The Accounting Review*, January 1975. Their arguments are repeated in I. Giddy, "Exchange Risk: Whose View?", *Financial Management*, Summer 1977. See also, H. E. Wyman, *op. cit.*

The first is that if the law of one price, i.e. purchasing power parity (PPP) prevails, changes in exchange rates offset changes in the local prices of physical assets. The latter, it is asserted, are therefore not exposed. However, the fact that a physical good has the same price everywhere as soon as a common numeraire is used *merely implies that its exposure is the same wherever it is located, not that it is zero.* Even if the foreign currency price of a physical asset located abroad, translated at the current exchange rate, is always equal to the reference currency price of an identical asset located at home, the asset will be exposed if the latter price changes when the exchange rate varies. Physical assets are unexposed under FASB–8 simply because they are arbitrarily posted at their foreign-currency acquisition cost and translated at the historical exchange rate: their reference-currency values therefore remain constant. In general, reference currency prices are not independent of exchange rates.[21] Whether one does anything about it or not physical assets are exposed.

The second is that if the Fisher relation holds, long term nominal assets such as foreign bonds will not be exposed. According to the Fisher relation, interest rates and exchange rates are inversely linked. Nominal assets dominated in a currency which the market expects to devalue must offer, by way of compensation, a higher nominal yield. The argument is then that long term nominal assets are not exposed because successive exchange rate variations will be compensated by simultaneous interest rate changes leaving the bearer (issuer) indifferent to the denomination of the asset (liability). This can only be the case, however, when the market perfectly anticipates the exchange rate change, i.e. under certainty, where there is no risk at all and therefore no risk exposure. Once exchange rates are uncertain they cannot be perfectly compensated by interest rates which are pre-specified in advance. The investor gets the contractual yield plus the capital gain or loss and in addition bears exchange risk, that is, unexpected reference-currency price variation due to a deviation of the exchange rate from its anticipated level. There is no reason to suppose that the net yield to maturity will be independent of the exchange rate. Nominal assets are generally exposed.[22]

Finally, practitioners have argued that, although physical and nominal assets may be exposed, these exposures can be ignored because deviations of exchange rates around purchasing power parity or interest rate parity seem to average to zero in the long run. If so, the story goes, the cumulative sum of exchange gains and losses should also equal zero over time. This argument, we think, is wrong. If hedging exchange risk is irrelevant, the reasons are different and have been discussed in Part 2. None has anything to do with the frequency distribution of exchange rate changes. The issue is only whether a firm can maximize its value or, better, reduce its probability of default over a sequence of future dates using one hedge for each date. The average exposure over time cannot condition these hedging decisions in any way. A firm with a zero probability of default can choose to take financial risks which do not raise that probability without reference to any exposure concept, average or otherwise.

5. Implementation: simulation and optimization

Implementation takes place in two stages: first simulation and then, possibly optimization. While the numerical example of the previous section was kept simple, simulation allows the greater complexity of the circumstances of individual firms to be incorporated.[23] The method is capable of wide application. The steps in the simulation stage are as follows:

A1. Specify a number of scenarios, i.e. future states of nature. Each scenario should be consistent with a value of each exchange rate and of other key economic variables which will affect the value of the firm in that state at the given target date or dates.

A2. For each scenario, calculate the end-of-period book value of the firm's net worth in that state. The result of the analysis will be a state-by-state distribution of these book values and the associated levels of each exchange rate and other key variables.

---

[21] Technically, it is relative prices, i.e. the price of one good relative to the prices of others in the same location, which have to be independent of the exchange rate for exposure to be zero. This is almost never the case. Thus, in our example, the Ffr devaluation was accompanied by a change in the relative prices of traded goods in France: the dollar price of the firm's good was held constant while the Ffr price of substitute goods made in France were equally unchanged. Consequently, sales to France, production and profits were all reduced. In principle, the value of the subsidiary's productive physical assets in the U.S. should also be affected and, by that token, partly exposed.

[22] Long term bonds may not, however, be 100% exposed. It all depends on the expectations formation processes which determine successive bond prices, see M. Adler and B. Dumas, "Exchange Risk, Exposure and the Relevance of Hedging," unpublished, 1978.

[23] A lead in the application of this technique was supplied by Gordon Donaldson, "New Framework for Corporate Debt Policy," *Harvard Business Review,* March–April, 1962. See also, F. S. Hillier, "The Derivation of Probablistic Information for the Evaluation of Risky Investments," *Management Science,* April 1963.

The simulation provides the basic data. One then has an option between two strategies: complete protection or a balancing of risk against return by diversification. We take each in turn.

B1. To identify exposure, establish the statistical link between the firm's net book value, the exchange rates and other variables by multiple regression. The regression coefficients of the exchange rates can be identified as the firm's exposures to each currency. Provided that the firm's value varies linearly with the exchange rates, these coefficients represent the amounts of the forward contracts that will render the value independent of the exchange rates. A different regression is required for each target date.

B2. There is no reason to suppose that a policy of covering all exposures will be optimal. It should be compared to the alternative of diversification.[24]

C1. From the simulation, calculate the expected net book value of the firm without forward cover and its variance. The objective is to discover the combinations of forward contracts in each currency which produce the highest expected value for a given variance or which minimize the variance for a given expected net worth.

C2. Experiment with various levels of forward cover. The book value of equity in each scenario will vary proportionally with the amount of the contract. Hence the expected net worth will vary linearly and its variance quadratically with the forward contract amounts.

C3. Use available quadratic programming techniques to compute the dominant strategies, i.e. the combinations of exposures and forward cover which minimize the variance at alternative levels of expected net worth. Additional (linear) constraints reflecting a firm's individual circumstances can be incorporated.

C4. Present the results in a form suitable for managerial review. For each combination of forward covers selected by the optimization programme tabulate: the expected net book value, its maximum and its minimum. As the expected value increases, so also will the spread between the two extremes.

D1. These options should be compared among themselves and with the alternative of complete cover (B1). The final choice can be made according to the treasurer's preferences.

Owing to the reporting requirements of FASB–8, many treasurers apparently feel impelled to choose a strategy corresponding to the most pessimistic scenario so as to reduce the likelihood of having to report translation losses. It is certainly possible to devise a simulation and optimization programme directed only at translation or accounting exposure. The method proposed in Part 4, however, is based on an analysis of the variations not in translation gains or losses but in net worth. A firm following a hedging strategy linked to this objective may well end up reporting significant FASB–8 exchange gains and losses. But these will be offset by losses and gains in other accounts. And, to reiterate, their appearance in financial statements apparently produces little additional variability in stock prices.

---

[24] The technique summarized below is well established. See, B. Lietaer, *Financial Management of Foreign Exchange: An Operational Technique to Reduce Risk,* (Cambridge, Mass., M.I.T. Press, 1971). For a simplified application, see also, H.C. Blackie, "The Choice of Currencies in Portfolio Management, *Euromoney,* December 1978.

CHAPTER VII

Conflicts in exposure management

A. Conflicts between income, cash and FASB-8

Corporations with overseas subsidiaries may have to make their decisions about exposures *after* a currency realignment has become probable, or foreign exchange controls have already been instituted. Because of such developments the corporation may not be able to restructure the subsidiary's balance sheet through local currency borrowing, investing in local currency assets, lead and/or lag payments or the repatriation of capital. The only timely action left may be hedging via the forward currency market. This, like any other exposure management technique, has its costs.

The cash, income and FASB-8 impact will vary according to whether the company decides not to hedge, to hedge on a before-tax basis or to hedge on an after-tax basis. Each of these strategies (if the hedge is properly structured) will minimize the impact of exchange rate fluctuations on *one* of the three variables (cash, net income or FASB-8 gain/loss) regardless of what happens to the future exchange rate, but will at the same time exacerbate the impact on the other two variables.

These conflicts are inherent in exposure management via the forward markets. We are analyzing them with emphasis on three variables: net reported income, FASB-8 gain/loss and cash flows. Each of these is analyzed both before and after tax, with emphasis on after-tax results.

The accounting treatment and cash impact—before and after tax—of a foreign exchange exposure and an offsetting hedge contract (when appropriate) are discussed in connection with a specific example with the following assumptions:

- A U.S. multinational company's subsidiary in country A has a net liability exposure of 1,000 local currency units (LC) on December 31, 19X0. This exposure remains unchanged throughout the accounting period. The translation rate on December 31, 19X0 is LC 1·00 = $1·00. The tax rate for the U.S. parent is 40%.
- On December 31, 19X0, the U.S. parent projects a substantial appreciation of the local currency over the next year.
- The exchange rate on December 31, 19X1 is LC 1·00 = $1·15.

The corporation has three courses of action available, depending on its objectives: (1) do nothing, (2) hedge on a before-tax basis, and, (3) hedge on an after-tax basis.

1. Deciding not to hedge

A company may be reluctant to risk cash to protect itself against a possible accounting valuation loss. In our example, the company decides not to hedge its net exposed liability of LC 1,000. Subsequently, as the exchange rate appreciates from LC 1·00 = $1·00 to LC 1·00 = $1·15 the translated value of that liability increases from $1,000 to $1,150, resulting in FASB-8 translation loss of $150 (see Exhibit 1). This loss is not tax deductible in the foreign country and is assumed not to reduce taxes in the United States. Consequently, the impact on net after-tax income is the same as the reported FASB-8 loss.

The foreign exchange loss in this example is thus determined solely by the spot exchange rate at the end of the accounting period.[1] It is a function of the exchange rate at maturity, as indicated in Chart 1. For instance, should the exchange rate depreciate to LC 1 = $0·90, the translation gain would be $100 (LC 1,000 × $1·00 − LC 1,000 × $0·90).

No immediate cash flow results. Yet, as the local currency liability has increased in dollar value, a potential loss does occur, in that, if the *parent company* decided to liquidate the net liability, it would have an outlay of $1,150 instead of $1,000. In this event the repayment of the local currency liability at a higher exchange rate may force the parent company to retain funds (reduce dividends),

---

[1] See paragraph 25 of FASB-8, for details refer to Chapter IV, Section A.

Exhibit 1—Subsidiary's balance sheet exposure and FASB-8 impact

		31/12/X0	31/12/X1
(1)	(Short) position	LC (1,000)	LC (1,000)
(2)	FX rate	$1·00/LC	$1·15/LC
(3)	Translated value	$(1,000)	$(1,150)
(4)	FASB-8 gain/loss		$(150)

or obtain additional funds (borrow) or generate additional revenues (raise prices) or a combination of the three.

2. Before-tax hedge

The company may be concerned about the reported FASB-8 (before-tax) gain or loss. It is willing to risk cash in order to minimize the FASB-8 impact. The parent thus purchases forward LC 1,000 at $1·05.

As Exhibit 2 shows, the FASB-8 loss resulting from the balance sheet position is the same as in the first example, i.e. $150 (line four). On the forward contract data, the FASB-8 gain is computed in accordance with FASB-8 and amounts to $150 (line eight). Hence, in this example, the foreign exchange loss on the exposed net liability is offset exactly by the foreign exchange gain on the forward contract. This is because the FX gains and losses on both—the balance sheet exposure and the forward contract—are computed on the spot-to-spot basis. As line nine shows, the total reported FASB-8 result in this case would be zero and this is true regardless of what happens to the exchange rate on December 31, 19X1.

Exhibit 2—Before-tax hedge: FASB-8 impact

Balance sheet exposure

		31/12/X0	31/12/X1
(1)	(Short) position	LC (1,000)	LC (1,000)
(2)	FX rate	$1·00/LC	$1·15/LC
(3)	Translated value	$(1,000)	$(1,150)
(4)	FASB-8 loss		$(150)

Forward hedge contract

		31/12/X0	31/12/X1
(5)	Amount bought forward	LC 1,000	LC 1,000
(6)	FX rate	$1·00/LC	$1·15/LC
(7)	Translated value	$1,000	$1,150
(8)	FASB-8 gain		$150

Consolidated

(9)	FASB-8 gain/loss (lines 4 + 8)	0

Although the company has accomplished its objective of eliminating the FASB-8 gain/loss by covering, it has affected its cash flow and net income. As Exhibit 3 indicates, *net after-tax income* has declined by $90. This is the sum of the FASB-8 loss of $150 on the net exposed liability to LC 1,000, the FASB-8 gain of $150 on the forward contract, the premium expense on the contract of $50, and the tax impact of the latter two (−$60 + $20). Cash flows are another consideration. In this situation the after-tax *cash inflow* resulting from closing the forward contract at maturity is computed by multiplying the amount of local currency bought by the difference in the contract rate ($1·05) and the spot at maturity ($1·15). This gain is taxable in our example at the rate of 40%.[2]

It is worth noting that, in the case of a before-tax cover, the decrease in the net income is smaller than in the case of an open position. This smaller decrease is further accompanied by a cash inflow of $60. This positive impact of a before-tax cover, however, should not be interpreted as if a before-tax cover automatically has a good effect on earnings and cash flows. As Chart 2 indicates,

---

[2] The cash impact can be computed also by adding the FASB-8 gain on the contract and the premium expense, both before and after-tax. In our example the contract gain is $90 and the premium expense $30, i.e. net cash inflow of $60.

Exhibit 3—Before-tax hedge: income and cash impact

Income impact

Balance sheet loss	$(150)
FX gain on contract	150
FASB-8 gain/loss	0
Tax expense (contract)	(60)
FASB-8 gain/loss less tax effect	(60)
Premium expense	(50)
Tax credit (premium)	20
Net income after tax	(90)

Cash flows

Purchase of local currency	$(1,050)
Sale of local currency	1,150
Cash flow—before tax	100
Net tax provision	(40)
Cash flow—after tax	$60

whereas earnings fluctuations have been reduced considerably (and the FASB-8 loss eliminated), cash costs may be significant. Should the spot at maturity fall anywhere below $1·05, cash outflows would result. For instance, should the currency move against the hedger's expectations and spot at maturity reach $0·80, the cash cost of eliminating the FASB-8 loss and reducing net income fluctuations would be $150.

3. After-tax hedge

The parent company may be concerned about the FASB-8 gain or loss adjusted for tax effects. It is willing to risk cash to minimize the after-tax impact of foreign exchange fluctuations (EPS impact) on the corporate entity. The parent thus buys forward LC 1,666·67—LC exposure divided by (one minus the tax rate)—at $1·05.

Exhibit 4—After-tax hedge: FASB-8 impact adjusted for tax effects

Balance sheet exposure

	31/12/X0	31/12/X1
(1) (Short) position	LC (1,000)	LC (1,000)
(2) FX rate	$1·00/LC	$1·15/LC
(3) Translated value	$(1,000)	$(1,150)
(4) FASB-8 loss		$(150)

Forward contract

	31/12/X0	31/12/X1
(5) Amount bought forward	LC 1,667	LC 1,667
(6) FX rate	$1·00/LC	$1·15/LC
(7) Translated value	$1,667	$1,917
(8) FASB-8 gain on contract		$250
(9) Tax on contract gain (40%)		$(100)
(10) FX gain on contract less tax effect		$150

Consolidated

(11) FASB-8 gain/loss adjusted for tax effects (lines 4 + 10)	0
(12) FASB-8 gain/loss (lines 4 + 8)	$100

Exhibit 4 shows the balance sheet data remaining the same, resulting in an FASB-8 loss of $150. The forward contract data (lines 5 to 10) differ in that the larger amount of LC purchased forward (LC 1,666·67) results in a larger FASB-8 gain, i.e. $250. In addition, the tax impact of the forward contract is shown, as the objective this time is to eliminate the after-tax impact (excluding premium

161

expense) of foreign exchange fluctuations. Hence, the FASB-8 gain of $250 on the contract is reduced by a tax expense of $100, resulting in an after-tax FASB-8 gain on the contract of $150. This gain thus offsets the loss of $150 (not taxable) on the balance sheet, resulting in a net FASB-8 gain/loss which exactly offsets the tax effects (line 11).

However, in this situation as FASB-8 gain of $100 will be reported (sum of FASB-8 gain of $250 on the contract and loss of $150 on the balance sheet liability), as FASB-8 gain/loss is reported on a before-tax basis.

Exhibit 5—After-tax hedge: income and cash impact

Income impact

Balance sheet loss	$(150)
FX gain on contract	250
FASB-8 gain	100
Tax expense (contract)	(100)
FASB-8 gain/loss adjusted for tax effects	0
Premium expense	(83)
Tax credit (premium)	33
Net income after tax	(50)

Cash flows

Sale of local currency	$1,917
Purchase of local currency	(1,750)
Cash flow before tax	167
Net tax provision	(67)
Net cash flow after tax	$100

The after-tax hedge implications are further analyzed in Exhibit 5. It is worth noting that, inasmuch as the FASB-8 gain/loss adjusted for tax effects has been fixed at zero, so has the net after-tax income been fixed at a negative $50. This is illustrated in Chart 3, where the net after-tax income remains at a loss of $50 regardless of what happens to the future spot.

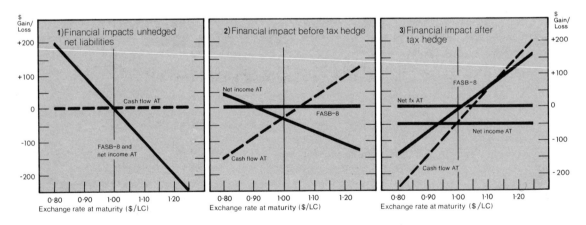

The potential cash flows resulting from the closing of the forward contract may be significant with an after-tax hedge. They are larger than with a before-tax cover, because the amount purchased forward is larger. Indeed, the higher the tax rate on the forward contract gain/loss, the larger is the amount of the after-tax cover and the potential cash flow resulting from the closing of the forward contract.

Any corporation considering this strategy should examine its willingness to manage its position actively. If the outlook for a currency should change completely from appreciation to depreciation—a real possibility in today's world—then one should consider reversing the cover, so limiting cash losses. This runs counter to the desire often expressed by corporate treasurers to square their positions and to match their risks.

162

Using the data presented above, FASB-8 gain/loss is likely to fluctuate most with no cover and least (theoretically) with before-tax cover (see Chart 4).

The net after-tax income impact, as in the case of FASB-8 gain/loss, is most volatile again with no cover (the two impacts are identical with no cover); before-tax cover decreases the volatility of net after-tax income; and, an after-tax cover decreases the volatility to zero. As mentioned above, in the latter case, the impact is fixed at the time the contract is entered into by the premium/discount expense/income (see Chart 5).

Finally, the cash flows are bound to be most significant with an after-tax cover, smaller with a before-tax cover and none with an unhedged position (see Chart 6).

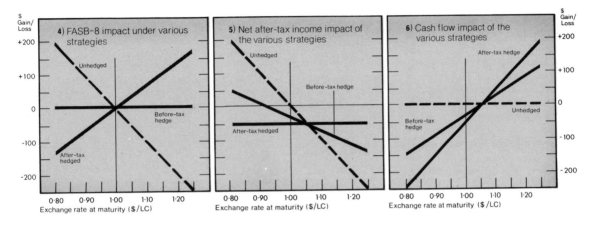

In the final analysis, a corporation can select an appropriate strategy depending on its objectives and its attitude toward risk. Should the objective be minimizing net income fluctuations, its earnings per share impact, it may be appropriate to cover on an after-tax basis if the cost in terms of premium/discount is acceptable. The cash costs of such strategies, however, may be significant. On the other hand, should the objective be minimizing cash outlays at the expense of EPS fluctuations, the appropriate strategy would be to stay open. Finally, if fluctuations of FASB-8 gains/losses are to be minimized, a before-tax cover will result in zero FASB-8 gain/loss regardless of the exchange rate on December 31, 19X1. The potential cash costs of this strategy are likely to be smaller than with an after-tax cover, but larger than with an unhedged position.

B. Subsidiary *vs.* consolidated entity: intercompany transactions

Intercompany flows may be hedged in a number of ways. But each achieves different objectives and may produce dramatically different and conflicting results for the subsidiary, parent and consolidated entities. How the corporation resolves these conflicts depends on the corporate objectives which, in turn, determine the organizational structure of the international treasury function. If emphasis is placed on smoothing the earnings-per-share reported in the consolidated quarterly statements, then the treasury function is likely to be centralized and corporate hedging of after-tax currency risks will be emphasized. If emphasis is placed on the financial performance of overseas operating divisions, then the treasury function is more likely to be decentralized and hedging by the overseas subsidiaries in local currency terms will be emphasized.

Throughout this chapter we examine the financial impact within the context of a single example. The example assumes that a subsidiary has on its books an intercompany payable of PC 10,000 to the parent on December 31, 19X0. It further assumes that the exchange rate between the local currency and parent currency is at par at the beginning of the exposure period, and that the LC devalues by 10% against the PC on March 31, 19X1. Finally, in order to simplify the presentation, we ignore premiums/discounts in the forward markets.

	Spot rate	3 months forward rate
31/12/X0	LC 1 = PC 1·0	LC 1·0 = PC 1·0
31/03/X1	LC 1 = PC 0·9	—

The exposures generated by the intercompany account and the related hedge are discussed strictly from an accounting point of view. First, they are discussed as if in a vacuum, without taking into consideration the asset financed by the payable. Second, they are analyzed in connection with financing of one type of asset. The analytical framework used in these situations may be used regardless of the type of asset financed.

1. No cover

In this case we assume that the corporation decides not to hedge the intercompany exposure at either the subsidiary or the consolidated level. Accordingly, gains or losses will be reported at the subsidiary and consolidated levels if the exchange rate between the local currency and parent currency changes during the exposure period. Given our assumptions of a 10% devaluation of the LC against the PC (i.e. PC revaluation of 11·11% against the LC) the relevant data is presented in Exhibit 1.

Exhibit 1—No cover

A. Subsidiary: exposure	31/12/X0	31/03/X1
(1) Exposure (PC)	(10,000)	(10,000)
(2) ER (LC/PC)	1·0	1·11111
(3) LC equivalent	(10,000)	(11,111·11)
(4) FX gain/(loss) B.T. (LC)		(1,111·11)
(5) Tax (40%)		444·44
(6) FX gain/(loss) A.T. (LC)		(666·67)

B. Consolidation after-tax: exposure		
(7) Exposure parent (PC)	10,000	10,000
(8) Exposure subsidiary (PC)	(10,000)	(10,000)
(9) Net consolidated (7) + (8)	0	0
(10) ER (PC/LC)	1·0	0·9
(11) PC equivalent of tax; lines (5) × (10)		400
(12) FX gain/(loss) A.T. lines (9) + (11)		400

Impact on subsidiary: As the parent currency appreciates against the local currency from LC 1·0 to LC 1·111, at maturity the subsidiary has to pay LC 11,111·11 instead of the original LC 10,000 to settle the intercompany transaction. The loss of LC 1,111·11 (line 4) results in a tax credit of LC 444·44 and an after-tax loss of LC 666·67 (line 6) for the subsidiary.

Consolidated after-tax impact: The subsidiary's tax credit of LC 444·44 is reflected in the consolidated books, yielding a consolidated after-tax gain of PC 400 (line 11). As indicated above this before tax exchange loss occurs only in local currency (line 4) and not in consolidation in dollars (line 9) whereas the reduction in the taxes of the subsidiary—assuming the credit can be used—is translated into dollars in consolidation.

Chart 1 presents the foreign exchange impact of this strategy graphically under various exchange rate assumptions, with the impact on subsidiary shown under item A and the impact on consolidation under item B.

Chart 1—No cover
A. Impact on subsidiary
B. After-tax consolidated impact

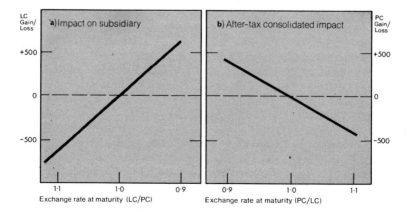

164

2. Decentralized hedge by subsidiary

As an alternative policy the corporation hedges the intercompany transaction at the subsidiary level. Anticipating an appreciating PC over the next quarter, on December 31, 19X0, the local manager buys PC 10,000 to cover the subsidiary's short exposure of the same amount. Given our assumption that the PC revalues by 11·11% on March 31, 19X1, the relevant data is presented in Exhibit 2.

Exhibit 2—Subsidiary's hedge

	31/12/X0	31/03/X1
A. Subsidiary: exposure		
(1) Exposure (PC)	(10,000)	(10,000)
(2) ER (LC/PC)	1·0	1·1111
(3) LC equivalent	(10,000)	(11,111·11)
(4) FX gain/(loss) B.T. (LC)		(1,111·11)
(5) Tax (40%)		444·44
(6) FX gain/(loss) A.T. (LC)		(666·67)
B. Subsidiary: forward contract		
(7) Amount bought (PC)	10,000	10,000
(8) LC equivalent; line (2) × (7)	10,000	11,111·11
(9) FX gain/(loss) B.T.		1,111·11
(10) Tax (40%)		(444·44)
(11) FX gain/(loss) A.T.		666·67
C. Subsidiary: combined data		
(12) FX gain/(loss) B.T.; line (4) + (9)		0
(13) FX gain/(loss) A.T.; (6) + (11)		0
D. Consolidation		
(14) Exposure (LC amount sold)	(10,000)	(10,000)
(15) ER (PC/LC)	1·0	0·9
(16) PC equivalent	(10,000)	(9,000)
(17) FX gain/(loss) B.T.* (9) × (15)		1,000
(18) Net income A.T.; line (13) + (17)		1,000

* FX gain of PC 1,000 is assumed not to be taxable.

Impact on subsidiary: By buying the parent currency forward, the local manager has eliminated the subsidiary's short transaction exposure in the parent currency. The loss on the PC payable is offset by a foreign exchange gain on the forward contract (lines 12 and 13). Accordingly, the subsidiary will report no foreign exchange gain or loss regardless of the exchange rate at maturity of the transaction, as illustrated in Chart 2-A.

Chart 2—Subsidiary's hedge
A. Impact on subsidiary
B. Impact on consolidation

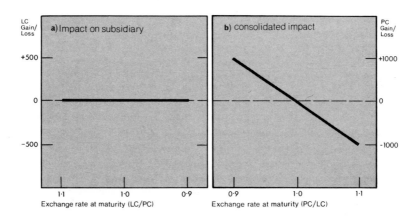

165

Consolidated after-tax impact: From the consolidated viewpoint, by buying PC forward the subsidiary simultaneously sold LC forward and thereby created a short exposure of LC 10,000 for the consolidated entity. This can be seen by tracing the effect of the forward contract. Before this contract there was no exposure in parent currency in the consolidated books of account as the PC receivable of the parent was offset by a PC payable of the subsidiary. The forward purchase of PC created an incremental short LC exposure in consolidation while eliminating the PC exposure at the subsidiary level. In the example this exposure will result in consolidated after-tax gains if the LC weakens against the PC, and losses of it strengthens, as illustrated in Chart 2-B.

3. Centralized hedge by parent company

An alternate to the subsidiary's hedge is the parent company hedge of the after-tax impact of intercompany flows. In our example, anticipating an appreciation of the local currency during the exposure period, on December 31, 19X0, the treasurer buys forward LC 6,666·67 to cover the subsidiary's tax exposure of LC 4,000.[3] The local currency, however, moves against his expectations, depreciating by 10% against the PC. This situation is presented in Exhibit 3.

Exhibit 3—Parent's after-tax hedge

	31/12/X0	31/03/X1
A. Subsidiary: exposure		
(1) Exposure (PC)	(10,000)	(10,000)
(2) ER (LC/PC)	1·0	1·1111
(3) LC equivalent	(10,000)	(11,111·11)
(4) FX gain/(loss) B.T.		(1,111·11)
(5) Tax (40%)		444·44
(6) FX gain/(loss) A.T.		(666·67)
B. Consolidation: exposure		
(7) Exposure (PC)—parent	10,000	10,000
(8) Exposure (PC)—subsidiary	(10,000)	(10,000)
(9) FX gain/(loss) B.T.		0
(10) ER (PC/LC)	1·0	0·9
(11) PC equivalent of tax; lines (5) × (10)		400
(12) FX gain/(loss) A.T.; (9) + (11)		400
C. Parent: forward contract		
(13) Amount bought (LC)	6,666·67	6,666·67
(14) PC equivalent; (10) × (13)	6,666·67	6,000
(15) FX gain/(loss) B.T.		(666·67)
(16) Tax (40%)		266·67
(17) FX gain/(loss) A.T.		(400)
D. Consolidation after-tax: exposure and contract		
(18) FX gain/(loss) B.T. (9) + (15)		(666·67)
(19) FX gain/(loss) A.T. (12) + (17)		0

Impact on subsidiary: The subsidiary's exposure data is analyzed in Section A of the exhibit. The subsidiary reports a before-tax loss of LC 1,111·11 and a tax credit of LC 444·44 (line 5), identical to the "no hedge" situation discussed above.

Consolidated after-tax impact: Again, as in the "no hedge" situation, the consolidated entity reports an after-tax gain of PC 400 (Section B), resulting from the translation of the increased tax credit of the subsidiary. The forward contract data is presented in Section C of the exhibit, and indicates an after-tax loss of PC 400 (line 17) for the parent. The after-tax gain on the exposure and the after-tax loss on the contract offset each other, and, as Section D indicates, the after-tax consolidated impact is zero (line 19). It will be zero regardless of the exchange rate at the maturity of the transaction, as illustrated in Chart 3-B.

---

[3] The tax exposure of LC 4,000 is computed in Chapter IV, Section D. The amount bought for after-tax cover = after-tax exposure of subsidiary/(1 − tax rate on forward contract) = LC 4,000/(1 − 0·4) = LC 6,666·67.

Chart 3—Parent's after-tax hedge
A. Impact on subsidiary
B. After-tax consolidated impact

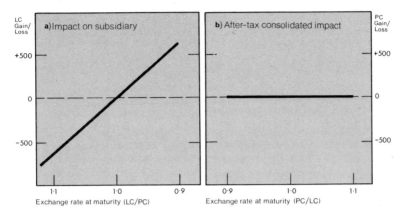

4. Co-ordinated hedge by parent and subsidiary

Each of the three strategies discussed above meets certain objectives and produces differing effects. The no hedge strategy leaves the subsidiary exposed on the transaction side and the consolidated entity from the after-tax perspective. The decentralized or subsidiary's hedge eliminates the subsidiary's transaction exposure, while, at the same time creating a short translation exposure for the consolidated entity. The centralized hedge, on the other hand, neutralizes the consolidated after-tax exposure; yet leaving the subsidiary's transaction exposure uncovered.

In the light of these imperfections, how should the corporate treasurer protect intercompany flows against foreign exchange fluctuations? A *co-ordinated hedge* may resolve the imperfections and conflicts identified above. Thus, in addition to the subsidiary's hedge of the transaction exposure (Part 2 above), the parent would cover the translation exposure of short LC 10,000 by purchasing local currency forward. This situation is presented on a pre-tax basis in Exhibit 4.

Exhibit 4—Co-ordinated hedge

A. Intercompany exposure
(1) Subsidiary: PC intercompany payable	(10,000)
(2) Parent: PC intercompany receivable	10,000
(3) Net intercompany exposure	0

B. Forward contract of subsidiary
(4) Subsidiary: PC amount bought	10,000
(5) Subsidiary: LC amount sold	(10,000)

C. Subsidiary's exposure
(6) Net exposure; (1) + (4)	0

D. Consolidated exposure
(7) Parent: amount bought	LC 10,000
(8) Parent: amount sold	(PC 10,000)
(9) Net consolidated exposure; lines (5) + (7)	0

With the two contracts in place, both entities have eliminated their exposures (lines 6 and 9) and any potential foreign exchange impact at the subsidiary and consolidated levels. Accordingly, from an *accounting point* of view, the company has achieved a perfect hedge, as illustrated in Chart 4.

5. Additional considerations

The above strategy implications must be qualified when applied to individual situations because of parent/subsidiary funding considerations. Stated differently, financing provided by the parent's receivable or loan may be used by the subsidiary to finance various types of assets. The exposure

167

Chart 4—Summary
A. Impact on subsidiary
B. After-tax consolidated impact

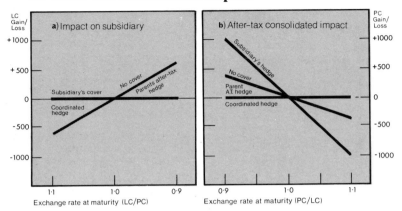

generated by these assets must, of course, be considered in tandem with the intercompany exposure. Assuming that the funds are used by the subsidiary to finance receivables denominated in local currency, the exposures and their impact are presented in Exhibit 5.

Exhibit 5—Financing of monetary asset denominated in LC

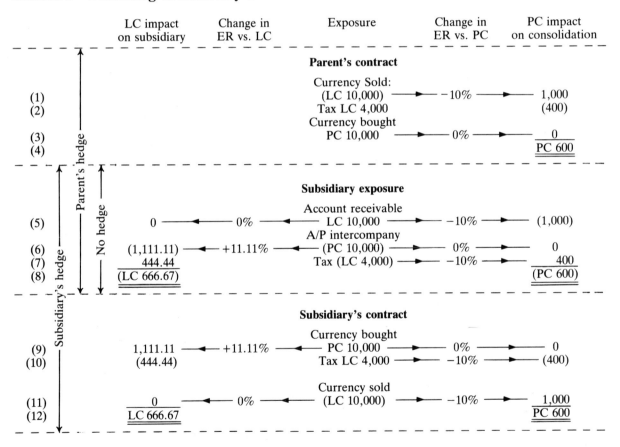

	LC impact on subsidiary	Change in ER vs. LC	Exposure	Change in ER vs. PC	PC impact on consolidation
			Parent's contract		
			Currency Sold:		
(1)			(LC 10,000) —— −10% ——		1,000
(2)			Tax LC 4,000		(400)
			Currency bought		
(3)			PC 10,000 —— 0% ——		0
(4)					PC 600
			Subsidiary exposure		
			Account receivable		
(5)	0 —— 0% ——		LC 10,000 —— −10% ——		(1,000)
			A/P intercompany		
(6)	(1,111.11) —— +11.11% ——		(PC 10,000) —— 0% ——		0
(7)	444.44		Tax (LC 4,000) —— −10% ——		400
(8)	(LC 666.67)				(PC 600)
			Subsidiary's contract		
			Currency bought		
(9)	1,111.11 —— +11.11% ——		PC 10,000 —— 0% ——		0
(10)	(444.44)		Tax LC 4,000 —— −10% ——		(400)
			Currency sold		
(11)	0 —— 0% ——		(LC 10,000) —— −10% ——		1,000
(12)	LC 666.67				PC 600

No hedge: If the receivable is denominated in local currency, the subsidiary is still short PC 10,000 before-tax (line 6) and would record a loss of LC 666·67 on an after-tax basis (line 8). The consolidated after-tax exposure is now the sum of the long translation exposure of LC 10,000 (line 5) and the short after-tax exposure of LC 4,000 (line 7). The after-tax consolidated impact is thus PC 600, as indicated by the middle panel and line 8.

Subsidiary's hedge of transaction exposure: Here, the subsidiary buys PC 10,000 (line 9) forward and

168

thereby eliminates its short transaction exposure of the same amount. From a consolidated point of view the short exposure of LC 10,000 on the contract is offset by the long balance sheet translation exposure of the same amount. The subsidiary's hedge has thus eliminated exposures at both levels. From a cash flow perspective, this can be seen as follows: at maturity of the contract, the subsidiary receives LC 10,000 delivers it for settlement of the contract for PC 10,000 which, in turn, it delivers to the parent company (see the two lower panels of the exhibit).

Parent's after-tax hedge: The parent company sells LC 10,000[4] (line 1) forward to cover its consolidated after-tax exposure of LC 6,000. In this situation, as the exhibit indicates, the translation loss of PC 1,000 and the tax credit of PC 400 (i.e. net loss of PC 600) are offset by the cash gain of PC 600 on the contract (line 4). The subsidiary's results are unaffected by the parent's hedge (see the two upper panels of the exhibit).

Co-ordinated hedge is inappropriate in this situation as the subsidiary's decentralized hedge is a perfect hedge for the consolidated entity as well as the subsidiary. In other words, the consolidated entity was originally long LC 10,000. When the subsidiary went short LC 10,000 (by buying PC 10,000 forward), it eliminated the consolidated LC exposure and concurrently offset the tax effect of the subsidiary's intercompany payable denominated in the parent currency. If—in addition to the subsidiary's purchase of PC 10,000—the parent bought or sold LC, it would generate exposures for itself. On the other hand, if—in addition to the parent's after-tax hedge—the subsidiary bought PC 10,000 to cover its exposure of PC 10,000 it would generate an additional exposure for the consolidated entity.

C. Subsidiary *vs.* consolidated entity: third party transactions

Foreign subsidiaries' currency exposures may be offset in the forward markets in a number of ways. The manner in which the exposure is hedged usually depends primarily on corporate objectives, and those objectives largely determine the organizational structure of the international treasury function. For instance, if the corporate objective is to reduce earnings-per-share (EPS) fluctuations, the corporate (parent) treasury would probably be responsible for offsetting the after-tax impact of currency fluctuations as reported upon consolidation. The exposure management function in this case should be centralized. If, on the other hand, the corporate objective is to expedite the evaluation of overseas performance, the local managers should be permitted to hedge foreign exchange risks of subsidiaries as measured in local currency terms. In that case the exposure management function would be decentralized. Finally, if the corporation wishes to achieve both objectives, only a co-ordinated approach to exposure management will both reduce EPS fluctuations and expedite evaluation of overseas performance.

It should be noted that only the accounting impact is dealt with here and the cash flow impact is not evaluated. This section discusses the hedging options open to a corporation with regard to its subsidiary's transactions *vis-à-vis* third parties denominated in third currencies. Within this context we compare the impact of four alternative strategies: (1) no hedge; (2) decentralized hedge, i.e. subsidiary's hedge of transaction exposure; (3) centralized hedge, i.e. parent's after-tax hedge of consolidated after-tax exposure; and (4) co-ordinated hedge, i.e. subsidiary's hedge of transaction exposure in tandem with parent's hedge of translation exposure.

Throughout the section we use an example of a £10,000 exposure on the books of a German subsidiary owned by a U.S. parent. We assume that all foreign exchange gains or losses in Germany are taxed at the rate of 40%, and to further simplify the presentation we ignore premiums and discounts in the forward markets. The authors believe all the hedges discussed herein are Paragraph 25 hedges under FASB-8. The exchange rate assumptions used are identical throughout and are as follows:

Exchange rate assumptions

Exchange rate on 31/12/X0: £1 = DM 3 = $1·5
Exchange rate on 31/03/X1:

Translation rate ($/DM)	Transaction rate (DM/£)		
	Weak £: DM 2·9	Stable £: DM 3·0	Strong £: DM 3·1
Weak DM: $0·45	£1 = $1·305	£1 = $1·35	£1 = $1·395
Stable DM: $0·5	£1 = $1·45	£1 = $1·5	£1 = $1·55
Strong DM: $0·55	£1 = $1·595	£1 = $1·65	£1 = $1·705

---

[4] The amount of after-tax hedge is computed as follows:

$$\text{After-tax hedge} = \frac{\text{LC } 6{,}000}{1-t} = \frac{\text{LC } 6{,}000}{0·6} = \underline{\underline{\text{LC } 10{,}000}}$$

These nine scenarios are represented graphically in Charts 1–5. Exhibits 1–5, however, present only the weak sterling/weak DM possibility as an example. The approach in the exhibits can be used for the other eight scenarios.

1. No hedge

In many cases, a company recognizes that it may incur foreign exchange losses and yet it may be reluctant to go into the foreign exchange market to cover exposed positions. Accordingly, in the following example neither the subsidiary nor the parent hedges the net exposed asset of £10,000 on the subsidiary's books. Subsequently, as the exchange rates (between sterling and the mark and sterling and the dollar) change, the subsidiary, the consolidated entity or both may report a foreign exchange impact, depending on the movements in the respective cross-rates. Assuming a decline of sterling from DM 3·0 to DM 2·9 and from $1·5 to $1·305 the relevant data is presented in Exhibit 1.

Exhibit 1—No hedge

A. Subsidiary	31/12/X0	31/03/X1
(1) Exposure (£)	10,000	10,000
(2) ER (DM/£)	3·0	2·9
(3) DM equivalent	30,000	29,000
(4) FX gain/(loss); B.T.		(1,000)
(5) Tax (40%)		400
(6) FX gain/(loss); A.T.		(600)

B. Consolidation		
(7) Exposure (£)	10,000	10,000
(8) ER ($/£)	1·5	1·305
(9) $ equivalent	15,000	13,050
(10) FX gain/(loss); B.T.		(1,950)
(11) ER ($/DM)		0·45
(12) $ equivalent of tax; (5) × (11)		180
(13) FX gain/(loss); A.T. (10) + (12)		(1,770)

Impact on subsidiary: From the subsidiary's viewpoint, as sterling depreciates by 3·33% against the mark, the receivable is now worth DM 29,000, resulting in a foreign exchange loss of DM 1,000 for the subsidiary (line 4). This loss is assumed to be tax deductible from German income producing an after-tax loss of DM 600 (line 6).

Consolidated impact: From the consolidated viewpoint, as sterling depreciates by 13% against the dollar, the receivable is now worth $13,050 resulting in a translation loss of $1,950 (line 10), which is assumed not to be tax deductible from U.S. income. The subsidiary's tax credit, however, is translated (in our case at the closing rate of $0·45) and consolidated and, added to the translation loss of $1,950, yields an after-tax consolidated loss of $1,770 (line 13).

After-tax exposure computations: Given the 40% tax rate in Germany, from a consolidated after-tax viewpoint 40% of the receivable is exposed to the $/DM exchange rate while the remaining 60% is exposed to the $/£ rate. This is because 40% of the subsidiary's loss constitutes a tax event in DM terms and will result in a tax payable or receivable in marks. The remaining 60% of the receivable maintains its sterling value from the consolidated point of view. Accordingly, the after-tax exposures and the related gains or losses in our example are computed as follows:

Exposure	ER ($/DM)	$ Before-tax equivalent	1 − tax rate	$ Equivalent after-tax	Change in ER ($/DM)	$ gain/loss
(1) DM 30,000	0·5	15,000	1	15,000		
(2) (DM 30,000)	0·5	(15,000)	0·6	(9,000)		
(3) DM tax exposure (40% of exposure)				6,000	−10%	(600)

Exposure	ER ($/£)	$ equivalent	1 − tax rate	$ after-tax	Change in ER ($/£)	
(4) £10,000	1·5	15,000	0·6	9,000		
(5) £ after-tax exposure (60% of exposure)				9,000	−13%	(1,170)
(6) Total after-tax impact						(1,770)

The net after-tax impact of negative $1,770 computed above (line 6) is identical to the after-tax loss shown in Exhibit 1 (line 13) under the weak DM/weak £ scenario. It can be interpreted as follows: if the receivable of £10,000 had been collected by the subsidiary on March 31, 19X1 and had been immediately remitted to the parent, it would have been worth $13,230 (*vs.* $15,000 on December 31, 19X0) in the consolidation; this value is the sum of the value of the receivable—$13,050 (£10,000 × $1·305)—and the dollar equivalent of the tax credit received by the subsidiary, i.e. $180 (DM 400 × $0·45). The outcome of the other exchange rate scenarios is presented graphically in Chart 1.

Chart 1—No hedge
(a) Impact on subsidiary (b) Consolidated impact ($/DM rate) (c) Consolidated impact ($/£ rate)

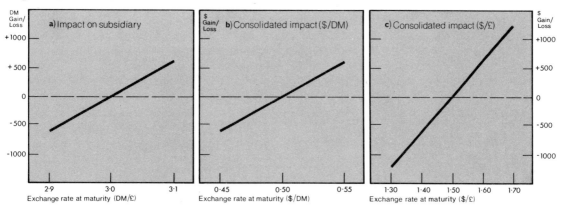

2. Decentralized hedge: subsidiary's hedge

In this situation the company's exposure management function is decentralized and the local manager is responsible for the subsidiary's net income after foreign exchange gains or losses. Accordingly, he has the authority to take cover at the subsidiary level in order to minimize foreign exchange losses of the subsidiary. In the following example, anticipating a depreciation of sterling against the mark, the local manager covers the subsidiary's transaction exposure of £10,000 by selling £10,000 against the mark. The impact of this strategy is summarized below and presented in more detail in Exhibit 2.

Exhibit 2—Decentralized hedge

	31/12/X0	31/03/X1
A. Subsidiary: exposure		
(1) Exposure (£)	10,000	10,000
(2) ER (DM/£)	3·0	2·9
(3) DM equivalent	30,000	29,000
(4) FX gain/(loss); B.T.		(1,000)
(5) Tax (40%)		400
(6) FX gain/(loss); A.T.		(600)
B. Subsidiary: forward contract		
(7) Amount sold (£)	(10,000)	(10,000)
(8) DM equivalent; (2) × (7)	(30,000)	(29,000)
(9) FX gain/(loss); B.T.		1,000
(10) Tax (40%)		(400)
(11) FX gain/(loss); A.T.		600
C. Subsidiary: net		
(12) FX gain/(loss); B.T. (4) + (9)		0
(13) FX gain/(loss); A.T. (6) + (11)		0
D. Consolidation		
(14) Exposure (DM)	30,000	30,000
(15) ER ($/DM)	0·5	0·45
(16) $ equivalent	15,000	13,500
(17) FX gain/(loss)		(1,500)

Impact on subsidiary: By selling sterling against the mark in the forward market, the local manager has eliminated the subsidiary's transaction exposure and the potential foreign exchange loss of DM 600 as follows:

- Exposure data (Section A)   FX loss A.T. (DM 600)
- Forward contract data (Section B)   FX gain A.T. <u>DM 600</u>

- Net foreign exchange impact (Section C)   <u>DM   0</u>

With a decentralized hedge, the subsidiary will report no foreign exchange gain or loss regardless of the DM/£ cross-rate at the maturity of the transactions. This is illustrated graphically in Chart 2(a).

Chart 2—Decentralized hedge
(a) Impact on subsidiary (b) Consolidated impact ($/DM rate) (c) Consolidated impact ($/£ rate)

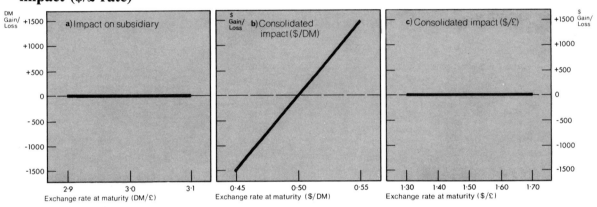

Consolidated impact: By selling sterling against marks the local manager has eliminated the sterling (transaction) component of the exposure but fixed the mark (translation) component of exposure for the consolidated entity as follows:

- Transaction exposure   £10,000
- Forward contract
  - (a) £ sold   (£10,000)
  - (b) DM purchased   DM 30,000

Returning to Exhibit 2, the consolidated exposure data is presented in Section D and indicates that the exposure of DM 30,000 results in a foreign exchange loss of $1,500 (line 17) with the weak DM assumption. A strong mark would result in a translation gain, for the consolidated entity, as illustrated in Chart 2(b). Finally, Chart 2(c) indicates that the dollar/sterling rate is irrelevant in this situation, as the pound exposure has been eliminated by the subsidiary's hedge.

3. Centralized hedge: parent's after-tax hedge

In this instance, the company is concerned about the consolidated foreign exchange impact adjusted for tax effects. Accordingly, the exposure management function is centralized at the company's headquarters with the objective of minimizing after-tax impact of foreign exchange fluctuations (EPS impact) on the corporate entity.

Forecasting declines of both the mark and sterling against the dollar, to cover after-tax exposures the global manager sells DM 17,142·86 and £8,571·43 against the dollar. Assuming a U.S. tax rate of 30% on gains/losses on forward contracts, the after-tax exposures and appropriate amounts of hedges are computed as follows:

- DM tax exposure = DM exposure × German tax rate on FX gain/loss = DM 30,000 × 0·4 = <u>DM 12,000</u>
- Amount of DM after-tax hedge = DM tax exposure/(1 − tax rate on forward contract) = 12,000/(1 − 0·3) = <u>DM 17,142·86</u>
- £ after-tax exposure = £ exposure × (1 − German tax rate on FX gain/loss) = £10,000 × 0·6 = <u>£6,000</u>
- Amount of £ after-tax hedge = £ after-tax exposure/(1 − tax rate on forward contract) = 6,000/(1 − 0·3) = <u>£8,571·43</u>

172

Exhibit 3—Centralized hedge

	31/12/X0	31/03/X1
A. Subsidiary: exposure		
(1) Exposure (£)	10,000	10,000
(2) ER (DM/£)	3·0	2·9
(3) DM equivalent	30,000	29,000
(4) FX gain/(loss) B.T.		(1,000)
(5) Tax (40%)		400
(6) FX gain/(loss) A.T.		(600)
B. Parent: exposure		
(7) Exposure (£)	10,000	10,000
(8) ER ($/£)	1·5	1·305
(9) $ equivalent	15,000	13,050
(10) FX gain/(loss) B.T.		(1,950)
(11) ER ($/DM)	0·5	0·45
(12) $ equivalent of tax; (5) × (11)		180
(13) FX gain/(loss) A.T.; (10) + (12)		(1,770)
C. Parent: forward contract 1 (DM)		
(14) Amount sold (DM)	(17,142·86)	(17,142·86)
(15) $ equivalent; (14) × (11)	(8,571·43)	(7,714·29)
(16) FX gain/(loss) B.T.		857·14
(17) Tax (30%)		(257·14)
(18) FX gain/(loss) A.T.		600
D. Parent: forward contract 2 (£)		
(19) Amount sold (£)	(8,571·43)	(8,571·43)
(20) $ equivalent; (19) × (8)	(12,857·14)	(11,185·72)
(21) FX gain/(loss) B.T.		1,671·42
(22) Tax (30%)		(501·42)
(23) FX gain/(loss) A.T.		1,170
E. Consolidation		
(24) FX gain/(loss) B.T.; (10) + (16) + (21)		578·56
(25) FX gain/(loss) A.T.; (13) + (18) + (23)		0

Consolidated impact: The impact of the global manager's actions is summarized below and is presented in detail in Exhibit 3 as follows:

- After-tax loss on exposure (Section B) — ($1,770)
- DM forward contract gain A.T. (Section C) — 600
- £ forward contract gain A.T. (Section D) — 1,170
- Consolidated after-tax impact (Section E) — $ 0

Chart 3—Centralized hedge
(a) Impact on subsidiary (b) Consolidated impact ($/DM rate) (c) Consolidated impact ($/£ rate)

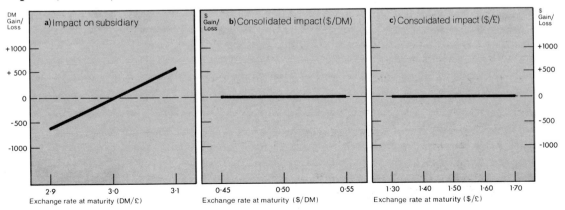

173

The global manager has succeeded in eliminating the consolidated after-tax exposure by forward sale of both DM and £ against the dollar and, accordingly, no consolidated after-tax foreign exchange gain/loss will be reported regardless of the dollar cross-rates against both pound and mark. This is illustrated in Charts 3(b) and (c).

Impact on subsidiary: The subsidiary's transaction exposure of £10,000 remains uncovered in this case and results in a loss of DM 600 for the subsidiary as shown in Section A and Chart 3(a).

4. Co-ordinated hedge: subsidiary's and parent's hedges

In this instance, the management is concerned about foreign exchange losses at all levels of the corporation. Accordingly, the company's exposure management function is characterized by a co-ordinated approach where each unit manages its own exposures. The global manager is thus responsible for the translation component of the exposure, while the local manager is responsible for the transaction component.

Assuming a co-ordinated hedge of the subsidiary's sterling exposure, a perfect cover is accomplished as follows. The local manager, concerned about a possible decline of sterling *vis-à-vis* the mark, sells £10,000 forward against the mark; at the same time, the global manager, aware of the German subsidiary's action, foresees a depreciation of the mark versus the dollar and sells forward DM 42,857·14 against the dollar. Amount of DM after-tax hedge = DM exposure/one minus tax rate on forward contract = DM 30,000/1 − 0·3 = DM 42,857·14. The impact of this strategy is summarized below and analyzed further in Exhibit 4.

Impact on subsidiary: By selling £10,000 forward, the local manager has eliminated the sterling component of the exposure and neutralized the subsidiary's potential after-tax loss of DM 600 as follows:

- FX loss on exposure (Section A)   (DM 600)
- FX gain on forward contract (Section B)   DM 600
- Combined impact (Section C)   DM   0

Consolidated impact: By selling DM 42,857·14 the global manager has neutralized the potential A.T. translation loss of $1,500 as follows:

- Loss on consolidated exposure (Section D)   ($1,500)
- Gain on forward contract A.T. (Section E) $1,500
- Net impact (Section F) $ 0

Chart 4—Co-ordinated hedge
(a) Impact on subsidiary (b) Consolidated impact ($/DM rate) (c) Consolidated impact ($/£ rate)

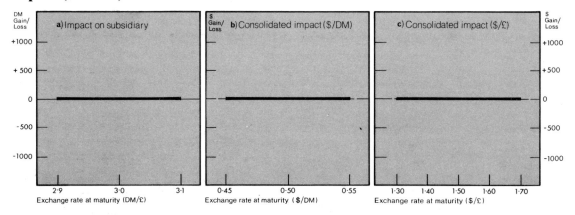

Chart 4 presents the situation graphically for both the subsidiary and the consolidated entity and indicates zero foreign exchange impact for either one regardless of cross-rate movements between the three currencies.

Exhibit 4—Co-ordinated hedge

	31/12/X0	31/03/X1
A. Subsidiary: exposure		
(1) Exposure (£)	10,000	10,000
(2) ER (DM/£)	3·0	2·9
(3) DM equivalent	30,000	29,000
(4) FX gain/(loss); B.T.		(1,000)
(5) Tax (40%)		400
(6) FX gain/(loss); A.T.		(600)
B. Subsidiary: forward contract		
(7) Amount sold (£)	(10,000)	(10,000)
(8) DM equivalent	(30,000)	(29,000)
(9) FX gain/(loss); B.T.		1,000
(10) Tax (40%)		(400)
(11) FX gain/(loss); A.T.		600
C. Subsidiary: net		
(12) FX gain/(loss); B.T.		0
(13) FX gain/(loss); A.T.		0
D. Consolidation: exposure		
(14) Exposure (DM)	30,000	30,000
(15) ER ($/DM)	0·5	0·45
(16) $ equivalent	15,000	13,500
(17) FX gain/(loss); B.T.		(1,500)
(18) Tax (0%)		0
(19) FX gain/(loss); A.T.		(1,500)
E. Parent: forward contract		
(20) Amount sold (DM)	(42,857·14)	(42,857·14)
(21) $ equivalent; (15) × (20)	(21,428·57)	(19,285·71)
(22) FX gain/(loss); B.T.		2,142·86
(23) Tax (30%)		(642·86)
(24) FX gain/loss; A.T. (22) +(23)		1,500
F. Consolidation: net exposure		
(25) FX gain/(loss); B.T. (17) + (22)		642·86
(26) FX gain/(loss); A.T. (19) + (24)		0

Summary

There are four strategies available for a corporation to manage a subsidiary's third party/third currency transactions: (1) no hedge; (2) decentralized hedge of transaction exposure; (3) centralized hedge of consolidated after-tax exposure: and (4) co-ordinated hedge of transaction

Chart 5—Summary
(a) Impact on subsidiary (b) Consolidated impact ($/DM rate) (c) Consolidated impact ($/£ rate)

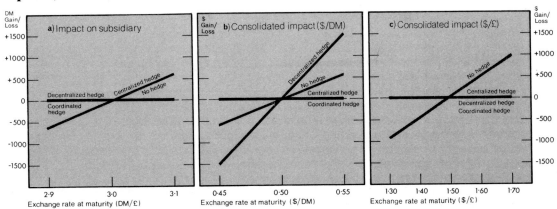

175

Exhibit 5—Summary and comparison

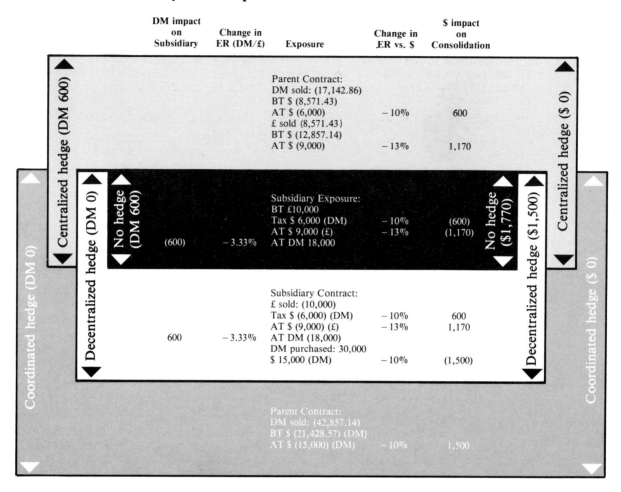

and translation exposures. The no hedge strategy leaves both the subsidiary and the consolidated entity exposed to all exchange rate movements. The second strategy, the decentralized hedge, where the subsidiary covers the transaction exposure, eliminates the transaction exposure for the subsidiary while leaving uncovered a translation exposure for the consolidated entity. The third strategy, the parent's after-tax hedge, eliminates consolidated after-tax exposures, while leaving the subsidiary's transaction exposure uncovered. Finally, the co-ordinated approach neutralizes all exposures at all levels. The impact of the four strategies is summarized in Exhibit 5 and illustrated graphically in Chart 5 under various exchange rate assumptions.

D. Covering in forward vs. spot markets

Two of the alternative techniques by which net exposed assets can be protected by corporations are: (1) forward cover, that is, a sale of the exposed currency in the forward market, and (2) spot cover, that is, a borrowing of the exposed currency in the amount of the exposure in the Eurocurrency market followed by an immediate conversion of the proceeds of the borrowing into the reporting currency and investment of the latter in a Euromoney interest bearing deposit.

Because the forward and Eurocurrency markets are arbitraged by the market participants, it is frequently assumed that the costs of hedging in the two markets are identical. This, however, is not generally true. It holds true only under some limited assumptions as to exchange rate movements. If the exchange rate at the maturity of the cover differs from the forward rate at the inception of the cover, the accounting costs of hedging in the two markets will differ. The cost differential is also affected by the relative level of interest rates in the Eurocurrency markets (higher rates mean a greater differential). The overall cost differential of hedging in the two markets may be substantial. This section discusses the foreign exchange, financial cost and net income implications of the two hedging techniques, with emphasis on after-tax results. (The net income and cash results are identical throughout this section, as both the exposure and cover are assumed to have the same maturity.)

176

The following general assumptions are used:

- The net accessible interest rate differential[5] between the local currency and the reporting currency reflects the net accessible premium/discount in the forward market for the same maturity. Spreads are ignored.
- Interest payments are due at maturity and there are no hidden costs associated with either of the two hedging strategies.
- Tax rates on foreign exchange gains or losses and all other income or expenses are the same and tax effects are accrued under both alternatives.
- The exchange rate changes at the beginning of the accounting period but after the forward contract or the Eurocurrency hedging arrangement has been entered into.

It is recognized that in reality things do not fall into place so neatly. For example, the premium/discount has no cash-flow effect until the maturity of the contract but interest sometimes has an earlier effect, and exchange rate changes do not happen in a manner which avoids the need to recognize exchange gain or loss on accrued interest and the related tax effects, if any. But more realistic assumptions on such matters would complicate the examples without helping to clarify the principles involved.

The foreign exchange and accounting implications of a foreign exchange exposure and the two hedging strategies are illustrated with the following specific assumptions:

- A U.S. multinational company has a receivable of LC 1,000 on 31/12/X0, which is collectable on 31/12/X1. The spot exchange rate on 31/12/X0 is LC 1·00 = $1·00 and the company's tax rate is 40%.
- On 31/12/X0 the company projects a depreciation of the LC over the coming year. On 01/1/X1 the LC is devalued to LC 1·00 = $0·75.

1. Forward cover

In the case of forward cover, the company decides to hedge its exposed receivable in the forward market. Accordingly, on 31/12/X0 it sells forward LC 1,000 for delivery on 31/12/X1 at $0·85. Exhibit 1 analyzes the foreign exchange, financial cost and net income implications of the foreign exchange exposure and an offsetting forward (sale) contract. Lines 1 to 5 show the company's balance sheet data and the related after-tax foreign exchange loss of $150. Lines 6 to 11 analyze the

Exhibit 1—Forward cover

Balance sheet	31/12/X0	31/12/X1
(1) Exposure (LC)	1,000	1,000
(2) Exchange rate ($/LC)	1·00	0·75
(3) $ equivalent	1,000	750
(4) Foreign exchange gain/(loss) before-tax		(250)
(5) Foreign exchange gain/(loss) after-tax		(150)
Forward contract		
(6) Amount sold forward (LC)	(1,000)	(1,000)
(7) $ equivalent; lines (2) × (6)	(1,000)	(750)
(8) Foreign exchange gain/(loss) before-tax		250
(9) Foreign exchange gain/(loss) after-tax		150
(10) Financial cost before-tax*		(150)
(11) Financial cost after-tax		(90)
Consolidated after-tax impact		
(12) Foreign exchange gain/(loss); lines (5) + (9)		0
(13) Net financial cost; line (11)		(90)
(14) Net income; lines (12) + (13)		(90)

* Discount to be amortized = (forward rate—spot at start of contract) × LC amount sold
= ($0·85 − $1·00) × 1,000 = ($150).

---

[5] "Net accessible interest differential—The difference between the interest rates which can actually be obtained on two currencies. This difference is usually . . . derived from external interest rates rather than domestic interest rates. These external rates, or Euro-rates, are free from reserve requirements (which would increase the interest rate) and from exchange controls (which would limit access to the money)." Quoted from Heinz Riehl and Rita M. Rodriguez, *Foreign Exchange Markets: a Guide to Foreign Currency Operations.* New York, McGraw-Hill, 1977.

impact of the forward contract, indicating an after-tax foreign exchange gain of $150 and a financial cost of $90. Lines 12 to 14 identify the overall impact of the balance sheet exposure and the forward contract. The foreign exchange loss on the exposed receivable is offset exactly by the foreign exchange gain on the forward contract because foreign exchange gains and losses on both—the balance sheet exposure and the contract—are computed on the spot-to-spot basis. The financial cost of covering the exposure is $90, that is, the net after-tax discount on the LC, and, accordingly, the net income effect is negative $90.

Chart 1—After-tax impact of forward cover

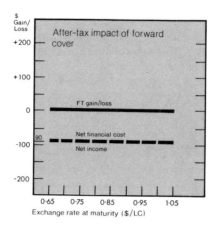

Chart 1 indicates that the outcome of this strategy will be the same (zero after-tax foreign exchange gain/loss and financial cost of $90) regardless of what happens to the exchange rate on 31/12/X1. In other words, the foreign exchange and financial impact were fixed at the time the corporation covered its exposure by the forward contract.

2. Spot cover

In the case of spot cover the company decides to hedge its exposed receivable in the Eurocurrency markets, borrows EuroLC 1,000, converts the proceeds into dollars and invests the funds in the Eurodollar market. Given an interest rate of 10% on the Eurodollar and the 15% discount on the LC in the forward market, the EuroLC interest rate would be 29·412%.[6]

Exhibit 2—Spot cover

Balance sheet	31/12/X0	31/12/X1
(1) Exposure (LC)	1,000	1,000
(2) Exchange rate ($/LC)	1·00	0·75
(3) $ equivalent	1,000	750
(4) Foreign exchange gain/(loss) before-tax		(250)
(5) Foreign exchange gain/(loss) after-tax		(150)
EuroLC borrowing		
(6) Amount borrowed (LC)	(1,000)	(1,000)
(7) $ equivalent; lines (2) × (6)	(1,000)	(750)
(8) Foreign exchange gain/(loss) before-tax		250
(9) Foreign exchange gain/(loss) after-tax		150
(10) Financial cost (LC) before-tax (interest rate 29·412%)		(294·12)
(11) Financial cost ($) before-tax; lines (2) × (10)		(220·59)
(12) Financial cost ($) after-tax		(132·35)
Eurodollar deposit		
(13) Financial revenue (10%) after-tax		60·00
Consolidated after-tax impact		
(14) Foreign exchange gain/(loss); lines (5) + (9)		0
(15) Net financial cost; lines (12) + (13)		(72·35)
(16) Net income; lines (14) + (15)		(72·35)

178

As Exhibit 2 shows, the foreign exchange loss and gain resulting from the balance sheet exposure and the EuroLC loan are the same as for the forward contract hedge previously demonstrated. The financial cost with this strategy, however, differs from the situation where the hedge was undertaken in the forward market. Given the interest rate of 29·412% on the EuroLC, the before-tax financial cost is LC 294·12 (line 10), which translated into dollars at maturity equals $220·59 before-tax (line 11) and $132·35 after-tax (line 12). The Eurodollar deposit results in after-tax financial revenue of $60 (line 13). Lines 14 to 16 identify the overall impact of this strategy. The total foreign exchange gain/loss is again zero, as both the balance sheet exposure and the EuroLC borrowing are valued on the spot-to-spot basis. The net financial cost is $72·35 and, accordingly, the net income effect is negative $72·35.

3. Comparing the two strategies

As the above analysis indicates, the two strategies are likely to affect the net financial cost differently.[7] Whereas with the forward contract cover the financial cost is fixed at the inception of the cover, this is not the case with the spot cover. The two variables that affect the eventual cost of hedging in the Eurocurrency market are the exchange rate at maturity and the level of interest rates in the Euromarkets.

Exchange rate impact: The dollar cost of the spot cover would be the same as that of the forward cover if the spot rate at maturity were identical to the forward rate at the inception of the cover to the same maturity. In other words, the cost in both cases would be $90. If the exchange rate at maturity is lower than the forward rate at the inception of the cover, the dollar cost of the EuroLC loan is lower because the interest payments at maturity are translated at an exchange rate lower than the forward rate.

This cost differential is computed as follows: LC interest payment × difference between forward and spot rates × (1 minus tax rate) = LC 294·12 × 0·1 × 0·6 = $17·65. The cost differential of $17·65 is the difference between the net cost hedging in the forward and Euromarkets, i.e. $90 and $72·35, respectively.

Although in the above example the spot cover was preferable, this is not necessarily the case in all circumstances. For instance, where the spot rate at maturity exceeds the forward rate at inception, the cost of the EuroLC loan will exceed the cost of the forward sale since the interest payment due in LC would have to be translated at the higher exchange rate.

This cost differential is illustrated in Chart 2. Referring to the chart, should the currency move against the hedger's expectations and spot at maturity reach $1·05, the financial cost of the spot cover would be $125·29 (over 12·5% on the original dollar-equivalent exposure) *vs.* a guaranteed $90 (or 9%) under the forward contract cover.

Interest rate level impact: The financial cost differential illustrated above is further compounded by the relative level of interest rates in the Euromarkets. The higher the interest rate on the EuroLC, the higher the amounts of interest payments that have to be translated at the new exchange rate at maturity.

The impact of the interest rate level on the financial cost of hedging in the two markets is illustrated in Chart 3. In the chart, the left hand scale plots the financial cost of the hedge in dollars and percentage terms, while the right hand scale tracks the financial cost differential of the two strategies. The financial cost of the forward contract is $90 (i.e. 9%) regardless of what happens to the exchange rate at maturity (see Chart 1). The financial cost of the spot cover, on the other hand, is a function of the exchange rate at maturity (discussed above) and the level of interest rates in the

---

[6] A large proportion of forward exchange contracts is matched by Eurocurrency deposits. One way a bank can guarantee a US trader a fixed prive on LC at some future date is to convert dollar deposits into LC. It then re-deposits the LC with another bank until the trader buys them with dollars. In our case this would be done as follows: 1. The bank sells forward to a company LC 1,000 @ $0.85. 2. To ensure a fixed price on the LC, the bank converts $772.727 ($1,000/1 + 0.2941176) into LC 772.727 and invests in EuroLC for the same maturity @ 29.41176%. 3. At maturity, the EuroLC deposit is worth: LC 772.727 (1 + 0.2941176) = LC 1,000. 4. At maturity the bank delivers to the company LC 1,000 in return for $850. Note: The proof of the mathematics is that if the bank invested $772.727 in Euro-dollar at 10%, it would have obtained at maturity: $772.727 (1 + 0.1) = $850. The covered interest arbitrage formula is as follows: $1,000 (1 + 10%) = LC 1,000 (1 + 29.41176%) × 0.85 $/LC.

[7] The reader should be aware that there are other alternatives for hedging in the Euromarkets. One of them would be borrowing the discounted amount of the local currency exposure so that the borrowing at maturity equals exposure at maturity. Under this alternative the net financial cost of the two strategies—forward cover and spot cover—would be identical. The accounting exposure, however, would not be eliminated, as by borrowing LC 772.727, the exposure of LC 1,000 would be merely reduced from LC 1,000 to LC 227·273.

Eurocurrency markets. As the chart indicates, the higher these rates are in percentage terms, the higher the amounts of LC payments which must be translated into dollars at the exchange rate at maturity. For instance, given the 15% discount on the LC in the forward market and the exchange rate of LC 1 = $0·75 at maturity, the financial cost differential would be between $10·59 (with 0% interest on the Eurodollar) and $28·24 (25% interest on the Eurodollar). Should the exchange rate move against the hedger's expectations and appreciate by 5% to LC 1 = $1·05, the financial cost of spot cover would be between $111·17 (0% interest on the Eurodollar) and $146·47 (25% interest on the Eurodollar) as compared to $90 with a forward contract cover.

Chart 2—After-tax impact of spot cover

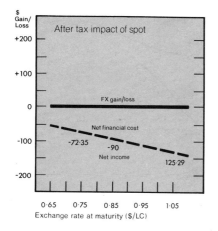

Chart 3—Comparing the two strategies

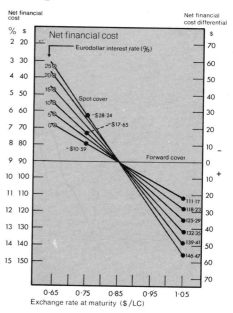

Summary

The two strategies are likely to affect reported earnings (and cash-flows) differently. The two variables that affect the eventual outcome are the exchange rate at maturity and the level of interest rates. If spot at maturity is $0·85 (same as the forward rate at the inception of the hedge on 31/12/X0), the financial costs in the two markets are identical. If, however, the exchange rate at maturity falls below $0·85, the costs of the spot cover are lower than the costs of the forward contract; if it stands above $0·85, they are higher. Finally, the higher the relative interest rate level, the larger the financial cost differentials.

In the final analysis, by entering into a forward contract, a corporation can lock in the costs at the time of the forward sale. On the other hand, by covering in the Eurocurrency markets, the corporation exposes itself to some additional risk in that accounting impact may be larger than originally anticipated.

CHAPTER VIII

Disclosure and management control

A. Disclosure

Before FASB-8 companies employed widely varying disclosure procedures. With a uniform and rational methodology, and sharp fluctuations in currencies, the impact of translation has been quite marked, and often of a surprising magnitude. Disclosure then becomes an important element of management.

The disclosure requirements of FASB-8 have been of little help to investors.

> "32. The aggregate exchange gain or loss included in determining net income for the period shall be disclosed in the financial statements or in a note thereto. For the purpose of that disclosure, gains and losses on forward contracts determined in conformity with the requirements of paragraphs 25 and 26 shall be considered exchange gains or losses."
>
> "33. Effects of rate changes on reported results of operations, other than the effects included in the disclosure required by paragraph 32, shall, if practicable, be described and quantified. If quantified, the methods and the underlying assumptions used to determine the estimated effects shall be explained (paragraphs 223–225)."

Beyond the requirements of #8 the voluntary disclosures of corporations have been minimal. Corporate complaints have been frequent and loud; ironically, those who complain have done little to teach the reader of corporate accounts. Analysts have also shown little enthusiasm for understanding the impact of currency movements. Nevertheless, there are a number of policies that corporate management should follow to inform and educate both investor and analyst.

1. Exposure by currency

First, exposure by currency should be disclosed in the annual report. At the moment, Exxon appears to be the only corporation to do this. Since Exxon's exposure is substantial, $4·1 billion at the beginning of 1980, and since currency swings have created major changes to earnings, knowledge of the exposure has been of inestimable value in anticipating losses. Thus, at the end of each quarter, or even monthly, one can calculate the gain/loss well in advance of an earnings release. The calculation for the September quarter is based on the previous year-end exposure, and the exposure may vary during the year. But such a calculation gives a reader direction and a rather good approximation of the amount in timely fashion.

All a reader has available in other cases is the long term debt by currency, found in the annual report. The working capital position, exclusive of inventory, is unknown. This may be important. Assume a multinational oil company operates in say, Angola, producing substantial earnings and owing the government income taxes. Those taxes are included in current payables, not long term debt, and if payable in the local currency, escudos, there is a substantial currency exposure not noted by the reader. An observer might think that Angola did not have a capital market of consequence and that there would be no long term debt denominated in escudos. Nevertheless, the tax liability has created significant exposure. In the case of Gulf, the Angolan tax liability in one period was responsible for half of the currency loss.

Similarly, our accounting model permits us to pick up equity earnings for 20–50% owned investments without any indication anywhere of the exposure of those investees by currency. For example, in one quarter Royal Dutch suffered a $309 million charge from translation of long term debt: an exposure that was indicated by the annual report. However, there was another $160 million charge as a result of translating equity interests.

At year end, where translation losses or gains have been substantial, a corporation may wish to show the amounts of gain/loss by currency. Together with the exposure by currency this would facilitate understanding of fluctuations and their impact. An obvious question to management might then be, "Why not repay, as others have done, the Swiss or German debt, which caused significant losses, and replace it with dollar borrowing?"

In Paragraphs 213–226 the Financial Accounting Standards Board explained the basis for its conclusions on disclosure. The Board believed "that management can best decide how information about the effects of rate changes in revenues and earnings should be described or quantified" (Paragraph 224). The Board went on to state that "Disclosing only exchange gains and losses if rate changes significantly affect reported revenue and earnings in a way or to an extent that can be determined would not, in the view of the Board, comply with the intent of paragraph 33 of this Statement".

To date the announced work on revising FASB-8 has been concerned with theory, such as the rate to be used, or the rationale for deferral of certain gains/losses. There has been little focus on disclosure. But it is clear that disclosure has been a minor part of #8 in practice and the needs of users would be helped by improved disclosure.

2. Tax effect

A second major disclosure need in currency translation is on understanding of the tax effect. Standard 8 does little to enlighten us on this point. Since taxes can reduce the impact of gains/losses by as much as 50%, it might be useful to have a better understanding of the tax effect.

In Paragraph 203 of #8, the FASB concluded that existing literature provided sufficient guidance about the need to provide deferred taxes. The complications have been such that an outsider has no guidance whatsover. In Paragraph 218, the Board bowed to the arguements of those who opposed disclosure of the tax effects; for one thing, such disclosure might imply the gain/loss was extraordinary!

3. Transaction impact

There is a third major area that needs disclosure: the transaction impact. The corporate community is outspoken on the impact of #8 creating accounting losses, but it says little on the longer term effect caused by strong local currencies being used to buy dollar denominated imports. The excuse has been that a currency change produces interrelated effects. Nonetheless, one might expect sophisticated corporate staffs to isolate variables and produce pertinent elements of use to readers.

The oil industry is unique in its exposure to this aspect. Oil is a dollar denominated product; major imports into consuming countries with strong local currencies (Europe and Japan) provide a textbook illustration of the long run impact of local currency strength reducing the cost of goods sold. The impact is felt long after the immediate change in currencies which produced the obvious translation loss. Indeed, one company that used to produce this material, Texaco, stopped disclosure of the currency effect on operating earnings on the grounds that the investor did not understand the information and was wrongly critical of the company as a consequence.

Note the following illustration one year:

	Exchange rate ($/DM)	January	Exchange rate ($/DM)	November
Sales realizations per barrel of products (DM)		32·76 DM		33·25 DM
Crude cost in DM	$·41792	30·39 DM	$·464994	27·31 DM
DM margin		2·37 DM		6·04 DM
Equivalent of dollar margin		$·99		$2·81

European refineries, running at perhaps 60% of capacity, plagued with major losses, began to move towards very significant profit levels as a consequence.

Thus, the effect of a currency change is immediate, perhaps producing a sharp translation loss in December of one year. But there is a long run effect, for the 12 months following, that may be of critical importance. Only disclosure of the transaction impact as well as the translation impact will provide the full story.

One company, Scholl, presented a very interesting profit and loss account in pounds sterling and dollars with an explanation of the effects on sales and earnings. But such innovative efforts are rare; instead, we have a litany of complaints that #8 is not meaningful.

4. Variance analysis

A fourth disclosure need is variance analysis. This would show the income statement changes attributable to volumes, prices, costs, as well as currency. Such a matrix must be essential to management thinking and must be done as a review of local operations. It helps the company to identify and measure the factors influencing the business. (See Section B below.)

182

Conclusion

As so little disclosure has been done in a voluntary fashion since FASB-8 was introduced, it is now time for the next step, mandatory disclosure requirements. Such steps would include:

(1) A table of currencies indicating the exposure involved. This facilitates an understanding as currencies change subsequently as to the translation impact that will be revealed when the earnings are announced.
(2) Gains/losses by currency for the period covered.
(3) The tax effect of translation gains/losses.
(4) While the translation gains attract so much attention, readers may easily lose sight of the longer term effect of the transaction impact, the benefit/harm to income stemming from the income statement.
(5) Variance analysis—the impact on operating profit of all factors, currency, volumes, prices, costs. Thus, proper perspective is achieved as to the factors causing a profit change.

With information of this sort, readers of financial statements would achieve understanding, the goal of financial reporting.

B. Profitability analysis: currency variance

One aspect of foreign exchange risk that is not easily comprehended in the area of exposure management is the impact of currency movements on the income statement, as presented by the parent company. A way has to be found to isolate the effect of currency movements when explaining the results of operations to management at the end of a given period, be it a month, a quarter, or the full year. The method usually adopted to explain periodic results is what is commonly referred to as variance analysis. The intent is to ascertain the factors having an impact on earnings, and how much each of these factors contributes to the change in results when two periods are compared. For the purpose of this section, it is immaterial whether we compare one period against a like period in a previous year, whether we compare a budget or profit plan with actual results, or whether we are making projections for the future. The technique is always the same and, if applied rigorously, it gives management confidence in the explanations offered.

1. Variance analysis concepts

Variance analysis can be made relatively simple or can be extended to include detailed and sophisticated approaches depending upon the requirements of management. For illustration purposes we assume a relatively simple approach, which is explained in detail, while the more sophisticated methods are only alluded to later in this section.

The two most common variances used by financial analysts are volume and price variances. We need these to analyze both revenues and costs, and the method is the same whether we deal with revenues or costs of sales. One way of arriving at a *volume variance in revenues* is to multiply the current unit selling price by the change in sales volume. Similarly, when we wish to establish the volume variance arising out of costs, we multiply the current unit cost by the change in cost volume. To arrive at the *revenue price variance,* we take the change in selling price and multiply it by the base period sales volume. The term base period relates to the period against which we make our comparison, be it the prior year, the prior month, or perhaps the profit plan. The *cost price variance* is computed similarly: the change in unit cost is multiplied by the base period volume. It is more descriptive to call the price variance relating to cost of sales a cost rate variance.

The foregoing variances give us the explanation as to what happened to the margin or gross profit realized in our business. Yet, in the simplest variance analysis one more aspect needs to be accounted for: namely, expenses. The easiest method is to compare current period expenses with those of the past or comparison period and call the result an *expense variance.*

It will be appreciated that this provides a very basic variance analysis only. More sophistication is frequently desirable and necessary. The price variance relating to revenues can easily be broken down into variances arising from price changes at the port of entry (assuming third party market prices are available) and the prices achieved at the final destination. Similarly, the volume variances can be divided between a true volume variance and the variance that arises from a change in the mix of products sold; moreover, a more elaborate variance analysis approach will include the change in volume related expenses as part of the volume variance. The cost rate variance can be calculated in such a way that management can ascertain the effect of cost changes based on current or replacement costs, while the analyst segregates those changes that are due to the vagaries of the inventory valuation system. Finally, the expense variance can be made more meaningful by differentiating between fixed expenses, maintenance, gain or loss on exchange, gain or loss on the sale of assets, etc.

To simplify our illustration, we utilize only the four basic variances (volume, price, cost rate and expenses); any other approach would make the understanding of currency impacts more complicated. Also, it should be noted that the formulas suggested above are those that have been found most useful by many businesses. Other formulas are possible and are recommended in various publications. No statement can be made as to the most "correct" calculation, as much depends upon the results that a given manager wishes to concentrate on or achieve.

2. Separation of conventional and currency factors

In order to arrive at an evaluation as to what the effects of currency were on income, it is necessary to go through the conventional variance analysis as described above and then ascertain by difference how currency movements affected the stated results. We have again to establish a convention to determine the base on which we make our comparisons. It has been found most practical that comparisons are made against the currency translation in force during the base period. Thus, for example, if the exchange rate in year 19X0 was LC 1 = PC 1, all local currency results of the current period are translated at that rate. In our example, we assume that the LC has depreciated by 10% and the exchange rate in year 19X1 was LC 1 = PC 0·9.

3. Local variance analysis

First, it is necessary to establish the variance analysis as it would be done by the local subsidiary or affiliate. The example we analyze is shown in Exhibit 1 and presents a simplified income statement of LC Company for the first quarters ended 31/03/X0 and 31/03/X1. During the first quarter of year 19X0 the company sold 1,000 units at LC 1; its unit cost was LC 0·50; it had expenses, interest and depreciation of LC 200, LC 25, and LC 50, respectively. In the first quarter of year 19X1, the company's sales rose to 1,200 units at a selling price of LC 0·95 per unit, and its costs dropped to LC 0·40 per unit. Expenses rose to LC 220 and interest charges to LC 30; depreciation was the same as in year 19X0.

Exhibit 1—LC Company

	1st quarter ended 31/03/X0	31/03/X1	Total	Variance analysis (LC) Volume	Price	Cost rate	Expense
Revenues	1000	1140	140	190	(50)		
Beginning inventory	(500)	(380)	120				
Purchases	(500)	(600)	(100)				
	(1000)	(980)	20				
Ending inventory	500	500	0				
Cost of sales	(500)	(480)	20	(80)		100	
Gross profit	500	660	160				
Expense	(200)	(220)	(20)				(20)
Interest	(25)	(30)	(5)				(5)
Depreciation	(50)	(50)	0				
Before-tax income	225	360	135	110	(50)	100	(25)

The first column of the variance analysis is a total column and shows the differences for each item in the income statement. The *volume variance* for revenues is computed by multiplying the change in sales volume, 200, by the current selling price of LC 0·95, which results in a variance of LC 190. The related volume variance applying to cost of sales is ascertained by multiplying the change in volume, 200, by the current unit cost LC 0·40. The result indicates that volumes added LC 80 to the company's costs. Therefore, our net volume variance is LC 110, relating to before-tax income. To identify the *price variance*, we take the base period volume of 1,000, multiply it by the change in selling price, a negative LC 0·05, and obtain a negative price variance of LC 50. The *cost rate variance* is LC 100, which we obtain by multiplying the base period volume of 1,000 with the positive change in cost of LC 0·10. Finally, the negative *expense variances* of LC 25 are shown in the last column.

The analysis of these results shows that the company improved its before-tax income by LC 135, which is made up, as follows:

	LC
Higher volumes accounted for	110
Lower prices reduced earnings by	(50)
The cost rate was lower by	100
Expenses were higher by	(25)
	135

In many situations it is unnecessary, meaningless or very difficult to extend the variance analysis to include the tax line. In most business situations, management can affect transactions in terms of pre-tax outlays only; prices to customers are always stated on a pre-tax basis and merchandise is normally paid for on a pre-tax basis. Moreover, tax calculations are frequently complex: companies avail themselves of accelerated depreciation for tax purposes, but not always for book purposes; in the United States and some other countries, depletion allowances for tax have a different basis from that used for shareholder reporting purposes; various inventory systems, such as stock relief in the United Kingdom or LIFO (last-in, first-out) valuation in many other jurisdictions apply to tax calculations, but do not always find reflection in book income—to mention just a few of the literally hundreds of book/tax adjustments that multinational companies face. Consequently, the variance analysis frequently stops on the before-tax income line and we respect this convention in this section.

4. Parent company analysis

Exhibit 2 extends the example discussed above to the parent company. The illustration has been expanded to show how LC Company's results would be reflected in the parent company's statements, if we assume an exchange rate of LC 1 = PC 1 in year 19X0 against a rate of LC 1= PC 0·9 in year 19X1.

The data in the PC column follow logically from the above exchange rate assumptions. Two lines call for further explanations. The beginning inventory shown for the quarter ended 31/03/X1 has to be converted at the historical rate of exchange in compliance with FASB-8. For purposes of this illustration, we are assuming that inventories are valued on a FIFO (first-in, first-out) basis and that the historical rate is the same as that of the previous year, namely, LC 1 = PC 1. The ending inventory has an average exchange rate of LC 1 = PC 0·9; the old inventories have been used up, and only the latest inventories are held in stock. The other line that shows an unusual exchange rate conversion is the one showing the depreciation expense; that item also follows the FASB-8 requirement of an historical conversion rate, which in our example is LC 1 = PC 1.

Exhibit 2—LC Company, a 100% owned subsidiary of PC Company

	1st quarter ended 31/3/X0			1st quarter ended 31/3/X1			Total	Variance analysis (PC)				
	LC	ER	PC	LC	ER	PC		Volume	Price	Cost rate	Expense	Currency
Revenues	1000	1.0	1000	1140	0.9	1026	26	190	(50)			(114)
Beg. inventory	(500)	1.0	(500)	(380)	1.0	(380)	120					
Purchases	(500)	1.0	(500)	(600)	0.9	(540)	(40)					
	(1000)		(1000)	(980)		(920)	80					
End. inventory	500	1.0	500	500	0.9	450	(50)					
Cost of sales	(500)		(500)	(480)		(470)	30	(80)		100		10
Gross profit	500		500	660		556	56					
Expense	(200)	1.0	(200)	(220)	0.9	(198)	2				(20)	22
Interest	(25)	1.0	(25)	(30)	0.9	(27)	(2)				(5)	3
Depreciation	(50)	1.0	(50)	(50)	1.0	(50)	0					
Before-tax income	225		225	360		281	56	110	(50)	100	(25)	(79)

Before considering the variance analysis of the parent company, we restate our principle of using the base period exchange rate as that which underlies our comparison. It reinforces the highly desirable result that the basic variance analysis at the parent company offices will look the same as that obtained by the local subsidiary or affiliate. Thus, if we look at the variance analysis columns of Exhibit 2, we note that the results of the analysis, namely, the bottom line for volume, price, cost and expense are exactly the same as those of Exhibit 1, except that all data are stated in PC. It should be stressed that this is solely due to an assumption of a base period exchange rate of LC 1 = PC 1. In all real situations this is most unlikely, but proportionately the results will always have to be the same.

Continuing with our illustration, we note that if we go through the analysis of our total revenue difference of PC 26, our volume and price variances of PC 190 and a negative PC 50, respectively, do not add up to the total of PC 26. As we have previously established that these identified variances are the appropriate ones calculated by the local company, the balance, a negative PC 114, must be due to currency. In other words, the weakening of the local currency versus the parent company currency has resulted in a translation into fewer parent company currency units. Of course, exactly the opposite is the case for cost of sales and expenses.

Our final conclusion is that, from a parent company's point of view, the total variance of PC 56 shows the same factors as the ones noted in Exhibit 1, only this time expressed in parent company currency, and that currency itself has caused the overall results to be lower by PC 79. This indicates that when a local currency depreciates in relation to the parent company currency, and where margins are positive, the translation process will result in lower earnings as shown in this illustration. By the same token, the opposite would happen if the local currency appreciated.

The summary presentation of the variance factors is as follows:

	PC
Volume	110
Price	(50)
Cost rate	100
Gross profit (margin)	160
Expense	(25)
Local operations	135
Currency	(79)
Total	56

As mentioned above, each one of these factors may be analyzed further. It is, for example, possible to segregate the currency effect between ordinary, or pure translation, and dual currency accounting. Dual currency accounting is practised for such factors, as inventories and fixed assets where books are kept in both LC and PC.

In this example, the dual currency accounting effect would be PC 43, which is arrived at, as follows: the opening inventory in year 19X0 was converted at a rate of LC 1 = PC 1; whereas, in year 19X1 the current exchange rate was LC 1 = PC 0·9, with an effect of reducing costs by PC 38. Similarly, depreciation was held constant, while a translation at the current rate would have reduced the charge by PC 5. Altogether, we have therefore overstated our costs and expenses by PC 43. As our overall currency variance is a negative PC 79, the pure, or total translation effect between the two quarters is a negative PC 122.

5. Intercompany transactions

It should be pointed out that the variance analysis presented in the foregoing paragraphs assumed that LC Company was independent as to its source of merchandise and that we could, therefore, take the LC analysis and transplant it to the PC analysis. If, however, LC Company were to obtain its merchandise from PC Company's resources, a different approach could be utilized as it would be inappropriate, from PC Company's point of view, to take the cost of sales variance of PC 30 and assign a currency factor to it. If the parent company is the sole supplier, it would be questionable to have a currency variance, and the cost rate variance would have to be adjusted accordingly. Exhibit 3 shows the difference in bottom line results that would be achieved if we determined in which country's currency a given transaction should be stated.

In this example, we assume that in LC Company's country the tax rate is 60%, while in PC Company's country the tax rate is 50%. We also assume that we have an option to determine whether the merchandise cost is expressed in LC or PC. Assuming that we are shipping merchandise from PC Company to LC Company and that the exchange rate has changed to LC 1 = PC 0·9 by the time payment is made for the merchandise, the illustration shows the difference in tax savings that would result in denominating this transaction in either LC or PC.

If the transaction is denominated in LC, and our base amount is LC 1,000, LC Company would make a payment of LC 1,000 to PC Company. PC Company would receive PC 900, and would therefore realize an exchange loss of 100, which would result in a tax benefit of PC 50. If, on the other hand, this same transaction were denominated in PC, LC Company would have to pay LC 1,111 in order to pay off its PC 1,000 debt. This payment would result in a loss on exchange of LC 111 and would yield a tax benefit of LC 66.

Exhibit 3—An intercompany merchandise transaction

Assumptions	LC	ER	PC
Tax rate	60%		50%
Exchange rate at title date		LC 1 = PC 1	
Exchange rate at payment date		LC 1 = PC 0·9	
Merchandise cost	1,000		1,000
Transaction is denominated in LC			
Payment by LC Company to PC Company	1,000		900
Loss on exchange	0		(100)
Tax benefit	0		50
Transaction is denominated in PC			
Payment by LC Company to PC Company	1,111		1,000
Loss on exchange	(111)		0
Tax benefit	66		0

It is obvious that denomination in PC is more advantageous to the consolidated financial picture of these companies. Even if allowance is made for the depreciation that has occurred in LC, the overall benefit of this denomination is readily apparent. To take advantage of this situation, the tax structures (and possibly commercial impediments) must be studied in order to determine whether, based on the forecast of likely currency movements, it is advisable to structure merchandise transactions in either the parent company's currency or in the currency of the various subsidiaries or affiliates affected.

Conclusions

To summarize variance analysis is a methodology which expands what has happened or what is likely to happen in the comparison of income statements for two different periods. As such, it reports on currency effects, but cannot guide as to future behaviour. By critically examining variance factors, especially the currency factor, an insight is gained into some operational matters which could have results with regards to exposure management.

As a final point, it should be noted that the recommended methodology should not be affected by any revisions of the techniques for translating local currency statements other than that the total currency variance will be different. The portion of the analysis which deals with the events that occurred in the country in which LC Company was located will not be affected if the recommended method is used.

C. Evaluation of overseas performance[1]

The development of an appropriate methodology for evaluating overseas operations is a topic of continuing concern. All too frequently, evaluation procedures are incompatible with a firm's goals and inappropriate to the lines of authority within the firm. Moreover, continuing volatility in the foreign exchange markets increases the difficulty of evaluating overseas performance consistently and equitably.

To assess the methodology multinational corporations (MNCs) use to incorporate exchange rate considerations in their evaluation process, Business International Money Report analysts recently surveyed 12 major corporations. The survey focused on the procedure these firms use to compare actual operating results with a projected budget. This is the most widespread technique for evaluating the performance of foreign operations.

1. Evaluating in local vs. parent currency

Seven out of the 12 respondents measure the performance of their overseas operations in both local and parent currencies. The five remaining firms evaluate in parent currency terms alone. Results expressed in local currency display a subsidiary's ability to perform according to local market criteria but ignore the impact of exchange rate fluctuations. Evaluation in parent currency terms includes the effect of variable exchange rates (provided different exchange rates are used in the

---

[1] Reprinted in part from the November 16 and 23, 1979 issues of Business International Money Report, with the permission of the publisher, Business International Corp.

projected budget and the operating results) and allows corporate headquarters to understand better the data reported by foreign operations, since they are expressed in a familiar currency. Thus, evaluation in both currencies can provide more information than what is yielded by reporting results in one currency alone.

2. Rates used in budgeting and tracking

When evaluating performance in parent currency terms the firm must determine which exchange rate to use for translating local currency budgets into home currency. Since projected budgets and actual results are being compared, the firm may use the same or different exchange rates for each. (See Exhibit 1.) The choice of exchange rate can influence the evaluation and actual operating decisions and therefore should depend on the company's goals and allocation of authority between headquarters and local operations.

Exhibit 1—Rate used to track performance relative to budget

	Initial	Projected	Ending
Initial	A–1 Budget on initial Track on initial	A–2 Budget on initial Track on projected	A–3 Budget on initial Track on ending
Projected	P–1 Budget on projected Track on initial	P–2 Budget on projected Track on projected	P–3 Budget on projected Track on ending
Ending	E–1 Budget on ending Track on initial	E–2 Budget on ending Track on projected	E–3 Budget on ending Track on ending

Rate used for determining budget (left axis)

The combinations along the diagonal (A–1, P–2, E–3) use the same exchange rate for budgeting and tracking. The shaded boxes (P–1, E–1 A–2, E–2) are illogical combinations. Survey results show that P–3 was the most popular combination, followed by P–2 and A–1.

Source: Donald R. Lessard and Peter Lorange, "Currency Changes and Management Control: Resolving the Centralization/Decentralization Dilemma," Accounting Review, July 1977, p 360.

The survey respondents were asked which exchange rate they used to project an operating budget and which was used at the end of the budgeted period for tracking actual performance.

- Six of the 12 respondents use a projected exchange rate for budgeting purposes and the actual rate at the end of the period for tracking purposes.
- Three firms compare projected rates at both stages.
- Two respondents utilize the rate in effect when the budget is first established for both budgeting and tracking purposes.

The distinction among methods is not always clear-cut, and a few of the firms use several combinations of rates. For example, one firm uses a projected rate to establish its budgets but then translates actual results twice, once using the projected rate and again using the actual rate. For this firm, performance evaluation is based on the projected rate and therefore does not take exchange effects into account. The actual rate is used to determine the exchange rate variance from the budget, but overseas operations are not held accountable for this discrepancy.

3. Advantages and disadvantages of projected rates

The majority of surveyed firms using a projected rate indicate their strong commitment to this rate by keeping it fixed regardless of subsequent currency movements. A few of the respondents update their projected rates when exchange rates change drastically. This step is appropriate when operating plans are flexible and can be adjusted to factor in the new data. The use of a projected rate in budgeting allows the firm to adjust its business or financial decisions in anticipation of the impact of exchange rate movements. Decisions open to the firm might include changing sales invoice prices or currencies, adjusting sources of inputs, production schedules, markets for outputs and borrowing sources, and hedging, leading or lagging certain receipts and/or disbursements as a means of shifting some funds from one currency to another.

Determining who sets the rate and how it is derived is one problem that can arise when using projected rates. For the sake of consistency, the unit held accountable for any resulting exchange rate variance should be primarily responsible for setting the rate. Since foreign exchange exposure management in the majority of MNCs has become centralized in the corporate treasury, that unit generally would set the rate. Indeed, the survey shows that in all but one case, projected rates were set at headquarters. The majority of these firms weighed the advice of foreign subsidiaries before projecting the rates.

In some cases, political considerations may result in a projected rate that does not reflect actual expectations of exchange rate movements. For instance, one firm noted that at times the projected rate was based on the desired profit in dollar terms. This can result in management accepting or rejecting projects that would not have been accepted or rejected if a less biased determinant had been used. One way to avoid this problem is to use the forward rate as the projected exchange rate.

4. Same *vs.* different rates

Survey results show that there is a fairly even split among respondents between firms that use the same exchange rate for both budgeting and tracking purposes and firms that use different rates. Using the same exchange rate effectively ignores the impact of any exchange rate fluctuation between periods. Thus, the method is similar to evaluating in local currency terms. This approach reflects management's desire to insulate the evaluation of overseas performance from the effects of exchange rate movements. Thus, the manager of an overseas operation would not be directly concerned with exchange rate changes and would be less tempted to make operating or hedging decisions that might not be optimal from the parent's point of view.

The use of differing exchange rates for budgeting and tracking purposes will produce a variance reflecting the difference between the figures. This variance quantifies the effect of exchange rates on performance. A comparison of a projected rate used for budgeting with the actual end-of-period rate enables the firm to examine the accuracy of its forecasting. The question then arises whether managers of overseas operations should be held accountable for this variance? If they are held accountable they may attempt to take countervailing measures that can be detrimental from the parent company's perspective (i.e. selling short a currency that other members of the same corporate group may need for payments).

Only two surveyed firms hold their overseas operations accountable for this variance. One of these firms, however, requires only that overseas managers explain how much of the variance was coverable through operating (as opposed to financial) adjustments such as price increases. This firm's treasury is held responsible for the impact of exchange rate changes remaining after the sub-operating adjustments are accounted for. Another firm, although not holding their foreign operations accountable for an exchange variance, noted that it requires foreign units to be aware of its impact. In a 1975 survey, five of the current respondents held their overseas operations accountable for any variance resulting form exchange rate fluctuations. Thus, the new survey shows a trend away from assigning accountability for exchange effects to foreign operations.

5. Minimizing exchange effects

A successful and consistent evaluation system will measure performance against a unit's ability and authority to meet that portion of the budget for which it is held accountable. If exposure management is centralized in, or at least coordinated by the corporate treasury (as is the case with most MNCs), that unit will normally be held accountable for minimizing the exchange rate effects which concern the corporation. If the firm is not concerned with some forms of exposure (e.g. it ignores translation exposure), no unit should be held accountable for it. On the other hand, if a firm's foreign operations are held totally accountable for profitability shortcomings attributable to exchange rate changes they should have the authority to take whatever actions they deem necessary to cover such loss.

In practice, there is considerable variety in the amount of authority granted foreign operations to take action guarding against exchange efforts. All surveyed firms give their foreign operations authority to compensate for, or anticipate exchange rate changes by raising prices. However, the subsidiaries' ability to do this depends on market conditions and government regulations and may be inadequate to cover losses resulting from exchange rate movements especially in the short run.

Alternatively, firms tend to be much more cautious in permitting foreign subsidiaries to use protective financial techniques, such as hedging on the forward market. One company surveyed holds its overseas managers accountable for exchange variances, giving them authority to use the forward market only if they conform to corporate guidelines. Another company does not hold its foreign operations accountable for the variance but gives its foreign subsidiaries the authority to take any measures necessary, including translation exposure, to cover exchange risks. A third firm gives foreign subsidiaries authority to cover transaction and translation exposures, but exercises strong control at the treasury level over the subsidiaries' hedging activities. In another case, local subsidiaries may cover transaction risks only, or conduct leading, lagging or other operational activities, but hedging translation exposure is always the responsibility of the corporate treasury unit. In the majority of surveyed firms, foreign operations do not have the authority to hedge transaction or translation exposure.

6. **Performance and profit**

Respondents' firms were also asked whether they distinguish between a measurement of a foreign unit's overall profitability and a measurement of the unit manager's operating performance. Most surveyed firms do make such a distinction. Surveyed respondents also reported the extent of the impact of FASB-8 on their evaluation process. Five of the surveyed firms state that FASB-8 does affect their evaluation process. The ruling's impact appears to be increasing, as three of these firms found FASB-8 to have little impact during a 1975 survey. Half the surveyed firms respond that FASB-8 is causing their company to emphasize local currency results as well as U.S. dollar results due to the distorting impact FASB-8 has on their translated gross profit margins. Three firms report FASB-8 is prompting them to make overseas operations more aware of exchange gains and losses now that these gains or losses must be recognized as income in the period during which they occur.

Bibliography

Adams and Henrey, Tax Consequences of Foreign Currency Fluctuations, *Tax Executive (July, 1978)*.

Aggarwall, Raj., Financial Policies for the Multinational Company. *Praeger & Co,* 1976.

Aliber, Robert Z., Exchange Risk and Corporate International Finance, London: *Macmillan,* 1978.

Bilson, John F.O., Forward Rates and Future Spot Rates: Some Multinational Evidence. Unpublished manuscript, University of Chicago, September, 1979.

Blackie, H. C., The Choice of Currencies in Portfolio Management, *Euromoney* (December, 1978).

Campbell, Jimmy and O'Connor, Walter F., Taxation of Foreign Exchange Activities of Commercial Banks. *The Tax Adviser,* 541 (September, 1976).

Dinur, Daniel D., Tax Consequences in Settlement of Currency Futures Unclear Despite Recent Decisions. 51 *Journal of Taxation* 282 (November, 1979).

Dukes, R. E., The Empirical Investigation of the Effects of FASB Statement No. 8 on Security Return Behaviour, *FASB* (December, 1978).

Duncan, W. Egerton, Effect of Restated E & P from Foreign Currencies to Dollars on Subpart F Income. 51 *Journal of Taxation* 34 (July, 1979).

Eitman, David K. and Stonehill, Arthur I., Multinational Business Finance. *Addison–Wesley Publishing Co.,* 1979.

Ensor, Richard and Antl, Boris (editors), Management of Foreign Exchange Risk. *Euromoney Publications,* 1978.

Giddy, I., Exchange Risk: Whose View?, *Financial Management,* Summer, 1977.

Henrey, Robert, Measuring the Impact of Currency Fluctuations. *Coopers & Lybrand,* 1978.

Henrey, Robert, Tax Consequences of Foreign Exchange Gains and Losses Within the Corporate Family. 37 *New York University Institute of Federal Taxation* 20–1 (1979).

Howlett, Keith, Forward Hedging Does Pay, Because the Long Run is too Long. *Euromoney, April 1977*: 83–85.

Jackson, Peter D. and Meagher, Michael B., The New Foreign Currency Recommendations. *Canadian CA magazine* of December, 1978.

Kohlhagen, Steven W., A Model of Optional Foreign Exchange Hedging Without Exchange Rate Projections. *Journal of International Business Studies,* 9, No. 2 (Fall, 1978): 9–20.

Lessard, Donald R. and Lorange, Peter, Currency Changes and Management Control: Resolving the Centralization/Decentralization Dilemma. *Accounting Review* 52, No. 4 (July 1977): 628–37.

Levich, Richard M., Analyzing the Accuracy of Foreign Exchange Advisory Services: Theory and Evidence. In Exchange Risk and Exposure: Current Developments in International Financial Management, edited by R. Levich and C. Wihlborg. *Lexington, Mass.: D.C. Heath and Company,* 1980.

Levich, Richard M., Further Results of the Efficiency of Markets for Foreign Exchange. In Managed Exchange-Rate Flexibility: The Recent Experience. *Federal Reserve Bank of Boston,* Conference Series No. 20, 1978.

Lieberman, G., A Systems approach to Foreign Exchange Risk Management. *Financial Executive* December, 1978, 14–9.

Mandich, D. R., Foreign Exchange Trading Techniques and Controls. *American Bankers Association,* 1976.

Moore, Michael L. and Kramer, John L., Tax Accounting Rules for Currency Translation. *International Tax Journal* 238.

Polk, Raemon M., Financial and Tax Aspects of Planning for Foreign Currency Exchange Fluctuations. 56 *Taxes* 131 (March, 1978).

Prindl, A., Guidelines for MNC Money Managers. *HBR*, January–February, 1976: 73–80.

Prindl, A., Foreign Exchange Risk. *John Wiley & Sons,* 1976.

Rhoades, Income Taxation of Foreign Related Transactions, *Matthew Bender* (1979).

Riehl, Heinz and Rodriguez, Rita M., Foreign Exchange Markets, A guide to Foreign Currency Operations. *McGraw-Hill,* 1977.

Rodriguez, Rita M. and Carter, Eugene E. International Financial Management. *Prentice-Hall Inc.,* 1976.

Calderon-Rossell, J. R., Covering Foreign Exchange Risk of Single Transaction, *Financial Management* (Autumn, 1979).

Schuck, Edward, Federal Income Tax Consequences of Foreign Currency Transactions and Fluctuations: Another Look. 26 *Tax Review* (1978).

Shapiro, Alan C. and Rutenberg, David P., Managing Exchange Risks in a Floating World. *Financial Management* 48 (September, 1976).

Tryon, Ralph, Testing for Rational Expectations in Foreign Exchange Markets. *Board of Governors of the Federal Reserve System, International Finance Discussion Papers.* No. 139, May 1979.

Watt, Hammer, Burge, Accounting for the Multinational Corporation, *Financial Executives Research Foundation (1977).*

Wyman, H. E., Analysis of Gains and Losses from Foreign Monetary Items: An Application of Purchasing Power Parity Concepts, *The Accounting Review* (July, 1976).

Foreign Currency Accounting, The Accounting Forum, Volume 47, No. 2, December, 1977.

Statement of Financial Accounting Standards No. 8, Accounting for Translation of Foreign Currency Transaction and Foreign Currency Financial Statements. *Financial Accounting Standards Board,* October, 1975.

Notes on contributors

Boris Antl—Assistant Vice President, Financial Consulting Services, Chemical Bank, New York

Michael Adler—Professor of Finance, Graduate School of Business, Columbia University, New York

Robert Ankrom—Treasurer, P.S.A. Peugoet–Citroen, Paris, France

Victoria D. Blake—Assistant Vice President, Corporate Finance Department, Citibank, New York

Mark Borsuk—Managing Consultant, Asia, Foreign Exchange Advisory Service, Chemical Bank

Paul R. Brenner—Member of the New York Bar and of the firm of Kelley Drye & Warren, New York

James Burtle—was formerly Vice President in the Economics Group of W. R. Grace & Co., New York, and is now Managing Editor of the *International Country Risk Review*, International Reports, New York

Charles Stephen Clegg—Director of International Finance, Avis, Inc., New York

John J. Costello—Member of the New York Bar and of the firm of Kelley Drye & Warren, New York

John G. Dickerson—Assistant Vice President, Morgan Guaranty Trust Company, New York

Dr. Jeffrey C. Donahue—Manager, Foreign Currency Operations, Union Carbide Corporation, New York

Shirley B. Dreifus—Assistant Vice President, Foreign Regulations Service, Chemical Bank, New York

Bernard Dumas—Professor of Finance, E.S.S.E.C., Cergy, France

Peter W. Eccles—Vice President, Corporate Finance Department, Citibank, New York

Peter A. Fegelman—Financial Analyst, Treasury Department, Continental Group. The articles are adapted from Mr. Fegelman's Master Thesis written at the Graduate School of Business Administration, New York University

Dr. Helmut Hagemann—Director, McKinsey & Co., Inc., Munich, Germany

Richard M. Hammer—Partner and National Director of International Tax Services, Price Waterhouse & Co. (National Office), New York

Robert J. E. Henrey—Partner in Charge of International Tax Consulting, Coopers & Lybrand, New York

Albert C. Henry—Senior Manager, Accounting Services, Price Waterhouse & Co. (National Office), New York

Alice B. Kerr, Senior Consultant, Foreign Regulations Service, Chemical Bank, New York

Richard M. Levich—Associate Professor of Finance and International Business, Graduate School of Business Administration, New York University, New York

Gerald F. Lewis—Controller of the Worldwide Marketing & Refining Division and Assistant Controller of Mobil Oil Corporation, New York

Gail Lieberman—Director, Performance Reporting and Forecasting, RCA Corporation, New York

Ralph J. Massey—Vice President and Treasurer, Chemco International Leasing Inc., Chemical Bank, New York

David Norr—CPA and Financial Analyst with Lieber & Co., New York. He served on the Accounting Principles Board

Jay B. Schwartz—Tax Manager, International Tax Services, Price Waterhouse & Co. (National Office), New York

Dr. Alan Teck—Vice President, Director of Financial Consulting Services, Chemical Bank, New York